T0383890

HOW TO LOSE A WAR

HOW TO LOSE A WAR

THE STORY OF AMERICA'S INTERVENTION IN AFGHANISTAN

AMIN SAIKAL

YALE UNIVERSITY PRESS
NEW HAVEN AND LONDON

For Mary-Lou, Rahima, Samra and Amina

For information about this and other Yale University Press publications, please contact:
U.S. Office: sales.press@yale.edu   yalebooks.com
Europe Office: sales@yaleup.co.uk   yalebooks.co.uk

Set in Minion Pro by IDSUK (DataConnection) Ltd
Printed in Great Britain by TJ Books Limited, Padstow, Cornwall

Library of Congress Control Number: 2024932811

ISBN 978-0-300-26624-5

A catalogue record for this book is available from the British Library.

10 9 8 7 6 5 4 3 2 1

Contents

Preface

The Afghanistan conundrum has been haunting the country's population and the world for nearly five decades. During this period, five ideological clusters from different points of the political spectrum and two world powers have sought to transform the country into a viable state. Afghanistan has transited from a monarchy to a republic to a people's democratic republic to an Islamic republic to an Islamic emirate, back to an Islamic republic and then back to an Islamic emirate. The country has also been invaded and occupied by the Soviet Union in the 1980s and subjected to a US-led intervention for two decades from 2001, along with Pakistan's continuing interference. No country in the modern world has changed hands as many times and in such a short period as Afghanistan. Ultimately, the country has entered its current darkest phase, for the second time, under the brutal religious rule of the ultra-extremist Taliban.

The last hope for stability, security and prosperity within a democratic framework came with the US intervention in response to the 9/11 Al Qaeda terrorist attacks on America. But the US and allied involvement was confounded by a number of key issues. They prominently include: America's inability to net its most wanted man, Al Qaeda leader Osama bin Laden, sooner rather than later; conflation of the Afghanistan campaign with the broader foreign policy goals of 'democracy promotion' and 'war on terrorism'; poor governance by Afghan ruling elites under the US watch; and Pakistan's Janus-faced stance against terrorism while promoting the erstwhile terrorist Taliban and their partners to undermine the US and allied campaign in Afghanistan, as well as Washington's strategy or lack of it in handling these variables against the backdrop of the prevailing and historical complexities of Afghanistan and its region.

This book explores the US-led intervention and its eventual failure within the framework of these variables, which have not received sufficient insightful attention. It narrates and discusses critically how the US's initial approach from a 'light footprint' changed to a 'heavy footprint' that widened and deepened its involvement in processes of state-building and, by the same token, led it to fall into the 'Afghan trap' from which it could eventually extract itself only in defeat. The return to power of the Pakistan-backed and Al Qaeda-linked Taliban in mid-August 2021 proved to be humiliating for the US and indeed its allies, and disastrous for the people of Afghanistan. The United Nations warned in July 2023 that once again Afghanistan was at mortal risk of giving rise to terrorist actions. How long this phase of Afghanistan's turbulent evolution will last and where it will lead as a source of tension and conflict in an increasingly polarized world is now a matter of conjecture, as neither the Afghan people nor the world have seen the end of the Afghanistan crisis.

In deciding to write this book, I was motivated by growing concerns that, despite the work that has been published on Afghanistan and the US-led intervention, some critical gaps exist in the literature. In its coverage, the book draws on years of my field-work, interviews with Afghan, regional and Western policymakers, practitioners, scholars and informed folk, as well as my extensive writing and publications on the subject in regional and international contexts. The many people with whom I have had endless discussions and debates inside and outside Afghanistan about the failure of the American-led intervention are too numerous to mention by name for a variety of reasons. Some, more specifically in the case of Afghan insiders, are still on active duty, while many others are in hiding or have joined the resistance. All of them know that I owe them enormous gratitude.

However, I must mention two people in particular: former US ambassador and commander of forces in Afghanistan Karl Eikenberry, and my brother, ex-ambassador Mahmoud Saikal. I am deeply indebted to them for their most valuable counsel and contributions to this volume, which otherwise would not have been initiated and eventually completed. Both have generously given me their time and insights, and have read the entire manuscript, adding to the uniqueness of this volume.

Equally, I am very grateful to Australian National University (ANU) emeritus professor Malcolm Gillies, a former colleague and Vice Chancellor of two British universities, for kindly, generously and meticulously reading the final draft of this manuscript and providing me with very enriching views and comments. In addition, I am enormously thankful to the Hon. Professor Gareth Evans, former Foreign Minister of Australia, ANU Chancellor and head of the International Crisis Group. During most of my academic career, he has been an inspirational source of support, knowledge and experience in world affairs.

Beyond this, my gratitude goes to three friends and colleagues, Professor Samina Yasmeen, Director of the Centre for Muslim States and Societies at the University of Western Australia, Professor Kumar Ramakrishna, Dean of the S. Rajaratnam School of International Studies at Nanyang Technological University, and Dr Greg Fry, Honorary Associate Professor of Pacific Affairs at the ANU. I cannot praise enough their warmth, generosity and scholarly standing. I am also very thankful to Philippa Hetherington for her research assistance on a piece prepared more than a decade ago and which I have now made use of. I am also indebted to Joanna Godfrey, the acquisition editor of Yale University Press, for being so patient, cheerful, encouraging and helpful to me throughout the life of this book.

In the case of this book and my previous publications, my partner and love of my life, Mary-Louise Hickey, has been instrumental in enabling me to get through this work. She has not only stood beside me every step of the way, but also applied her enormous skills as a very accomplished editor to make my work readable and comprehensible. She has done so with patience, understanding and dedication. All my work is dedicated to her and my three most loving and accomplished daughters, Rahima, Samra and Amina, and to the two most recent additions to the family, Hendrik and Nina. Writing this book also coincided with the long illness and passing of my younger sister, Maliha Saikal, a former diplomat and Arabist, from cancer, a tragedy that one cannot easily overcome while the spirit of her kindness and affection still swirls around us.

Abbreviations

AAF	Afghan Air Force
ACKU	Afghan Center at Kabul University
AICC	Afghanistan Inter-Ministerial Coordination Cell
ANA	Afghan National Army
ANASF	Afghan National Army and Security Forces
ANDSF	Afghan National Defense and Security Forces
ANP	Afghan National Police
ANSF	Afghan National Security Forces
BSA	Bilateral Security Agreement
CDC	Community Development Council
CE	Chief Executive
CENTCOM	Central Command
CIA	Central Intelligence Agency
CLJ	Constitutional Loya Jirga
COIN	counterinsurgency
DDR	disarmament, demobilization and reintegration
ECC	Electoral Complaints Commission
ELJ	Emergency Loya Jirga
EU	European Union
FATA	Federally Administered Tribal Areas

FBI	Federal Bureau of Investigation
GDP	gross domestic product
ICG	International Crisis Group
IEC	Independent Election Commission
IECC	Independent Electoral Complaints Commission
IS	Islamic State
ISAF	International Security Assistance Force
ISI	Inter-Services Intelligence
ISIS	Islamic State of Iraq and Syria
IS-K	Islamic State-Khorasan
JEMB	Joint Electoral Management Body
LOTFA	Law and Order Trust Fund of Afghanistan
NATO	North Atlantic Treaty Organization
NCA	National Coalition of Afghanistan
NDS	National Directorate of Security
NGO	non-governmental organization
NRF	National Resistance Front
NSP	National Solidarity Programme
NTM-A	NATO Training Mission-Afghanistan
NUG	National Unity Government
OEF	Operation Enduring Freedom
OIC	Organisation of Islamic Cooperation
OPEC	Organization of the Petroleum Exporting Countries
PC	Provincial Council
PDC	Provincial Development Committee
PDPA	People's Democratic Party of Afghanistan
PRT	Provincial Reconstruction Team
RAWA	Revolutionary Association of the Women of Afghanistan
RSM	Resolute Support Mission
SCO	Shanghai Cooperation Organisation
SEAL	US Navy Sea, Air and Land

ABBREVIATIONS

SIGAR	Special Inspector General for Afghanistan Reconstruction
SNTV	Single Non-Transferable Voting
TTP	Tehrik-e Taliban Pakistan
UAE	United Arab Emirates
UINFSA	United Islamic National Front for the Salvation of Afghanistan
UN	United Nations
UNAMA	United Nations Assistance Mission in Afghanistan
UNDP	United Nations Development Programme
UNESCO	United Nations Educational, Scientific and Cultural Organization
UNOCAL	Union Oil Company of California
UNODC	United Nations Office on Drugs and Crime
UNSCOM	United Nations Special Commission
USAID	United States Agency for International Development
WHO	World Health Organization

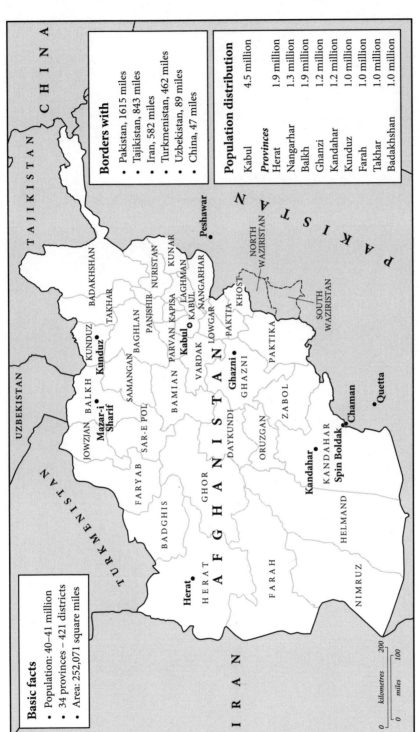

Basic facts
- Population: 40–41 million
- 34 provinces – 421 districts
- Area: 252,071 square miles

Borders with
- Pakistan, 1615 miles
- Tajikistan, 843 miles
- Iran, 582 miles
- Turkmenistan, 462 miles
- Uzbekistan, 89 miles
- China, 47 miles

Population distribution

Kabul	4.5 million
Provinces	
Herat	1.9 million
Nangarhar	1.3 million
Balkh	1.9 million
Ghazni	1.2 million
Kandahar	1.2 million
Kunduz	1.0 million
Farah	1.0 million
Takhar	1.0 million
Badakhshan	1.0 million

Map of Afghanistan

Introduction

Big Power, Small War

Afghanistan – a land of superb and rugged beauty . . . [with] a spirit which through the centuries has meant that [the country] has been unconquered and unconquerable.

Richard Nixon[1]

The former United States vice-president and subsequent president, Richard Nixon, made this remark when welcoming Afghan Prime Minister Mohammad Daoud on the occasion of his first official visit to Washington on 24 June 1958. At that time, neither Nixon nor any American leaders could possibly imagine that one day the US would find it compelling to intervene[2] in the 'unconquerable' country and there fight the longest war in American history. Yet that day came, shortly after Al Qaeda's attacks on the US on 11 September 2001 (hereafter referred to as 9/11), killing 2,977 people, plus nineteen hijackers[3] who, in a murder-suicide mission, slammed planes into New York's World Trade Center, the Pentagon in Washington, DC, and a field in Pennsylvania. The event – comparable to Japan's strike on an American naval base at Pearl Harbor sixty years earlier – shook the world's most powerful state to its core.

Backed by allies inside and outside the North Atlantic Treaty Organization (NATO), along with widespread global sympathy, the conservative Republican administration of the recently elected President George W. Bush launched a retaliatory military campaign within a month against Al Qaeda and its protector, the Pakistan-backed Taliban ultra-extremist Islamic regime that had ruled most of Afghanistan since mid-1996. This marked the start of the 'Afghan War' that the US, in President Bush's words, 'did not ask for, [and] did not want', but which was imposed on it.[4] However, this was also the war that, in 2021, the US and, for that matter, NATO lost after two decades of involvement, resulting in the return to power of the Al Qaeda-linked Taliban. It cast a long shadow over America's world power status and its fight against terrorism, changed the regional strategic texture in favour of the US's adversaries, and created titanic consequences for the people of Afghanistan.

The question of where the US and, for that matter, its allies went wrong has been widely debated. Different perspectives from varying ideological, geopolitical and strategic vantagepoints have emerged in response. The central concern of this study is specifically to explore and expose those aspects of the US-led Afghanistan campaign that have not been addressed and analysed with the degree of insightfulness that they deserve. In a nutshell, the book focuses on what caused the US, along with its allies, to move from an initial 'light footprint' approach to a heavy focus on state-building, thus becoming entangled in a long war from which it could not extract itself in any other way than to make an embarrassing exit in defeat of the very original objectives of its invasion. It explores the fragility of the US Afghanistan campaign in relation to Afghanistan's historical and prevailing intricacies, and the 'hunt for Bin Laden' and its conflation with America's wider foreign policy agenda of 'democracy promotion' and 'war on terrorism' to preserve America's global power status that set the tone for the campaign from the outset. The failure to net the Al Qaeda leader, Osama bin Laden, and his main operatives early enough; to secure a reliable and effective Afghan leadership and workable system of governance; to halt Pakistan's predatory behaviour; and to pursue an appropriately long-term military strategy to deal with unforeseen contingencies could not but play a central role in derailing the American campaign.

Sole world power status

The tragic events of 9/11 came at a particular juncture for the US in world politics. America's superpower rival, the Soviet Union, had disintegrated and the Cold War as we knew it had ended a decade earlier. The US had claimed the triumph of democracy and free enterprise capitalism over Soviet communism and a socialist mode of development, elevating its own position as the world's sole super-power.[5] These developments had emboldened the forces of the 'Right' in the US that had been seeking to shape America's foreign policy posture according to a unilateralist, and ideologically and geopoliti-cally assertive, agenda since the Republican presidency of Ronald Reagan in the 1980s. While held at bay during the Democratic administration of President Bill Clinton (1993–2001), a major oppor-tunity to advance American ideological and geopolitical objectives came with the advent of Bush's administration in January 2001. Three of the 'Right's' elements powerfully interlocked to dominate and determine American foreign policy priorities.

First was the neoconservative group, led by such ideologues as Paul Wolfowitz, Deputy Secretary of Defense, Richard Perle, Chairman of the Defense Policy Board Advisory Committee, and William Kristol, well-known writer and commentator.[6] Second were the born-again Christian and evangelist movements, personified by President Bush himself. Third was the ultra-nationalist cohort, embodied by Vice-President Dick Cheney and Secretary of Defense Donald Rumsfeld. Although hailing from different backgrounds, these minority forces shared a common ideological platform and belief in what can be termed a 'doctrine of power reality'. The central point of their argument was that, as the mightiest state on earth, the US should exert its economic and military power to rebuff its adversaries and export American democracy, in the first instance, to the Middle East and then to the rest of the world. They further contended, although for different reasons, that the US should stand behind the state of Israel as the most sacred and reliable Judeo-Christian and democratic ally in the Middle East.[7]

In a common cause, they advocated for regime change in oil-rich Iraq. Saddam Hussein's dictatorship was widely detested and demonized. It had functioned as a thorn in the side of the US since its August 1990 invasion of the Western-backed, oil-wealthy Emirate of Kuwait, which the US, supported by a regional coalition, had successfully reversed six months later. Changing Iraq into a friendly democratic ally was to provide the US with a bridgehead to alter the political landscape against the hostile and defiant forces across the region, with one eager eye turned on Iran's Islamic 'fundamentalist' regime.[8] Iran was once a critical pillar of *Pax Americana* in the region, from 1953 until the Iranian revolution of 1978/79 that toppled the pro-Western monarchy of Mohammad Reza Shah Pahlavi, enabling the monarch's key religious-political opponent, Ayatollah Ruhollah Khomeini, to transform the country into an Islamic Republic and a hotbed of political Islamism, with an anti-US and anti-Israel posture.[9] The higher goal of the three interlocking elements was to ensure the preservation and strengthening of the US position as the only global power, with the idea that the twenty-first century would be dominated by America, not any other power, particularly China, which was then in the process of emerging as a military and economic competitor.

The Hainan Island incident

An early sign of the Bush administration's assertive foreign policy posture became evident in the so-called Hainan Island incident. On

1 April 2001, an air collision between a sophisticated US Navy spy plane and a Chinese jet fighter 80 km south-east of China's Hainan Island forced the American plane to land in China with twenty-four crew on board.[10] Beijing blamed the US for the episode over China's territorial waters, but Washington claimed that the Chinese jet was aggressively tailing the American plane in international airspace and demanded the immediate and unconditional release of the plane and its crew. The incident rapidly developed into an international crisis. Bush declared: 'Failure of the Chinese government to react promptly to our request [for the return of the plane and its crew] is inconsistent with the standard diplomatic practice and with the expressed desire of both our countries for better relations.'[11] After eleven days of tense deadlock and Washington's expression of regret over the loss of the pilot of the Chinese plane, Beijing released the American aircrew. However, the matter did not rest there.

While China inspected the spy plane's state-of-the-art equipment and handed over its disassembled parts on 31 July, Washington pursued a relentless policy of escalating pressure on China, condemning its human rights violations and threatening to block its entry into the World Trade Organization. Two weeks after the release of the American crew, Bush made a more explicit commitment than any of his predecessors to Taiwan's defence, declaring that if China attacked the island, the US would help Taiwan defend itself 'whatever it took'.[12] This was despite the US having recognized China as the legitimate representative of the Chinese people and adopting a 'one China policy', with China replacing Taiwan as the permanent member of the United Nations (UN) Security Council in October 1971, reinforced by President Nixon's historic visit to China in February 1972.

The US response to Al Qaeda's attacks

Thus, even before 9/11, the Bush administration's foreign policy had taken an upward trajectory in pursuit of building a US-centric world order. Al Qaeda's mega-terrorist operation, which was designed to undermine the US's economic, military and political power, and which killed mostly Americans but also nationals from ninety other countries, constituted an unprecedented challenge that no American leader could brush off. Yet it also opened the arena for the Bush administration to cement America's post-Cold War global leadership.

As Richard Clarke, the US counterterrorism czar (1998–2003) reveals, for many years the American political, military and intelligence establishments had been increasingly apprised of Al Qaeda and its founding leader, the wealthy, anti-US, Saudi Islamist dissident, Osama bin Laden. The US had planned several times to target Bin Laden. However, each time the plan had not been executed, largely due to 'risk-averse' considerations, mainly at the instigation of the Central Intelligence Agency (CIA). Thus Clarke concludes that important opportunities were missed that could have prevented not only Al Qaeda's 9/11 attacks, but also several before it on American targets in the second half of the 1990s.[13]

Al Qaeda's enabler – the Taliban – emerged on the Afghanistan horizon from mid-1994 and assumed power two years later. While alert to the dangers of this group, Washington was cautious about taking decisive action against them as well. In the late 1990s, American diplomats based in the US embassy in Islamabad, along with policymakers in Washington, had engaged with some elements of the group for the purpose of information-gathering and potentially inducing the militia to sever ties with Al Qaeda and cease sheltering Bin Laden and his leadership team. Although the Taliban were happy to interface with US diplomats for recognition, they were not prepared to change their ultra-theocratic practices or agree to American requests to break their alliance with Al Qaeda, particularly given the personal bonds between the Taliban leader Mullah Mohammad Omar and Bin Laden.[14] In the process, Washington failed to act decisively against Al Qaeda's growing strength, with Ayman al-Zawahiri and his militant Egyptian Islamic Jihad joining the group shortly after September 2006. Al-Zawahiri rapidly emerged as Bin Laden's lieutenant and Al Qaeda's main ideologue, and subsequently succeeded Bin Laden following the latter's killing in a special US operation in 2011.

The question confronting Washington over 9/11 was how to respond, given the breadth and width of the attack and its intended humiliation of the US. The Bush leadership had several options. One was to treat 9/11 as a criminal act and resource Interpol to hunt down its masterminds and bring them to justice, but not declare war. A leading advocate of this approach was Gore Vidal, an American writer, public intellectual, and strong critic of the Bush leadership. He argued:

> Although every nation knows how – if it has the means and the will – to protect itself from thugs of the sort that brought us 9/11, war is not an option. Wars are for nations not rootless gangs. You put a price on their heads and hunt them down. In recent years, Italy has been doing that with the Sicilian Mafia; and no one has yet suggested bombing Palermo.[15]

Vidal also regarded 9/11 as a colossal failure of US intelligence, a view echoed by many others, including Senator Richard Shelby, who, in a 2002 congressional hearing called it 'an intelligence failure of unprecedented magnitude'.[16] This was especially so, given the history of Al Qaeda's deadly attacks on American targets.

Another option was to lean decisively on Pakistan to curtail all links with Al Qaeda and the Taliban. Washington was aware that Pakistan's military or, more specifically, its powerful Inter-Services Intelligence (ISI), operated virtually as a 'government within a government', and that it orchestrated and supported the Taliban, facilitated the Taliban–Al Qaeda alliance, and used radical Islamism as a foreign policy tool.[17] If these groups could be prevented from using Pakistan's territory for cross-border movements into Afghanistan, it could force them to surrender at a time when Afghanistan's other neighbours had shunned the Taliban and closed their frontiers with the country.

However, these two options were regarded as logistically very difficult to implement and were not conducive to the Bush administration's wider global agenda. The full support of Pakistan would have been needed for Interpol to penetrate Afghanistan deeply and pervasively to locate and capture Al Qaeda leaders and core operatives, who were strongly guarded by their own well-armed militia and Taliban protectors. Compelling Pakistan to disown the Taliban and, by implication, their Al Qaeda allies was not practical either, given Pakistan's heavy investment in the group. Although Islamabad publicly sided with the US against terrorism, President General Pervez Musharraf had already described Pakistan's support of the Taliban as a national 'security imperative' for Islamabad.[18]

The third option that the Bush administration adopted was an 'intervention' as the most effective way to achieve its Afghanistan-related and wider objectives. The initial plan was to pursue a 'light footprint' approach and act in conjunction with the anti-Taliban resistance alliance of the United Islamic National Front for the Salvation of Afghanistan (UINFSA) to present the intervention as an indigenous-backed act of liberation. The convenient way to access Afghanistan was through the north-east border of the country with Tajikistan. This area was under the control of the UINFSA, which Islamabad had dubbed the 'Northern Alliance'.[19] The UINFSA had been organized and led by the Mujahideen commander Ahmad Shah Massoud, who had valiantly fought the Soviet occupation in the 1980s and opposed the Taliban and Al Qaeda. Massoud was assassinated by Taliban-backed Al Qaeda agents two days before 9/11 as a prelude to the event. His fighters and supporters were therefore eager and willing to do whatever was necessary to see the end of what they generally regarded as Pakistan's proxy rule in Afghanistan.

After the Taliban's rejection of US demands to hand over Bin Laden, the Bush administration launched a military campaign,

'Operation Enduring Freedom', on 7 October 2001. The top priority was to go after Bin Laden by either capturing or killing him, and to destroy Al Qaeda. But in the process, there was no choice but also to dismantle the Taliban regime and 'stabilize' Afghanistan. Washington had not originally intended to fight a long and costly war in Afghanistan; it wanted to do only the bare minimum. It did not want to get involved in the difficult task of nation- or state-building and thus potentially be led into a 'quagmire', as happened to the British and Soviets in the nineteenth and late twentieth centuries respectively. Deputy Secretary of Defense Wolfowitz, one of the leading architects of the US strategic planning for Afghanistan, made this very clear in a congressional hearing in June 2002.[20]

However, despite its early military success in dispersing Al Qaeda and toppling the Taliban but not defeating them, the US was confronted with a situation that led it into the so-called 'Afghan trap', just as the British and Soviets had experienced before. After two decades of very costly human and financial investment in state-building and military operations, with NATO and non-NATO allied input, the US found itself with little choice but to bow out of Afghanistan. It did so based on signing with the Taliban what was widely regarded as the flawed 29 February 2020 peace agreement (formally called the Agreement for Bringing Peace to Afghanistan). This agreement guaranteed a US and allied withdrawal, but not a political settlement of the Afghanistan conflict. It left the fate of the country in the hands of the vulnerable protégé government in Kabul and its defence forces that the US and its allies had helped build at a very high price. As the foreign troop pull-out accelerated, neither could survive the Taliban onslaught for even a few days beyond mid-August 2021 – just short of the date designated by President Joe Biden to mark the twentieth anniversary of 9/11. The Afghan armed and security forces as well as the administrative apparatus rapidly disintegrated – a lot sooner than President Ashraf Ghani had warned in January 2018, saying that the Afghan National Army would not last more than six months without US support. However, the commander of US forces at the time, General John Nicholson, rejected this idea, claiming that the US could still win Washington's longest war.[21] Ghani and his predecessor, Hamid Karzai, played their part in the process. In the end, while finding himself in the position of an 'emperor without clothes', Ghani broke his repeated promise to the Afghan people that he would never leave them; he fled the country, along with his close aides, completely losing his dignity.

The cost and casualties of the war were less than those in Vietnam, but the humiliation that the US and its allies suffered arguably exceeded that of the Vietnam fiasco some five decades earlier, as well as that of Iraq following the Afghanistan intervention. The defeat reflected badly not only on the US but also on NATO, which was supposed to be the world's most powerful military alliance, and other US allies. It emboldened America's main regional and global adversaries, such as Iran, Russia and China.

Yet the worst outcome was the return to power, from mid-August 2021, of the very forces that the US and its allies had sought to uproot: the Taliban in combination with the Haqqani network and their continued linkages to Al Qaeda. Pakistan celebrated the development, although at the risk of the Taliban victory rebounding on itself as a fragile state. And Al Qaeda and the Taliban's rival terrorist group, the Khorasan branch of Islamic State (IS-K), which had become active in Afghanistan from 2016, could not hope for more favourable opportunities.[22]

Prior to the Taliban's resumption of power, some policymakers and analysts inside and outside the US expected the Taliban 2.0 to be more nuanced and cognizant of the imperative not to repeat their previous repressive, misogynistic and draconian religious rule, especially in light of the pro-liberalist mode of change and development that Afghanistan experienced under the US watch. They included Zalmay Khalilzad, who, in his final position as the US special representative for Afghanistan reconciliation, concluded the February

2020 peace deal. Providing a time-based exit of US and allied forces, the agreement incentivized the Taliban as never before to accelerate their march towards power. The assertion that the Taliban had changed and that their renewed rule would be more nuanced proved to be fanciful.

The Taliban's return

The renewed rise of the Taliban occurred against the backdrop of two significant dimensions of Afghanistan. On the one hand, the US and its allies had helped change the country's political and developmental landscape, introducing some pro-Western features. On the other, political and Islamic traditionalism, ethno-tribal diversity, social and economic disparity and injustices, widespread poverty, corruption, insecurity, and a state–society dichotomy still remained dominant. As such, modern Afghanistan had endured many painful and destructive transitions since its emergence more than two and a half centuries before. At no point had it evolved as more than a weak and, in many ways, primordial state, with strong but differentiated micro-societies, whose vulnerabilities were compounded by its strategic crossroads geographical location and outside power interventionism.

Lacking appropriate governance and resource-rich foundations, Afghanistan had never really been able either to stand on its own two feet or to ward off successive outside actors from attempting, unsuccessfully, to tame it according to their ideological and geopolitical preferences. Afghanistan had survived as a kind of rentier entity during most of its existence.[23] Not surprisingly, since the early nineteenth century, many of Afghanistan's leaders held power with the backing of an outside actor – imperial Britain, Soviet Russia and the United States – not to mention Pakistan's buttressing of the Taliban when the group has been both in and out of power.

Internal weaknesses and foreign interventionism mutually reinforced one another to keep Afghanistan in the perpetual political, developmental and security doldrums. The only period in which the country enjoyed relative stability and peace was between 1930 and the mid-1970s. That was largely due to a certain power-based arrangement that the monarchy of the time managed to forge against the backdrop of the flexibility provided, at first by a reduction in the traditional Anglo-Russian rivalry and subsequently by the vagaries of the US–Soviet Cold War competition.

Even so, Afghanistan had never experienced anything like the first and second round of the reign of the Taliban. Taliban 2.0 have essentially weaponized Islam in accordance with their own version of the faith as the basis of their power and legitimacy to impose once again their unique draconian rule, devastating the country. Their so-called interim government, representing mainly the Ghilzai tribe of the ethnic Pashtuns, who have historically formed the largest minority in Afghanistan, has been led by erstwhile terrorist figures, most of them on the UN's blacklist and some wanted by the US Federal Bureau of Investigation (FBI). It has lacked an acceptable level of national and international consensus and legitimacy, and proven to be repressively exclusionary and discriminatory. By applying draconian edicts and laws, it has brutally stripped women and girls of all their rights, including education, work and freedom of movement, ostracized non-Pashtun minorities – the Hazaras and Tajiks (the Panjshiri branch, in particular) – with measures that have potentially amounted to massive human rights violations and episodes of ethnic cleansing, and silenced any form of dissent or opposition.[24]

Beyond this, it has engaged in a wholesale Islamization of the country according to its own particular Taliban-centric interpretation and application of Islam, which has no parallel in any other Muslim country. Most of the educational forums and institutions, including universities, have been pressured to conform to the Taliban's Islamic and power whims, with the specific aim of transforming Afghanistan into a unique, theo-political, totalitarian state. The current Taliban leadership has shown as much dedication as when the group was previously in power to creating a political, social and cultural order in the image of what one of its own generals, Muhammed Mubin Khan, has called 'mullahocracy'.[25] It contains many of the very people whose crass actions included the destruction in March 2001 of Bamiyan Province's Buddha statues, which dated back to the fifth century AD, ostensibly as they were deemed to be 'un-Islamic', with no respect for their historical and cultural significance.

Further, this is the first time in the history of Afghanistan and, indeed, of the world, that an erstwhile terrorist group, in continued solidarity with the perpetrators of 9/11, has assumed power while inheriting a massive military machine courtesy of the US and its Afghan allies. In its disorderly and chaotic retreat, the US left behind some $7.2 billion[26] worth of military equipment, including light and heavy weapons, ammunition, drones and a fleet of jet fighters and helicopters,[27] empowering the Taliban to build and equip a 150,000-strong defence force. The group has also publicly announced a plan to create a brigade of suicide bombers[28] – a means which they successfully deployed against the US, its allies and Afghan government forces, as well as civilian targets.

The Taliban's mixed Deobandi-Salafist version of Sunni Islam is not practised elsewhere in the Muslim world, is rejected by the fifty-seven-member Organisation of Islamic Cooperation and councils of *ulema* (the learned scholars of Islam), and is condemned by the international community. As the US and its allies have found it politically and ethically repugnant to continue their reconstruction and economic aid through the Taliban authority, the Afghanistan economy, banking system, social services, most importantly health and education, industrial enterprises and employment opportunities have virtually dried up. Many of the country's limited pool of educated people have either fled or been imprisoned or killed by the Taliban. House searches, persecution and killing of the remaining administrative and security members of the previous US-backed governments have become a common daily occurrence. So have the disappearance and flogging of women and men who have potentially and actually resisted the Taliban impositions.

Afghanistan has sunk into the biggest humanitarian crisis in its recorded history. It has become a begging bowl of the world, with some 95–98 per cent of its estimated 38–40 million population dependent on international handouts, suffering from 'record levels of hunger'[29] to the extent that some families have sold body organs, kidneys in particular, or a child, in order to feed the remaining siblings. Death from preventable starvation, malnutrition and diseases has been rife. According to the Global Hunger Index, in 2022 Afghanistan ranked 109 out of 121 countries.[30] The Taliban leaders have persistently blamed the US and its allies for Afghanistan's miserable state, while refusing to admit that their extremist nature and disposition have been primarily responsible. A report of the UN Analytical Support and Sanctions Monitoring Team concludes:

> The Taliban, in power as the de facto authorities in Afghanistan . . . have reverted to the exclusionary, Pashtun-centred, autocratic policies of the administration of the late 1990s. . . . The link between the Taliban and both Al-Qaida and Tehrik-e-Taliban Pakistan . . . remains strong and symbiotic. A range of terrorist groups have greater freedom of manoeuvre under the Taliban de facto authorities. They are making good use of this, and the threat of terrorism is rising in both Afghanistan and the region.[31]

President Biden, who presided over the last stage of the chaotic US withdrawal, justified his action by claiming that the US had achieved its main goal – to prevent another 9/11. He intimated that this was the only objective that had driven the US to embark on, and persist with, its Afghanistan campaign.[32] Yet the chairman of the Joint Chiefs of Staff, General Mark Milley, branded the Afghanistan war a 'strategic failure'.[33] Looking back at America's Afghanistan campaign, former US Ambassador Karl Eikenberry has argued that perhaps, following the US overthrow of the Taliban regime, Afghanistan should have become a 'UN trusteeship'.[34]

Big powers' loss of small wars

This is not the first time that a major or big power has lost what by all accounts can be classified as a small war. Many examples abound in history. In the twentieth century, the French and the US were defeated in Indo-China, as were the Soviets in Afghanistan. These powers' conventional military superiority, capable of prevailing in a war with another state, did not fare well against insurgents' asymmetrical or guerrilla campaigns or other means of military struggle.

In most historical cases, several factors have invariably advantaged the insurgents against the superior, mechanized military of an imposing power. These factors have included the insurgents' ability to easily blend in with the local people, whether in an urban or rural setting; to cope with subsistence living; to exploit the people's suffering inflicted on them by military and cultural misconduct and the impositions of a colonial or invading power; and to make maximum use of the weaponry salvaged from the enemy. Their capabilities are enriched and resilience enhanced to stay in the fight for as long as necessary when they are supported by an outside actor – whether big or small. A historical survey of modern times shows that ultimately the power imbalance has mostly worked in favour of the insurgents in pursuit of 'liberationist' causes. In a very deft article, Andrew Mack states:

> In guerrilla warfare in the classical sense, the 'people sea' forms a sanctuary of popular support for the 'guerrilla fish'; in urban guerrilla warfare the anonymity of the city provides protection. Operating in uninhabited areas and supplied from without . . . the insurgents may simply rely on the mountains and forests to conceal and protect them.[35]

The Taliban benefited from all these variables, except in two areas. First, they have not had the same degree of popularity that, for example, the Viet Cong enjoyed as a liberationist movement against the US or that the Mujahideen possessed as Islamic jihadist groups fighting against the Soviet Union. A majority of the Afghan people had previously experienced the Taliban's rule and feared its return, although the group's appeal among segments of their Pashtun kindred should not be underestimated.[36] This was especially so as the conflict dragged on and the US and allied forces resorted to the application of increased firepower, and search-and-destroy missions, resulting in cultural and human rights violations. Second, since their burgeoning in late 1994, the Taliban have been widely viewed inside Afghanistan and outside the country as a Pakistani proxy force. These two issues were instrumental in preventing the Taliban from gaining any meaningful measure of internal and external legitimacy during their previous rule, and that remains the case since their return to power.

The US-led defeat epitomized the way a major power can lose a small, anti-insurgency war. The Taliban-led insurgents were not the better-organized, trained, equipped, fed or clothed force. Nor were they supported by a world power (the US) as were the Afghan Mujahideen during the Soviet occupation of Afghanistan in the 1980s. Although nuclear-armed, Pakistan was and continues to be a fragile state. Its political, economic, financial and security woes have peeled away its ability to be regarded as even a middle power.[37]

Sources and organization

The US handling of the Afghanistan conflict, along with studies of the complex aspects of Afghanistan's landscape, have generated a large volume of literature, covering various aspects of the phenomena from different standpoints by policymakers, academics, journalists and popular writers from inside and outside Afghanistan. The field is saturated with monographs, articles and reports published in English and in Afghanistan's two main indigenous languages, although mostly in Dari/Persian rather than Pashto, not to mention other mediums. This makes the task of writing another book without too much overlap very arduous.

However, as stated earlier, the objective of this book is more specific. As such, the book does not aim to provide a detailed study of Afghanistan's complex history, or social and cultural terrain, or foreign relations. Nor does it try to give a comprehensive picture of the Taliban and their affiliates in terms of their ideological disposition, organizational structures, internal divisions and *modus operandi* in conducting a robust and enduring resistance to the US and its allies, as well as the governments in Kabul under America's patronage. Nor does it aim to give an exhaustive study of Pakistan's role and that of other regional actors in Afghanistan's changing fortunes. While referring to these issues when appropriate, they have been covered at various levels of depth and breadth by many other scholars and observers in both historical and contemporary terms.[38]

The book draws not only on many existing primary and secondary sources as well as field interviews conducted over the years, but also on the eyewitness accounts and highly relevant information of several insiders from the Afghan and American sides, particularly Mahmoud Saikal and Karl Eikenberry, respectively.

Mahmoud Saikal was a key participant and player in his country's political, developmental and strategic fortunes during most of his adult life, especially over the past three decades. He held important government and non-governmental positions, including as deputy foreign minister (2005–6) and ambassador to the UN (2015–19). He resigned twice from senior government positions in protest at Afghan governments' misguided policies and corruption. His copious notes of developments in the form of a comprehensive diary unveil what has so far remained hidden from the public eye.

Karl Eikenberry, a retired US Army lieutenant-general, was the US ambassador to Afghanistan (2009–11). He also served two tours of military duty in the country as US security coordinator for Afghanistan and chief of the Office of Military Cooperation-Afghanistan (2002–3), and as commander of the US-led coalition forces (2005–7). He was intimately involved in the execution and policy-setting of the US campaign, with a very deep policy understanding and lived experience of the Afghanistan conflict. After his military career, he was director of the US Asia Security Initiative at the Walter H. Shorenstein Asia-Pacific Research Center, Stanford University (2011–19).

As a result, the book is enriched with insights that, to the best of my knowledge, have not been seen previously. For me, the book is also the culmination of long years of academic study of Afghanistan, where I was born and raised, and its region. In this volume, I draw on some of my previous work.[39]

In its coverage, the book analytically narrates the historical context, primarily to explain the fundamental variables that have traditionally affected Afghanistan's turbulent evolutionary journey and rendered the task of state-building in the country back-breaking, as a way of providing the necessary background to the kind of Afghanistan that the US took on. The issues of the US intervention and the Bonn process, by which Afghanistan was set on the course of building a post-Taliban system of governance against the backdrop of the Bush administration's wider foreign policy agenda of 'democracy promotion' and the 'war on terror', are elaborated. Dysfunctional governance under Hamid Karzai, the decay of the National Unity Government, and the debilitating Ashraf Ghani presidency are discussed, as well as other challenges of state-building in relation to the opium crisis, the economy, the status of women and social services. The US's strategy and security-building processes and their shortcomings in dealing with unanticipated developments, including Pakistan's Janus-faced behaviour, are analysed. The volume concludes with highlights of some of the core findings of the study, including a brief look at where the main players in the Afghanistan theatre ended up and what lessons could be learned.

Note: The advent of the rule of Taliban 1.0 and 2.0 has sparked an extensive debate about the nature and exclusiveness of the group. The discussion, mostly among non-Pashtuns on social media, has centred on questioning the validity of the terms and names by which Afghanistan and its diverse population are identified and described. Some have objected even to the use of the names 'Afghanistan' and 'Afghan', arguing that they essentially refer to the 'land of Pashtuns' and the 'ethnic Pashtuns', whereas Afghanistan is truly a country of minorities, made up of many ethnic, linguistic, cultural and sectarian elements – a feature which is elaborated in chapter 2. There is also a controversy about whether one of the main languages of Afghanistan should be called Dari or Persian, and whether the Taliban should be called a rebel/terrorist or insurgent entity. However, in order to avoid confusion and misunderstanding, this study uses the standard and widely accepted versions, spelling and translation of names and terms. Thus, 'Afghanistan' refers to the whole country within its current borders, 'Afghan' means every inhabitant – Pahstun and non-Pashtun – of Afghanistan, Dari denotes a Persian derivative, and the Taliban are described as both an erstwhile terrorist and insurgent entity.

2

The Historical Context

We found greater cause to admire the Afghans in their taste in
swords than for their chemical studies.

Alexander Burnes[1]

Every country in the contemporary world has tragic tales and
events about their historical evolution, but few have experienced
as much hardship as Afghanistan. From its emergence in the mid-
eighteenth century, the country's journey has been marked by too
many cataclysmic episodes of instability, insecurity, bloodshed, autocratic rule of one kind or another and multiple foreign interventions.
Afghanistan is distinctively the only country on the globe that has
been 'invaded' by all three major powers of the last two centuries –
Great Britain, the Soviet Union and the United States. Each of these
powers has forcefully sought to tame or shape the country in accordance with its ideological and geopolitical preferences, but each has
failed and retreated in defeat. In the aftermath of every intervention,
Afghanistan's mosaic and mostly impoverished Muslim population
have been left to fend for themselves in an environment where often
'strongmen' or elites have assumed power from different ends of the
political and religious spectrum to rule the country. Even then, very

few rulers have been able to stay in power without the backing of a regional or international actor, and most have been killed or exiled by one another.

Rulers' personal and family interests as well as tribal and ethnic loyalties have frequently been prioritized over the country's need for a viable system of governance and mode of social-economic development that could generate solid foundations for national unity and a degree of self-sufficiency whereby Afghanistan would be far less vulnerable to internal upheavals and foreign interventions. The dominant faith of Islam, and ethno-tribalism and sectarianism, as well as ideologies in the country have frequently been used in different ways for power grabs and legitimation or *jihadi* (combative) actions. Religion has rarely been applied within an *ijtihadi* (reformist) framework for progressive and forward-looking developments according to the changing times and conditions.

The country has never enjoyed the status of a state or polity where there has been what Philip Pettit calls 'a rough balance of power between the rulers and their subjects: between decision makers and decision takers'.[2] By the same token, it has never achieved statehood or the conditions of being a state in the modern sense of the term. The country has generally survived and been recognized as a political and territorial country where repressive authoritarianism and a concomitant political culture have persistently been the order of the day. The rulership has generally been determined by the ruler's ability to outmanoeuvre his rivals and command a sufficient degree of support from a circle of loyalists, based on family, tribal and ethnic or ideological connections, who have formed the nucleus of his security and administrative apparatus of one kind or another, as well as from a foreign power within either a patron–client or an implicit interdependent relationship. Rulers have exercised power independent of the society. As such, Afghanistan's history and destiny have generally been shaped by ruling individuals and elites rather than their subjects. The country has scarcely experienced appropriate and effective processes of not necessarily nation-building but rather state-building, given that the country is comprised of diverse 'nations'. It has mostly been deprived of an enduring political order, national stability, security and unity, with social justice and economic equity to guard against internal disorder and outside predatory meddling and actions.

Four variables

Let us look at this in the context of four interrelated variables that have historically and invariably influenced Afghanistan's evolving internal and external settings: its crossroads strategic location; social and cultural diversity; domestic power rivalry and 'political dualism'; and outside interventionism. These fundamentals, constituting a binding theme, have historically led Afghanistan to evolve as no more than a primordially weak state with strong micro-societies at the best of times. For most of its existence it has been in an almost perpetual state of disorder. Indeed, a great many scholarly studies have covered these variables either individually or as part of larger national and regional portrayals. However, the task here is to analyse them interrelatedly and critically, though as briefly as possible, in order to set the scene for the kind of Afghanistan that the United States took on, but from which it eventually retreated.

Strategic location

As a landlocked country, the strategic importance of Afghanistan stems mainly from its geographical location at the crossroads of Central, South and West Asia, as well as the Far East. The country's borders, enveloping it currently between Pakistan, Iran, Tajikistan, Uzbekistan, Turkmenistan and China, were mostly fixed between 1893 and 1948, though not all satisfactorily. The border with Pakistan (the longest of all), which was inherited from British India, has been most contentious. Afghanistan's geography has been an asset and a curse for it. On the one hand, it has given it the potential to be a beneficiary of regional and global competition under the right circumstances. On the other, it has made it dependent on the mercy and goodwill of its neighbours and at the same time vulnerable to them and to world powers in pursuit of often conflicting interests. Consequently, arguably Afghanistan has often been the focus of more regional and international attention and intervention than otherwise would have been the case.

This locational aspect has led scholars to describe Afghanistan as an embryonic 'hub of connectivity',[3] part of 'the heartland of Eurasia', a 'geographical pivot of history',[4] a 'highway of conquest',[5] part of 'a pivot of the world's security',[6] and at the same time 'unconquerable' and a 'graveyard' for those powers that have sought to dominate it.[7] Additionally, Afghanistan has been praised for its natural beauty and hospitality for those who have sought refuge in it, and labelled 'the Switzerland of Asia'.[8] It has indeed lived up to all these descriptions at different moments in its history. But otherwise, it has been largely pre-industrial, with only meagre trained manpower and industrial output, although with a considerable amount of natural resources. In recent times, US and Afghan sources have estimated that the country possesses $1 trillion worth of valuable minerals buried deep under its harsh and treacherous terrain – an issue which is detailed in chapter 6.

Social-cultural diversity

Afghanistan's society is a mosaic. Without engaging in a genealogical or sociological analysis, which has been copiously carried out by many other Afghanistan specialists, it suffices for our purpose to say that the country's population is a tapestry of various ethnic, tribal and sectarian groups. Each has historically functioned as a micro-society or mini-nation based on shared ancestral, social, cultural and linguistic heritage, where identity and loyalty are generally deter-mined at family, clan, tribe and ethnic levels, more often than not at the expense of inter-group relationships and bonds of national unity.[9]

The ethnic Pashtuns or 'Afghans' or Pathans (as they are called on the Pakistan side of the border) have traditionally formed the largest minority in the country. Most of Afghanistan's rulers, including the Taliban, have come from this group. In the absence of any reliable census, it is estimated that the Pashtuns have historically formed about 42 per cent of the country's roughly 40 million population today,[10] of which, as of 2020, 26 per cent were urbanized and the remainder led a rural life. Derived largely from Indo-European stock, the Pashtuns[11] populated the adjoining regions along the two sides of today's Afghanistan-Pakistan border some nine centuries ago. In Afghanistan, they largely coalesced in the southern region of Kandahar. There has been some controversy about the Pashtuns' ancestral origins. The Scottish statesman and historian Mountstuart Elphinstone (1779–1857), touted a theory that the Pashtuns originated from the last tribe of Israel and therefore descended from Jewish ancestors.[12] But this theory has widely been rejected. A prominent Afghan historian, Mohammad Ali (*b.* 1925), sides with a majority, claiming that the Pashtuns' language of Pashto 'bears no resemblance to Hebrew or any other Aramaic language'.[13] However, while possessing a broad feeling of solidarity or what the noted Arab historian and sociologist Abdurrahman bin Mohammad ibn Khaldun calls *Asabiyyah*,[14] the Pashtuns have by no means always been a united ethnicity. They have functioned as a cluster and have been divided between two macro-tribes – the Durrani or Abdali and Ghilzai – with each composed of several families, clans and sub-tribes, inhabiting mostly southern and eastern Afghanistan along what has been the border with Pakistan since the creation of the latter in 1947.[15]

In both tribes, individual members' identity, loyalty, and codes and norms of behaviour have often been determined vertically from family upward. As Anatol Lieven argues, 'loyalty to family, clan and tribe always took precedence over loyalty to the Afghan state',[16] though this has had limited applicability to some of their educated and urbanized elements in recent times. The Durrani cluster, and mostly its sub-tribe of Mohammadzai, formed the core ruling elite in Afghanistan from the time of Amir Dost Mohammad Khan (who ruled between 1826 and 1839, and 1843 and 1863) until 1978, except for a brief period in 1929.

On the other hand, the Ghilzais only rose to power with communist presidencies of Noor Mohammad Taraki (April 1978–September 1979), Hafizullah Amin (September–December 1979) and Mohammad Najibullah (May 1986–April 1992), as well as the controversially elected presidency of Ashraf Ghani (2014–21). The Taliban leaders and their commanders and foot soldiers also hail from the Ghilzai tribe. The two tribes have harboured rivalry and have occasionally been in conflict with one another, though when threatened from outside, they have in the past presented a common front with a sense of ethnic solidarity.

After the Pashtuns, the Tajiks form the second largest minority in Afghanistan. Descending from ancient East Iranian people of Central Asia, or what some historians have called the 'Aryan race', they constitute an estimated 27 per cent of the population, followed by Hazaras of Mongol origin (about 9 per cent), Uzbeks (9 per cent), Aimak (4 per cent), Turkmen (3 per cent) and Baluchis (2 per cent), with the rest, including Kirgiz, constituting smaller minorities.[17] Except for the Baluchis, who have predominantly been located in the south, all the other groups have traditionally been concentrated in northern, central and western Afghanistan, bordering the Central Asian Republics of Tajikistan, Uzbekistan and Turkmenistan, as well as Iran. Kabul (the capital since 1776) has grown to be a melting pot. It is located to the south-east of the Hindu Kush ranges that stretch from western and central to north-eastern Afghanistan, virtually bisecting the country between north and south. The non-Pashtun groups are also subdivided along the lines of locality, exhibiting distinct social, linguistic and cultural norms and practices. Whereas the Pashtuns speak different dialects of the Pashto language, depending on their residential locations, the Tajiks speak varying dialects of Persian (formally named Dari in 1964).[18] Pashto and Dari have officially assumed national prominence, with Dari having evolved as the main language of administration, literature, and creative and performing arts. The morphological dichotomy between the Pashtuns and the Tajiks has historically mirrored a social divide in Afghanistan. Despite differences between these two larger minorities and smaller ones, they have shown a culture of peaceful coexistence when benevolent and inclusive rulers have come to power, although not so often as to result in enduring norms of national unity.[19]

Afghanistan is indeed a land of minorities and a patchwork of distinct social and cultural micro-societies, with most of them having had the capacity to function as self-contained entities to a noticeable degree. Complicating this demographic profile is that just about all these micro-societies have had, as is the case up to the present, extensive cross-border ties with Afghanistan's neighbours. Consequently, whatever transpires in terms of stability and instability in Afghanistan can potentially concern the country's neighbours and cause them to engage in interventionist action.

The religion of Islam has been a common thread running through the micro-societies but has not provided for the degree of uniformity and enforceability at the micro-level to bridge the country's entrenched social cleavages, for two important reasons. The first is sectarian division: 80 per cent of the population follow the relatively flexible Hanafi school of Sunni Islam, although in varying shades, the same as in neighbouring Pakistan, and about 15 per cent adhere to the Shia sect of the religion, with most of them being followers of the Twelve Imams, as in Iran. In contrast to Iran, where Shia Islam has underpinned the operation of state and society since the advent of the Islamic government in 1979, Islam in Afghanistan has been upheld during most of its history as a state religion. The country was declared an Islamic state for the first time in April 1992, followed by the Taliban renaming it the Islamic Emirate from September 1996 to December 2001, and again from August 2021.

However, the Islam that historically prevailed in Afghanistan was generally moderate and largely followed at the village level. It was practised as a faith and way of life without most of the population being deeply versed in the fundamentals and exegesis of the religion. At the mass level, most of the adherents – largely illiterate – could hardly comprehend the holy Qur'an in classical Arabic. They acquired an understanding of the religion primarily from their families, *madrassas* (religious schools), local preachers and imams (prayer leaders), who were traditionally on the government's payroll and greatly subordinate to the ruler of the time. While this is not to claim that elements of the religious establishment did not engage in politicking and pose challenges to the central authority, it is important to note that radical or extremist political Islamism in different shades has been a recent phenomenon in the country. It burgeoned with the formation of Islamic resistance groups, the Mujahideen (Islamic strivers/fighters), who fought against the Soviet-backed communist rule and Soviet invasion for more than a decade from April 1978, and the advent of Taliban rule prior to the US intervention and after its retreat. It is sufficient here to say that, given the above reasons, Islam has traditionally not been able to play a determining role in bridging social and cultural diversity, and generating a widespread consciousness for national unity, even when it has been deployed as an ideology of power legitimation or resistance or change, to which Afghanistan has been subjected throughout its history.

'Political dualism' and outside interventionism

Two other variables that have catalytically interacted with the strategic location of the country and its mosaic population have been inter- and intra-dynastic rivalry and inner ruling elite dualistic power hostility, based on tribal, ethnic, cultural, ideological and personality differences, and outside interventions. Since its foundation, Afghanistan has experienced only two periods of relative stability and security: from 1747 to 1793, and from 1930 to 1973. Let us turn to a brief discussion of how these periods evolved, what bolstered them and what undermined them, and what transpired in between, to highlight the conditions favourable to state-building in Afghanistan.

From the outset, muddying Afghanistan's road to statehood was the process by which the country was founded and by the politics of 'royal dualism' in the age of British colonialism and rival Tsarist Russian expansionism. The country's foundational nucleus was not laid down on a multi-ethnic consensual basis. It came into existence as a primordial Pashtun creation. Leading the process was Ahmad Khan – a prominent ethnic Pashtun from the Sadozai clan of the Abdali Durrani tribe. He was a notable warrior and organizer, who had distinguished himself in the service of the Persian King Nadir Shah Afshar. After the latter's assassination in 1747, Ahmad Khan returned to his tribe in southern Afghanistan where he convened a gathering or *jirga* ('council', in the Pashtun tradition) of the 'notables' of the Durrani and Ghilzai tribes in Kandahar and forged a Pashtun ethno-tribal confederation. This formed the core of what coalesced as Afghanistan or the place of Pashtuns, with Ahmad Khan as the paramount chief and king. The authority of Ahmad Khan was not immediately recognized throughout Afghanistan. He relied on conquest, the dictums of 'divine right' and 'divide and rule', and the politics of co-optation and alliance and counter-alliance to achieve it.[20]

From the capital Kandahar, he rapidly succeeded in building a patriarchal Pashtun-centric dynastic form of rule over what became known as the Durrani empire, stretching from today's north-eastern and south-eastern Iran to eastern Turkmenistan and north-western India. His power structure was dominated by his tribal loyalists. While assuming the titles of the Shah (king) and the Durr-e Durran (Pearl of Pearls), his rule came very close to the Weberian ideal of patrimonial rule, in that his power was fundamentally personal and independent of any objectively rational goal. Ahmad Shah, as he was now known, did not develop new common legal and political frameworks to transcend the traditional boundaries of various micro-societies.[21] Thus, the way Afghanistan was forged, and the manner in which Ahmad Shah ruled and homogenized the country at a macro level, engendered a sense of Pashtun political and ethnic primacy, providing the basis for some Pashtun figures to claim the rulership of Afghanistan as their natural right up to the present.

Yet, Ahmad Shah's imperial domain did not survive for long after his death in 1773. Like most powerful, wealthy and affluent Muslim males of his time, Ahmad Shah was polygamous. In Islam, a man is conditionally permitted to take up to four legal wives at the same time, although there is no firm ruling on the number of concubines, for 'politics or pleasure'.[22] Ahmad Shah had taken three wives, producing several sons as full and half-brothers, with each being eligible to claim the throne. In the absence of a clear leadership succession procedure, the monarch could designate any of his sons to succeed him. His choice was influenced not only by a son's ability but also by his mother's status, in terms of whether she was very beautiful and assertive or linked to a powerful family or tribe or group. The impact of royal polygamy has often been overlooked by scholars of Afghan politics and society. But, as we will see, it has proven to be one of the most destructive causes of conflict and instability in Afghan history.[23]

Ahmad Shah's favourite was his second eldest son, Timur, from his first wife. Shortly before his death, he pronounced Timur as his heir without consulting his tribal council, which backed his eldest son Sulaiman, the governor of Kandahar. This set off a dynastic power struggle in which Timur made his brother flee to India. Timur had previously gained administrative experience as governor of several cities in Punjab. Upon becoming Timur Shah, he shifted the capital to Kabul, closer to the heart of the empire, and managed to keep the diverse imperial domain almost intact. However, in the process, he had to ward off challenges, not only from his brother but also from ethno-nationalist uprisings in different areas of the empire, especially on the part of the Sikhs, who were increasingly becoming assertive. The multiple campaigns that he unleashed sapped most of his energy and resources, causing the Durrani empire to weaken from within and lose territory at its peripheries, thus moving towards an imperial decline.

When Timur Shah passed away in 1793, he left behind twenty-nine sons from ten wives, several of whom contested the throne. During the struggle for power, the Durrani domain was dealt a serious blow by the rise of Sikh nationalism under Ranjit Singh, the first Maharajah (Great Ruler) of the Sikh Empire (1801–39). He defeated the Afghans, securing the north-western part of the Indian subcontinent. The loss of a sizeable chunk of the Durrani empire to the Sikhs had a domino effect and showed that the Afghans were not invincible.

From that point, internal power rivalries, distrust, betrayal, the breaking of oaths of loyalty and agreements, treachery, political and social unrest, rebellion and disintegration, and foreign intervention came to be a dominant feature of Afghanistan's evolution. Few rulers came to assume power free of dynastic feuding and conflict, at least until 1973, and intra-elite personal and factional power struggle thereafter. Most rose to rule with the direct or indirect support of a foreign power, and were either brutally deposed or assassinated or exiled.[24] Timur Shah's rival sons were patronized by two competing powers of the time – Great Britain and Tsarist Russia. The former pursued a colonialist forward policy,[25] and the latter sought to advance its own regional ambitions during most of the nineteenth century. Afghanistan was intermittently plunged into devastating internal strife, functioning as little more than a cluster of feuding principalities, with Kabul, Kandahar and Herat as capitals of warring full and half-brothers and their supporting tribal groups. Atrocities reached such heights that siblings killed, imprisoned or exiled one another. Power also changed hands between branches of Durranis and Ghilzais, although the former remained dominant. This scenario recurred periodically throughout the twentieth century, although in different ways and varying intensity, spawning political dualism and intergenerational power struggles.

Internal strife was fuelled by a growing Anglo-Russian rivalry, which was conducted within what the British diplomat Arthur Conolly dubbed the 'Great Game' in 1840, a term which Rudyard Kipling popularized in his novel *Kim*, published in 1901. It involved the two powers' competitive diplomatic, political, and espionage and counter-espionage activities for regional influence from Tibet to Istanbul. Afghanistan, along with Persia and Central Asia, formed the territories that the rival powers sought to leverage as a buffer against one another. Each imperial power, although Britain more so than Russia, backed and manipulated rival claimants to the Afghan throne and tribal and ethnic groups to advance their geopolitical interests. Their interventionism, in turn, reinforced Afghanistan's internal turmoil. Thus, although Afghanistan was never technically colonized, the internal and external variables fed on one another to thwart the country's potential to consolidate into a viable state.

Russia advanced across the Central Asian steppes close to Afghanistan's present northern borders, and the British constantly sought to act as king-makers in Afghanistan. They played off different throne aspirants and ethnic and tribal chiefs for their conflicting interests just as much as these actors were keen to leverage one of the powers for their benefits. An illustrative example was during the reign of Amir Dost Mohammad Khan, who held the throne twice (1826–39 and 1843–63). He founded the dynasty of the Durrani's Barakzai branch and was regarded as an independent-minded and forward-looking ruler, who reunited Kandahar and Herat with Kabul under his leadership. The British were initially receptive towards the Amir, as he was content to have the British on his side. However, when he sought to recover Peshawar from a defiant British India, he expediently courted Russia. The British, who wanted the Afghan king to be a staunch ally, launched a military expedition against the

Amir and backed one of Timur Shah's compliant sons, Shah Shoojah, who had earlier been dethroned, causing the first Anglo-Afghan War (1839–42). But their elevation of Shah Shoojah to the throne was only temporary, as the British suffered a humiliating defeat.

In a similar vein, the British invaded Afghanistan once more in 1878, during the reform-inclined reign of Amir Shir Ali Khan (1863–79), a son of Dost Mohammad Khan, who governed amid a power struggle with his brothers. Shir Ali's resistance to British demands for Afghanistan to accept a permanent envoy in Kabul was perceived as the Amir siding with Russia. The British launched a military campaign, igniting the second Anglo-Afghan War (1878–80). Although Shir Ali died in 1879, the conflict spilt over into the following year. Despite contention and turmoil, the Afghans were able to harness their combative strength, born out of their honorific customs and harsh and austere environment, to protect their traditional spirit of freedom. G.P. Tate notes:

> Between the Russian Dominions in Asia and the Indian Empire of Great Britain, Afghanistan is placed, like a nut, between the levers of a cracker. The notoriously unwholesome quality of the kernel, however, will perhaps continue to preserve it from being shared by its powerful neighbours.[26]

The British still could not give up on Afghanistan against perceived Russian expansionism. They backed a grandson of Dost Mohammad Khan, Abdur Rahman Khan, to take the throne. Abdur Rahman Khan had previously lost a power tussle with Shir Ali and taken refuge in Central Asia, placing himself under Russian protection, in January 1869. Originally an opponent of the British, his bitter living experiences in Tashkent made him distrustful of the Russians. In the wake of Shir Ali's passing, and the ensuing chaos amid resistance to the British invasion, he returned to Afghanistan. Leveraging his anti-Russian sentiments, the British promptly negotiated an agreement with him, whereby he took the throne in July 1880 and the British assumed control of Afghanistan's finances and foreign policy, and withdrew their forces to Kandahar in the full knowledge that now they had a friendly king in power in Kabul.

National homogenization and awakening, reform and rebellion

In the midst of the interactive internal strife and outside encroachments, nonetheless certain leaders of varying characteristics emerged who took steps in their own ways to build a sovereign Afghan state. Amir Abdur Rahman Khan, who became known as the 'Iron Amir' for his repressive rule (1880–1901), made some progress in this regard. Launching a ruthless Pashtun-driven process of 'internal imperialism', he centralized power, subordinated micro-societies to his rule and established the basis for an administrative structure.[27] Meanwhile, the British determined the Durand Line in 1893, delineating the border between Afghanistan and British India, which served subsequently as a serious bone of contention between Afghanistan and Pakistan.

After dying of natural causes in 1901, Abdur Rahman was succeeded by his eldest son Habibullah Khan, by right of primogeniture, while outmanoeuvring other crown contenders. Building on his father's legacy, he launched a phase of modest modernization, ushering in some basic industries, social services – including education and health – and press innovation. While maintaining British support, he opted for a *modus vivendi* with an unstable Tsarist Russia, which was shaken by its defeat in the 1904 Russo-Japanese War and the abortive revolution a year later. Habibullah's reign marked a period of national awakening, opening a limited space for a small group of intelligentsia, from which emerged the 'Young Afghans', who called for constitutionalism and modernization only to face an uphill struggle to make an impact in the coming decades.[28] Habibullah was assassinated in February 1919 in a plot that most likely involved his son, Amanullah Khan (from his first and most influential wife), who had an association with the Young Afghans.[29]

Amanullah faced challenges from his uncle and one of his brothers but managed to neutralize them and assume the throne, displaying a burning and impatient nationalist desire to change Afghanistan into a modern, constitution-based and fully fledged independent state along Western lines, a path that was concurrently being pursued by the founder of modern Turkey, Mustafa Kemal Ataturk. Amanullah started his reign by launching the third Anglo-Afghan War in early May 1919, whereby he was able to prompt Britain to agree finally, although reluctantly, to Afghanistan's independence. Adopting a liberalistic constitution in 1924, he initiated a radical and ambitious programme of fundamental political, social and economic reforms, including promotion of women's rights and monogamy. He enabled a group of young Afghan women to be educated in Turkey, and his wife, Soraya, donned Western clothes. He was the first monogamous leader of Afghanistan. In short, his goal was essentially to pull Afghanistan out of a largely medieval way of functioning to a twentieth-century standard. Aiding him in the military and security spheres was his Minister of War Mohammad Nadir, the head of the Mohammadzai Musahiban family. In reformist ideas, he enjoyed the wisdom, enlightenment and advice of a leading thinker, Mahmoud Tarzi, who was also his father-in-law. Previously, under Habibullah Khan's rule, the Musahiban and Tarzi families had been exiled to India and Syria respectively.[30]

Certain changes in the region and beyond also helped Amanullah, who assumed the title of king in 1926, in his reformist zeal. They included the growing nationalist movements in British colonies, most relevantly in the Indian subcontinent, which made London more inward-looking; nationalist reformist trends that swept parts of the Muslim domain, as in Turkey, Persia (called Iran from 1932) and Egypt; and Tsarist Russia's transition to the Soviet era in the wake of the Bolsheviks' 1917 seizure of power, led by Vladimir Ilyich Lenin. The latter's prompt recognition of Afghanistan's independence, and extension of friendship and support to Amanullah at a time when the British still harboured resentment towards him, came in handy. These developments, and a lull in the traditional Anglo-Russian rivalry largely due to the two powers' domestic preoccupations, encouraged Amanullah to accelerate the pace of his reforms.

The breadth and speed of his changes, however, rocked the conservative and divided Afghan society, causing growing opposition from the forces that touted his reforms as anti-Islamic and contrary to Afghanistan's cultural and social norms and values. By the mid-1920s, Amanullah's rule was besieged by widespread ethno-tribal rebellions and betrayal by some members of his inner circle, whose personal power ambitions and rivalry were of the pattern that had historically marred Afghanistan's governance. As the country was plunged into civil war, Amanullah found it necessary to go into exile and abdicated in January 1929 in favour of his brother, Inayatullah Khan. But the latter's rule lasted only a very short time before an illiterate Islamic Tajik warrior, Habibullah Kalakani (known as *bache-i saquo*, or 'son of a water carrier') claimed the throne and declared himself king.[31] This was the first time that a non-Pashtun had assumed power. Amanullah, a frustrated and failed modernizer, lived in Italy until his death in Zurich in 1960.[32]

Politics of gradualism and dualism

Kalakani was unacceptable to the Pashtuns and was betrayed by some of the very people around him who had undermined Amanullah. The Musahiban elder brother Mohammad Nadir, who had been exiled to France in 1926 due to differences with Amanullah, returned through British India in early 1929 to rescue the throne. Accompanied by his two full brothers, who were later joined by his two half-brothers, and backed by the British, he raised a cluster of kindred Pashtun tribal fighters and defeated Kalakani's forces. Despite an Islamic/Qur'anic agreement with Kalakani not to harm him if he surrendered, in the old Afghan tradition Nadir hanged Kalakani, together with several of his close aides, letting their bodies dangle for days in Kabul as a warning to any other opposition. For doing this, he gained the title of Nadir-i-Ghadar (Nadir the traitor).

Nadir's declaration as king or shah in October 1929 inaugurated his dynastic rule. His reign marked the beginning of the longest period of relative national harmony and security in Afghanistan, although not one free of intra-royal family rivalry. Descending from the royal family of Amir Dost Mohammad Khan, Nadir Shah's father, Mohammad Yusuf Khan, had three sons from one wife – Mohammad Nadir, Shah Mahmoud and Shah Wali – and two sons from another – Mohammad Hashim Khan and Mohammad Aziz Khan. Having experienced sibling power struggles with devastating consequences for Afghanistan in the past, Nadir wanted to avoid this happening again. He opted for a balance between the two branches of the royal family by appointing his two full brothers, Mahmoud and Shah Wali, as War Minister and ambassador to Britain respectively, and his two half-brothers Hashim and Aziz as prime minister and ambassador to Russia and shortly thereafter to Germany, respectively. Maintaining the tradition of patrimonial rule, he reinstituted a Mohammadzai-centred autocracy with the monarch wielding absolute power. He purged those who had served Amanullah in senior positions and subordinated or marginalized any form of actual or potential opposition. When his rule was challenged by rival Ghilzai tribes, as well as by some of the other non-Pashtun minorities – Uzbeks and Hazaras in particular – the uprisings were forcefully suppressed.

Nadir Shah called off Amanullah's policy of accelerated, liberal-oriented modernization in favour of top-down controlled processes of evolutionary change and development which he deemed more suitable for Afghanistan's conditions. He focused on building a strong army and other rule-enforcement agencies, and passed a constitution in 1931, enshrining the powers of the monarch and Islamic codes of governance and behaviour. His reforms prioritized administrative structures and social and economic development, stressing the importance of education, public health and industrial innovation. Although centralist, he seemed to be consensual as a prerequisite for generating national unity. On the external front, he pursued a pro-British posture but also good neighbourly relations with the USSR within an officially declared foreign policy of neutrality. He took advantage of the slowdown in the Anglo-Soviet rivalry, as dictator Joseph Stalin intensified his domestic power consolidation and Britain found it imperative to deal with increased unrest in its colonies and cope with the fallout from the Great Depression of 1929.

Nadir Shah was assassinated in November 1933 by a Hazara student, Abdul Khaleq, who had family and ethnic grievances against him. Khaleq, his entire family and many from his ethnic group were executed. Like Amanullah, Nadir had been monogamous. Prime Minister Hashim and War Minister Mahmoud swiftly moved to avoid the chaos of previous leadership successions by crowning Nadir's eldest son, the Afghan- and French-educated Mohammad Zahir, then aged nineteen, who became Zahir Shah. But since the new king was young and inexperienced, Hashim, backed by Mahmoud, wielded all the executive power. Hashim was accorded respect for his seniority in the context of the Afghan culture. Consequently, Zahir Shah was only nominally the king, while Hashim took charge of running the country. He built on Nadir's policy of domestic gradualism in the form of two steps forward and one step back in national development, with a foreign policy of neutrality.

However, two aspects of his prime ministership are worth emphasizing, for their long-term impact on the course of Afghanistan's evolution. One was the broadening of the country's foreign relations, as the United States finally, after much lobbying, opened its embassy in Kabul in 1942. This paved the way for America's modest financial and developmental aid at a time when Britain's power was waning in the region, culminating in the partition of the Indian subcontinent colony in 1947 into the independent states of Hindu-dominated

India and Muslim-majority Pakistan. The ensuing border disputes and rivalry between these two states spawned a lasting source of regional instability and world concern.

The second was the rivalry between the two branches of the royal family. Hashim had favoured Zahir's coronation for the sake of dynastic continuity, but he was well disposed towards his two full nephews, Mohammad Daoud and Mohammad Naim, sons of Aziz, who was killed during his ambassadorial mission by an Afghan student in Germany, in June 1933. Hashim took the two under his tutelage and made sure that they were well looked after. Of the two brothers, French-educated Daoud turned out to be more politically savvy and ambitious. Under Hashim, he served consecutively as governor of the eastern provinces and the southern province of Kandahar, as well as commander of the Central Forces, enabling him to gain administrative and military experience, crystallizing his political drive.

Afghanistan's neutrality was maintained during the Second World War, but under pressure from the Allies, Kabul severed relations with the Axis powers. Hashim was criticized for this by those elements of the Afghan intelligentsia who opposed Britain for all its past misdeeds in Afghanistan and valued German friendship. He resigned due to ill health in favour of his half-brother Mahmoud in 1946, and died three years later. His departure opened the arena for Daoud to advance his leadership aspirations. He started various political and popular machinations to achieve his goal, sparking another intra-royal family power rivalry that eventually led Afghanistan down the path of devastating turmoil from the early 1970s to the present. How did this come about?

Mahmoud was a milder and more consensual figure than Hashim in his political and social interactions. At the urging of Hashim, Mahmoud appointed Daoud, who was married to King Zahir's eldest sister,[33] as defence minister, then two years later as interior minister, followed by a short ambassadorial post in France and then as commander of the Central Corps of the Afghan Armed Forces. This gave Daoud the opportunity to build a patronage power base and engage in such behind-the-scenes activities as to undermine his half-uncle's leadership. He finally made a handshake deal (as is customary in Afghan culture) with the king to push Mahmoud out on the proviso that, if Daoud was made prime minister, the king would be able to exercise his constitutional powers and the two could work together to accelerate Afghanistan's modernization. Mahmoud resigned in September 1953, but once Daoud succeeded him, he did not remain loyal to the deal, reviving the old Afghan politics of dualism.[34]

Daoud was essentially an autocratic, socialist-oriented, nationalist modernizer, although with no ideological interest in Marxism-Leninism per se. He seemed more of a reformer who desired to achieve what King Amanullah had failed to accomplish. While isolating King Zahir and running the country as he deemed suitable, his period of prime ministership stood out for its efforts primarily in the areas of social reform, economic and infrastructural development, and women's emancipation. He placed greater stress on a resolution of the dispute over the Durand Line and support for a Pashtun separatist movement for the creation of an independent state of Pashtunistan (in alliance with Afghanistan) out of Pakistan's North-West Frontier and Baluchistan provinces, for two purposes: to enable Afghanistan to gain direct access to international waters; and to promote a Pashtunist-based nationalism as an instrument of power and to impose national unity at home. While ensuring that the political and military leader-ship remained in the hands of his Mohammadzai clan, he allowed the Tajiks a substantial share in the administrative, educational, literary and artistic life of the country. As an integral part of this formula, he stressed the importance of the development of the Pashto language – equal to that of the more widely spoken Dari – as one of the two offi-cial languages of Afghanistan. He did so, even though he personally, along with many other members of the royal family, had been urban-ized and spoke mainly Dari. Daoud's policies nonetheless shifted Afghanistan's relations with Pakistan to a more confrontational level, which worried the non-Pashtun minorities, whose elements figured strongly, along with many educated Pashtuns, in the small but growing and active intelligentsia in the country.

To achieve his domestic and foreign policy objectives, Daoud needed outside financial, economic and technological aid, and a strong military to deal with any ethno-tribal backlashes and to stand up to Pakistan. He was fully cognizant of what frustrated Amanullah's reformist efforts. At first, he approached the US for help in 1954. Washington responded negatively because Afghanistan was not critical to its strategic interests at that time. This led him to turn to the Soviet Union. Moscow welcomed his request with open arms. As Nikita Khrushchev stresses in his memoirs, his leadership feared America's intrusion into Afghanistan as part of its policy of containment of the USSR at the height of the global Cold War.[35] Moscow's provision of military and economic aid, and its backing for Afghanistan in the border dispute with Pakistan, prompted Washington also to warm to the need for a neutral Afghanistan, although refusing to do anything that could offend friendly Pakistan. Ultimately, Daoud was able to play off the two powers and attract aid from both, but it was the Soviet Union that became the dominant provider. Within a decade, Moscow funded and constructed many infrastructural and industrial projects, and the Afghan armed forces became predominantly Soviet-equipped and trained. With this came Soviet military and civilian advisors, as well as the training of Afghan personnel in both spheres in the USSR, laying the foundations for Soviet political influence. Daoud resigned in 1963 over his costly push for Pashtunistan that had resulted in border skirmishes with Pakistan and the latter's closure to Afghan transit. But he departed on the basis of another handshake deal with King Zahir to enable him to make a comeback when politically appropriate.

Daoud's departure at last enabled the king to assert his authority and, in turn, block Daoud's future power ambitions. He appointed a non-royal (the first in Afghan history) – German-educated Dr

Mohammad Yousuf – as prime minister, promulgated a new pro-democratic constitution in 1964, containing a provision that banned members of the royal family from assuming ministerial positions, de-emphasized the Pashtunistan issue and opened a new phase known as an 'experiment with democracy' in Afghan politics. None of these measures pleased Daoud, who now used his retirement to plot against the king. He exploited his relations with certain receptive elements within the royal family, governmental structures, parliament and the military for revenge. For reasons of pure Realpolitik, he enhanced ties with a tiny pro-Soviet political faction, Parcham (Banner), led by an old Moscow-backed Marxist hand, Babrak Karmal, who, along with some of his informal party members, was elected to the lower house of parliament in the first parliamentary elections in 1965 since the adoption of the new constitution. Publicly, Daoud refrained from siding with Parcham when it was joined by the rival but also very small pro-Soviet faction, Khalq (Masses) in forming the People's Democratic Party of Afghanistan (PDPA). But he and his supporters quietly took advantage of their demands for more political reforms and freedoms in opposition to the monarchy.

An advantage to him, too, was the political infighting and uncertainty generated by the emergence of opposition groups to the PDPA, such as the pro-Maoist group, Shuli Jawaid (Eternal Flame), and an Islamist movement that coalesced around a political movement called the Jamiati Islami Afghanistan (the Islamic Society of Afghanistan). Two prominent figures of the Jamiat were Burhanuddin Rabbani and Ahmad Shah Massoud from the Tajik ranks. Rabbani was an Egypt-educated theologian who subsequently led the Jamiat, and Massoud emerged as a famed, home-grown Jamiat commander.[36] They both believed in a progressive Islamist transformation of Afghanistan and subsequently fought the Soviet occupation of the country (1979–88) and the Pakistan-backed Al Qaeda-allied Taliban. Splitting from Jamiat was the Hezbi Islami, under the Pashtunist Gulbuddin Hekmatyar, who preached an extremist version of Islamic activism.

These developments, plus King Zahir's reluctance to ratify the parliament-endorsed political party bill for fear of losing some of his powers, caused unprecedented political and social fragmentation, mirroring the diverse nature of Afghan society. Daoud and his supporters skilfully exploited the situation. When the 69-year-old King Zahir was on a visit to Italy for his health, Daoud, in alliance with Parcham, staged a successful palace coup on 18 July 1973.[37]

Still, it is worth stressing that the period between 1930 and 1973 marked the longest – and an unprecedented – period of peace in Afghanistan, with the country's government consolidating what could be described as approximate to a primordial functioning state. By the mid-1960s, the capital Kabul exuded a noted degree of cultural, social and developmental vibrancy, and the city's tranquillity was reflected across the nation. One could move freely and securely across the city, limited only by the majestic mountains surrounding it. Cyclists could peddle around the country and tourists could safely visit it on bus trips from Kathmandu to Munich. While still predominantly Muslim, traditional and poverty-stricken, with a very slow pace of modernization, Afghanistan had become known for not only its natural beauty and people's hospitality, but also its serene environment. Women's emancipation, along with modern primary, secondary and tertiary education for both males and females, with Kabul University as a co-educational institution, as well as the arts, theatre, print and electronic media, had become measures of its progress. The country stood as a model of neutrality in world affairs, being a founding member of the United Nations (1946) and of the Non-Aligned Movement (1955). Afghanistan's ambassador to the UN, Abdul Rahman Pazhwak, was elected to the presidency of the UN General Assembly in 1966. Kabul was named as a possible site for the Vietnam peace talks in 1969, although due to a lack of sufficient facilities it was passed over for Paris. This is not to claim that Afghanistan was advancing beyond being a pre-industrial developing country. To the contrary, it still suffered from poor governance and malpractice at all levels. It was foreign-aid dependent, and top-down corruption was a problem, involving the royal family, but not on a large and pervasive scale.[38]

Zahir Shah's 'experiment' with democracy, involving parliamentary elections as limited and primitive as they were, attracted a rare degree of international press coverage. *Time* published a lengthy piece in December 1965, praising the country's move in a democratic direction: 'Neither [Hashim] Maiwandwal [the second civilian prime minister, 1965–7],[39] nor his King believes that democracy will come easily to Afghanistan. In a nation where violence is still the code . . . the process will be long and hard.' It quoted Maiwandwal: 'There are risks involved in instituting democracy at this time. . . . But they are calculated risks. The people will have to come to understand more about the processes of law.' It concluded:

> That is just what the U.S. would like to see. Afghanistan has always been a buffer between Russia and the Indian subcontinent. As such, it must remain neutral. American aid ($300 million v. Russia's $700 million) is dedicated to promoting that neutrality – and to building democracy as well.[40]

Two factors stand out as contributing to the serenity of the period. One was the post-Second World War polarization of global politics under the aegis of two rival superpowers, the US and the USSR. The Cold War underpinned a predictably stable global order, despite being punctuated by several wars in the South, with American and Soviet direct or proxy involvement. This enabled a neutral country like Afghanistan to exercise more independence in the conduct of its internal and foreign affairs, and to play off rival powers to its advantage. The other was the success of the Afghan ruling elite, despite its internal divisions, in generating a loose but workable triangular framework of relations between the monarchy, the religious establishment and local power-holders or 'strongmen', within which the micro-societies were carefully placed and where their interactions with the centre and one another were reasonably defined. In brief, the monarchy acted as the repository of national power, authority and sovereignty, with a focus on promoting national cohesion, identity and security, and with control over national finances and foreign relations. It pursued a minimalist interventionist approach to micro-societies, providing them with the necessary space to conduct and regulate their internal affairs in conformity with their particular conditions. The system was by no means conducive to lifting Afghanistan from a position of being a least developing and, by and large, a rentier (that is, foreign-aid dependent) country. It nonetheless contained a degree of internal elasticity and external flexibility that allowed it to function as a respectable sovereign actor in a difficult neighbourhood within a relatively stable bipolar international order.

Transition from monarchy to republic

However, this framework was smashed, partly by the coup of 1973. Daoud declared Afghanistan a republic, abolishing the historically entrenched monarchy, around which the concept of power, authority and public attachment had traditionally swirled. Along with it, he also ended the prime ministership of the Pashtun reformer Musa Shafiq, whom the king had appointed in December 1972 to move Afghanistan further along the path of modernization. With Master's degrees from Al-Azhar University in Cairo and Columbia University in New York, Shafiq was well-versed in Islamic and Western ideals and practices and well-positioned for the task at hand. During his short tenure, one of his important achievements was to settle the dispute with Iran over water distribution from the Helmand River, as outlined in the Afghan-Iranian Helmand-River Water Treaty of 1 July 1973.[41]

Daoud promised a brighter and more prosperous future. While upholding Afghanistan's policy of neutrality, he affirmed the country's close friendship with the Soviet Union, mainly as part of a deal with Parcham, while singling out Pakistan for differences over the border dispute and the right of Pakistan's Pashtuns to self-determination. He suspended the 1964 Constitution and dissolved its prescribed organs, including the parliament, claiming they were the foundations and chains of corruption and dysfunctionality.[42]

Despite his public utterances about ushering in 'true democracy', Daoud set out to move Afghanistan along a highly centralized pro-socialist mode of development as a sovereign and neutral state. He unfolded a substantial programme of economic and social reforms, and diversification and expansion of Afghanistan's relations. But as an autocrat he surrounded himself largely with sycophants, many of whom proved to be incompetent and self-interested. He could not tolerate sharing power with anyone and his partnership with Parcham was more an act of political expediency than commitment.[43] Nor could he accept any form of subordination to the USSR or any other power, despite having been responsible for laying the foundations for Soviet influence in Afghanistan during his prime ministership. As he became increasingly cognizant of the threat from the rear – the Soviet Union – he sought to slacken his alliance with Parcham and de-emphasize the Pashtunistan issue that had alarmed pro-Western Pakistan and Iran.

Daoud's attempts to reduce his vulnerability to Parcham and the Soviet Union[44] and concurrently to turn his back on Islamist groups as 'dark forces', proved to be very costly for him. He tried to mitigate the repercussions by improving relations with Pakistan and turning for aid to Washington, and to the leaders of oil-rich Iran, Mohammad Reza Shah Pahlavi, and Libya, Colonel Muammar al-Qaddafi. But this, along with his friendship with the anti-Soviet Egyptian President Anwar al-Sadat, did not pay off as expected. US Secretary of State Henry Kissinger visited Kabul on 1 November 1974, but could not fully digest Daoud's desperate need for support to cool down relations with the USSR. Washington directed Kabul to the Shah of Iran as America's main ally and regional gendarme.[45] The Shah promised $2 billion in aid, but could only provide $20 million before he was embroiled in a revolution and overthrown in January 1979. No assistance came from Qaddafi or Sadat either. Moscow viewed Daoud's policies as a serious attempt to break Afghanistan away from Russia's influence and abrogate its massive economic, financial and military investment in the country, amounting to $2 billion during the period 1955 to 1978, compared to America's $500 million, mostly made up of non-military aid, during the same period.[46]

Transition to 'communism' and the Soviet invasion

Consequently, Parcham and Khalq revived their mid-1960s alliance within the PDPA, possibly at Moscow's urging, to wrest power from Daoud. When Daoud moved against the PDPA leaders and jailed some of them, their supporters in the armed forces (in which the Soviet advisors were embedded) staged a violent coup on 27 April 1978. They were spurred on by Hafizullah Amin, a Wisconsin University-educated Pashtun Marxist, who oversaw the PDPA's liaison with the military. In the operation, Daoud and most members of his family were killed. After being rescued from jail, the PDPA leaders hailed the end of what they termed the corrupt and oppressive Nadir dynastic rule, and declared Afghanistan a democratic republic with fraternal ties to the Soviet Union. This began a new but very turbulent transition in Afghanistan's historical journey in the context of the US–Soviet Cold War rivalry.

The political dualism, with multi-dimensional manifestations, that had characterized the course of Afghan politics, governance and development took a new turn. The unholy Parcham–Khalq alliance within the PDPA could not endure for too long.[47] Both factions lacked popular and historical legitimacy, and administrative experience. Their leaders and followers within and outside the military came from diverse backgrounds, with different ideological and political approaches. Although projecting themselves as revolutionary Marxist-Leninists, most were more so in style than substance. As mentioned earlier, Parcham was led by Babrak Karmal, who was of Durrani Pashtun heritage and highly urbanized, speaking mainly Dari rather than Pashto. He was encircled by like-minded colleagues, but from varying social strata. They included Anahita Ratebzad – well-educated and widely rumoured to be Karmal's mistress – and politically ambitious heavyweight Mohammad Najibullah, who hailed from the Ahmadzai branch of the Ghilzai tribe, and who could eloquently speak in both Dari and Pashto. Karmal and his supporters acted like the Mensheviks, the moderate wing of the Russian Social-Democratic Workers' Party, which Lenin and his radical Bolshevik supporters outmanoeuvred following their seizure of power in 1917. They recognized that conditions in Afghanistan were not ripe for a Marxist revolution and had pursued a *modus vivendi* with the ruling establishment until such time as circumstances would change in favour of such an event.

On the other hand, the Khalq was a hard-core Ghilzai Pashtunist group, led by a largely self-educated, self-styled romantic revolutionary, Noor Mohammad Taraki, and his cunning and power-hungry Leninist-cum-Stalinist lieutenant, Hafizullah Amin. The group acted largely in the Bolshevik tradition and sought urgent and forceful transformation of Afghanistan into what they perceived as a socialist and communist state. Despite their bitter differences, the two groups initially announced a unity government, with Taraki as president, Karmal and Amin as two deputy prime ministers and in the case of the latter, also foreign minister, Najibullah as head of the State Intelligence Service (Khadamat-e Aetla'at-e Dawlati – KHAD, the equivalent of the Soviet KGB)[48] and Ratebzad as deputy head of state. Other cabinet posts were divided among the two factions. Moscow had favoured Parcham over Khalq as being more in line with its interests, but now immediately recognized the new government with an expression of full support.

Yet the PDPA's factional unity was a mirage. Amin despised Karmal and wanted all the power for himself and his Khalqi supporters. Within weeks he installed his devotees, including members of his wider family and Ghilzai clan, in the administration and military, and outwitted the Parcham leaders. At first, he exiled them as ambassadors; subsequently he sacked them on corruption charges and imprisoned them, then undertook a purge of Parchamis in the government. However, Moscow kept Karmal and his exiled colleagues in storage (with Karmal in a town outside Prague) for possible future use, as it was not fully confident of Amin's loyalty. The PDPA became increasingly entangled in factional fighting and the politics of repression as a reflection of its own insecurity. Compounding the situation was its forceful centralization of power and rapid unfolding of secularist social, cultural and economic changes in the name of the socialist development of Afghanistan, which were viewed by most Afghan people as repugnant in relation to their entrenched traditions and Islamic beliefs and values. A backlash from the micro-societies resulted in uprisings in different parts of the country and in the government's augmented repression.

Meanwhile, as the PDPA was tearing itself apart and could not cope with the backlash, it became increasingly dependent on all-round Soviet aid. Under the Brezhnev Doctrine, named after the Soviet leader at the time, Leonid Brezhnev (1964–82), the Communist Party of the Soviet Union was required to assist any needy fraternal party in another country, so Moscow kept escalating its advisory, economic and military involvement in support of the PDPA's rule.

Public discontent gave rise to the formation of Islamic resistance forces (the Mujahideen). The main and primarily Sunni Mujahideen groups emerged in two distinct radical and traditionalist political Islamist categories. The radical groups were Gulbuddin Hekmatyar's Hezbi Islami (Islamic Party), Abdul Rab Rasul Sayyaf's Ittihadd-e Islami (Islamic Union), and Mohammad Yunus Khalis's Hezbi Islami (Islamic Party). The traditionalist groups were Mohammad Nabi

Mohammadi's Harakati-i Islami (Revolutionary Islamic Movement), Sibghatullah Mojaddei's Jabha-i Nejat-i Milli (National Liberation Front) and Sayid Ahmad Gailani's Mahaz-i Milli (National Front). In between the two categories stood Jamiati Islami Afghanistan. They were all active participants in a declared *Jihad* (Islamic holy war) against the PDPA and its Soviet backers, for attempting to transform Afghanistan into a 'Godless' communist state.

However, whereas the ethnically Tajik-based Jamiat was the largest Mujahideen group expounding a version of progressive Islamism, the other groups were mostly Pashtun. Hekmatyar's, Khalis's and Sayyaf's groups came mainly from the Ghilzai tribes and stood for a variety of radical Islamisms, including Saudi Wahhabism, as advocated by Sayyaf, who had nurtured a special relationship with Riyadh and received funding from that source. The other three were relatively small and pro-monarchist, supporting the restoration of Zahir Shah's monarchy. All the groups, except for Jamiat, grew to be dependent on and vulnerable to predominantly Sunni Islamic Pakistan, which was now regarded as a frontline state against the spread of Soviet influence from Afghanistan and was favourably disposed to the United States. There were also three smaller Shia resistance groups, representing some of Afghanistan's Shia minority. They were aided by the Iranian Islamic regime under the leadership of Ayatollah Rohullah Khomeini, who labelled the US 'the Great Satan' and the USSR 'the Smaller Satan', but nonetheless found the latter politically more congenial than the former.[49]

Meanwhile, the PDPA was drowning in self-destruction. Even its dominant Khalq faction could not maintain internal unity. There was never a happy political marriage between the politically naive Taraki and the ambitious and ruthless Amin. In the past, Amin had described his relations with Taraki as inseparable like 'nail and flesh'. He used this to consolidate his personal power, which alarmed Taraki and some of his loyalists within the party. Returning from a Non-Aligned Summit in Cuba, Taraki stopped in Moscow in early

September 1979 for a meeting with the Soviet leaders, who by now had become highly suspicious of Amin. A plot was hatched to get rid of Amin. But since the latter had a mole in Taraki's entourage, following the president's return to Kabul, a bloody showdown took place in the presence of the Soviet ambassador, in the presidential palace (Arg). Amin prevailed, detaining his boss, and shortly thereafter suffocated him on the lower ground floor of the Kooti-Baghcha building of the palace. He declared himself the new president and head of the PDPA on 14 September 1979. In a politically cunning move, while calling for more Soviet help, he expediently sought to negotiate a power-sharing deal with Hekmatyar, who was widely regarded at the time as an Inter-Services Intelligence (ISI) client and 'Pakistan puppet'.[50] He also made overtures to the US in a meeting on 27 October 1979, with the US chargé d'affaires, Archer K. Blood,[51] despite the deterioration of Kabul–Washington relations since the kidnapping and killing of American ambassador Adolph Dubs in Kabul, in a botched Afghan security operation in February 1979. These developments alerted the Brezhnev leadership to the possibility it might lose Afghanistan to the US.

Moscow was faced with the difficult choice of either intervening (under the Brezhnev Doctrine) to save the PDPA regime or letting it go. But the Kremlin could not possibly accept the prospect of a Western-backed Mujahideen Islamic government replacing that of the PDPA, particularly given the proximity of the USSR's predominantly Muslim Central Asian Republics. In addition, Iran was already being placed under radical Islamic rule and Pakistan was experiencing vigorous Islamization under General Zia ul-Haq.

Although the Soviet Politburo had rejected a proposed invasion in early 1979, Brezhnev decided to bypass a full meeting of the decision-making body. Together with four other Politburo members, including the defence minister, he opted for invasion,[52] despite some of the military generals recommending the contrary, with the aim of replacing Amin with Karmal and strengthening the PDPA rule. It was thought that Soviet troops would be able to stabilize the situation within a year or so before most would be withdrawn as had happened previously in the Soviet East European satellite states. This was not to be the case. The invasion, which began in late December 1979, opened a new phase in Afghanistan's tragic history. As Soviet troops poured in, ultimately numbering 105,000, they killed Amin, and empowered Karmal and his Parchami colleagues, which only resulted in the cementing of Parcham-dominated PDPA rule, not necessarily party unity.

Moscow claimed that its dispatch of 'a limited contingent of troops' was at the invitation of the very Afghan government whose head it eliminated. The move sparked a debate in Western policy-making and academic circles as to whether the Soviet invasion was a defensive, pre-emptive or offensive act, which was reflected in the pages of the *New York Times* at the time.[53] Yet the weight of opinion in Washington leant towards the view that it was offensive, purporting that Moscow could use Afghanistan as a springboard to realize its long-standing plan for regional domination.

Democratic President Jimmy Carter, who had hitherto been pursuing a policy of détente with the USSR, called the invasion 'a callous violation of international law and the United Nations Charter' and 'an extremely serious threat to peace'. He stressed the 'strategic importance' of Afghanistan (something that Washington had overlooked in the past) and condemned the Soviet move as a 'stepping stone to possible control over much of the world's oil supplies' from the Persian Gulf.[54] Even so, Carter was careful not to overplay his hand.[55] He decided on a relatively modest programme of aid to the Mujahideen and Pakistan. However, the invasion certainly provided a compelling reason for the hardline Republican President Ronald Reagan (1981–9) to accelerate military, financial and logistic support for the Mujahideen through Pakistan, and also to lavish Islamabad with vast amounts of military, financial and economic assistance (amounting to $10 billion over the next decade) to combat the Soviet 'evil empire'.[56]

The Kremlin clearly overestimated the potential for unity within the PDPA. The Khalqi members continued to undermine their Parchami counterparts, and the US availed itself of a unique opportunity to draw the Soviets into a long bloody conflict as part of its long-standing policy of containment of the USSR – as indicated by Carter's national security advisor, Zbigniew Brzezinski.[57] The CIA closely coordinated and cooperated with the ISI in channelling aid to the Mujahideen groups. America's total military, economic and financial assistance to the radical Mujahideen groups amounted to more than $20 billion between 1981 and 1992. This was supplemented by $1.2 billion from Saudi Arabia between 1981 and 1986 alone.[58] Indeed, as then Saudi chief of intelligence Turki bin Faisal Al Saud conveyed to the author, Saudi aid to the Mujahideen and their successors, the pre-9/11 Taliban, amounted to $24 billion between 1981 and 2001.[59] The CIA also played a critical role in coordinating efforts from New York, Cairo and Riyadh to attract foreign fighters for the Mujahideen's jihad.[60] These included Osama bin Laden, who brought money and fighters to participate in the jihad as an Islamic 'obligation', and to forge his Al Qaeda network in Pakistan. Further, the US and Saudi Arabia provided funding for numerous *madrassas* (religious schools) in Pakistan to ensure a steady supply of Mujahideen manpower from among the Afghan refugees.[61]

For a while, the Soviet forces performed reasonably well by protecting the major cities, strategic points, main lines of communications and border entries, and by dominating the sky at the increasing cost of Mujahideen and civilian lives. The Soviets also invested enough resources to keep the Afghan economy afloat and to build several infrastructural and industrial projects as symbols of Afghanistan's socialist transformation. However, with Soviet leaders Brezhnev, Yuri Andropov and Konstantin Chernenko dying on the job one after another, finally the youngest Politburo member, Mikhail Gorbachev, succeeded to the Soviet presidency in 1985. The USSR was by now politically, economically and financially a sinking ship.

While trying to save it through a process of vigorous reformation, Gorbachev could see that his country was involved in a prolonged, resource-draining and unwinnable Afghan war, leading him to describe Afghanistan in early 1986 as a 'bleeding wound'.[62]

The Reagan administration made sure to turn this wound into a defeat for Soviet communism. The US's supply of shoulder-firing Stinger missiles and the UK's furnishing of Blowpipe missiles to the Mujahideen by mid-1986 provided the resistance forces with effective cover against Soviet air power, enabling them to shoot down a Soviet plane every couple of days. Gorbachev was left with no option but to seek a military exit. Given the heavy Soviet investment in the war, his preference was for an honourable disentanglement through a political settlement or 'afghanization' of the war. Since Karmal had proved ineffective, Moscow replaced him in November 1987 with Najibullah, who had emerged as more politically savvy, intellectually sharp, and potentially capable of reshaping the PDPA government in tune with Moscow's changing interests. Najibullah announced a number of policy measures, including altering the PDPA's name to Watan (Homeland), in order to entice the Mujahideen and their outside supporters into a process of national reconciliation and participation, although under his leadership. He also warned the world that: 'If fundamentalism comes to Afghanistan, war will continue for many years. Afghanistan will turn into a centre of world smuggling for narcotic drugs. Afghanistan will be turned into a centre for terrorism.'[63] But it all came too late.

Najibullah's brutality as head of KHAD had already blackened his reputation. His efforts to generate factional unity within the PDPA produced no results. He faced persistent party disunity, as exemplified by the March 1990 bloody coup against him by his Khalqi minister of defence, Shahnawaz Tanai. Although the coup failed and Tanai escaped to Pakistan to join the Hekmatyar group,[64] it clearly showed the depth of the ongoing Parcham–Khalq factional animosity. Meanwhile, the Mujahideen were not united either. The Hekmatyar and the Rabbani or, more specifically, Massoud, groups were locked in serious rivalry on personality, ethnic and visionary grounds. The former sought power to change Afghanistan into an extremist Islamic country with ISI's support, and the latter acted in pursuit of an independent, sovereign, enlightened Islamic Afghanistan.

The lack of a united, reliable and effective Afghan partner on the ground, plus a divided anti-systemic armed opposition, including three Iranian-backed Shia-dominated groups, which the US and its allies did not support, scuttled any chances of a viable political settlement for the Soviets. In the end, Moscow settled for a negotiated deal, known as the Afghan Geneva Peace Accords, signed on 14 April 1988 by the Najibullah and Zia ul-Haq governments, with the Soviet Union and the United States acting as its guarantors. The accords, in which the Mujahideen had no direct input, provided for a Soviet troop withdrawal within less than a year, with no ceasefire or curtailment of arms supplies by the two major powers to their Afghan clients in place.

Nonetheless, the last Soviet soldier left Afghanistan on 15 February 1989.[65] As provided for by the Geneva Accords, Moscow continued life-saving support for the Najibullah government, and the US maintained its aid to the resistance and Pakistan. Najibullah's government survived for another three years, for two main reasons. First, the Soviet withdrawal removed the focus of the Mujahideen's semblance of unity, leading them to intensify their internal power struggle. The main catalyst here was ISI's favourite, Hekmatyar, who treacherously sought to target Massoud's forces. Second, US interest in the Afghan conflict began to wane. Washington had achieved its main objective of causing the Soviet defeat by proxy, comparable to what the Soviets had helped North Vietnam inflict on the US. In effect, it entrusted Islamabad with the task of managing the post-Soviet Afghanistan transition.

Transition to Islamic republic

The USSR's disintegration in December 1991 heralded not only the end of Soviet communism and support for the Najibullah government, but also the end of the Cold War, and the dawn of a new era for the US to claim a unipolar world. It was clear that, despite its ideological and political machinations, the Kabul government had reached the end of its rope. Some of the heavyweights around Najibullah became concerned about their own survival. They included Foreign Minister Abdul Wakil and army chief General Mohammad Nabi Azimi,[66] who found it expedient by early 1992 to sacrifice Najibullah and transfer power to the opposition. But the question was, to whom? They had a choice of three: Hekmatyar, the northern Uzbek warlord, Abdul Rashid Dostum, whom Najibullah had used as a non-Pashtun to take on his Pashtun opponents in the south, or Massoud. Given their disgust with Pakistan's role and mistrust of Hekmatyar and Dostum, and their unsavoury reputations, Wakil and Azimi negotiated with Massoud, whose forces took over Kabul in late April 1992. Najibullah sought asylum in the UN mission in the capital. The UN Secretary-General's representative for Afghanistan, Benon Sevan, who had been tasked with negotiating a peace settlement, and the Indian ambassador to Afghanistan, Hamid Ansari – both sympathetic to Najibullah – tried to rescue him but were unsuccessful. He was captured and brutally killed by the Taliban in 1996.

However, since Massoud was disinclined to be at the helm but keen to see a Mujahideen government taking over, he soon found himself in the midst of a bloody internecine conflict. The Pakistan-based Mujahideen leadership agreed to the formation of an Islamic government and leadership succession procedure, but the question of who should lead and for how long led to underlying discord. Initially, they expediently assigned the leader of a pro-Zahir Shah group, Sibqatullah Mujaddedi, to be the transitional president for two months, followed by a four-month term of Rabbani, at the end of which a grand assembly (Shura-i-Ahal-i-Hal wo Aqd) was expected to elect a new head of state. However, once Mujaddedi took over, he did not want to relinquish power. He was an anti-communist religious figure from a pious family that had not always played a constructive role in Afghan politics. As the defence minister of the new government, Massoud desired the implementation of the agreed procedure for the sake of a smooth power transition, national unity and a stable political order. When Mujaddedi, who had previously praised Massoud, was forced to leave office, he damned the latter. Meanwhile, other claimants – the Pakistan-backed Hekmatyar and Iran-supported Hezbi Wahdat (representing the Shia groups) led by Ali Mazari – decided to bid for power. Afghanistan was plunged into an internal conflict or what many have called a civil war, although there was nothing civil about it; it was very bloody and destructive.

Afghanistan's neighbourhood

The scramble for power also drew in Afghanistan's neighbours, as they aided and abetted different warring factions according to their conflicting interests. Although both Pakistan and Iran, and to some extent the Central Asian Republics, as well as Turkey and India, played a part, Pakistan proved to be the main villain. General Zia ul-Haq had delegated Pakistan's Afghanistan and Kashmir policies to the ISI as far back as 1982, with an emphasis on the use of radical Islamic groups as a foreign policy instrument in pursuit of expanding Pakistan's regional geopolitical and strategic interests, largely in rivalry with its arch regional foe, India. He wanted to benefit from Pakistan's support of the Afghan resistance groups, and for hosting some 3 million refugees. Zia's Afghanistan policy had all along been closely tied to nurturing the idea of 'strategic depth', whereby Afghanistan could be used as a useful backyard in the event of another war with India. He keenly entertained the idea of merging southern Afghanistan, including Kabul, into Pakistan, from the Hindu Kush ranges to the Afghan-Pakistan border, which would also put an end to the Durand Line dispute and squash a revival of the concept of Pashtunistan.

Zia was killed in a mysterious air crash on 17 August 1988, but his policies remained ingrained with Pakistan's military and ISI, which have directly or indirectly ruled Pakistan to the present day. The military has operated as an 'Inc.' in the life of the nation, with control of Pakistan's nuclear arsenal. Anatol Lieven describes Pakistan as 'an army with a state'.[67] The military has played a double-edged role in the conduct of the country's internal and external settings. On the one hand, it has held Pakistan back from developing a viable, stable and enduring democratic system of governance with a level of social and economic development whereby national productivity can meet the needs of rapid population growth (231 million in 2021). On the other, it has served as a central force in keeping together the country's four disparate national groups – the Punjabis, Sindhis, Baluchis and Pathans or Pashtuns, plus the Muhajirs (those who migrated to Pakistan from India in the wake of the 1947 partition of the Indian subcontinent). It is widely believed that, without the military's determining hand, Pakistan could implode, for the way that the common religion of Islam has been used and practised in the creation of Pakistan and its domestic and foreign policies has not been sufficient to bridge the ethnic and cultural cleavages in the way the founder of the country, Mohammad Ali Jinnah, had intended.

To achieve Zia ul-Haq's Afghanistan policy objectives, Islamabad heavily armed its favourite proxy Hekmatyar in order to attack Kabul to oust and replace the Rabbani government. In the ensuing conflict, it was reported that Hekmatyar's forces destroyed half of Kabul, which had hitherto been largely preserved, and thousands of its inhabitants were killed between April and September 1992 alone. For that, Hekmatyar became known as 'the butcher of Kabul'. The Massoud forces battled Hezbi Islami of Hekmatyar and Hezbi Wahdat, which acted at times in coordination based on an understanding between Islamabad and Tehran. In the ferocious fighting, all sides, including Sayyaf's Ittihadd-e Islami, committed unspeakable human rights violations.[68] Ultimately, they could not dislodge the Rabbani–Massoud government, but managed to prevent it from consolidating and gaining control over the country. This was the second time in Afghan history that two Tajiks had reached the helm with a national agenda. But this was not acceptable to many Pashtun leaders or to Pakistan, which found the nationalist stance of Rabbani and Massoud contrary to its interests.

Transition to an Islamic emirate

When, finally, Islamabad realized that Hekmatyar lacked popularity inside Afghanistan, vacillated between being pro and anti-US, and on occasion ingratiated himself with Iran, it decided to raise a fresh force to realize its goal of a subordinate Afghanistan – the Taliban.[69] Reportedly 'fathered' by Pakistan's interior minister, Major General Naseerullah Babar, the Taliban leaders were mainly tutored in an extremist Deobandi version of Salafi-Wahhabi Sunni Islam whose foot soldiers were young Afghan refugees recruited from largely US- and Saudi-funded Pakistani *madrassas*. They first appeared on the Afghanistan scene in the second half of 1994. With Pakistan's full logistical and material support and strategic guidance,[70] they were able to cut their way through to Kabul by fighting, buying off various local power-holders and exploiting an exhausted population who were desperate for peace and security. By September 1996, they had compelled Rabbani and Massoud to evacuate their forces to Massoud's native Panjshir enclave, where he rebuilt a resistance network to the Taliban. The politically swinging Hekmatyar, whom the president had appointed prime minister shortly before in an attempt at national unity and stability, was also evacuated by Massoud. Upon taking over Kabul, the Taliban declared Afghanistan an Islamic emirate, enforcing an unprecedentedly draconian medieval-type theocratic order.[71]

However, the Taliban needed money and manpower. The wealthy and pious Bin Laden was the man of the hour. He had been disowned by Saudi Arabia for his criticism of the Saudi regime as a US puppet and for his opposition to Riyadh's decision to allow the US to deploy half a million troops on 'Islam's holy soil', where the two holiest sites of Mecca and Medina are located, to launch the August 1990 Iraqi invasion of Kuwait. After spending six years in friendly Sudan from 1991, Bin Laden made *hijra* (migration – styled after that of Prophet Mohammad from Mecca to Medina in 622) through Pakistan to Afghanistan under the very receptive Taliban regime.

Bin Laden and the reclusive Taliban leader, Mullah Mohammad Omar, forged an alliance whereby the former provided the latter with money and manpower from the Arab world, and the latter furnished the former and his Al Qaeda operatives safe sanctuary in Afghanistan, enabling them to establish their terrorism training camps or what they called 'universities'. It is widely believed that the Al Qaeda–Taliban alliance could not have materialized without the ISI's critical linking role. Pakistan was the only country whose borders were wide open to the Taliban and Al Qaeda leaders to crisscross without any inhibitions. Afghanistan's other neighbours had closed their frontiers with the country. Pakistan was the first state to recognize the Taliban regime, followed by only two more, Saudi Arabia and the United Arab Emirates (UAE). The main reason for Saudi Arabia's recognition was its historical strategic ties with Pakistan and its sympathy for a like-minded Sunni Islamic movement. The UAE leant towards the Taliban for largely geostrategic reasons. The Taliban expounded an anti-Shia and therefore anti-Iranian posture. The UAE had had a major territorial dispute with Iran since the latter's takeover from the emirates of Sharjah and Ras al Khaimah of the three strategic islands in the Persian Gulf – Abu Musa, and Greater and Lesser Tunbs – as part of a deal between Tehran and London in the wake of British withdrawal from East of Suez in 1971.[72]

The financial assistance of these two oil-rich kingdoms, plus Pakistan's all-round support and lucrative income from the cultivation of poppies to produce heroin that made Afghanistan one of the largest suppliers in the world, proved instrumental in enabling the Taliban to expand their territorial conquest into northern Afghanistan. Within two years, they gained control over about 80 per cent of the country. In northern Mazar-i-Sharif in August 1998, they not only defeated Dostum but, as part of their anti-Shia stance, they also killed eleven Iranian Consulate personnel. The incident brought them to the brink of a major conflict with Iran, which was only avoided by successful mediation on the part of UN Secretary-General Representative for Afghanistan Lakhdar Brahimi.

Under the watchful eyes of the Taliban and ISI, Al Qaeda plotted and executed several anti-US operations. These included attacks on American embassies in Kenya and Tanzania in August 1998, with some 200 American and African personnel killed and about 4,500 wounded, and the bombing of the USS *Cole* navy destroyer at the port of Aden in October 2000 that killed seventeen American sailors and made a big hole in the ship. With regard to the embassy bombings, the Clinton administration, which had failed to act decisively when warned by US intelligence about Al Qaeda's anti-US objectives, retaliated by firing Tomahawk cruise missiles at two targets: what it regarded as Al Qaeda facilities in Khartoum, Sudan, and training camps in Khost Province in eastern Afghanistan. It also strengthened a regime of sanctions against the Taliban. But none of these measures proved effective. In Khartoum, the missiles destroyed a pharmaceutical factory, and in Afghanistan they killed a number of Al Qaeda's trainees but missed Bin Laden, who had already left the site.[73] As for the USS *Cole*, President Clinton, who was embroiled in the Monica Lewinsky affair at the time and had come to the end of his second term in office, could not take any further action against Al Qaeda.

However, the US cruise missile attack scuttled a deal which was in the making between the Taliban and Saudi leaders about the former handing over Bin Laden to the latter. Turki bin Faisal Al Saud had visited Mullah Mohammad Omar and was responsible for managing the deal. But the missile attack angered Omar, who condemned the US for violating Afghanistan's sovereignty[74] and halted the negotiations. In return, Riyadh withdrew its recognition of the Taliban government. Meanwhile, the main obstacle to the Taliban–Al Qaeda alliance and its Pakistan supporters subjugating all of Afghanistan was Massoud's resistance. He successfully countered the Taliban and their allies from north-eastern Afghanistan and forged a wider anti-Taliban and anti-Al Qaeda coalition known as the United Islamic National Front for the Salvation of Afghanistan (UINFSA). Islamabad dubbed the latter as the 'Northern Alliance' to indicate that it represented only non-Pashtuns, although the Front included several Pashtun dignitaries. The Rabbani government also thus managed to retain its international recognition and the Afghan seat at the UN. Meanwhile, strongly sensing a danger from the Taliban–Al Qaeda alliance backed by the ISI, during a visit to Europe at the invitation of the European Parliament, Massoud gave a clear warning at a press conference on 4 April 2001 of the tragedies that the world could face arising from the situation in Afghanistan.[75]

The Clinton administration's approach to the Taliban was full of ambiguity. On the one hand, it was careful not to engage in any policy actions that would alienate a nuclear-armed but fragile Pakistan nor to dismiss the Taliban altogether, as US officials had established informal contacts with the group. On the other, it was wary of the Taliban as a dark Al Qaeda-allied Islamic force, whose theocratic order was highly barbaric and especially discriminatory towards women. During a visit to Pakistan in November 1997, Secretary of State Madeleine Albright slammed the Taliban's policies as 'despicable',[76] discriminating against women and minorities, and running Afghanistan as a medieval fiefdom, and First Lady Hillary Clinton and several Hollywood celebrities spoke strongly against the Taliban's treatment of women. This was effective and the US Senate passed a resolution on 5 May 1999, calling on President Clinton not to recognize the Taliban government. A similar resolution was introduced in the House of Representatives shortly thereafter. This was in contrast to Zalmay Khalilzad's earlier recommendation that: 'It is time for the United States to reengage' Afghanistan under the Taliban,[77] which this author later cautioned against.[78] But at the same time, the US administration was not prepared to assist Massoud in his struggle with the Taliban and their supporters. Whether the Clinton administration could or should have done more to contain Al Qaeda and their Taliban harbourers decisively has been a matter of debate, but my own view was that it should have.[79]

Whatever the case, against this background of Afghanistan's historical and in many ways tragic evolution, Al Qaeda was able to orchestrate its major 9/11 operation. Had Afghanistan been developed as a viable state with a durable and appropriately participatory system of governance capable of harnessing national unity and prosperity, and free of outside interventions and invasions, the Taliban would not have been able to assume power, nor would the country have become a seriously disrupted or failed state and a hub for international terrorism. By the same token, the US would not have found it necessary to invade a country whose conditions had traditionally denied the invaders any degree of tangible success.

The Afghanistan that the US took on in late 2001 had been shattered, not only by twenty-three years of bloody, destructive warfare, pushed back in time under the rule of the Taliban, it had also come through a very turbulent historical journey since its inception. Before the US, two other world powers had sought to dominate and change Afghanistan but had failed. In spite of its progress in the previous seven decades, it was still one of the poorest and least developed countries in the world. In 2000, Afghanistan's gross domestic product (GDP) was $3,532 million; it ranked 134th out of 195 countries and its GDP per capita was $181.[80] It had very poor social services, especially in the areas of education and health. Many of its citizens died of preventable and curable diseases, and life expectancy was one of the lowest in the world, while its literacy rate stood at approximately 15 per cent.[81] The lack of trained manpower was acute. The extremist, discriminatory and misogynistic rule of the Taliban had reduced it to an extraordinary level of backwardness. Every time, under one regime, that a small intelligentsia had emerged from the midst of a very limited educated pool, it was suppressed or decimated by the succeeding ruler or his ideological cluster. This had deprived Afghanistan of the capability needed to move it beyond an almost perpetual state of internal divisions, as well as severe political, social and economic stagnation, and to guard it against outside interventions. As already mentioned, the country had evolved only for a short period in its history as a weak, prototype state with strong micro-societies. These societies functioned in a loose relationship with one another and the central authoritarian, but divided, ruling elite in Kabul – an elite which had persistently been riddled with family feuds, power rivalry, distrust, and an attitude of being forever out to get one another. After the end of monarchical rule in July 1973, Afghanistan had violently swung from one extreme to the other on the ideological and political spectrum, bewildering the citizens who were left not knowing what to expect or how to fend for themselves in an environment where one crisis after another kept striking them.

3

Intervention, Post-Taliban Democratization and the 'War on Terror'

If men's sense of economic cleavage is greater than their sense of common nationality, if religious or social or race or colour cleavages are too strong, if there are permanent social minorities, a healthy democracy is so far impossible.

A.D. Lindsay[1]

The US Afghanistan campaign and its objectives have been widely debated from different perspectives in the policy and public arenas. The dominant view projects that the George W. Bush administration acted primarily to punish Al Qaeda, liberate Afghanistan from the medieval-style tyrannical rule of Taliban and help the people of that war-torn country to live in peace and security, free of terrorism. While confident of what a fraction of American power could accomplish in a country like Afghanistan, Washington's initial intention was to achieve its objectives at minimal costs and length of time. It wanted to avoid getting 'bogged down' in the country as had happened previously to the Soviets and the British. Hence its original opposition to engaging in 'nation-building' or to unfold a 'Marshall Plan' for Afghanistan. A 'light footprint' approach was preferred to carry out the Afghanistan mission.

However, Washington could not proceed as was originally envisioned. Many factors accounted for its plans being derailed. When examined against the backdrop of Afghanistan's historical and prevailing conditions, as explained in chapter 2, four proved critical in leading the US and its allies into the 'Afghan trap': the US's failure to decapitate and round up Al Qaeda and uproot the Taliban within the early days of Operation Enduring Freedom; the Bush administration's conflation of Afghanistan's transition with its foreign policy agenda of 'democracy promotion' and the global 'war on terror' as mutually reinforcing variables; the dysfunctional post-Taliban system of governance, along with America's lack of a reliable and effective partner on the ground; and the US's incongruous strategy in dealing decisively with the Taliban-led insurgency and its main external patron, Pakistan, in a zone of intense regional tensions and rivalries. This chapter focuses on the first two factors, with the third factor discussed in chapters 4 and 5, and the fourth in chapter 7.

Intervention, obsession with Bin Laden, mission creep

The apocalyptic attacks of 11 September 2001, on the World Trade Center in New York and the Pentagon in Washington, DC, as well as a failed attempt on the White House by Osama Bin Laden's Al Qaeda network, occasioned a sea-change in US foreign policy and the fortunes of Afghanistan.[2] The attacks were as multi-dimensional in their impact as the US response turned out to be. They targeted the heart of America's economic, political and military power, shattering the belief in America's invulnerability and that of its allies around the world. The global standing of the US was challenged in an unprecedented manner and on a scale that the country had not seen since Japan's attack on Pearl Harbor in 1941. The hawkish Republican Bush administration found it imperative to respond.

There are not many insightful studies available detailing systematically the precise nature and breadth of the debate that took place, and how a final decision to intervene in Afghanistan was reached in the White House. Bob Woodward provides some insights in his book *Bush at War*, based on interviews with President Bush, members of his war cabinet and a host of security advisors who advised the president from political and military vantage points, although not always in harmony with one another. For example, while the CIA director George Tenet constantly assured the president of victory, with his organization taking the lead,[3] Defense Secretary Donald Rumsfeld questioned what would come after the initial phase of military success and his deputy Paul Wolfowitz raised the issue of not descending into a quagmire.[4]

Whatever the influence of those views, the president was in a hurry to make a decision, for both domestic and foreign policy reasons. He needed to restore the confidence of the American public in their government, not only to protect them, but also to reassure the world of America's global power and reach. Following the Taliban's refusal to meet Washington's demand to turn over Bin Laden, there was little time to draw up a comprehensive strategy or plan of action, not only to achieve America's immediate objectives but also, and more importantly, to deal with what might arise in the medium to long term. By all accounts, ideas of pressuring Pakistan, the Taliban's sponsor, to do the job, or sending a contingent of American Special Forces through Pakistan to capture Bin Laden and his main operatives, were not given any serious consideration. The intervention option was adopted in haste as most practical. Washington could count on the support of the largely non-Pashtun United Islamic National Front for the Salvation of Afghanistan (UINFSA) or 'Northern Alliance' and indeed a majority of the people of Afghanistan who craved freedom from the Taliban's ruthless ultra-theocratic rule.

Enjoying a surge in global sympathy, President Bush warned the world of the spectre of international terrorism and declared America's determination to deal with it decisively. He cautioned those regimes that could potentially stand in the US's way by famously proclaiming

'either you are with us, or you are with the terrorists', which by implication meant that if any regime did not support the US, it would face
America's wrath. More specifically, the main target was the military
regime of General Pervez Musharraf.[5] Reportedly, Musharraf was
bluntly told by US Deputy Secretary of State Richard Armitage that
if Pakistan defied Bush's warning, it should 'be prepared to be
bombed . . . to the Stone Age'.[6] As Musharraf recounts, he had little
choice but to support the US and let down Pakistan's Taliban clients[7]
and, by implication, their Al Qaeda ally, although this did not turn
out to be a lasting change (as is explained later, see chapter 7).

The US commenced the intervention with Operation Enduring
Freedom on 7 October 2001. The Bush administration's consensus at
the time was that it could ensure the success of its Afghanistan
campaign within a policy approach based on an assumption that it
would defeat the Taliban and Al Qaeda, and change Afghanistan
with a minimum amount of combat, or political and reconstruction
investment. In its military aspect, the campaign involved a two-
pronged operation from the north and the south. The northern
approach was spearheaded by CIA operatives, backed by a contingent of Special Forces, using the provision of military support and
the distribution of cash to rapidly win the cooperation of the leaders
of the UINFSA forces, who were more than willing to avenge Ahmad
Shah Massoud's killing and see the end of the Taliban's reign of terror
in the name of Islam. Washington's policymakers were keen for the
campaign to be seen as Afghan-led and owned. Nonetheless, the
ground operations were instrumentally assisted by a very effective
application of massive US air power, as authorized by Vice Admiral
Willy Moore, commander of the navy's Fifth Fleet based in Bahrain,
at the instruction of Central Command (CENTCOM) and
Washington. They successfully shocked the Taliban, destroyed the
militia's limited number of military targets, including command and
control centres, and means of communication, paved the way for the
UINFSA militias to gain territory, and forced the Taliban fighters to

retreat towards Kabul and their heartland in the south, Kandahar in particular. Within less than six weeks, the UINFSA fighters were able to take over the northern provinces and enter a Taliban-depleted Kabul on 14 November 2001. The Taliban regime was toppled and their Al Qaeda allies dispersed, giving confidence to the Bush leadership that everything was proceeding smoothly. As for the Pashtun-dominated southern provinces, UINFSA was restrained from entering them for reasons of ethnic and political expediency.

That task fell on the US southern operation, headed by Major General Jim Mattis, the recently appointed commander of the Marine Task Force 58. Mattis was a long-standing Marine officer, well-versed in the history of wars. While anticipating a full 'invasion' of Afghanistan to 'kill' the perpetrators of 9/11 and their Taliban protectors, he swiftly coordinated with the Fifth Fleet, the CIA, the US Navy Sea, Air, and Land (SEALs) and Major General Farooq Ahmed Khan, the planning chief for the Pakistani military,[8] which had thus far patronized the Taliban, and launched attacks from naval ships in the Arabian Sea via the skies of Pakistan's Baluchistan Province. The objective was to establish Camp Rhino south of Kandahar, where the bulk of the Taliban forces 'were falling back in disorder'. Within days, Mattis's 4,000-strong Marine contingent landed in Camp Rhino.

As Mattis was cognizant of the need to have – at least symbolically – a Pashtun leader on his side in confronting the Taliban, he found that person in Hamid Karzai, whom he described as 'calm, confident, and content, and in league with our Special Forces'.[9] A well-educated, urbane figure, Karzai came from an established Popalzai branch of the Pashtun Durrani tribe. His father, Abdul Ahad Karzai, was a prominent figure in Afghan politics, serving as deputy speaker of the National Assembly under King Zahir Shah. He was assassinated in Quetta, Pakistan, in 1999. While his assassins were never found, two Taliban were suspected. In opposing the Soviet invasion, Hamid Karzai had backed the Mujahideen's resistance and worked as chief of the office of the pro-Zahir Shah Sibghatullah Mojaddedi, leader of

Jebh-e Nejat-e Melli (National Liberation Front) group. As mentioned in chapter 2, Mojaddedi later acted as president for a very short period in the first Mujahideen-led Islamic government after the fall of the Soviet-installed communist rule in Kabul in April 1992.

Karzai joined the Mujahideen government as a deputy foreign minister but, after a year of service and a short period of detention for being distrusted by the new UINFSA military leader Mohammad Qassim Fahim, he left for the United States in 1994, where his brothers ran lucrative hospitality businesses. While there, he developed relations with the CIA and the Taliban, who nominated him as their first representative to the UN – an offer that he declined. Instead, he supported Massoud in opposition to the Taliban. While backed by the US and accompanied by, as Mattis puts it, '[a]n eleven-man Special Forces team'[10] and a 150-strong fighting force of fellow Pashtuns, Karzai played a visible role in providing a Pashtun face to the Camp Rhino operation and, for that matter, the US intervention. His role paralleled that of his counterparts in northern Afghanistan. By mid-December 2001, Mattis's forces had captured the Kandahar airfield, which had been built with US aid in the 1960s. Karzai, along with another Pashtun figure, Gul Agha Sherzai, and his 2,000-strong contingent, was able to claim the liberation of his birthplace, Kandahar. At one point in the process, he was injured in an explosion of 'a two-thousand-pound bomb' dropped in error by a B52, some 200 km north of Camp Rhino, on 5 December 2001. Karzai refused to be evacuated, as his injury was not life threatening, but the 'casualties were severe'.[11] Dozens of Karzai's Pashtun fighters, along with several Americans, were killed and injured.[12] At another point, he was encircled by the Taliban, only to be rescued by American Special Forces.

Meanwhile, the Taliban and Al Qaeda were seriously unsettled by the speed with which their main power base crumbled. Some of the Taliban's commanders and most of their foot soldiers, who could not be differentiated from the public, simply melted away into Afghanistan's war-ravaged and treacherous landscape. Many of their leaders and operatives, along with those of Al Qaeda, fled Kandahar. The main escape route out of Afghanistan open to them was towards Pakistan. Most significantly, America's prime target and the trigger of its intervention, Bin Laden, whom President Bush wanted 'dead or alive', managed to flee, together with 2,000 of his fighters, to the cave complex of Tora Bora in the White Mountains in eastern Afghanistan near the Khyber Pass. Bin Laden had built reasonably well-equipped and well-fitted hide-outs in the caves for just such an eventuality.

Mattis claims that he and his Marine forces were ready to go after them, but to his profound disappointment he never received the order from CENTCOM. He bitterly complains that whatever options he offered for capturing Bin Laden were stonewalled. According to Mattis, CENTCOM commander General Tommy Franks opted for Afghan fighters 'loyal to warlords from the north' to do the job. Franks' idea, Mattis claims, was to show the 'Afghans fighting their own war' and to avoid Americans repeating the Soviet mistakes 'by blundering around those mountains and gorges with armor battalions chasing a lightly armed enemy'.[13] Hazrat Ali, a controversial and unreliable warlord from a small Pashayee minority from eastern Afghanistan, was entrusted with the task.[14] Mattis had no confidence in such figures to do the job. He argues that they were 'poorly equipped and strangers among the locals ... [and] proved incapable of closing with the tough, desperate Al Qaeda fighters'.[15] The Tora Bora fighting lasted from 6 to 17 December 2001, without success. Hazrat Ali was accused of betraying the Americans and allowing Bin Laden and his entourage to escape into the rugged tribal border areas of Pakistan in exchange for money.[16] Thus, Al Qaeda, the Taliban and their Pakistani supporters retained their capability to reinvent themselves and make a comeback to fight at the earliest opportunity.

The failure to capture or kill Bin Laden proved extremely consequential. It laid down the very early foundation of troubles of the Afghanistan campaign, setting the scene for the US and, more specifically the CIA, to engage in a frantic search for the fugitive Al Qaeda leader and members of his inner circle. As Karl Eikenberry says, this led to an obsession with 'get Bin Laden'[17] as the number one priority and to 'mission creep'. Initially, the US funded and equipped Afghan groups to assist its Special Forces in the hunt for Bin Laden, although without the necessary foresight as to how these groups would eventually be disarmed or incorporated into an Afghan national army under a post-Taliban system of governance. But all efforts yielded no result. By 2009, a US congressional report stated:

> The failure to finish the job [to kill Bin Laden] represents a lost opportunity that forever altered the course of the conflict in Afghanistan and the future of international terrorism, leaving the American people more vulnerable to terrorism, laying the foundation for today's protracted Afghan insurgency and inflaming the internal strife now endangering Pakistan.[18]

Affirming these points, Bush's National Security Advisor Stephen Hadley subsequently noted:

> We succeeded in displacing Al-Qaeda from Afghanistan and going after them under two administrations in Pakistan. And what happened was the capacity of Al-Qaeda, then, to do those kinds of 9/11 kinds of activities degraded, but it then metastasized, if you will, to a number of regional organizations that had regional objectives but actually were infused with the Islamist ideology.[19]

The hunt for Bin Laden and the quest to ensure that Afghanistan would not emerge again as a source of terrorism led to the expansion of US involvement from the originally intended 'light footprint' approach to half-hearted, confused and very costly 'heavy footprint' state-building processes. This also entailed a divergence in the US's approach between the political masters' aim – a relatively short and light Afghan mission – and the military's longer-term security concerns about the re-activation of Al Qaeda while its leadership and that of the Taliban were at large.

Even so, the first year of the intervention marked a calmer period across Afghanistan. A fear of American firepower and the immediate deployment of an International Security Assistance Force (ISAF) by NATO allies to provide security for Kabul certainly overwhelmed the rise of any serious internal challenges. Not only did the Taliban and their affiliates find themselves mostly restrained, but so too did a range of criminal gangs – drug traffickers, contraband operators and people smugglers – as well as a variety of local opportunist and corrupt power-holders popularly known as *jangsalars* or 'warlords', who were still potentially in a position to wield considerable extraction and dispensation power. A general air of optimism settled on the Afghan public and, indeed, in Washington. President Bush wasted no time in announcing to the American public and the world that US power had triumphed, and that Afghanistan was liberated from terrorist groups, with his senior aides appearing very buoyed up about the success of America's mission and the future of Afghanistan. In his 2002 State of the Union address, President Bush heralded the dawn of a new era for the US and Afghanistan:

> The American flag flies again over our embassy in Kabul. Terrorists who once occupied Afghanistan now occupy cells at Guantanamo Bay. And terrorist leaders who urged followers to sacrifice their lives are running for their own. America and Afghanistan are now allies against terror. We'll be partners in rebuilding that country. . . . Our progress is a tribute to the spirit of the Afghan people, to the resolve of our coalition, and to the might of the United States military.[20]

In his 2003 State of the Union speech, he claimed: 'In Afghanistan, we helped liberate an oppressed people. And we will continue helping them secure their country, rebuild their society, and educate all their children – boys and girls.'[21]

Democracy promotion and democratic state-building

Following on the tail of the security concerns regarding the removal of the Taliban and debasement of Al Qaeda was the burning question of how the US, its international partners (including the United Nations) and Afghan allies could turn Afghanistan from a seriously disrupted or, in the opinion of some analysts, 'failed state',[22] into a long-term, stable, secure and functioning state. Prior to the intervention and in its immediate aftermath, the Bush leadership shunned the idea of nation-building along the lines of what the US had instigated in relation to post-Second World War Japan and Germany.[23] It was wary of being caught in an ongoing conflict in Afghanistan; hence Washington's initial 'light footprint' approach in a belief that in partnership with some US-backed indigenous groups, a reasonably limited American troop deployment and operation could yield sufficiently satisfactory results. In an early commendation of this approach, Deputy Secretary Wolfowitz, stated:

> We did not become bogged down in a quagmire, unlike the British in the 19th century, or the Soviets in the 20th. Nations that arrive in Afghanistan with massive armies tend to be treated as invaders, and they regret it. Mindful of that history, General Franks has deliberately and carefully kept our footprint small to avoid just such a situation. On balance, our partnership with indigenous forces has been very positive and continues to be so . . . our success in Afghanistan has contributed to the larger campaign [war on terrorism].[24]

Concurring with Wolfowitz on this point at the time were not only the president but also Vice-President Dick Cheney, Defense Secretary Rumsfeld and National Security Advisor Hadley, who all appeared to believe in America's military might as a problem solver and expected the initial force deployment to smooth the way for turning Afghanistan around. Although in the same testimony

Wolfowitz pointed out that there would be successes and setbacks for a period, Washington's official estimation was that the Afghanistan mission could be accomplished within a relatively short timeline with moderate human and material costs. Secretary of State Colin Powell dismissed the suggestion of a Marshall Plan for Afghanistan, saying 'Afghanistan is not Western Europe after World War II . . . [t]he amounts are not going to be comparable. We can do a lot with a lot less money than people might think.'[25]

This 'light footprint' approach was hampered not only by an underestimation of the complexity of Afghanistan's internal and external settings (as explained in chapter 2) but also by the Bush administration's emphasis on two foreign policy priorities: 'democracy promotion' and the 'war on terrorism'. The first priority essentially dictated that Afghanistan should be endowed with a democratic system of governance. The second led the US to engage in direct and proxy military operations across a swathe of countries, of which Iraq was identified as the most urgent and significant. Along with an obsession with finding Bin Laden, these two variables played a critical role not only in undermining America's initial military successes in Afghanistan but also in dragging the US and its NATO allies into a wider and deeper involvement in the country, at staggering human and material costs for them and for the Afghan people in the years ahead.

Let us first look at the issue of democracy promotion that underpinned the US's ideological and political efforts, along with those of many educated Afghan allies, in shaping the post-Taliban system of governance that proved unworkable and played a key part in derailing America's Afghanistan project. In the debate among decision-makers in Washington as to what political direction Afghanistan should take, the advocates for changing the country along the lines of an American model of *democratic* 'state-building' prevailed. With neoconservatives leading the way (Wolfowitz was a key figure), it was envisioned that building a democratic state in Afghanistan was vital for global security; it would help stem a perceived tide of Islamic extremism and thus protect America's democracy and national interest as the sole superpower. As such, the Afghanistan mission was integrated with the wider project of spreading liberal political institutions and values abroad as central to what added up to the 'Bush Doctrine'.[26]

Democracy promotion was upheld as integral to fighting terrorism. The idea was that the more countries that were democratized, the less space there would be for terrorism or any form of violent extremism or hostile actions against the United States and its allies. Bush articulated this point succinctly in an address to the United States Military Academy at West Point on 1 June 2002:

Our Nation's cause has always been larger than our Nation's defense. We fight, as we always fight, for a just peace – a peace that favors liberty. We will defend the peace against the threats from terrorists and tyrants. We will preserve the peace by building good relations among the great powers. And we will extend the peace by encouraging free and open societies on every continent.[27]

In reinforcing this point more specifically in relation to democratizing Afghanistan, Bush later remarked:

Our goal in Afghanistan is to help the people of that country to defeat the terrorists and establish a stable, moderate, and democratic state that respects the rights of its citizens, governs its territory effectively, and is a reliable ally in this war against extremists and terrorists.[28]

The process of building a 'democratic' system of governance started with a conference, convened in Bonn, Germany, in early December 2001. Although held under the auspices of the United Nations, it was largely driven by Afghan participants and the United States, with the objective of mapping the path for establishing a constitutional system of governance that possessed all the necessary democratic trappings as central to building a new stable, secure, and progressive Afghanistan. The outcome was announced in the form of the Bonn Accords, officially titled 'Agreement on Provisional Arrangements in Afghanistan Pending the Re-Establishment of Permanent Government Institutions' on 5 December, which was promptly supported by the UN Security Council.[29]

A great deal of literature has examined these accords and the subsequent processes by which key benchmarks for state-building were set out to be met in the two and a half years following the conference, although this was 'hardly enough time to turn a traditional and failed state into a democracy'.[30] Even so, for the purposes of this book, it is imperative to take a fresh detailed analytical look at the accords (henceforth called the Bonn Agreement) and their implementation, for they laid the cornerstone for a political order and state-building that reflected the agenda of the Afghan delegates and that of the Bush administration, although not necessarily in accord with the harsh realities of Afghanistan.

The Bonn Agreement and process

The UN-brokered talks in Bonn were chaired by Lakhdar Brahimi, the UN Secretary-General's special representative for Afghanistan, and included four anti-Taliban Afghan groups. One was the UINFSA, the main Afghan ally of the US and coalition forces in Afghanistan during the intervention. This group represented Burhanuddin Rabbani, who was still formally the president and did not attend the conference, and was largely made up of non-Pashtun elements such as Tajiks, Uzbeks and Hazaras, with mixed claims to different versions of political Islam.[31] The other three were the 'Rome group', involving the three small conservative Mujahideen movements mentioned in chapter 2 and associated with ex-King Zahir Shah, who was not personally present at the conference; the 'Cypress group' (a group of exiles with ties to Iran); and the 'Peshawar group' (made up of mostly Pashtun exiles based in Pakistan).[32] The Taliban had no direct representation, but Pakistan was a participant and in a position to reflect the group's interests. Participants in the conference also included, most importantly, the Islamic Republic of Iran, Russia and China.

The Bonn Agreement came about largely as a joint Afghan-US-induced and UN-legitimated inter-elite compromise deal among these Afghan groups. It resulted from much behind-the-scenes cross-ideological, cross-ethnic and Realpolitik bargaining, as well as a rare instance of cooperation between two long-standing arch foes – the United States and Iran. The US delegation was led by veteran diplomat James Dobbins, aided by Afghan-American Zalmay Khalilzad. Since Dobbins' knowledge of Afghanistan was limited and he hardly dealt with the country's various power groups, Khalilzad was the man of the hour. His long-standing involvement in Afghanistan and interaction with various power elements in the country, and his ability to speak his mother tongue Pashto as well as competent Dari, came in very handy. The Iranian delegation, representing the reformist government of President Mohammad Khatami (1997–2005), was headed by the country's UN ambassador, Javad Zarif, who skilfully leveraged Iran's friendship with UINFSA to persuade its delegate to moderate its demands. He also let Dobbins know of his government's desire to improve relations with the US, although Dobbins' message to Washington in this respect fell on deaf ears.[33]

The Bonn Agreement outlined plans for an interim administration, an Emergency Loya Jirga (ELJ) (grand assembly) to select a transitional administration to succeed the interim administration in June 2002, and a Constitutional Loya Jirga (CLJ) to discuss and endorse a new constitution. It also set a timeframe for the holding of elections, both for the head of state and for the legislative body. It laid the groundwork for the development of a system of democratic government and drew up a clear (if ambitious) timeframe for the transition of Afghanistan from failed state to functioning democracy.

It also endorsed, in response to UINFSA's demand, the establishment of an international peacekeeping force in Kabul, which the UN Security Council approved on 20 December 2001. This force – ISAF – was to number between 3,000 and 5,000, composed of NATO allies and led by Britain.

Further, it settled the contentious question of who should lead the interim administration. The 'Rome group' initially backed a non-Pashtun, Abdul Sattar Sirat, who had served as justice minister and deputy prime minster under King Zahir Shah. But since Sirat was an ethnic Uzbek, he was not favoured by the Pashtun delegates. The UINFSA delegation was divided: half wanted Rabbani (who, from Kabul, directed that the issue be settled inside Afghanistan), and the other half, headed by Yunus Qanuni, backed by Qassim Fahim and Abdullah Abdullah, who all assumed key ministerial positions in the interim government, favoured a compromise – Karzai – much to Rabbani's discomfort. The impasse reached the point of the conference breaking up. So as not to miss this momentous opportunity, US Secretary of State Powell instructed Dobbins to 'keep them [the delegates] there; lock them up if you have to'.[34] The US's favourite was Karzai, who it kept promoting as most suitable. Karzai was endorsed as the compromise choice to lead the interim administration. As corollary to this, the conference also approved the names of a twenty-nine-member cabinet for the administration, with UINFSA occupying half of it.

As well as setting down a timeline for the restoration of government and the instigation of electoral processes, the Bonn Agreement provisioned for a Supreme Court and gave the interim administration authority to set up more courts as required. The re-establishment of the rule of law was considered one of the vital steps towards the construction of a stable government in Kabul. The drafters at Bonn also dictated that the 1964 Constitution of Zahir Shah should be reinstated until such time as an appointed committee could work to draft a new constitution, minus those provisions that were inconsistent with the Bonn Agreement and Afghanistan's international obligations.

Reinstatement of the 1964 Constitution allowed the interim authority to begin operating within a set legal framework very quickly. But since the provisions in that constitution and the Bonn Agreement regarding the drafting of the *new* constitution were inadequate, the transitional administration was given the task of establishing a constitutional commission; yet the mode of appointment, mandate and composition of this commission remained undefined.[35] This led to considerable confusion when the time came, in 2002, to draft the new constitution, a process further outlined below.

Much of the literature examining the Bonn Agreement is divided between those who argue that the timetable it set was too ambitious, calling for elections too quickly after the fall of the Taliban, and those who believe that only the rapid institutionalization of democratic procedures outlined at Bonn could save Afghanistan from becoming, once again, a 'failed state'. From the perspective of the legitimacy of the Bush administration's democracy promotion project, it was imperative that the intervening forces be seen to be forging a democratic path for Afghanistan as quickly as possible, if only to garner support for the asserted reconstruction and 'humanitarian' aims of Operation Enduring Freedom. Thus, arguably, US eagerness for state-building in Afghanistan contributed to a rushed and overly ambitious roadmap at Bonn, which, although ostensibly overseen by the UN and Brahimi, was influenced by a US delegation ideologically committed to 'democracy promotion'. As an active member of the neoconservative clique in Washington, no one was more instrumental in this respect than Khalilzad.

Traditional legitimation of the transitional government

While many international commentators were left with the impression that the Bonn Agreement had given existing elites a disproportionate share of power in the interim administration, it was hoped that the ELJ, convened to select the transitional administration, would ensure a level of representativeness in government until elections could be held.[36] As mentioned in chapter 2, a jirga is a traditional Pashtun assembly or council. A 'Loya Jirga' is a grand council, and typically adjudicates a number of legal issues from property rights to tribal foreign policy and relations with other governments (both national and international).[37] The Loya Jirga had approved the five previous constitutions of Afghanistan (1923, 1931, 1964, 1977, 1987) although, with the possible exception of the Loya Jirga of 1964, they had mostly been docile, unassertive bodies whose job was to rubberstamp the dictates of the leader.[38] For the 2002 ELJ, the procedure for the selection of delegates was complex; traditional leadership councils known as *shuras* met to choose electors, who then cast ballots for Loya Jirga delegates from their district. Khalilzad, who was now the US special presidential envoy for Afghanistan, touted the Loya Jirga as an 'ancient democratic tradition'.[39] Critics, however, questioned the democratic credentials of the Loya Jirga, pointing out that the *shura* that made decisions pertaining to potential delegates at the grassroots level were made up of (all-male) elders 'considered to represent the respected or powerful families in a given region'.[40]

The ELJ nonetheless managed to choose a transitional leader and transitional administration in June 2002.[41] Karzai was confirmed as transitional leader, a position he was to occupy until the elections planned for 2004. On 19 June, the final day of the ELJ, Karzai named a government, with the three key security portfolios of the defence, foreign and interior ministries going to prominent former UINFSA members, and the transitional administration was formed.

Some observers hoped that the transitional administration would be more representative of the ethnic and cultural heterogeneity of Afghan society than its interim counterpart. But once again the government which emerged mirrored the security and strategic concerns of Karzai and his American backers.[42] Many delegates complained that they had felt intimidated by members of the security services who were reported to have been present inside the ELJ tent, undermining the notion that the electoral process was free and fair.[43] In addition, Khalilzad was accused of twisting the arm of former king Zahir Shah, to convince him not to stand for transitional leader, leaving the way open for Karzai to win.[44] Countering this claim, Khalilzad pointed out that the king was never interested in taking up the position as head of state.[45] However, I was told by the king's youngest son, Mirwais Zahir, at a conference in Bonn in September 2008, that his father could have been open to persuasion, if Washington had strongly backed him. It is important to note here that Zahir Shah would have been favoured by a majority of the delegates at the Bonn Conference to head the interim administration. He was the only figure who could have been the focus of national unity, for most Afghans were nostalgic about the degree of stability and security that had marked his reign. Although in his late eighties, he was still respected widely, among the Pashtuns in particular, as the father of the nation (Baba-e Millat), a title with which he was officially honoured later. As such, a momentous opportunity was lost. The impression that the US delegation was exerting influence behind the scenes tarnished the legitimacy of the ELJ in the eyes of many in Afghanistan.[46]

The legal rationale framework

Many of the problems faced in the convening of the ELJ resurfaced just a few months later, when the CLJ convened to discuss and approve a constitution put forward by a drafting committee Karzai had appointed. The draft produced by the committee was based heavily on the 1964 text. Prior to the CLJ, copies of the draft were distributed throughout the country by the United Nations Assistance Mission in Afghanistan (UNAMA), with the process involving consultations with citizens in thirty-two provinces, as well as large refugee populations in Pakistan and Iran.[47]

There was considerable international scrutiny of the proposed constitution, particularly in the US, where the key questions for many were the role of Islam in the future Afghan state and the protection of international norms of human rights. In 2003, the US government-affiliated RAND Corporation published conference proceedings, the central concern of which was the extent to which the constitution drew on Islam – and in particular *shari'a* – as a source of law. While the editors of the conference proceedings agreed that referring to Islam in the constitution was unavoidable and necessary to ensure widespread support for the new political framework in Afghanistan, they suggested a cautious attitude towards the enshrining of Islam as a source of law, pointing to the atrocities committed during the Taliban rule in the name of Islam.[48] This focus on the role of Islam in the proposed constitution was reiterated in the US media coverage of the lead-up to the CLJ, obscuring other pressing issues such as the balance between the centre and periphery in the Afghan state, and the differences between the advocates of centralized and decentralized government in the ethnically and tribally divided country.[49]

The draft constitution presented to the CLJ was reviewed by a constitutional commission whose members were handpicked by Karzai. It was viewed by many in Afghanistan as Karzai's attempt to consolidate power in his own hands, backed by the US, who believed a strong centralized state would make Afghanistan more amenable to American interests. As one Afghan academic cynically observed: 'Every regime in Afghanistan has had its constitution; this will be the Americans' constitution.'[50] The concentration of power in the presidency prompted 'nearly universal criticism in Afghanistan from across the political spectrum'. Groups such as Jamiati Islami, Junbish-i Milli and Hezbi Muttahed-e Melli lined up in opposition to the heavily presidential weighting of the draft constitution.[51] Abdul Rashid Dostum and fellow regional leaders such as former Mujahideen figures Ismail Khan from Herat, Mohammed Atta Noor from Mazar-i-Sharif and Qassim Fahim (who Karzai appointed as minister of defence in the interim administration) were vocal about their support for a hybrid federalist model of government that would devolve more power to the regional leaders and governments.[52]

However, the pro-Karzai factions, who argued for a strong presidential system of governance and cautioned against the risk of power fragmentation, won the day. The constitution stipulated a strong executive arm and therefore a highly centralized system of governance. Little consideration was given to the fact that a strong presidential system in the Afghan context would be dangerous in two important respects. First, it would perpetuate authoritarianism by enabling the executive to dominate the legislative and judicial organs of the government, thus reducing their role as checks on the executive. Second, it would typically produce one winner and many disgruntled strongmen losers with a capacity to challenge, undermine or otherwise manipulate the victor, and force the latter to engage in unsavoury practices in order to maintain power.[53]

Another controversial issue was the question of language, often considered a marker of ethnic identity in multi-ethnic Afghanistan. After much tense debate over whether Pashto should be given more weight than Dari, it was decided that the two languages would jointly remain the official languages. In addition, six others (Turkmen, Uzbek, Pashai, Baluch, Nuristani and Pamiri) were mentioned as official in regions where they were the 'dominant language'. While the Pashtun delegates were insistent on state employees being fluent in both national languages, this was opposed by their Tajik delegates and dropped. But in return, it was agreed that the national anthem would just be sung in Pashto.[54]

In a traditionally Muslim country, the role and administration of the judiciary also arose as a point of disagreement. The draft constitution cited Islam as an important influence on the formation of Afghan law, but also placed considerable emphasis on secular sources of law, such as international human rights treaties, and democratic norms such as the rule of law and gender and ethnic equality.[55] The

RAND Corporation had made it clear that the Americans would not be amenable to a constitution based primarily on the dictates of Islamic law. In the lead-up to the CLJ, several groups were calling for a greater role for Islam than they suspected would be advocated for by the constitutional commission. Members of Jamiat and Ittihadd-e Islami called for the words 'Islamic state' to be used in the constitution, as well as some reference to the *hijab* (women's veil), while a group of Islamic scholars led by Deputy Supreme Court Justice Fazel Ahmad Manawi advocated *shari'a* as the sole source of law in Afghanistan.[56]

Ultimately, a compromise was reached between the more secular outlook of the draft constitution and the Islamists within the CLJ. A number of provisions referencing Islam in the draft were retained, such as one which declared that: 'In Afghanistan, no law can be contrary to the beliefs and provisions of the sacred religion of Islam.'[57] Freedom of religion was also constitutionally enshrined, although freedom to act according to one's religion was invalidated if such acts were contrary to the law.[58] The Supreme Court was given powers of judicial review; this was key as '[t]he great struggle between conservative clerics and more moderate elements within Afghan society will not be settled in this Constitution but in its subsequent interpretation.'[59]

While much attention was focused on the internal disputes between pro-Karzai, ethnic Tajik and Uzbek factions in the CLJ, equally relevant to the nature of the democracy project in Afghanistan were the procedures governing the jirga itself, the process by which it was run and the extent to which it could be considered a representative body. Even more than the ELJ, the utility of the CLJ as a symbol of American success in bringing democracy to Afghanistan rested on its status as a fair, representative and unbiased organ of government. However, a number of non-governmental bodies attending the jirga, as well as journalists and other commentators, reported considerable intimidation, aggressiveness and even violence among delegates; women in particular seem to have been singled out as targets of this behaviour. Many women were verbally abused and were frightened to vote in case of repercussions from local warlords;[60] and the delegates who wished to oppose prominent powerbrokers were evicted from meetings or threatened with violence.[61] There were claims of bias and intimidation, particularly by the American delegation at the CLJ, undermining the assertion that, in Khalilzad's words, democracy was 'bubbling up' in Afghanistan.[62]

The CLJ was hailed a significant achievement by a number of US government and non-government figures. As the 502 delegates approved a new constitution on 3 January 2004, the legal foundations were laid for a highly centralized presidential governmental structure, with a bicameral parliament: a lower house or House of the People (Wolesi Jirga) to be elected through a national vote open to all men and women over the age of 18, and an upper house or House of Elders (Meshrano Jirga), one-third of which was to be appointed by district councils, one-third by provincial councils and one-third by the president. The structure reflected more an American democratic model in conformity with the Bush administration's democracy promotion agenda rather than being in accord with the needs of Afghanistan. Any federalist form was dismissed, more specifically a centralized-decentralized one, whereby the powers of the central government would be proportional to the investment of greater sovereignty in micro-societies that could otherwise feel alienated from the political system in an ethnically heterogeneous country.[63] However, the next step was to hold elections, for the president and then for the Wolesi Jirga, which were scheduled for June 2004.

The presidential system

The final stage in the implementation of the Bonn Agreement, and the one which arguably received the most media attention in the US, Europe and Australia, was the staging of elections for the president and the legislature. The Bonn Agreement required that free and fair elections be held 'no later than two years from the convening of the emergency Loya Jirga', that is, by June 2004. However, the lack of infrastructure and insufficient security for the huge undertaking of two concurrent elections in 2004 led to the postponement of the presidential elections until October 2004, and the parliamentary elections until September 2005.

According to article 62 of the constitution, candidates for the role of president had to be Afghan citizens, Muslim, and no less than forty years old when they put themselves forward. In addition, no one convicted of crimes against humanity could nominate themselves for president.[64] In May 2004, the Karzai government passed an Electoral Law which further outlined the procedure for the election of the president. In order to win the election outright, a candidate had to win more than 50 per cent of the vote; if no candidate achieved this, the two highest polling candidates would take part in a second round, the winner of which would be declared president.[65] According to these provisions, an election for the president was called for 9 October 2004.

The administrative and security effort, and the costs involved in organizing the elections, which were met by the US and its allies, were enormous, given Afghanistan's rugged landscape, the poor state of the means of communication and the inaccessibility of many remote parts outside the main cities. A number of internal and external bodies helped the transitional government to convene the election. These included the Afghan-run Joint Electoral Management Body (JEMB), established by the Electoral Law to establish policy guidelines, approve procedures, and exercise oversight over the electoral processes. JEMB was assisted by two US organizations funded by the Reagan-founded National Endowment for Democracy, namely the National Democratic Institute and the International Republican Institute, as well as UNAMA. The National Democratic Institute and USAID also took on a civil society domestic election monitoring component. American and international organizations thus played a significant role in the organization and monitoring of Afghan elections, a fact which both supported the Bush administration's claims that the US was deeply involved in the Afghan democracy process, and implicated them in any potential failures of the electoral process.

In the end, the 'two-round system' outlined by the Electoral Law proved unnecessary in Afghanistan's first post-Taliban election, as Karzai won the vote with 55.5 per cent, negating the need for a run-off. His closest rivals were Qanuni, a UINFSA member and Tajik candidate from the Panjsher Valley with 16.3 per cent and Mohamed Mohaqqeq, a Shia Hazara candidate from Hazarajat with 11.7 per cent. With an overall majority, Karzai was officially elected President of Afghanistan for a five-year term. Despite high rates of illiteracy, unfamiliarity with democracy and persistent instability in the country, 8.1 million Afghans had voted in the election in the hope of a better life. This constituted 70 per cent of those registered to vote.[66] As observed by international monitors, the election was largely free and fair (despite some controversies, most notably a problem with the system by which people who had voted were marked with indelible ink).[67] Karzai's victory, whereby he was able to cross ethnic lines and receive votes from non-Pashtun Afghans, was considered by many a victory for ethnic pluralism, although other commentators noted that his high polling may also have been influenced by the fact that he was implicitly backed by the US, against whom there was as yet limited resistance.[68]

The legislature

While the presidential election had occurred without any major upsets, the much larger election for the parliament was an even bigger challenge. The elections for the 259 members of the Wolesi Jirga were an enormous undertaking, involving 160,000 polling staff who manned 26,500 polling stations in 8,300 locations throughout

Afghanistan.[69] Once again, JEMB, the UN, and international and domestic security forces were involved in the coordination of the elections. According to the constitution, a quota system was put in place to ensure women won at least 25 per cent of seats.

In the lead-up to the election, much debate surrounded the voting system to be used for the selection of candidates. International democracy promoters associated with the UN, independent think-tanks and other non-governmental organizations (NGOs) pushed for a party-based system, whereby political parties would pre-select candidates and the voters would vote by party, rather than candidate, at the polling booth.[70] Political parties are often considered a bulwark of democracy development, but the Karzai leadership and many of its supporters feared that such an approach would lead to existing ethnic and tribal factions dominating electoral proceedings.[71] As a result, a Single Non-Transferable Voting (SNTV) system was put in place. This system – used only in a few countries, such as Vanuatu and Jordan – is notorious for its perversity. It is simple on the surface, as it makes it easy to count the ballot papers and gives an opportunity for independent candidates unaffiliated with any party to win seats. But it can produce bizarre outcomes. According to this system, voters cast ballots for individuals not parties. In the end, the SNTV system encourages the election of the best-organized candidates with large networks, resources, and high profiles, and can actually make it more difficult for minority groups and independent opinions to be expressed in parliament.[72]

The SNTV system contributed to the emergence of a fragmented legislature in the September 2005 parliamentary election that was largely unrepresentative of the votes cast. Only an estimated 2 million of the 6 million votes cast were for winning candidates, resulting in over 4 million 'wasted votes'.[73] Social and religious conservatives, including a number of 'strongmen', were the largest group elected to the parliament although they did not constitute a majority. Also, large groups of traditionalists and liberals were elected. In addition, sixty-eight women were elected, nineteen more than the 25 per cent required by the quota system.[74] The turnout was much lower than expected, compared to the high turnout for the presidential elections; 57 per cent of registered voters placed a ballot, a significant decrease from the 70 per cent at the presidential election.[75] This was partly due to the confusion surrounding ballot papers,[76] but largely due to the growing disillusionment with the electoral process, after the successful presidential election had failed to bring about an increase in security and stability in Afghanistan,[77] as discussed in chapter 7.

Nonetheless, the election of the Wolesi Jirga, and with it the completion of the roadmap outlined at Bonn, was presented by many in the Bush administration and segments of the US and international media as an unmitigated success. It was cited as a justification of the US decision to intervene in Afghanistan; not only had US forces removed a terrorism threat to the US, but they had completely reformed Afghan politics and thus fulfilled a humanitarian mission. Khalilzad declared that the elections were evidence of Afghanistan's emergence as a 'moderate and democratic society'[78] and the success of American attempts to 'lay the foundation on which a democratic society can be constructed'[79] in a post-conflict environment. Bush personally congratulated Afghanistan on the successful parliamentary elections which he declared a major step forward in Afghanistan's development as a democratic state governed by the rule of law. An editorial in the *Wall Street Journal* the day after the elections declared that 'this is one battle in the war on terror that we are clearly winning'.[80]

Yet even as members of the Bush administration and its supporters were confidently declaring Afghanistan's transition to a working procedural democracy, some NGOs, scholars, journalists, commentators and other politicians were pointing to inherent flaws in the process by which Bonn had unfolded.[81] They included accusations of intimidation and vote-buying involved in the two Loya Jirgas, the impact of weak security on the ability of many to vote, particularly in unstable regions in the Pashtun-dominated south, the lack of protection given to women and other minorities, which silenced many who might have otherwise wanted to play a more active role in the consultative and decision-making processes, and the dangerous potential for conflict as a result of a heavily centralized and powerful executive arm based in Kabul, rather than a system that would help to enfranchise provincial and minority sections of Afghan society. Thus, far from solving the democracy deficit in Afghanistan, the Bonn process and the manner in which it was enacted had left the country in a state 'between stability and volatility',[82] with an inherently flawed governance structure.

The regional power vacuum

In the period since the culmination of the Bonn process, the disconnect between the centre and periphery in Afghan politics emerged as one of the most serious challenges to the development of democracy in the country. On the one hand, a highly centralized government with administrative structures based in Kabul was seen by many as crucial to the success of the 'state-building' project in the country, as was evidenced by the emphasis the US and its backers put on this outcome during the Bonn process. On the other hand, this focus led to a governance vacuum in the provinces, even though rural areas, in particular, were in desperate need of stable government to administer reconstruction and development programmes, and strong local government was traditionally recognized by democracy promoters in the US as a pillar of the democratization process in post-conflict societies.[83]

Officially, the highest form of local government in Afghanistan's provinces was the provincial council (PC), and elections for the thirty-four provincial councils (*Woleyati Shuras*) were held at the same time as those for the Wolesi Jirga in September 2005. However, these councils had only advisory roles, and no real power to make decisions on a local level. Leadership roles, such as provincial governors, district commissioners and mayors were appointed by the president, and were thus often used as important bargaining chips in winning the support of various regional powerbrokers for the central government in Kabul, rather than providing democratic representation for a province's citizens.[84]

Nonetheless, the PCs were technically given a mandate to oversee two important areas: provincial-level development and the monitoring of provincial administration.[85] In light of the intense focus on rural Afghan development by international aid agencies, the control of provincial development should have put the PCs in control of large budgets and given them considerable room to influence the direction of reconstruction projects. However, the reconstruction was actually overseen by Provincial Development Committees (PDCs), separate bodies which were appointed rather than elected, and which coordinated the activities of the Kabul-based ministries in the provinces, as well as monitoring development projects. The relationship between the elected PCs and the appointed PDCs was ambiguous and this undefined relationship contributed to confusion over the correct channels through which to organize reconstruction projects.[86] To add to the confusion, in 2003 the Afghan government established the National Solidarity Programme (NSP). This was a development programme run by local communities which was designed to provide an inclusive framework by which Afghan citizens could 'identify and implement projects that directly respond to their needs'.[87] Once again, the relationship between the Community Development Councils (CDCs) that operated the NSP and the elected PCs remained undefined, and this ambiguity undermined the transparency of Afghanistan's government structures.

Apart from highlighting the complexity of Afghanistan's post-Taliban reconstruction process, the inadequate delineation of the separate function of the PCs, the PDCs and the NSP raised two other important points. The first was the interaction of elected bodies and international NGOs in Afghanistan. The NSP's CDCs were very dependent on international NGOs, without whom they could not undertake the reconstruction projects for which they were designed. This gave NGOs inordinate influence over the CDCs, which were, in turn, the unelected counterpart of PCs which were then left with little agency of their own to monitor development. This situation arguably resulted not only in a lack of clarity in provincial administration, but also represented the bypassing of elected bodies by external, often non-Afghan organizations in the development process.

The second problem highlighted by the ambiguity surrounding the role of the elected PCs was the continued emphasis on centralized, rather than locally devolved, power in Afghan administration. While the Kabul-based government had made some attempts to reform the disordered provincial administration, ultimately weak regional power helped the development of a strongly centralized government. This was evidenced by the formation of the NSP itself, which essentially took control of development projects from the PCs and placed them in the hands of a Kabul-based body. Meanwhile, the Kabul government was unable to maintain control over the provinces in the absence of strong, elected provincial leadership, which undermined democratic structures outside the capital. This was one of the most serious of the negative results of the US push for centralized government during the Bonn process: a government could neither meet the needs of Afghanistan nor provide evidence for US claims to be 'promoting democracy' in Afghanistan.[88]

The best outcome achieved by the Bonn process was a kind of basic *procedural* democracy – that is, the development of democratic state institutions, the holding of elections, the writing of a constitution and the creation of the executive, legislative and judicial wings of government. As for transition to *substantive* democracy, involving the reform of civil society, increased protection of human rights of Afghan citizens, particularly women and ethnic minorities, and increased social stability through successful reconstruction projects, the issue was left largely ambiguous and undefined. Neither the Afghan side, nor the US government, nor international bodies such as the UN or NATO chose to draft a specific plan for the development of a functioning civil society or the improvement of human rights, increased liberty or freedom from violence for the Afghan people.

Civil society incorporates groups and networks of people who operate in the space between individuals and the state or government. Democracy promoters have generally stressed the importance of the advocacy of NGOs, as key bodies to lobby for improved human rights and provide local civic democracy education.[89] The US democracy promoters in Afghanistan put emphasis on supporting purely *secular* NGOs, as the context of the global 'war on terror' perceivably targeted 'political Islamism', leading US NGO workers and aid officials to shy away from giving support to overtly Muslim organizations.[90]

Finally, the blurring of civilian and military action, reflected partly in the creation of provincial reconstruction teams (PRTs), run by US and various allies in different provinces, greatly influenced the activities and public perception of civil society in Afghanistan. As part of their operations, US forces strategically matched military interventions with humanitarian campaigns to win over the 'hearts and minds' of the population, thus appropriating the language of development and civil society and allying it with an often violent military campaign.[91] In doing so, they created a degree of distrust and suspicion of civil society actors, both foreign and Afghan, among the wider Afghan population. The fact that many Afghan NGOs popped up as fronts for raising funds from the US and allied donors for local power-holders or power groups made the operations of these bodies in general quite murky. Concurrently, there was a mismatch between Western NGOs, which often used a secular language to put forward their promotion of human rights and civil liberties for Afghan citizens, and the local population, which was embedded in an indigenous, religious and ethno-tribal culture.

War on terror and invasion of Iraq

The Afghanistan intervention was also, from the beginning, recipro-
cally linked to what President Bush declared to be the 'war on terror'.
The success of one was conditioned on the triumph of the other. In
other words, the greater America's achievement in spreading its
brand of democracy, the less room there would be for anti-US
terrorism and fanaticism in the world. The Afghanistan campaign
was launched as the first salvo in this wider war, which was waged
not on an identifiably fixed target but rather on a moving object,
which was defined by Washington as a terror network or group across
some sixty countries. The war on terrorism was touted in universal
terms, but it was two-dimensional in its aim and application.

At one level, it was specifically directed against Al Qaeda and its
affiliates, and similar organizations from Afghanistan to the
Philippines to Yemen. President Bush and his officials deployed such
terms as 'Islamic' or 'Islamist' terrorism as the main target of US
operations. They used these terms interchangeably, irrespective of
the difference in their meanings. Whereas Islamic implies that the
religion of Islam itself endorses terrorism, Islamist denotes a follower
of Islam who upholds Islam not just as a faith and way of life but also
as an ideology of societal transformation that constitutes Islamism.
Most Islamists reject violence as a means to achieve their objectives,
as they condemned 9/11. There is a minority among them who resort
to violence as a *modus operandi* and manifest a violently radical or
extremist interpretation and application of political Islamism for
notional goals. Exemplifying this category were and still are Al
Qaeda, the Islamic State of Iraq and Syria – ISIS (also called Daesh or
al-Dawlaal-Islammiya fil al-Iraq wa al-Sham), and the Taliban.

President Bush and British Prime Minister Tony Blair certainly
emphasized the sanctity of Islam and made it clear that they were not
against the religion per se, but rather against those who misused and
abused it for their violent, self-serving notional ends. Yet this was not

how some of the other leading European and American political figures saw it. For example, Italian Prime Minister Silvio Berlusconi publicly exalted Western civilization as superior to that of Islam, as it 'has guaranteed well-being, respect for human rights and – in contrast with Islamic countries – respect for religious and political rights'. He also hoped 'the West will continue to conquer [Muslim] peoples, like it conquered Communism'.[92] Many other opinion-makers and commentators echoed such remarks in the Western media in one form or another.[93] This invariably played into the hands of the very groups and forces that the US was seeking to eliminate or marginalize and offended many faithful across the Muslim domain. It provided oxygen to Al Qaeda, the Taliban and their affiliates and supporters, allowing them to paint US actions as anti-Islam and to expand their circles of recruitment and operations.

At another level, the war on terrorism had a subterranean geopolitical objective. It was to target America's main adversaries in the Middle East. The dictatorial rule of Saddam Hussein in oil-rich Iraq was top of the list and the Islamic regime of the equally oil-rich Iran figured prominently below it, while, for example, the friendly fundamentalist Wahhabi regime of Saudi Arabia, whose nationals formed the bulk of the 9/11 perpetrators, was spared. President Bush, Vice-President Cheney, Defense Secretary Rumsfeld and Deputy Defense Secretary Wolfowitz were very keen, from the early days post-9/11, to identify a linkage between that event and Saddam Hussein's regime to target Iraq. In fact, President Bush wanted to act at the same time as Operation Enduring Freedom unfolded in Afghanistan as an extension of the war on terror and the democracy promotion agenda.[94] But the president was held back by the need to build a case for action. The Iraqi dictator, whom the US once courted as an Arab bulwark against the hostile Iranian Islamic regime and to whom Rumsfeld had personally conveyed a letter from President Ronald Reagan in December 1983 to win his friendship,[95] had become America's nemesis since his August 1990 invasion of the pro-US, oil-wealthy Emirate of Kuwait. Under President George H.W. Bush (1989–93), a US-led coalition had liberated Kuwait within six months of the invasion, but the decision not to prosecute the war for a longer period to get rid of Saddam Hussein's rule left the Iraqi dictator as a thorn in the side of Washington. The main reason for not toppling Saddam Hussein was the lack both of a UN Security Council resolution and of an alternative to replace him, as the Iraqi opposition was very divided in exile and Saudi Arabia feared that his elimination would boost the regional position of its rival Iran.

Although very weakened domestically and unable to exercise sovereignty over northern and southern Iraq due to the US-led allies' imposition of air exclusion zones, Saddam Hussein was still able to pose challenges to America, reportedly including a failed plot to kill Bush Senior during a celebratory visit to Kuwait in April 1993. President Bill Clinton had responded to the plot with a cruise missile strike on the Baghdad headquarters of those officers who were allegedly commissioned to execute the event.[96] But this was not enough of a punishment for Bush Junior. In addition to harbouring a personal vendetta,[97] he was motivated by three considerations to move against Saddam Hussein. The first was to realize the neoconservatives' idea of transforming Iraq into a democracy and to spread the gospel of democratization to the rest of the Middle East. The second was, in spite of the administration's repeated denials, to enable the US to gain leverage over Iraq's ownership of 10 per cent of the world's oil reserves and to garner influence within the Organization of the Petroleum Exporting Countries (OPEC) in pursuit of wider geo-economic and geopolitical objectives of the US as a world power. Former chairman of the US Federal Reserve Alan Greenspan (1987–2006) alludes to this point, claiming that he proposed the idea to the White House. He scoffs at the Bush administration's denial, saying 'I'm saddened that it is politically inconvenient to acknowledge what everyone knows: The Iraq war is largely about oil.'[98] The third was to operate from Iraq so as to destabilize the Iranian Islamic regime and its only

Arab ally, Syria, and the proxy force of Hezbollah in Lebanon. In fact, even prior to the 9/11 attacks, 'the Pentagon had been working for months on developing a military option for Iraq'.[99] Hence Bush's famous designation of Iraq and Iran, along with North Korea, as an 'axis of evil' in his 2002 State of the Union address.

As such, the war on terrorism was initiated to target not only Al Qaeda, the Taliban and their affiliates, elusive though they were, but also America's geopolitical adversaries – whether religious or secular – and to export democracy to the Middle East. Highlighting the danger of the Saddam Hussein regime, the Bush leadership joined forces with that of Blair to claim that, based on credible intelligence, the Iraqi dictator possessed weapons of mass destruction, even though the United Nations Special Commission (UNSCOM) had investigated and destroyed Iraq's WMD following the reversal of the invasion of Kuwait. They also alleged the existence of a cooperative relationship between Al Qaeda and Saddam Hussein's regime, and therefore the latter's involvement in 9/11, even though Saddam Hussein's secularism stood in stark opposition to Bin Laden's religiosity. While almost all of America's NATO and non-NATO allies were content to back America's Afghanistan campaign as a good cause, neither they nor the UN Security Council were willing to support the Bush administration on Iraq. Core European allies, most importantly France and Germany, and some close regional friends, including Saudi Arabia and Egypt, cautioned Washington against it.

Regardless, the Bush administration, backed by only two allies, Britain and Australia in a 'coalition of the willing', prioritized Iraq over Afghanistan and launched an invasion of the country on 20 March 2003, while the Afghanistan situation was still very fluid, with its political and security landscape extremely fragile. The Iraq invasion toppled Saddam Hussein's regime but in the process also destroyed the Iraqi state. Against the backdrop of a massive power vacuum, for which the US had no viable political strategy, an Iraq deeply divided along ethnic and sectarian lines was rapidly transformed from a strong dictatorial state with suppressed societies into a weak state with strong societies. Within two years of the invasion, a growing bloody resistance, partly led by an Al Qaeda allied group, the Sunni Islamic State of Iraq, and partly by Iran-backed Shia groups, pulled the US forces into a ferocious insurgency. To quell it, the US escalated force deployment and operations at very high human and material costs to the Americans, not to mention British losses, as well as incalculable damage done to the Iraqi people and society. America's actions also involved moral degradation, given the atrocities that US troops committed.[100] While Rumsfeld had boasted that the US had the capacity to fight two to three wars at the same time, America's war of choice in Iraq proved otherwise. The Iraqi invasion, which many analysts have described as a bigger strategic fiasco than that of Vietnam,[101] diminished America's democratic and world power status. It entailed costly implications for the Afghanistan campaign, as critical assets were diverted from Afghanistan to Iraq. In the words of Congressman Eliot L. Engel:

> We got distracted by the war in Iraq under an administration whose priority [shifted to] defeating Saddam Hussein, not an end game in Afghanistan. . . . We changed missions, changed priorities, and lost sight of what was once considered 'the just war'.[102]

The transfer of resources to Iraq was most acutely evident in three areas. The first was in the realm of troop deployment. At the time of the Iraq invasion, the Afghanistan situation was still very fluid and fragile. Reconstruction work to move the country forward to a kind of viability had just begun. Realistically, no one could be confident of the workability of the Bonn process to establish an effective political order as a foundation for building a united, democratic and prosperous Afghanistan, as pressed for by American democracy promoters and embodied by Khalilzad. Despite an eerie calm in the country through 2002, the US and its allies had managed to gain control over only a very limited land surface, and the security situation was brittle. The challenge of the Taliban and several other anti-systemic groups was on the rise, stretching the capacity of the small contingent of American Special Forces and the CIA operatives, along with ISAF, to deal with them. Karl Eikenberry notes, 'we needed more capable forces for fighting and training the Afghan army' and 'US forces faced a shortage of both intelligence and military resources in Afghanistan'. The issue could not be eased by relying on Afghan security forces as, by early 2003, a mere 4,500 had been trained and equipped. Eikenberry states that as early as the second half of 2002, Washington seemed to have become very focused on Iraq and thus prioritized the latter over Afghanistan.

Meanwhile, the US Department of Defense seemed to be poorly cognizant of what was now required to help Afghanistan build its own armed and security forces; and this was not the time for the US military 'to let their eyes off the evolving security situation in the country'. Eikenberry recalls a very telling incident in this respect. Several months before the American invasion of Iraq in March 2003, an army major general who was leading efforts to build a new Afghan Army, requested to United States Central Command that the active duty US Army infantry brigade responsible for the training mission be replaced when it was due for rotation by another active duty unit. Although his request was supported by the US three-star commander of coalition forces –Afghanistan, the request was turned down by USCENTCOM. Instead, he was told that he would get a National Guard brigade.

> The Guard and the reserves are supposed to be the equal to the active force, but of course there's no way that they can be. They are citizen soldiers who train one weekend every month and then two weeks every year and you can't translate that into the competence and proficiency of a regular army which is 24/7. . . . The fact that we couldn't get an active infantry brigade committed to the training of the Afghan army indicated that already Afghanistan was now being subordinated to Iraq.[103]

This was in preparation for invading Iraq even well before a final decision had been made on the invasion. Thus, at a time when there was a shortage of troops in Afghanistan and more capable forces and resources were required for fighting and training the Afghan Army, the US launched Operation Iraqi Freedom, relegating the Afghanistan campaign to secondary importance.

For the Bush administration, Iraq rapidly became the main battleground, with more urgency and commitment of resources to address what it branded as a chief threat to the US in the war on terror and the ensuing insurgency. US troop deployment rapidly escalated to 130,000 in that theatre (accompanied by 45,000 British soldiers and 2,000 Australian service members), sadly at the cost of meeting the need for force augmentation in Afghanistan. As Richard Clarke notes, a considerable amount of combat resources were diverted, involving even 'the US Special Forces who were trained to speak Arabic, the language of al Qaeda, [who] had been pulled out of Afghanistan and sent to Iraq. . . . In fact, of the combined U.S. forces fighting the "war on terrorism" in the Afghan and Iraqi theaters, only about 5 percent were in Afghanistan' at the time.[104]

The second was in the sphere of human and satellite intelligence platforms. The CIA, which was very focused on pursuing Bin Laden and his main functionaries and on fighting global terrorism, had to shift much of its resources to Iraq. As argued by a former CIA analyst and regional expert Lisa Curtis, 'Unfortunately, shortly after we routed the Taliban, then more attention began going towards the war in Iraq.'[105] The CIA was now directed to train one eye on hunting Bin Laden and his main operatives and the other on Iraq. On the one hand, it was required to intensify efforts to search deep inside Pakistan to hunt down Al Qaeda's leaders and their main agents, who were actively plotting and executing plans against American targets in Afghanistan and beyond. On the other, it was becoming deeply involved in helping the Iraq operations and containing the raging insurgency that developed and beset that country.[106] As the insurgency in Iraq picked up dramatically in 2004/5, so did the CIA's involvement. Some of the satellites which had been focused on Afghanistan to provide valuable data regarding opposition movements and activities, and guide the coalition forces in that country, were directed to provide intelligence for the Iraqi theatre. The Afghanistan campaign was now subordinately entangled with the struggle against both the Iraqi invasion and global terrorism.

The third was in the sphere of airborne platforms. The growing commitment to Iraq reduced the US's resource capability for precision strikes against targets in Afghanistan. American forces in Afghanistan needed drones for intelligence reasons and combat missions as well as aircraft and attack helicopters, but they were all largely diverted to Iraq.[107] By the time the US decided to withdraw its forces from Iraq, starting in 2009 and finishing by the end of 2011, Afghanistan's overall security state was on a downward spiral. Yet it was too late to return the resources from Iraq, as most had already been committed to strengthening the Iraqi defence and security forces ahead of the American pull-out.

The Bush administration's intertwining of the Afghanistan campaign with the broader foreign policy objectives of democracy promotion and the war on terrorism, along with the failure to decapitate Al Qaeda and the Taliban in the early phase of the intervention, proved critical in defining and expanding the US role in Afghanistan in a direction that had not originally been intended. Its Afghanistan campaign was shaped more by bigger foreign policy goals than by what was achievable in that country with a clear eye on its complex historical and prevailing realities. Still, Washington expected its efforts to engender an appropriate post-Taliban system of governance under reliable and effective leaders whereby the US and its allies could make an early military exit with a degree of success. But what transpired further endangered America's Afghanistan project, setting it on the path towards failure, despite policy adjustments by President Bush and his successor.

4

Dysfunctional Governance

The Hamid Karzai Era, 2001–14

[I]t may be easier to raise a puppet king to a throne, than to keep him there firm in his seat. Woe to any government whose strongest or only puppet is the sword of the stranger!

A.L.O.E.[1]

The Bonn process and its implementation to democratize Afghanistan, despite early optimism for its success, could not deliver a governance system and state-building venture that would provide the United States and its allies with a credible, effective and, above all, accountable partner on the ground. Although presented within the traditional Afghan frameworks of consultation and endorsement, what it produced hardly constituted indigenous grassroots viability. It primarily reflected the interests of the US democracy promoters and war on terrorism advocates in support of preserving and strengthening America's world power status and that of the Washington-backed Hamid Karzai-led elite. The US allies followed suit. Over time, Karzai's leadership and governance proved incompetent, with its composition and behaviour more in accord with the traditional political and cultural practices that had historically impeded Afghanistan's transformation into a modern functioning state.

With the first Afghan presidential and parliamentary elections out of the way, there seemed to be a general sigh of relief on the part of the instigators of the Bonn process. They thought Afghanistan was now on a promising course of democratic change and development as an American success story. However, President Karzai did not turn out to be a man on whose administration the Afghan people could depend for generating good governance and national cohesion, which could instrumentally assist the US and its allies in their transformative Afghanistan campaign.

No doubt, Karzai took the helm at a very difficult time. He was entrusted with the unenviable task of turning Afghanistan into a viable state under the prevalent harsh conditions and in conformity with Washington's expectations. In Shakespearian terms, Karzai certainly was not 'great but greatness was thrust upon him'.[2] Yet he was assigned a task that would have been enormous even for a great man. Nonetheless, he was in a unique position to do a better job of his mission than finally eventuated under his leadership. He enjoyed extensive and unprecedented international support and faced no imminent internal threats. He had Washington's full support and protection, and the consensus and backing of the Afghan elites who had endorsed the Bonn Agreement. When Karzai arrived at Kabul airport in late December 2001 to head the interim government, he was warmly welcomed by the leaders of the United Islamic National Front for the Salvation of Afghanistan (UINFSA), whose forces provided him initial protection. But shortly thereafter, he relied on an American Special Forces unit to guard him. After a while he realized that being guarded by Americans was a bad look, and that unit was replaced by a trusted Afghan praetorian elite corps. Responsibility for his government's security and that of the capital Kabul soon rested with the International Security Assistance Force (ISAF) – a 5,000-strong contingent deployed by the US NATO allies, as authorized by United Nations Security Council Resolution 1386 on 20 December 2001.[3] Despite all the challenges facing his administration and the country, he was in a position to be innovative in the construction of a new Afghanistan.

The Karzai–Khalilzad duet

Karzai was, however, inexperienced in the art of governance and leadership and depended on the US for moving forward. This led him to work intimately with Zalmay Khalilzad, especially when the latter was US special presidential envoy for Afghanistan (2001–3) and, more importantly, US ambassador to the country (2004–5), in shaping Afghanistan's destiny. Sharing a common Pashtun background, the two had known each other since the mid-1990s, when Khalilzad was a paid advisor to the Union Oil Company of California (UNOCAL, owned by Chevron since 2005). Khalilzad was involved in liaising between UNOCAL and the Taliban rulers for the construction of a gas pipeline from Turkmenistan through Afghanistan to Pakistan and India.[4] As he says, the two 'had become friends over the years'. While US envoy, he 'spent hundreds of hours with Karzai' and Karzai included him even in 'his meetings of Afghan officials ... [and he] was the first and last person with whom Karzai would speak before making decisions'.[5] Khalilzad also claims that Karzai was nostalgic about Afghanistan's 'golden age' of the 1960s and 1970s, and wanted to restore it, but '[t]he problem was that he wanted America and the rest of the world to do it'.[6] Karzai cherished the fact that Khalilzad enjoyed a direct line of communication to the White House, enabling him to pick up the phone and talk to President George W. Bush or his senior staff, thus bypassing Washington's bureaucratic layers to get what he wanted – something that gave him extra personal power in policy recommendations and actions. In Karl Eikenberry's words, Khalilzad 'certainly during the Bush administration had a huge influence on [US] thinking about Afghanistan' and 'Karzai seemed to require Zal's [Zalmay's] presence as more of a security blanket and somebody who could help him interpret the US, though at the same time ... he did not entirely trust him'.[7]

Karzai indeed relied very heavily on Khalilzad in shaping his interim and transitional administrations, and domestic and foreign policy perimeters. Thus, the Karzai–Khalilzad duet essentially set the direction and pace for Afghanistan's transformation. But, in this relationship, there was a serious power imbalance where behind the scenes Khalilzad was in the driver's seat more than Karzai. On the one hand, Khalilzad represented the intervening power, was answerable to Washington, and was responsible for defending and promoting its interests; and in that he was also influenced by his close association with the neoconservative group that had become a dominant force in Bush's administration, which basically emphasized the rebuilding of Afghanistan in the US's image. Karzai, on the other hand, was supposed to be primarily responsible to the people of Afghanistan, and wished to be seen not as a puppet but a dedicated nationalist leader. Yet he was vulnerable to US power for, as Khalilzad writes, Karzai's 'authority depended on the protection and reliability of the United States'.[8] All this meant that Karzai's interaction with Khalilzad and, for that matter, with Washington, was one of acute dependency. Indeed, Khalilzad's influence on Karzai and in shepherding Afghanistan through its transition was so great that he was dubbed by some in Kabul as the 'Viceroy'.[9] The dependent nature of this relationship led many to view Karzai as an American sheriff. Over time, this was instrumental in generating distance between Karzai and some of the independent strongmen, especially within UINFSA. These figures, who had fought the Soviets and the Taliban, could not easily be as trustful of Khalilzad, whom they saw more as an American rather than an Afghan, although publicly they were polite to him and sought to have him on their side – a cultural norm among many Afghans ambitious for power and status.

During his first two years in office, Karzai appeared cognizant of the need to build a cross-ethnic and cross-sectarian administration as a basis for national unity and fruitful governance. This occurred mostly during the period when James Dobbins opened the American

Liaison Office in Kabul (17 December 2001) and directed it for a few months before Robert Finn was appointed US ambassador (March 2002 to August 2004). These two career diplomats advised Karzai and conducted their relationship with him in a professional manner. During their tenure, Karzai displayed a notable degree of inclusiveness in the make-up of his cabinet and in some of the other senior governmental appointments, despite having recruited a good number of them from Afghan expatriates in the West, based on personal contacts, due to a limited pool of trained personnel available domestically at the time. He showed an inclination to be forward-looking and to avoid the pitfalls that had marred Afghanistan's past. However, sadly, after winning the 2004 election and with the arrival of Khalilzad as US ambassador, who was always influentially in the background, Karzai felt confident and found it desirable and expedient to remedy his client status and revisit traditionalism by clawing back some of his earlier liberalist tendencies in order to enhance his position. He fell back on the traditions of Afghan rulership by personalizing and *ethnicizing* rather than institutionalizing politics for the common good. Though the evidence does not suggest he was personally enriching himself, it is hard to deny that his style and policies gave rise to a politics of patronage, corruption, inefficiency and disregard for the rule of law in both civilian and military spheres.[10] He failed to invest sufficiently in civilian law enforcement; the Afghan National Police force that evolved proved to be ineffective and suffered from nepotism and corruption.[11]

Decaying rule

Incrementally, Karzai started to behave like a Pashtun *khan* or tribal leader. Using his constitutional executive powers and international support, he resorted to running his administration fundamentally along the lines of the patronage network that he fostered, based on political favour or disfavour.[12] He surrounded himself mostly with political, ethnic and business entrepreneurs and powerbrokers. They included his full and half-brothers from the large Karzai family. Many of his aides from the diaspora and inside Afghanistan turned out to be more interested in safeguarding their positions of power and privilege than in boosting national unity, reconstruction and security. They largely acted as self-seeking, corrupt functionaries rather than visionaries, with little inclination for strategic thinking and planning. Karzai invoked the constitution and stressed the importance of the rule of law only when they suited his political and power needs. Otherwise, in accord with the Afghan traditional political culture, he willingly overlooked them when it came to protecting and preserving his own position and those who aided him to do so.[13]

As Karzai's sense of vulnerability to internal dissension and foreign pressure grew, he spent most of his time in the presidential palace,[14] only occasionally venturing to provinces, over many of which his writ barely ran, earning him the popular title of 'mayor of Kabul'.[15] In the absence of effective presidential-led coordination and communication, some of his ministers simply turned their ministries into disconnected and largely ethnic-based fiefdoms. A commission was appointed for public service reform, but few firm steps were ever taken to create a unified, functioning administration and public service, armed with a well-trained and effective bureaucracy. Various highly paid foreign firms were hired to help organize and improve standards in different branches of administration, but the volumes of recommendations that they produced gathered dust on the shelves of different ministries without being implemented. Nepotism – an historical practice – continued to be the order of the day. Most of the political, administrative and military appointments that Karzai made were based on family, tribal, ethnic and factional connections rather than on merit.[16] The 'old guard' continued to deprive the better-educated generation of young Afghans, arising from within the country or coming from the diaspora, of the necessary opportunities to play an effective role in the country's transition. Many of those who had initially come from abroad with genuine intentions based on love for the country started to leave in desperation within the first few years of the Karzai administration.[17]

Despite earlier downplaying the role of ethno-tribalism to bring about national cohesion and solidarity, under his personal impulses and those of lobbyists around him, Karzai increasingly appeared to privilege his own ethnic Pashtuns, including in the composition of the Independent Election Commission (IEC).[18] As such, Afghanistan shifted towards a politics of ethnic imbalance, causing growing concern among the non-Pashtun segments of the population, whose opposition to the Taliban's rule had been partly stirred by the repressive and discriminatory policies of this mainly Pashtun group. Although there is no evidence to suggest that Karzai personally engaged in monetary self-enrichment, 'concerns about corruption and malpractice could scarcely be assuaged by the rise of a Karzai cartel, dominated by close relatives of the president'.[19] Until his assassination by his head of security in July 2011, the president's half-brother, Ahmad Wali Karzai, had a reputation as the 'Kingpin of Kandahar', and was accused of being an 'extortionist and drug-trafficker extraordinaire',[20] something that President Karzai rejected as 'a lot of rubbish'.[21] Karzai's four remaining full and half-brothers, in particular Qayum, Mahmood and Shah Wali (who replaced Ahmad Wali in Kandahar as elder of the Karzai family and leader of his Populzai tribe), were allegedly involved in highly lucrative economic, commercial and industrial dealings (with considerable investments abroad, Dubai in particular) and political machinations. Not surprisingly, there were also signs of alleged financial and business squabbles among the president's brothers, especially between Mahmoud and Shah Wali.[22] Their sudden wealth, which amounted to millions of dollars, was very suspicious, as several brothers were reputed to be deeply involved in many illicit activities. Whoever carried the surname Karzai reaped maximum benefit from his or her association with the president, who did not hesitate to protect them whenever necessary.[23]

Also rapidly blossoming under the president's leadership was a post-2001 nouveau riche class. It formed a comprador elite who enriched themselves from illegal financial and commercial deals, avoiding any oversight by Afghan or UN or US watchdogs through various machinations, at times threatening any potential whistle-blowers. This elite was made up of government officials, business entrepreneurs, local administrators and anyone else who had connections or influence with power-holders, who could enable and protect them. They came from different ethnic backgrounds and operated within a context of ethnic or inter-ethnic favours given or withheld. The closer an elite member was to the president and other sources of power, the greater was that person's opportunities to accumulate wealth. Dubai was a haven in which to bank their money, invest in luxury property and hold lavish gatherings for some Afghan government officials, parliamentarians and persons with valuable connections. As one source put it, 'at a time when the United States and its allies . . . [were] spending . . . to prop up' Karzai's fragile government, the volume of outflow into Dubai was 'estimated to total well over $1 billion a year', which 'stirred concerns' for US officials to the effect that 'funds have been diverted from aid'.[24] This was happening in a country that was still one of the poorest in the world, with a gross domestic product (GDP) of just $18 billion in 2011 and a great majority of its people living in abject poverty. Towards the end of Karzai's era, little of the billions of dollars which flowed into the country, mostly from the US but also from other donors in support of governance, reconstruction, humanitarian and security objectives, trickled down to the masses.[25]

The president's office was privileged, funded annually and intermittently by the CIA,[26] MI6[27] and the Iranian government, along with many government aides and senior public servants, especially those from the diaspora, who also drew lucrative salaries from foreign sources.[28] This tarnished the president's reputation as he was seen as being a leader on 'the payroll' of foreign intelligence services.

Karzai publicly tried to weather the scandal by claiming that the payments were to cover the expenses of his office and to serve the interests of the country.[29] But the Afghan people historically viewed such a leader as a disgrace and a 'foreign stooge'. Some analysts compared Karzai with one of his nineteenth-century predecessors, Shah Shuja Durrani, who assumed the rulership of Afghanistan twice – from 1803 to 1809 and from 1839 until his assassination by one of his courtiers in 1842. He was renowned for being on the British payroll and for having been the servant of a foreign power.[30]

Rampant corruption seeped into the everyday lives of the Afghan people. In 2010, the United Nations Office on Drugs and Crime (UNODC) claimed that 59 per cent of Afghan citizens saw corruption as the most prominent problem for the country. More indicative of trends was the fact that 80 per cent of rural dwellers believed corruption had significantly increased from 2005 to 2010.[31] Afghans claimed that 40 per cent of the time they had contact with senior politicians they were solicited for a bribe. During 2009, one Afghan out of every two had to pay kickbacks to a public official. In that year, Afghans as a whole paid out $2.5 billion in bribes, accounting for an astronomical one-quarter of Afghanistan's GDP.[32] Disputes in a village, for example over water, were traditionally settled through mediation. Elders of the area refrained from calling a government official to mediate because he would have demanded a bribe. Instead, they asked a Talib to perform the task as he did it on an Islamic basis, without any monetary benefit.[33]

Under international pressure, especially from such main donors as the US and the European Union, Karzai was finally prompted in 2009 to make an effort to tackle the issue of corruption through pay and grading reforms, involving an increase in Afghan National Army (ANA) and Afghan National Police (ANP) salaries.[34] But two facts indicated that money alone was not sufficient to root out this endemic malaise, which became embedded in all levels of government and society. First, government operating budget expenditures had doubled between 2006 and 2010.[35] Second, as reported in 2012 by UNODC, large sums demanded in bribes by enforcement officials suggested that greed, rather than necessity, was often the major motivation.[36]

The difficulty of eradicating corruption in a country where domestic politics and international interests were so closely intertwined yet often conflicting was significant. Two cases were exemplary in this respect. The first involved Mohammad Zia Salehi, the chief of administration for the Afghan National Security Council and a close Karzai confidant. Salehi was investigated for corruption after wiretapping caught him soliciting a bribe.[37] Although Salehi was quickly released from prison (through Karzai's personal intervention)[38] and charges were soon dropped, the event caused considerable embarrassment to the United States and particularly the CIA, on whose payroll Salehi seemed to have remained at least until 2011.[39] The second case involved Khalilullah Ferozi, chief executive of the Kabul Bank, whose $900 million deposits were embezzled in 2011. A member of the nouveau riche and a 'pillar' of the Afghan business establishment, Ferozi had been running the bank along with the bank's former chairman, Sherkhan Farnood, 'as a giant pyramid scheme'. When the fraud was discovered, Ferozi was supposedly placed under house arrest, yet was free to continue living his rich life. He was able to receive a journalist in a luxurious hotel in Kabul to assure the world that he had done great things, including making 'investments' in Dubai, for Afghanistan. His arrest was fake and he was implicitly protected by powerful figures to whom he had offered loans on favourable terms, notably Karzai's vice-president, Mohammad Fahim, and Mahmoud Karzai.[40]

Executive–legislature rupture

Meanwhile, Karzai used his executive powers not only to intervene in the judiciary to protect family members and aides but also to marginalize parliament's role in the processes of governance.[41] He did little to build an effective working relationship between the executive and legislative branches. Through his minister of parliamentary affairs, Mohammad Ghulam Farooq Wardak (2006–8), who also served as minister of education for a much longer period, Karzai sought to incapacitate parliament, thereby making it his tool, rather than seeking to strengthen it as an effective arm of the government and a genuine check on executive power. He frequently exploited the Wolesi Jirga's internal divisions, reflecting essentially the political and social heterogeneity of the country, to gain the support of its members through patronage and nepotistic practices, and to prevail over the chamber and override its legislative responsibilities and decisions whenever he found it desirable to do so. The relationship between the two sides became unnecessarily adversarial and distrustful. He rarely withdrew any of his cabinet nominees who could not obtain sufficient votes of confidence from the Wolesi Jirga and left them in acting positions for long periods. For example, in 2007, the Wolesi Jirga gave a vote of no-confidence to Foreign Minister Dr Rangin Dadfar Spanta, but Karzai kept him in office until 2010. Also, in the latter year, the legislature rejected two-thirds of his cabinet nominees,[42] and many of them again in the following year, but the president simply ignored the rejections.

The parliamentary election of 2010 served only to deepen the executive–legislative divide.[43] Accusations of systematic fraud, ballot stuffing and intimidation led the UN-backed Electoral Complaints Commission (ECC) and Afghan-led IEC to act on a claim about the marginalization of the Pashtun vote, with the IEC discarding 1.3 million ballots out of 5.6 million cast,[44] and the ECC disqualifying twenty-one winning candidates. Soon afterwards, Karzai protested a perceived lack of Pashtun representation in the lower house. Under pressure from domestic constituents and the international community, he eventually swore in the new parliament in January 2011, yet he continued to question the latter's legitimacy. He established a

Special Court on Election Complaints, a body outside the jurisdiction of the Afghan courts, to question the election process and the IEC's activities.[45] According to a study by the Afghanistan Research and Evaluation Unit, the 2010 parliamentary election and subsequent intra-governmental squabbling damaged even further the legitimacy of the government and electoral institutions in the eyes of the people.[46] Only in August 2011, after months of sustained international pressure, did Karzai annul the special court and acknowledge the legitimacy of the IEC.[47]

The growing lack of trust between the executive and legislative branches seriously undermined the processes of building inter-institutional cooperation and institutionalization against the entrenchment of personal politics in Afghanistan. The centrality of political personalities, as opposed to political institutions, in Afghan political culture remained a deep-seated issue for political stability and continuity. As before, political institutions rose and fell with personalities, instead of governing and regulating the behaviour of these individuals.

Highly damaging political intrigues, rivalries and malpractices permeated Karzai's administration at all levels. There were serious rifts even within his inner circle. For example, in 2010, he found it politically expedient to force two of his top security officials – Pashtun Minister of the Interior Hanif Atmar and Tajik head of Afghan intelligence Amrullah Saleh, who were both at that time perceived by Washington as capable individuals – to resign over their failure to stop a rocket and suicide attack on a peace jirga, and policy differences. The main reason was that they disagreed with Karzai over his style of leadership and overtures to the Taliban, while there was no broad cabinet or national consensus on the issue.[48] Karzai had increasingly voiced a strong concern about the difficult predicament of his fellow Pashtuns and had pushed desperately for a political deal with the Taliban, whom he persistently called his 'brothers'. Saleh, and to a lesser extent Atmar, opposed such a deal at any cost, prompting them to join the political opposition.

Administration defects and lack of direction

Ultimately, Karzai presided over not only a highly corrupt and dysfunctional government, with limited control beyond Kabul, but also a very divided and conflict-ridden governing elite. The control by 'strongmen' over vast swaths of Afghan territory was an additional obstacle to centralized government, as many such figures were often at odds with the Karzai government. Meanwhile, Karzai's administration was vulnerable to penetration by opposition factions and various foreign intelligence services at both civilian and military-security levels. His cabinet discussions and decisions were allegedly leaked within hours. This, in turn, fed into Karzai's paranoia and sense of vulnerability. His growing conviction of the existence of plots against him further exacerbated his increasingly authoritarian tendencies.[49]

The inefficiencies of Karzai's government contributed significantly to its poor reputation among the international community and the Afghans themselves. The inability of the government to effectively allocate resources had as much to do with failings at a governmental level as it did with instability in the provinces. In particular, the lack of an overall direction and communication between the various tiers of government and external agencies severely restricted effective resource allocation. The disconnect between the executive and legislative branches often paralysed action. Given all this, it was therefore no surprise that when NATO assessed local governance in roughly 120 districts across the country in 2010, it was rated 'unproductive' in one-third of the districts, 'dysfunctional' in one-quarter, and in seventeen districts was simply described as 'non-existent'.[50] An 'unproductive', 'dysfunctional' or, even worse, 'non-existent', government presence was unlikely to inspire local or international confidence in the Karzai administration. Karzai often bitterly complained about foreign aid not being channelled through his government, but the main reason for this was that neither the US nor its allies could fully trust the government, given the rate of corruption and malpractice within it.

Ideologically, the Karzai government did not have a clear direction either. What did it stand for? Was it a pro-Western, secular pro-capitalist democracy with an Islamic face, capable of meeting the preferences of the United States and its allies, but unsupported by most of the Afghan people who were unable to identify with it? Or was it a blend of Western and Afghan values and practices, topped up by assorted Islamic traditions of authoritarianism, viewed with confusion and ambivalence by a majority of the Afghan population? The answer depended on Karzai's changing mood and circumstances. While often urbane in his approach, he was prone to changing his mind abruptly. Being unpredictable fed into public confusion and uncertainty and caught the US and its allies off-guard.

Public disenchantment

The public grew progressively more disillusioned with the Karzai administration. This was most visible among the citizens in the main urban centres, especially Kabul. The population of the capital doubled to over 5 million within a decade of the US intervention, as growing insecurity (discussed in chapter 7) and less than desirable levels of poverty forced increased migration from the country to the cities. Many began to question the efficacy of billions of foreign aid dollars for reconstruction and humanitarian purposes, not to mention the US and allied military expenditure that, in the case of the US alone, averaged $300 million a day.[51] Donations, along with reconstruction and military expenditure, certainly sustained the Karzai government, enabled some of his relatives and officials in positions of power and influence to fill their pockets and bank accounts abroad, and allowed the nouveau riche to live it up. This also benefited a number of foreign companies and their domestic subsidiaries, as well as America's military-industrial organizations. But, overall, it did little to lift the population of Afghanistan out of widespread poverty.

Having experienced so much turmoil and misery under five contrasting ideological groups and governmental systems since the mid-1970s, most of the public were left to live with uncertainty and insecurity, prompting them to fend for themselves and their families. Consequently, problems at the elite level were echoed within the population at large. Many ordinary citizens, compelled to ensure their own self-preservation, engaged in a variety of activities involving deceitful and corrupt practices.[52] Sadly, the result of this was that parts of Afghan society became, in many ways, as dysfunctional and corrupt as the government. While in many aspects the state–society dichotomy became entrenched, at least in this respect the two came to have much in common. The governmental and societal elements who wanted to serve their country with loyalty, dedication and sincerity found themselves on the fringes, frustrated about the direction Afghanistan was taking but void of resources and opportunities to make corrective differences.

The 2009 presidential election and Karzai's strained relations with Washington

Despite Karzai's growing unpopularity, or perhaps because of it, he appeared to have gained mastery of the art of political subterfuge, duplicity, patronage, co-optation and divide and rule. He is alleged to have used his office and foreign resources not only to protect his family but also to enhance his re-election chances. In addition to enlisting the support of various 'strongmen' with influence among different ethnic and tribal communities, irrespective of their suitability or qualifications, including Abdul Rashid Dostum, he resorted to splitting prominent families that could possibly undermine his electoral ambitions. Concerned about the influence of Ahmed Shah Massoud's family and its Panjshiri devotees, he caused a split within them by selecting one of Massoud's less-known brothers, Ahmad Zia, who had little government experience or record of service, as his running mate in the August 2009 presidential election. Through such mechanisms and alleged widespread vote-rigging in his favour he won that election.[53] Under the constitution, a president was eligible to run for two four-year terms, with the expiry of each term on 21 May. Karzai extended his first term by three months without a constitutional and parliamentary mandate. His cronies reportedly engaged in considerable irregularities, including stuffing ballot boxes and discounting votes to ensure his success. Under pressure from the international community, Karzai finally agreed to a second round against his main political rival, Abdullah Abdullah, who was foreign minister in Karzai's interim and transitional governments, but ultimately refused to meet Abdullah's calls for a fair and free run-off. He declined Abdullah's demand to fire the head of the IEC, who was accused of being a Karzai crony and of being involved in the vote-rigging, prompting Abdullah to withdraw from the run-off in protest. As a result, Karzai was declared the victor. Karzai's triumph was based on winning a little more than half of the 4 million votes cast out of 12 million voters registered. This result could hardly be seen as providing resounding legitimacy, particularly after the UN-backed election watchdog commission and the ECC found that 1 million of the 4 million votes were null and void.[54]

Concerns about electoral irregularities led the most senior American diplomat and deputy special envoy at the UN mission in Afghanistan, Peter Galbraith (a Democrat), to go public on the issue of widespread fraud in Karzai's favour and call for a thorough investigation. This resulted in a dispute with his mild-mannered, conciliatory Norwegian boss, Kai Eide and Galbraith's removal from his post.[55] Galbraith's move angered Karzai. From that point, relations between him and Washington took a downward turn, as the two sides lost confidence in each other.

The messy presidential election and its outcome, public disenchantment with the Karzai administration and the US failure to bring a marked improvement in living conditions for a majority of Afghans came against the backdrop of a new occupant in the White House, Democratic President Barack Obama, whose first term began in January 2009. Obama could not share Bush's optimism about Afghanistan or see the way forward with Karzai to a military victory. Despite having declared, during his presidential campaign, that the Afghan war was one of necessity and the Iraq war one of choice, he had by now developed serious reservations about the Afghanistan mission. Along with Vice-President Joe Biden and some other senior figures in the administration and Congress, Obama had grown concerned about the open-endedness of the US involvement. He intended to find a way out of this very costly war, already the longest in American history. The conflict had reached a point whereby it was no longer politically or financially sustainable and militarily winnable – something that the USSR had experienced two decades earlier. But, given America's hefty investment and reputational issues, he preferred to see an end to the war in a responsible and honourable way. To address the issue, in late January 2009 Obama appointed the experienced diplomat Richard Holbrooke as special representative for Afghanistan and Pakistan, and in the following month Michèle Flournoy, as Under Secretary of Defense for Policy, who crafted the administration's counterinsurgency policy in Afghanistan, and ordered a comprehensive review of the US Afghanistan policy.

The final evaluation of American policy was made by a White House Review Committee in February 2009, chaired by Bruce Riedel, a veteran CIA officer, also commissioned by Obama. In view of this final review, which came at a time when the political and security situation was worsening and American public support for the Afghan war was waning, in March 2009 Obama announced the dispatch of 4,000 troops and additional aid workers to Afghanistan, with increasing aid to Pakistan to entice it to be more cooperative.

However, in the northern summer of 2009, the appointment of General Stanley McChrystal as commander of US and NATO forces in Afghanistan changed the picture. McChrystal initiated another reassessment that ended with his request for an additional surge of 40,000 US troops.[56] This was on top of some 70,000 American troops and close to 50,000 allied service members already deployed. McChrystal's request generated intense and animated internal deliberation within the US political and military leaderships, including those on the ground in Afghanistan, which are discussed in detail in chapter 7. Here, it suffices to say that finally President Obama agreed to an extra 30,000, but with certain conditions, marking a turning point in US Afghanistan policy. In an address to the nation on 1 December 2009, he stated:

> I have determined that it is in our vital national interest to send an additional 30,000 U.S. troops to Afghanistan. After 18 months [that is, by mid-2011], our troops will begin to come home. These are the resources that we need to seize the initiative, while building the Afghan capacity that can allow for a responsible transition of our forces out of Afghanistan.[57]

He also alluded to the incompetence of the Karzai government and set new standards to which it would be held responsible, stating:

> The days of providing a blank check are over. President Karzai's inauguration speech sent the right message about moving in a new direction. And going forward, we will be clear about what we expect from those who receive our assistance. We'll support Afghan ministries, governors, and local leaders that combat corruption and deliver for the people. We expect those who are ineffective or corrupt to be held accountable.[58]

The revised policy, for the first time, set a date for initiating the withdrawal of US and allied troops from Afghanistan, thus making it a time- rather than a conditions-based pull-out, which was exactly what the Taliban and their supporters wanted. All they needed to do was wait. While disassociating from the term 'war on terror', the policy firmly signalled a shift in US and allied operations from counterterrorism to counterinsurgency (COIN), with four major objectives in support of a political settlement of the Afghan conflict. The first was to bolster the capacity of the Afghan National Security Forces (ANSF), including the army, police, and border guards, to take over combat operations from the US and NATO allies. One proposal at the time was to increase the ANSF troops from over 90,000 to more than 400,000,[59] but Washington agreed to 100,000 fewer, to be funded mostly by the US to the tune of $4.1 billion annually. This also involved building and equipping an air force 8,000-strong in terms of personnel. The second was to protect the population centres. The third was to exert greater pressure on Pakistan to close its safe havens and halt logistical support to the Taliban. The fourth was to leave a small transitional residual American and NATO troop contingent for a further year, which from 1 January 2015 would be known as the Resolute Support Mission (RSM). The RSM was to have no combat and only a self-defence role, operating primarily in support and training of the Afghan National Army and Security Forces (ANASF), though the Special Forces' frontline activities against Al Qaeda terrorism would continue with no time limit. The central but unspoken aim of the new policy was to *afghanize* the war, despite the fact that this mode had not worked previously for the US in Vietnam or the Soviets in Afghanistan; and to achieve a respectable political resolution to the Afghanistan conundrum.

The implied criticism of the Afghan government in this policy reset could only further irritate Karzai, who now resorted to playing his nationalist or, some might argue, Pashtunist nationalist card by voicing increased objections to the manner in which the US military operations and reconstruction aid were conducted. He complained that instead of targeting the real sources of the Taliban's support in Pakistan, the US and allied operations resulted in unnecessary casualties and customary humiliation of many innocent Afghans and destruction of their villages and livelihood, particularly in the Pashtun-dominated south. Regarding this point, Karl Eikenberry says that Karzai was probably quite justified in his objections.[60] But there was also another consideration at work. Karzai had already established back-channel contacts with the Taliban, who had signalled an interest in some kind of power-sharing arrangement, provided he distanced himself from the US. That is when Karzai started publicly calling the Taliban his 'brothers'.[61] He further complained about the US bypassing his administration on military operations and reconstruction aid, while failing to recognize that the US could not trust his government because it was riddled with corruption and infiltrated by Taliban supporters as well as hostile foreign intelligence services, including those of Iran and Russia.

After the Enduring Strategic Partnership Agreement Between the United States of America and the Islamic Republic of Afghanistan was signed in Kabul on 2 May 2012, providing a long-term frame-work for the Afghanistan–US relationship after the drawdown of American forces, Karzai hardened his position on signing the follow-up Bilateral Security Agreement (BSA), which was to be negotiated within a year. The BSA was required to formalize the status of some 10,000 US troops who were to remain in Afghanistan after the end of the international combat mission in 2014. It was to become opera-tional from 1 January 2015, 'until the end of 2024 and beyond'.[62] Karzai argued that since the US had not brought peace to Afghanistan, it was not appropriate for him to sign off on it. He made his signing conditional on the US proving its good intentions by keeping its soldiers out of Afghan homes, and promoting peace talks with the Taliban. To solidify his refusal, he convened a Loya Jirga of 2,500 handpicked participants in late November 2013 to scrutinize the BSA. But even when the Jirga defied him and approved the agree-ment, he declined to sign it, urged on by the Taliban.[63]

Karzai showed increasingly erratic signs in his behaviour. Eikenberry, who during his ambassadorship to Afghanistan frequently met with Karzai, says that the president was well-known for his 'swinging moods'. Karzai increasingly proved very frustrating for President Obama and many senior American policymakers and implementers. The president 'had reached a point with Karzai where he was just exasperated by every phone call and interaction with him'. In Eikenberry's view, following the toppling of the Taliban and expulsion of Al Qaeda, the US would have been better off if it had refrained from a transformative involvement in Afghanistan and placed it under a 'UN trusteeship' as a better way of managing its transition.[64] However, it was too late for any of these options, and the news about possibly getting rid of Karzai could only feed his paranoia and harden his anti-US rhetoric.

As troublesome as Karzai had become for the Obama administration, the latter had little or no choice but to put up with him. After all, he was an elected leader, irrespective of his flawed election, and there was too much at stake. So, the administration decided to wait for the end of Karzai's presidency and the election of his successor in 2014, with an earnest desire to be able to reset Afghanistan's direction.

Under Karzai's leadership, no solid foundations were laid for a bright future as most citizens had hoped. The goal of national unity, good governance, rule of law, and social and economic prosperity as the building blocks for state-building remained elusive. Despite the influx of hundreds of billions of dollars in foreign financial, reconstruction and humanitarian aid, and military expenditure in Afghanistan from 2002 to 2014, by the end of Karzai's presidency, the treasury could not have been emptier with the government facing a shortage of cash. Karzai's finance minister, Hazrat Omar Zakhilwal, who was widely alleged to be very corrupt (although he denied this),[65] and who served after Karzai as Afghanistan's ambassador to Pakistan from 2016 to 2018, was telling the world that they needed more money to be channelled through the government.[66]

While no firm institutional foundations for political stability and national unity were forged under Karzai in partnership with the international community, more specifically the US and its NATO and non-NATO allies, this leaves the question of where Afghanistan stood in relation to certain other pressing issues confronting the processes of state-building. Most importantly, they included the status of narcotics, the economy, women, human rights, social services, education and health in particular, and democratic freedoms. These variables are discussed in chapter 6.

Karzai primarily owed his elevation to power and enduring authority for thirteen years to US support and the initial trust and cooperation of the UINFSA. During most of his reign he was the face of America's intervention. Yet he grew to be a distrustful and strong critic of the US. He ultimately blamed the US for Afghanistan's misfortunes under his leadership. In an interview of 2022, he said he took 'full responsibility for the corruption and bribes in the delivery of services. . . . But the big contracts, big corruption, in hundreds of millions of dollars or millions of dollars, was clearly a United States of America thing.' He contended that 'the United States . . . bears ultimate responsibility for the fate of Afghanistan'. He further claimed, '[t]he war in Afghanistan was not our war . . . I was not a partner of the United States in that war against Afghan villages and homes. I changed from the moment I recognized that this war that is fought in the name of defeating terrorism is actually a war against the Afghan people. I called the Taliban "brothers" for that reason.'[67] Yet, the Taliban persistently rejected his government as a US puppet and refused to deal with him directly. In summing up Karzai's legacy, Shashank Bengali of the *Los Angeles Times* aptly wrote:

> The elegant man who once charmed the world and embodied the hope of his nation is leaving behind a government ravaged by corruption, an economy dependent on international donors, a badly frayed alliance with the United States and a population still vulnerable to a stubborn Taliban insurgency.[68]

If the US and its allies as well as those Afghans who were genuinely concerned about the state of affairs expected the post-Karzai situation to improve, they were to be disappointed, as worse was yet to come.

5

Dysfunctional Governance

The Ashraf Ghani Era, 2014-21

[T]he rulers should be identified with the people; that their interest
and will should be the interest and will of the nation.

John Stuart Mill[1]

The looming 2014 presidential election heralded a much-needed
opportunity to reset Afghanistan's political order as a fundamental prerequisite if the country was to transition into an endur-
ingly stable and secure functioning state. By now, many across the
political spectrum of Afghanistan and in the US political, military
and intelligence elites could clearly see that the governance system
based on the Bonn process had not produced, under Hamid Karzai,
what was required to move Afghanistan forward. Washington's whole
approach to state-building and the efforts of Afghan reformists,
involving development efforts on multiple fronts, at growing human
and financial costs, was in many ways in tatters. Inheriting a very
problematic legacy, the Afghan political opposition and President
Barack Obama and his team eagerly anticipated that the 2014 election would deliver a more effective and reliable Afghan leadership
and government whereby some necessary adjustments could be
made to put Afghanistan on a more promising path and enable the

US and its allies to make a respectable and responsible military exit from the country. However, this did not happen. Once again, the Afghan political opposition and the US were confronted with as many, if not more, roadblocks as during Karzai's rule, which continued to hamper Afghanistan's processes of state-building in its turbulent historical journey.

The election

Karzai's second term was constitutionally due to expire in May 2013, but he extended it for another year to the growing dismay of his political opponents, who questioned the legality of this and the president's motives. The first round of elections for his successor was finally held on 5 April 2014. The US, the European Union (EU) and the UN, along with many Afghan leaders and voters, strongly hoped for a relatively smooth and clean process, and results that could place Afghanistan on a more positive state-building trajectory within a democratic framework. In other words, the new president was expected to make serious progress, against all odds, in the areas where Karzai had faltered, and to act efficaciously and reliably in assisting the US and its allies, as well as other international partners, to put the Afghanistan project back on track. As a leading presidential aspirant, Abdullah Abdullah and many members of his entourage, composed of largely well-educated, pro-democracy and worldly elements, shared this sentiment. They longed for a more well-ordered campaign than had eventuated in the 2009 election, and for fraud-free results.

According to one of Abdullah's most senior advisors at the time, Mahmoud Saikal, there was a great deal of optimism in Abdullah's camp, and indeed in the wider community, that the democratic path outlined in the 2004 Constitution, was probably the only workable option for Afghanistan under the circumstances, provided that it was not corrupted and violated for self-serving power purposes. As is evident from Saikal's copious and hitherto unrevealed notes, he (along with many colleagues) strongly sensed that Afghanistan had reached a historical turning point of sink or swim. In other words, the country desperately needed a publicly mandated leader who could emerge from a credible electoral process and serve the cause of national unity and stability, thereby solidifying a workable democratic system of governance in the face of past and present impediments.

Saikal was well placed to make this call. He was profoundly versed in his country's conditions and the complexities of its regional and international situation, and had served it in various capacities over a long period. Despite his optimism and considerable investment of time in a credible electoral process, the election campaign and its results were manipulated by those who gave preference to personal power ambitions over national needs. What transpired was worse than the precedent set by the 2009 election. The outcome grieved not only Saikal but also many of his like-minded colleagues, a cross-section of the Afghan people and the US and its allies. It is important to provide a detailed exposé of this election and where it ended, partly based on Saikal's first-hand accounts, corroborated and supplemented by other reliable sources.

Of the original twenty-seven presidential candidates, the Independent Election Commission (IEC) disqualified most, with eleven left on the ballot. They included Karzai's eldest brother, Qayyum, as an independent, and Karzai's National Security Advisor Zalmai Rassoul, also as a Pashtun independent. Several candidates, including Qayyum, withdrew, partly because they did not do well in the opinion polls, which were conducted by US polling agencies, and partly out of a desire to strengthen the votes of other fellow Pashtun candidates. In the end, Abdullah and Ashraf Ghani emerged as the two leading candidates. Preliminary results of the first round were scheduled to be announced two weeks later and, if inconclusive, the second round was to be held six weeks later. Before analysing the situation leading up to the first round, its results and what transpired afterwards, it is important at this point to briefly profile the two front runners.

Ghani hailed from the Ahmadzai branch of the Ghilzai Pashtun tribe, sharing a common tribal heritage with the Taliban and the former Soviet-backed president Mohammad Najibullah (1986–92) (see chapter 2). Born in Afghanistan's Logar Province in 1948, he completed his secondary education in Kabul before departing for tertiary education in the late 1960s at the American University of Beirut, where he was a contemporary of Zalmay Khalilzad, followed by a PhD at Columbia University. He pursued an academic career as an anthropologist and economist mostly at Johns Hopkins University, with a stint at the World Bank.

Ghani returned to Afghanistan in 2002 as an advisor to the United Nations Special Representative for Afghanistan Lakhdar Brahimi (October 2001–December 2004). As an intellectual, Ghani's focus was on state-building and transformation. Having suffered earlier from a serious illness, he was now keen to play a role in Afghanistan after long years of secular living in the US. Karzai appointed him as finance minister in his first cabinet, where he reformed the Afghan currency and introduced a tax system. He was widely touted as an efficient technocrat and administrator, but at the same time was highly temperamental and impatient, exhibiting frequent bouts of anger, with a sense of intellectual superiority. After Karzai dropped him from the cabinet in his second term, Ghani took up the role of chancellor/president of Kabul University with an unfulfilled ambition for higher office.

While hurt by Karzai's action, Ghani became highly critical of the president and his family for their self-interested exercise of power and alleged misdeeds. In an encounter with the author during his visit to Singapore in January 2007, he bitterly complained about Karzai's incompetence and especially lambasted Hekmat Karzai – a cousin of the president – for having risen from a nobody to assuming, on the back of Karzai's name, a diplomatic position in the Afghan embassy in Washington in 2002. Even so, Hamid Karzai nominated him for the position of Secretary-General of the UN in 2006, as he did not wish to alienate him as an influential fellow Pashtun. Ghani failed in his UN bid but made history for being the first Afghan to run for the highest office of the world body. It brought him much publicity inside and outside Afghanistan. Although he came fourth in the 2009 presidential election with only 3 per cent of the votes, the experience provided him with a platform to try again in 2014. In between, he served, with Karzai's support, as chair of the Afghan Transition Coordination Commission, which was in charge of the transition of security policies and responsibilities from US and allied forces to the Afghan National Security Forces (ANSF, also known as the Afghan National Defense and Security Forces – ANDSF). According to a source close to him, he was able to use his position to gather an election war chest in the order of millions of dollars.

As Ghani's appetite for power grew, so too did his need to align himself with Islamic and Afghan traditions as much as possible. He resorted to Islamic dispositions, ensuring that his long prayer beads were always publicly visible. Like Karzai, who dressed in attire that exhibited the ethnic multiplicity of Afghanistan, Ghani discarded his Western outfit in favour of Afghan traditional clothes, topped with a Pashtun turban whenever politically and socially desirable. On occasion, he projected himself in the style of Mahatma Gandhi in his speaking manner and social demeanour.

However, ultimately he could not be the man of the people in a traditional society where religious credentials, cultural familiarity, and fluency – not only in Pashto but also Dari – in addressing the masses really mattered. While gaining the title of 'theorist-in-chief',[2] his secularist nature and lack of sufficient grounding in Islam and the Dari language handicapped him considerably. He often failed to pronounce Qur'anic terms and verses correctly, which, together with his awkward translation of English sayings, often made him the subject of public ridicule. For example, during his presidency he once said 'I am like a kite whose string is in the hands of the people . . . [who] can take me high . . . [or] pull me down.'[3] During a lecture at a university in Tajikistan in March 2021, while praising the great ninth-century Farsi poet Rudaki as someone who still determines 'the pulse of the feelings of all Dari speakers', he read incorrectly one of Rudaki's most famous lines.[4] He was hardly well equipped to lead a government, although he had demonstrated considerable ability as a minister and administrator.

Nothing, however, could dent his ambition to lead Afghanistan, for which he had also built a network of American friends and admirers who kept promoting him as a deep thinker, an intellectual, and somewhat of a genius who was well qualified to reform broken states. To this effect, together with Clare Lockhart, he founded a Washington-based non-governmental organization (NGO), the Institute for State Effectiveness in 2006, and published a book on how to fix failed states.[5] In a 2013 poll he was named as one of the top 100 thinkers in the world.[6] In reference to this point, former US Secretary of State Mike Pompeo subsequently wrote:

> Ghani's years in the West had made him masterful at gaming American lawmakers and nonprofit organizations. He also spent extravagantly on lobbyists. I say with no exaggeration that Ghani had more friends inside the District of Columbia than he did in Afghanistan.[7]

His claim to exceptionalism put him at odds with not only many of his fellow Afghan political leaders and strongmen but also someone like Khalilzad. The latter was always able to pull rank over Ghani during his official appointments, based on his close links with Bush and many other Republican heavyweights in Washington. The symbiotic relations between the two worked very badly from the beginning to the end, especially when Khalilzad was appointed in September 2018 by President Donald Trump as US special representative for Afghanistan reconciliation to end America's involvement in its longest war, as discussed later.

Abdullah was very different from Ghani in terms of background, personality and approach. Born in Kabul in 1960, as mentioned earlier, he came from a Kandahari Pashtun father and a Panjshiri Tajik mother. After graduating from Kabul University as an ophthalmologist, he initially practised in Kabul, but moved his practice to Panjshir during the jihad against the Soviets and their surrogates. His professional and trans-ethnic profile appealed to Commander Ahmad Shah Massoud, who incorporated him into his team as an aide, and he rose to the position of defence spokesperson for the Massoud-led resistance. During the Massoud-backed Burhanuddin Rabbani government, he shifted to foreign affairs and subsequently served as foreign minister of that government when the Taliban assumed power in Kabul from mid-1996. His inter-ethnic heritage and fluency in the two main official languages, Dari and Pashto, and his urbanized upbringing and jihadi experiences, together with his continuous presence inside Afghanistan, equipped him with an ability to interact patiently with diverse fellow citizens irrespective of their differences, and to nurture good relations with the outside world. He stood for enlightened Islam and was well-versed in the religion. While possessing a remarkable memory and skill in oral communication, he lacked a talent for structured teamwork and any zest for reading detailed works or embracing sound advice. As Mahmoud Saikal relates, he was 'poor at reading documents properly, and in carefully weighing up words and sentences ... [compared] to Ghani [who] was strong in this area ... [and] read things carefully'.[8] He also fell short of being a visionary, strategic thinker, system-builder and administrator. He exhibited a sense of vulnerability and servitude to Washington, and nurtured a strong penchant for stylish and expensive Western clothes, giving him a reputation as one who was more interested in appearance than substance.

Initially, Karzai was keen to extend his term beyond 2013, arguing that three transitions (security, political and economic) in one term of office was impossible and that it was important for him to continue his presidency during the security and economic transitions. He was reluctant to sign the election laws and set a timeline for the presidential elections. He faced resistance from the Afghan political opposition as well as the US administration and the wider international community. In December 2011, a small delegation of the National Coalition of Afghanistan (NCA, the largest political opposition group), headed by Mahmoud Saikal, travelled to Germany and, on the sidelines of the second International Afghanistan Conference in Bonn met with over ten delegations, including those from the UN, the US, China, the EU, France, the UK and the United Arab Emirates. During these meetings, the NCA delegation stressed the need for strengthening the rule of law, improving governance, restoring the credibility of the electoral process and pursuing reconciliation with justice, from a position of strength. Karzai finally committed himself at the July 2012 Tokyo Conference on Afghanistan to 'conduct free, fair, transparent, and inclusive [presidential] elections in 2014 and [parliamentary elections] in 2015'.[9]

The 2014 presidential election campaign commenced in earnest in the second half of 2013, when voter registration was opened by the IEC. The election was funded entirely by outside donors, with the US a key contributor. In an almost customary political action, candidates who wanted to depict themselves as dedicated to national unity, selected two running mates based on ethnic and sectarian diversity to obtain votes from a cross-section of the Afghanistan population. Ghani opted for Abdul Rashid Dostum, the head of the predominantly Uzbek National Islamic Movement, and Sarwar Danish of the Shia Hizbi Wahadat Islami. Abdullah chose Mohammad Khan[10] of the Pashtun Hezbi Islami (Arghandiwal faction) and Mohammad Mohaqiq of the Shia Hizbi Wahadat Islami Mardum-e Afghanistan. Although none of the vice-presidential choices had totally clean hands as they had been involved in the politics of conflict either for or against one another, Dostum was the most notorious. Ghani's choice was astonishing, raising the question as to why a well-educated and worldly person should opt for an illiterate warlord, reputed for his bloody record of alleged disloyalty and unsavoury activities since the days of the rule of the People's Democratic Party of Afghanistan (PDPA; see chapter 2). His main redeeming feature was that he could bring 1 million votes from the Uzbek minority.

Ghani and Abdullah entered the campaign in earnest, although Abdullah had a greater degree of optimism about his chances of success this time. Both candidates had assembled good teams, containing some well-educated and political thinkers. Ghani's inner circle included such pro-Pashtunist elements as Hamdullah Mohib and Haneef Atmar.

Mohib emerged as a young Ghani loyalist almost overnight, virtually from nowhere. He hailed from a Pashtun family in eastern Afghanistan and was educated in Britain after his family fled Afghanistan following the Soviet invasion. Having earned a degree in computer engineering, he lacked a background in politics, governance and diplomacy. However, during the election campaign, he apparently showed exceptional manipulative skills in vote tallying in favour of Ghani as a fellow Pashtun. This, along with his subsequent demonstration of strong political nous, endeared him to Ghani. When Ghani later assumed the presidency, he appointed Mohib as ambassador to Washington and shortly thereafter as national security advisor, to the surprise of many.

Atmar, on the other hand, was a political veteran, who had worked with different foreign humanitarian and aid agencies prior to 2001 and served in different ministerial positions under Karzai's presidency. He showed a flair for strategic thinking and combative political ambitions but was prone to changing alliances when it suited him. His differences with Karzai had resulted in him losing his position as minister of interior affairs in 2011 (see chapter 4).

Abdullah's team reflected the nation more broadly than Ghani's. It was multi-ethnic in its make-up and operated within the framework of a 120-member consultative *shura* (council). The core group of this *shura* consisted of those who had opposed the Soviet occupation, resisted Taliban rule and actively taken part in the reconstruction and development of Afghanistan after the fall of the Taliban regime. They genuinely believed that the only path for Afghanistan's salvation under the prevailing conditions was via a democratic system. They were cognizant of political manipulation by Karzai and Ghani. They also felt strongly that a clean election would not only result in a smooth transition of power but could also provide a unique opportunity to break down some of the traditional practices that had historically hamstrung the country, which were based on ethno-tribal, cultural and sectarian differences and rivalries, as well as the dictum that a Pashtun must always lead Afghanistan.

With this as a core element of his reformist platform, Abdullah officially launched his campaign in March 2014. While attracting unprecedentedly large enthusiastic crowds at his rallies, he was widely welcomed not only in the northern provinces but also in other provinces, including the Pashtun-dominated south, indicating the breadth of his cross-ethnic and cross-sectarian popular appeal. Ghani's campaigning and popularity were limited largely by his inadequate linguistic and religious projections, but like Abdullah, he too campaigned on a democratic platform, arguing that he was the only person capable of leading the country in its hour of need. He was assured of US support, given his long-standing American citizenship and connections, as well as his solemn promise to ratify the Bilateral Security Agreement (BSA) should he be elected – something that Abdullah had also pledged to do in the event of electoral victory.

As the campaign intensified, there was concern about security, but the US, its allies and the UN sought to alleviate this by ensuring maximum protection for the candidates and voters. Despite this, Abdullah's campaign came under numerous attacks. A list submitted to the United Nations Assistance Mission in Afghanistan (UNAMA) by Mahmoud Saikal records twelve of those attacks occurring in different provinces between 1 February and 15 March 2013, killing nine and wounding seven. Beyond this, the Abdullah camp wondered about Karzai's role in the process, given all of the allegations around him of dubious political behaviour. There was concern about the possibility of him influencing the election in favour of Ghani, not because he was very fond of the latter but mainly due to traditional bonds of ethnic solidarity. They also sensed an unacceptable degree of hyperbole on the part of Ghani's team, including Atmar, who promoted their candidate as an exceptionally intelligent reformer and state-builder, and therefore the natural choice to lead Afghanistan during the next phase of its democratic development. Regardless, the general consensus within Abdullah's camp and indeed the wider politically active landscape was that, with the international community's eyes focused on the race, this election would be a turning point for Afghanistan.

The election and its results turned out to be anything but fair. The picture initially looked promising. Despite the Taliban's rejection of the election and warnings to the public to act against it, 12 million voters registered and an estimated 7 million cast their votes in the first round of the election in early April. The voters were concentrated in Kabul and the northern and western provinces. The turnout was lower in the southern and south-eastern provinces as they formed the nucleus of the Taliban activities. In spite of many problems, including a shortage of ballot papers in several of Abdullah's strongholds, the 5 April 2014 elections were, from Saikal's perspective, probably the best exercise of democracy in the history of Afghanistan. In the preliminary results announced by the IEC on 26 May 2014, Abdullah had 44.5 per cent and Ghani 31.5 per cent of the votes. With neither candidate winning 50 per cent, a run-off was scheduled for 14 June.[11] Abdullah survived a suicide bomb attack targeting his convoy in Kabul on 6 June. After a considerable delay, the IEC declared the preliminary run-off results on 7 July. It reported that 8.1 million people voted – questionably higher than the first round – giving Ghani 55.27 per cent and Abdullah 44.73 per cent: an outcome that confounded the Abdullah camp's expectations and opinion polls' predictions.

Abdullah and his team challenged the results and lodged complaints with the Independent Electoral Complaints Commission (IECC), based on what they believed was solid documentary and recorded evidence of fraudulent action in support of Ghani. They accused the IEC, especially its CEO Ziaulhaq Amarkhil, who had persistently voiced pro-Pashtun sentiments, as one of the main culprits. The police had found Amarkhil travelling with thousands of blank ballots without a security escort. He was also recorded asking IEC officials in different provinces to 'take sheep to the mountains, stuff them and bring them back' – a reference that Abdullah's campaign team said was to ballot stuffing. Abdullah also demanded proof of the IEC's claim that 8.1 million people voted in the run-off and called for a thorough vetting of all the votes in certain eastern and southern provinces where violence had severely limited the ability and number of people who could vote.[12]

Amerkhil resigned, denying any wrongdoing, and Ghani and his camp took the run-off figures as sacrosanct. Their refusal, and that of the IEC, to budge set off another major political crisis, larger than that of 2009. The US, the EU and the UN, which were keen to see a workable and face-saving result, pressed the parties to resolve their differences urgently. However, negotiations dragged on for weeks, involving numerous meetings between the two parties and international stakeholders without any tangible results. With no resolution in sight, Abdullah threatened to withdraw from the process. Meanwhile, Karzai was hovering in the wings. While urging the two sides to smooth out their differences, he and his supporters concurrently saw an opportunity to form an interim government – a proposition that neither Abdullah nor the Obama administration would find acceptable.

By now it had become clear to many in Washington that Afghanistan's path to a democratic future was crumbling, and that America's military disentanglement from the protracted war was in serious jeopardy. Ghani, who was viewed at the time in Washington as a serious, intelligent and capable figure, stood firmly by his commitment, in the event of his becoming president, to sign the BSA, which would regularize the status of American forces, whatever their size and whatever the nature of their involvement, for almost another decade. From Washington's perspective, the issue was no longer whether Afghanistan would become an enduring democracy. It was rather whether the country was now going to have an elected leader on whom the US could rely for the BSA ratification and continuation of the planned troop drawdown, and who would be able to take responsibility for managing Afghanistan's affairs without enduring US and allied combat support.

The situation evolved to a point of desperation, not only for the Abdullah camp but also the Obama administration. Mahmoud Saikal, who was centrally involved in almost all the countless meetings that were held with foreign envoys, US officials and their EU and UN counterparts, records that his initial impression was that these stakeholders wanted to take the run-off results at face value and leant towards Ghani as an easy way out of the crisis.[13] But the Abdullah team's insistence on a thorough recount of votes and addressing the possibility of fraud for the sake of the integrity of the democratic process and political stability stood in their way. This viewpoint was shared by many in the US Republican Party. During a meeting with Abdullah in Kabul on 3 July 2014, Senators John McCain and Lindsey Graham, in the company of the US commander in Afghanistan Joseph Dunford Jr, and Saikal, backed Abdullah's right to ask for a vote recount. Graham said to Abdullah: 'You have every right to demand an audit. It is hard for us to support the outcome of the election without an audit. When the time comes, and the audit is over, and you lose, your behavior will be important, and that will impact our decision.' McCain said: 'We were encouraged by your views, and we hope that a proper audit will make you come back to the process. Whatever the result, you have a major role to play.'[14]

Saikal records that, under the circumstances, Abdullah faced a choice between three options: to declare his own government; to let Ghani win on what he believed was a fraudulent basis at the cost of making a mockery of the democratic process; or to reach a compromise for some kind of mutually acceptable coalition government. Given the sensitive situation, the latter option appeared the best, and something towards which Washington was now seriously moving. US Secretary of State John Kerry, who had gained marked familiarity with Afghanistan's conditions and who had come to know and dealt with many of its leaders, found it necessary to embark on a carrot-and-stick diplomatic mission for a resolution of the crisis. He offered to mediate – a well-worn traditional mechanism of conflict resolution in Afghanistan. This brought him twice to Kabul within a month for face-to-face, and if necessary forceful, discussions and negotiations.

In an 11 July 2014 meeting, Kerry said to Abdullah:

I was here in 2009, and I worked hard on those elections. I know that you are frustrated. We believe that we should finish the process properly and so does President Obama. The most important thing for the country is that we can get together. I said the same thing to Ghani. We have to find some compromise. What we need is legitimacy. The government that emerges must be the government of all. I am a friend of Abdullah, but I am impartial. We need a government that we can work with. The worst thing would be for a candidate to walk out and make his own government. We will put forward no dollar, no soldier if that happens. I have a reputation for being fair.[15]

In subsequent meetings, while shuttling between Abdullah and Ghani, Kerry acknowledged that fraud had taken place and the need for a thorough audit of votes. He put a compromise plan to both

Abdullah and Ghani on the basis of which evolved the concept of a government of national unity. He told Abdullah:

> I want you to understand that tonight [12 July] is one of the most important meetings in Afghanistan's history. I know your anger, frustration and mistrust. I know there has been fraud and corruption, not only now, but in previous years too. . . . I am known as a pretty straight shooter. If I say something, I tell the truth and I keep my word. If [you] and your team don't accept what is on the table [a 100 per cent audit to which Ghani had agreed as against Abdullah's demand for opening only those ballot boxes that were highly suspicious], you will hurt Afghanistan and you will steal . . . the chance to become President [and there will not be] a legitimate President . . .[16]

He cautioned Abdullah against walking away from the process and declaring his own government, saying:

> If you walk away, you will force me to be against you. I will be frustrated by the lost opportunity. If we were disregarding you, you would have the right to be angry, but we are not. If Afghanistan cannot bring this together, then the world will walk away. You could be one month away from the UN declaring Abdullah President. You want Abdullah to be President and for Afghanistan to remain united. There is only one way to do this legally. Trust this document that Abdullah himself has negotiated. Trust [UN Special Envoy and Head of the United Nations Assistance Mission in Afghanistan] Jan Kubis. Trust myself and trust President Obama. I am asking you as a friend to trust me. We will not allow anyone to play tricks. American soldiers did not come here and die, and US taxpayers did not invest billions of dollars, to see the Afghan election fail, so, I appeal to you to keep it together. Nothing will fall apart if you so choose. Ghani is afraid of this agreement. He knows he may lose.[17]

Kerry was able to bring Abdullah and Ghani together on 12 July for an exclusive tripartite meeting, after which the three emerged smiling. They had agreed on two documents. One was a political framework for a government of national unity, and the other was technical, outlining the handling of the audit. Now the question was the implementation of the two agreements. Saikal notes:

> It was our [Abdullah's] team that had been jumping up and down about fraud. Therefore, we were after speed in the process. The other [Ghani's] side was sitting still, saying that all was rosy, and that they didn't need to move [acting as if they have won the election]. They did everything possible to slow things down and exhaust the process. Meanwhile, this was in the interest of Karzai, in order to continue his Presidency.[18]

This assertion of Saikal's is confirmed by multiple sources, including Gul Agha Sherzai, who in a meeting with Kerry on 11 July, characterized Karzai as fraudulent. He said, 'Your intelligence should show that Karzai has been instrumental in engineering the fraud. He also helped to establish Ghani's team. There was fraud during the first round, too. We had won the election, but Karzai turned the result down. He doesn't want us to succeed in Afghanistan. Thank you for your recommendations . . . to establish a unity government.'[19]

Mahmoud Saikal recalls that Karzai was extremely agitated and not happy with US mediation. According to Saikal, Karzai told Abdullah that 'he [Karzai] and Ghani were taking foreigners out of the process [and] that Abdullah had brought them back'.[20] However, action on the political and technical agreements opened a new phase of negotiations and bargaining. The political deal was to involve a 50/50 power-sharing arrangement and the audit needed to be conducted freely and fairly by the UN. But Saikal asserts that Ghani's side started haggling over who should get what, who should chair the cabinet meetings, and how and what the audit should cover, causing unnecessary delays and frustrations, while the country badly needed an elected leader and government to take over from Karzai and his administration. The process once again entailed numerous negotiation meetings between not only the two parties, but also Abdullah's team and envoys of foreign stakeholders, the US in particular, with special representatives for Afghanistan and Pakistan James Dobbins and Daniel Feldman, and Obama's advisor Jeffrey Eggers, who were now the top US troubleshooters. Saikal's notes contain hour-by-hour and day-by-day details of all the meetings. They are extremely valuable in terms of understanding how different parties conducted themselves, precisely what they discussed and how the situation once again prompted President Obama to telephone both Abdullah and Ghani on 25 July to urge them to get on with it. In a twenty-minute telephone call to Abdullah, Obama made it clear that he was interested in making the political framework work. He told Abdullah 'call me anytime that you need to. Secretary Kerry can come to Kabul. We are following the UN audit.' Abdullah stressed that 'the equal commitment of the two parties is crucial. The audit process is very slow.' Obama: 'I will talk to Ghani. We want to work with you and your supporters. I hope you haven't removed the change to the parliamentary system from the text. At the moment you have the most influence on the situation. If there are things wrong it is best to appeal to Ashraf Ghani.'[21]

Arriving in Kabul on 8 August, Kerry met with Abdullah and his team on that day, urging Abdullah to stay on course. He emphasized that:

> Democracy is not easy. We are trying to protect everybody's voice. ... Unfortunately, what happened, happened [i.e. fraud], despite my advice five years ago. Electoral reform is needed. ... I met Karzai. Afghanistan is completely stalled in the water. There is no government.

He continued:

The economy is poor. Pakistan is not helping. [Major] General [Harold] Greene [deputy commander of Combined Security Transition Command-Afghanistan] was shot. We have a common challenge: Who is the President in the next few weeks? Too much blood has been shed. Too many troops have been killed. Billions of dollars have been put forward by the US. We are proud of it. Women, business, children going to school, the gains, and you [Abdullah] have a big part in that too. . . . [You] compromised on the audit and the political framework. What happens in the next 3–4 weeks is important. Jan Kubis and the UN are working hard on a fair audit. The leaders need to come up with an Afghan document on a unity government. I lost the US Presidential election to George [W.] Bush by 59,000 votes. I could have made it difficult, but I didn't. I am going to ask to help to have a President. If not, Congress will not pass money to a country where the leaders cannot form a national unity government. We did everything. ISAF [International Security Assistance Force] brought the boxes. No audit has ever been done at this high a level. If we can't get this done, I don't know what else we can do. Now we must all act like statesmen. UN standards will apply. We will not allow the IEC to undermine this.[22]

As Abdullah increasingly appeared amenable (a thread of his personality), Kerry concluded the meeting by saying that he would talk to President Obama at 4.30 p.m., telling him that 'things are moving'. He also said to Abdullah that:

Everyone is the leader [in the political framework]. It's time to stop attacking each other. One man is President, the other is a powerful man needed to bring Afghanistan together. It will help all your followers to see the big picture. The path ahead has both political and technical pieces. Afghanistan has a great future if you [and Ghani] work together.[23]

However, there did not seem to be a meeting of minds between Abdullah and Ghani. Abdullah insisted on 50/50 parity in a national unity government and an audit of the election with the results made public. As put by Atmar, Ghani's side did not interpret 'parity' as meaning 'equality'. Saikal wrote:

> At that point, I could see that the Americans, the UN and the Europeans were beginning to inject in their own minds, as well as ours, that Ghani should be the President. This would be with or without the audit results. This is why we assumed that there was a plot. This conspiracy held that no matter what we did, somehow they would force the outcome of the second round in favour of Ghani. . . . We couldn't see a degree of fairness in their handling of the negotiations, and in particular, of the audit process. We assumed at that time that perhaps John Kerry himself was genuine, but that the people within the UN or the intelligence services were part of the conspiracy.[24]

These views were also reinforced by former chief of the National Directorate Security, Amrullah Saleh, whom Ghani later selected as his vice-presidential running mate in the 2019 election. That election brought about another political crisis even worse than that of 2014, as discussed shortly.

Meanwhile, a NATO summit meeting was scheduled to be held in Wales on 4 September. Afghanistan was to be discussed and represented. Kerry and British Prime Minister David Cameron used the need for this representation to pressure Abdullah and Ghani to finalize a political deal before the outcome of the audit so that Afghanistan would be represented at the highest level. But there was still no agreement between them. Karzai sent his defence minister to the summit. The best Saikal could do was draft a joint letter in the name of Abdullah and Ghani in appreciation and continued support of NATO, which was sent to Ghani through

Atmar, who added a couple of paragraphs. This letter was circulated to NATO members.

Government of National Unity

In the final analysis, Abdullah relented by allowing Ghani to claim the presidency, while he himself assumed a new non-constitutional position as chief executive (CE) in a National Unity Government (NUG), which had no precedent in Afghanistan's history. As provided for in the NUG agreement, the CE's position was to be the equivalent of prime minister. For this change in title to occur, a constitutional amendment was required. The two protagonists also agreed that the results of the election should remain inconclusive and not be publicly announced. In bargaining over whether the president or the CE should chair the weekly cabinet meetings, Ghani insisted that it fell within his ambit. Regarding the filling of cabinet and other senior governmental appointments, the CE expected it to be on a 50/50 basis, but Ghani insisted on a 60/40 arrangement. This once again required intervention by the US, the EU and the UN. Kerry had to re-enter the fray to encourage and cajole both sides to reach an agreement in order to ensure the workability, legitimacy and inviolability of the NUG. Prime Minister Cameron also played his part in this respect by calling on Ghani and Abdullah to do the right thing.

After several weeks of on-and-off negotiations, outside interventions and missing the deadline for the NATO summit, the NUG was formally inaugurated on 29 September 2014, with Ghani sworn in as president and Abdullah as CE. As his first act in office, Ghani signed (with Abdullah's agreement) the BSA on 30 September 2014. The speed of its enactment drew a sigh of relief in Washington and allied capitals, promising a new era of cooperation between Ghani and Abdullah. It was regarded as a 'remarkable' achievement.[25]

President Obama congratulated the two leaders via video. In late October, he formally invited Ghani and Abdullah and their delegations for meetings in Washington. The visit took place during 22–26 March 2015 and Obama personally welcomed them to the White House on 24 March. As the White House put it in a Joint Statement:

> The visit offered an opportunity to renew U.S.–Afghan relations, review the joint achievements of the last 13 years in Afghanistan, and to discuss the actions each country needs to take to ensure that the social, economic, security and human rights gains over that period are sustained and advanced . . . to enable the Afghan National Defense and Security Forces (ANDSF) to address the significant security challenges facing Afghanistan and the wider region.

The two sides also 'reiterated their commitments under the U.S.-Afghanistan Enduring Strategic Partnership Agreement (SPA) and the U.S.-Afghanistan Security and Defense Cooperation Agreement (also known as the Bilateral Security Agreement, or BSA) to advance common objectives in these and other areas'.[26]

Ghani and Abdullah not only expressed their gratitude for America's support and sacrifices but also offered their solemn promise to work together for the good of Afghanistan and US–Afghanistan relations. Mahmoud Saikal was a member of the delegation and participant in all the meetings. He notes that, while seeming relieved not to have to face Karzai anymore, Obama strongly but politely emphasized to Ghani and Abdullah the need to ensure the success of the NUG and reminded them of the responsibility that they faced in Afghanistan's march towards a brighter future. He recalled the very costly US and allied military sacrifices and massive reconstruction, and promised America's continued political, economic and financial aid, with the proviso of a troop drawdown continuing as planned. The delegates returned to Afghanistan with a degree of relief on the part of most citizens that a more positive era was on the horizon.

However, it is baffling to some that the architects of the NUG thought that such a government could actually work, and could improve on Karzai's dubious legacy. From the start, its viability was questionable. It lacked any historical precedent; Afghan leaders had rarely worked in harmony. Even during the longest period of stability, under the rule of Nadir Shah's dynasty (1930–78), the politics of dualism and rivalry eventually eroded it from within. The NUG came to be subjected to the same dictates in the light of Ghani's political ambitions and intransigence.

Ghani and Abdullah were polar opposites. Apart from their personality and background differences, and differentiated outlooks on the political spectrum, the NUG's fundamental problem was two-fold. First, while the position of the president was clearly defined as all-powerful in the constitution, there was no provision in it for that of the CE. For the CE's position to formally be changed to prime minister, a constitutional amendment was needed and this could only be initiated by the president. Ghani refused to act on this throughout the nearly five-year extended life of the NUG and the agreement lacked a practical implementation mechanism to enforce the measures needed. During the negotiations, the parties, including Abdullah, had played down a Saikal proposal for a powerful quadrilateral commission, composed of authoritative representatives of the two camps, the UN and the US or another country, experienced in these matters, to meet regularly and enforce the provisions of the agreement. However, the proposal was not taken on board. Instead they made do with a provision in the NUG agreement that disputes over the interpretation of the agreement be 'resolved through consultations between the parties'. The UN and the US signed the agreement as mere witnesses. Second, as was widely understood by Abdullah's side and that of the US, the EU and the UN, the NUG was to be based on a 50/50 power-sharing arrangement. The president and the CE were expected to fulfil the arrangement in close consultation and cooperation with one another. This meant that all cabinet and senior governmental, including military, posts, as well as state domestic and foreign policy decisions, were to be agreed upon jointly. But since the president was in a constitutionally more powerful position as head of state and commander-in-chief of the armed forces, Ghani frequently overrode any of Abdullah's choices or proposals that did not suit Ghani's own power interests.

Abdullah had garnered cross-ethnic and cross-sectarian votes in the elections, and was keen to see that reflected in the composition of the NUG in all appointments at the central and provincial levels. But Ghani seemed more interested in building his own personal power. Despite his American education and work experience, he engaged in a strategy of micro-management, power-centralization and 'clique' rule. While preaching democratic ideals and values, he certainly appeared to be more in tune with the traditional practice of the personalization and *ethnicization* of politics than was required to promote an inclusive and responsible system of governance. As Jennifer Murtazashvili writes, '[r]ather than strengthening state institutions, Ghani again mimicked his predecessors, creating parallel bodies and decisionmaking mechanisms to get around the levers of government'.[27]

In projecting himself as the champion of the younger Afghan generation of men and women, Ghani preferred many of his fellow Pashtuns, more specifically young but largely inexperienced, to fill a majority of important policy, administrative, bureaucratic and defence and security positions. He showed a strong tendency towards ensuring that the levers of power remained in the hands of the Pashtuns.[28] While saturating the presidential palace with Pashtun loyalists, in the process, he viewed the regional powerbrokers of the non-Pashtun minorities in the northern province as impediments to his efforts to build a personalized state. He sought to disempower them by exploiting divisions among them through various political and power machinations. These elements, most coming from the United Islamic National Front for the Salvation of Afghanistan

(UINFSA), included the Balkh Province governor Atta Mohammad, whom he fired in 2017, and Salahuddin Rabbani, son of former Mujahideen president Rabbani and foreign minister in the NUG, as well as one of the leaders of Jamiati Islami Afghanistan, who in the end acrimoniously resigned from his ministerial post.[29] Most importantly, he spared no effort to build a strong base of influence within the armed and security forces by appointing and rotating his loyalists, irrespective of their qualifications and experience. Ultimately, it was all about Ghani, whose authoritarian actions resulted in his growing public isolation.

On the foreign policy front, Ghani acted independently of the CE on a number of initiatives. For example, in mid-2015, he resorted to a policy of propitiation towards Pakistan to allay the country's 'concerns, real or perceived, with regards to its interests in Afghanistan.'[30] In this, he aimed to entice the Taliban to negotiate a political deal with him and to induce the Pakistan-based maverick Gulbuddin Hekmatyar to join him in what was perceived by many as an attempt to create a Pashtunist front. His approach to Pakistan failed as Islamabad and the Taliban leadership viewed the NUG as American-made and Ghani as untrustworthy. But it nonetheless worked with Hekmatyar, who had become more or less a spent force in the face of Islamabad's investment in the Taliban. Along with his Hezbi Islami fighters, he moved into Kabul in early May 2017. Ghani accommodated him with much fanfare and luxurious living in the capital in the expectation that he would strengthen his power position. Hekmatyar, known as 'the butcher of Kabul' for his failed power-driven bombardment of Kabul in 1992, proved to be no more than an opportunist and a vacillating spoiler.

Ghani's initiative to kowtow to Islamabad and bring Hekmatyar on board, on the surface had the CE's backing, but there were resentments in the CE's inner circle, including from Saleh, who was distrustful of Pakistan and Hekmatyar, and Mahmoud Saikal, who wanted an apology by Hekmatyar to his victims and disarmament of his forces to be included in any agreement signed with him. They viewed Islamabad's and Hekmatyar's support of the Taliban as part of a long-standing design to ensure that Afghanistan operated under Pakistan's shadow and according to its interests. This was so, despite Islamabad's repeated friendly and conciliatory public statements in support of peace and stability in Afghanistan and brotherly relations with the country. When Ghani's pro-Pakistan moves did not pay off, he sought to play his India card by emphasizing Afghanistan's friend-ship with India. Afghanistan had signed a strategic partnership agreement with India in October 2011, as it had done with several other friendly countries, although with little or no effect. But this policy shift only infuriated Islamabad, prompting it to enhance rather than diminish its instrumentalization of the Taliban.

Nonetheless, as Ghani's appetite for power grew, Abdullah found himself with less room for manoeuvre. It was as if he believed that his mild manner and good relations with Washington would help pres-sure Ghani to honour the NUG agreement. He seemed keen not to be blamed for wrecking the NUG. Over time, he failed to act decisively and systematically to force Ghani to set up the required process for constitutional change to formally entitle him to be prime minister. He kept deferring to Washington as a source of support vis-à-vis Ghani rather than harnessing his own resources to check Ghani's power moves. He appeared content with preserving his CE status and acting as a man of the people, even as it seemed to many that Ghani was working around or disregarding the NUG agreement as it suited him.

The two sides ultimately could not see eye to eye on many appoint-ments and policy issues. Nor could they balance their personal poli-tics against what was required to promote national interests. The culture of personal and ethnic politics, flouting or averting the rule of law, rampant corruption,[31] administrative dysfunction and nepotistic practices that had characterized Karzai's administration continued unabated.[32] Ghani's anti-graft calls and promises of reform produced more sound than bite.

The efforts by Kerry to prevent Afghanistan from sinking into a political morass and ensure that the US and its allies had a dependable partner on the ground for an honourable US and allied exit did not pay off. Afghanistan's politics once again took the traditional form that had historically prevented it from becoming consolidated as a secure, stable and self-reliant state. Washington's experiences with the Karzai administration and the NUG could only lead it to tone down further its earlier endeavours to place Afghanistan on a democratic course of change and development as an effective US ally. All the US now wanted was to have a government in Kabul that could enable it to find a way out of the country. Yet worse was to come with the 2019 presidential election, when the two protagonists – Ghani and Abdullah – were set to battle it out once more.

The 2019 presidential election

Not surprisingly, this time Afghanistan was gripped by a greater political crisis. The electoral reform that was supposed to take place under the NUG agreement had not been implemented and Ghani had rewarded the alleged culprits of the 2014 election fraud with plum government jobs, appointing Amarkhil as senior advisor to the president and later as governor of Nangarhar and state minister for parliamentary affairs. Alarmed by these developments and to ensure that the next election was free of fraud, on 23 July 2018, as a result of the perseverance of Mahmoud Saikal, the president of the UN Security Council issued a statement emphasizing 'the need to address remaining challenges and to accelerate progress in electoral preparations, which requires without further delay the completion of outstanding issues'.[33]

The election was originally planned to take place in April 2018, but the IEC postponed it three times for various reasons, making some observers nervous about whether this election was going to be any more transparent than the two before it. The poll was finally held on 28 September 2019 amid the Taliban's rejection of it and warnings to voters not to participate, although there was less violence than had occurred in previous elections. Initially, seventeen contestants were declared qualified, but in time the field narrowed down to President Ghani versus CE Abdullah. Voter turnout was far lower than in the previous polls. Only 1.6 million out of 9.7 million people registered cast their votes. Voter disillusionment, security fears and the surge in fighting accounted for the low number. The IEC delayed the release of the preliminary results several times, raising suspicions of fraudulent behaviour by the IEC, whose chair and some members of which were appointed by Ghani. When the IEC at last released the preliminary results on 22 December 2019, they favoured Ghani with a little over 900,000 compared to Abdullah's just over 700,000. Abdullah rejected the results because he believed that the election had again been rigged by Ghani's side, triggering another election dispute and political crisis, this time of mammoth proportions.

On this occasion, the White House was under the impulsive and neo-nationalist Republican Donald Trump (2017–21). He had been a long-standing critic of America's Afghanistan war and was keen to see the end of it as soon as possible. During his 2016 election campaign, Trump had denounced the war as a 'terrible mistake',[34] and a 'total disaster',[35] but after taking office he was urged by his national security team, especially National Security Advisor H.R. McMaster and Defense Secretary James Mattis, who had both served in Afghanistan as military officers and were very familiar with the conditions in the country, to increase rather than reduce the number of US troops in view of the security deterioration in the country. He not only authorized the US military to drop what was at that time the largest non-nuclear bomb (the GBU-43/B Massive Ordinance Air Blast) in eastern Afghanistan in April 2017, though with no serious effect on the insurgents, but also, in a revised Afghanistan policy in late August 2017, announced 4,000 additional troops to bring the situation in the country under control. However, he accompanied this with a pledge to end a strategy of 'nation-building' and instead make the US withdrawal conditions-based, addressing 'the terrorist threat that emanates from the region'.[36] He also added that Pakistan must stop providing safe havens for terrorists who threaten America. While short on specifics, he said:

> I share the American people's frustration. I also share their frustration over a foreign policy that has spent too much time, energy, money, and most importantly lives, trying to rebuild countries in our own image, instead of pursuing our security interests above all other considerations.[37]

Trump's new strategy lacked proactive diplomacy to neutralize regional hostilities. Instead, he pulled out from the July 2015 Iran nuclear deal, launched trade wars with China and intensified confrontation with Russian forces in Syria. This caused Pakistan, China, Russia and Iran to coalesce against the presence of US/NATO forces in Afghanistan and give the Taliban fresh diplomatic and military boosts. As his new strategy faced serious obstacles, Trump could not hold back his personal conviction about the futility of the Afghanistan campaign. He was firmly convinced that the war and America's involvement in Afghanistan's reconstruction were getting nowhere, leading him to opt for a total US military exit from the country by the end of his presidential term. By now the number of American troops had dwindled from a peak of over 100,000 to 8,500 under Obama's drawdown. Trump told his newly appointed Secretary of State, Mike Pompeo, 'to get the hell out of Afghanistan', and 'I don't want to see anyone or anything left behind.'[38]

Pompeo says he started searching for 'the right person to help lead our diplomacy' in pursuit of fulfilling Trump's order. 'Everyone said, "You'll choose Zal," and then added, "He'll be a pain in the ass for you, but he is your best choice." They were right on both counts.'[39] In September 2018, he turned to the old Republican hand, Zalmay

Khalilzad, who despite having had a reputation 'for freelancing and secrecy', had 'grown up in Afghanistan and was an ethnic Pashtun',[40] and therefore capable of paving the way for a military exit, preferably through a political settlement of the Afghanistan conflict. As Trump's hardline National Security Advisor John Bolton (2018–19) – also Khalilzad's friend – points out, Trump did not know Khalilzad personally,[41] although they had had a brief encounter when Khalilzad introduced Trump in one of his 2016 campaign speeches. Khalilzad was nonetheless appointed, at Pompeo's urging, as the US special representative for Afghanistan reconciliation in September 2018. He set out in earnest to fulfil the wishes of the president and Pompeo, both of whom spoke almost with one tongue on all issues.

Khalilzad's top priority from the start was how to reach a political deal that could fulfil Trump's request to bring troops home, but in a timely manner, to serve two purposes. One was, as Pompeo puts it, 'to honour the sacrifices of nearly two entire decades and protect Americans against terrorism', based on a strategy of reaching an agreement with willing segments of the Taliban, in order to preserve the Afghan state; address Pakistan's interests so as to prevent Islamabad from undermining an Afghan reconciliation process; and publicly emphasize that America's military presence was conditions-based, and that its pull-out would happen only when the Taliban had fulfilled their end of the bargain in any deal.[42] The other unspoken objective was to achieve the military exit in a manner that could aid Trump win the 2021 presidential election with a claim that he ended America's military involvement in an unwinnable war in an honour-able and responsible way.

For this, Khalilzad initially promised to work for a comprehensive political settlement, based on a ceasefire across Afghanistan, inter-Afghan dialogue and negotiations, a US–Taliban peace deal, and the conditional withdrawal of foreign forces. He appeared to want the process to be seen as Afghan-owned and driven, but it was clear that he was in the driver's seat to achieve essentially what Trump wanted.

In his mission, Khalilzad's approach resembled that of former National Security Advisor Henry Kissinger in his negotiations for the withdrawal from the Vietnam fiasco fifty years earlier. Kissinger negotiated a peace agreement with the North Vietnamese Politburo member Le Duc Tho in Paris in January 1973, without the participation of the South Vietnamese government.[43] As it turned out, the deal primarily enabled the US to make a military exit, empowering North Vietnam and the Viet Cong to overrun the South, humiliating America, rather than resulting in a political settlement between North and South Vietnam.

After twenty months of many meetings with Taliban representatives in Doha, headed by the group's former deputy leader Mullah Abdul Ghani Baradar, recently released from a Pakistani jail at the instigation of Washington, and regional shuttle diplomacy,[44] Khalilzad could not achieve his original aim. He failed to forge an interlocking Afghan national and regional consensus for a comprehensive settlement. While excluding Tehran as US enemy number one from his consultations, irrespective of its standing as a critical regional player, and while being double-crossed by Islamabad, the best he could accomplish was a bilateral peace deal with the Taliban, signed in Doha on 29 February 2020.[45] Formally called the 'Agreement for Bringing Peace to Afghanistan between the Islamic Emirate of Afghanistan Which is Not Recognized by the United States as a State and is Known as the Taliban and the United States of America' (hereafter referred to as the Doha Agreement), it basically addressed the Taliban's fundamental demands in return for very little. First, the agreement was negotiated and sealed without direct participation of the NUG in the process, which fulfilled the Taliban's rejection of Ghani and the NUG as legitimate. NUG leaders had to be content with Khalilzad briefing them however he saw fit. Second, as the 'Islamic Emirate of Afghanistan' was mentioned nearly two dozen times in the accord, the US legitimized the Taliban over the NUG as its main partner in peace and therefore as the critical force in determining the future of Afghanistan. Third, the US agreed to the withdrawal of all American and allied forces from Afghanistan within fourteen months of the signing of the Agreement – the Taliban's most cherished goal. Fourth, the US undertook to free 5,000 Taliban core fighters from Afghan jails, enabling them to rejoin their co-fighters for the final battle against the Kabul government.

In return, the Taliban only pledged not to allow Afghan soil to be used for hostile actions against the United States and its allies, despite having little control over most of Afghanistan at the time, and released 1,000 Afghan soldiers from their detention. The deal did not provide for a universal ceasefire, but only for one between the Taliban and the foreign forces, leaving the militia to battle the Afghan forces. The question of whether the Taliban were legally bound by the agreement to negotiate an intra-Afghan political settlement was left open to conjecture. Washington hailed the agreement as a landmark pact and pathway to inter-Afghan dialogue for a final political settlement, whereas the Taliban treated the issue as discretionary. The agreement was not very different from the 1973 Vietnam peace agreement or the 1988 Geneva Peace Accords that provided for the US and USSR withdrawals from Vietnam and Afghanistan, respectively. Both of those deals failed to result in political settlements, instead leaving the interventionist powers humiliated.[46]

However, parallel to the signing of the Doha Agreement and in order to compensate the Afghan government for its lack of participation in negotiating the deal and to reassure it of continued support, NATO Secretary General Jens Stoltenberg and US Secretary of Defense Mark Esper flew to Kabul. They attended, along with Ghani and Abdullah, a ceremony in which they applauded the signing of the 'Joint Declaration between the Islamic Republic of Afghanistan and the United States of America for Bringing Peace to Afghanistan,'[47] and the Doha Agreement. In his remarks, Ghani welcomed the Doha Agreement and expressed a readiness to work with it.[48]

Later, as the implementation of the Doha deal unfolded, the NUG leaders, most importantly Ghani, were hurt by their exclusion from the process and unhappy with the agreement, which Khalilzad had shown them only once to read – without its attachments – prior to its conclusion.[49] As a first sign of displeasure, Ghani initially insisted that the Taliban prisoners were under his government's jurisdiction and therefore they could only be released as part of a negotiated settlement between his government and the Taliban. However, the Trump leadership, through Khalilzad, left him with no choice but to comply. Ghani must have been pained by a perception that it was Khalilzad who was in charge, which partly explained his hardening attitude towards Washington from that point.

Dialogue and negotiations between an inclusive delegation, representing the government and all stakeholders from inside Afghanistan, and the Taliban was supposed to start shortly after the signing of the US–Taliban agreement, but did not materialize for some time. When it finally started, in July 2020, the Taliban were not in a rush. They turned their intermittent meetings with the government-led delegation in Doha into a talking shop without any tangible results. The Taliban and their Pakistani patrons were fully aware that while the NUG had not worked since its inception, it was now ineffective and in total disarray.

Meanwhile, as mentioned earlier, Afghanistan was in political turmoil over the disputed results of the 28 September 2019 election which declared Ghani as the winner with less than 1 million votes in a country with a population of some 40 million. Afghanistan now scored another first in its history, with the two protagonists claiming parallel presidencies, reminiscent of the situation in the nineteenth century when Afghanistan was at one point divided into three ruling principalities (see chapter 2). Washington once again had to lean on the rivals to resolve the impasse.

Amid his reconciliation with the Taliban, Khalilzad mediated between Ghani and Abdullah to settle their differences, but to no avail.

Ghani and Khalilzad interacted with a degree of public courtesy but, as mentioned before, their relations seemed persistently undermined by rivalry and distrust; each likely viewed himself as intellectually and politically superior to the other, although Khalilzad always possessed the upper hand as the envoy of the patron power. In early March 2020, Ghani and Abdullah held parallel swearing-in ceremonies – the former declared the position of CE defunct, and the latter refused to recognize the former's presidency. Khalilzad nonetheless attended Ghani's oath of office event, signalling Washington's support for him. Afghanistan, unprecedentedly, had two presidents at the same time – a farcical development that brought stiff American intervention.

Reflecting frustration and a determination to ensure troop withdrawal as planned, in a hastily arranged trip, Pompeo flew to Kabul on 22 March 2020 to mediate. In contrast to Kerry's carrot-and-stick diplomacy in the 2014 dispute, Pompeo arrived to bang heads together without wasting much time. He met with both disputants but had little time for either. He subsequently wrote, 'both led cartels that stole millions of dollars in aid money from the United States. That corruption at the highest levels limited our ability to exit successfully.'[50] However, he reserved most of his venom for Ghani, regarding him as 'a total fraud who had wasted American lives and was focused solely on his own desire to stay in power'. He accused him of having 'bribed more voters and vote counters than the other candidates' during the 2019 election.[51] He also reportedly claimed that Ghani 'stole' the election.[52] When the two political rivals did not relent, Pompeo issued a damning statement:

> The United States is disappointed in them and what their conduct means for Afghanistan and our shared interests. . . . Their failure has harmed U.S.–Afghan relations and, sadly, dishonors those Afghan[s], Americans, and coalition partners who have sacrificed their lives and treasure in the struggle to build a new future for this country.[53]

He threatened to recommend to Trump that 'we should exit the country immediately, beginning with the elimination of the roughly $5–6 billion per year in foreign assistance that we were providing at the time'.[54] Even so, this time Ghani, who had worked hard to build a power base of loyalists in the armed and security forces and administration, was absolutely determined not to have Abdullah within the government structure. However, in the wake of Washington's pressure and with mediatory help from Karzai and another heavyweight, Abdul Rasul Sayyaf, he finally agreed to a resolution very much on his terms.

In a new arrangement, Ghani was confirmed as the constitutional president, and a non-constitutional position was created for Abdullah as chair of the High Council for National Reconciliation, outside the government structure. Abdullah's consolation prize also granted him permission to nominate half of the members of the cabinet, to be approved by the president. Thus, Ghani succeeded in keeping Abdullah outside the executive structure with no direct involvement in the government.[55] The strong presidential system of governance that had not suited or served Afghanistan well was once again confirmed, and its associated problems remained in place to be exploited by those in power and in political and armed opposition.

Despite the indignity of having assumed the presidency with less than 1 million votes, Ghani had no personal qualms over his political legitimacy. He took advantage of his incumbency, as he had before, to build what many regarded as his autarchy. He rapidly moved to reshuffle the civilian and military sectors by elevating more of his devotees to executive, administrative and armed and security positions, and rotated them as he saw fit. The Trump administration distrusted and loathed Ghani. As Pompeo says, Trump and Mullah Baradar, with whom the president spoke by phone on 3 March 2020, had 'one thing in common: both of them hated Ghani'.[56] This meant that, once again, the US was deprived of the kind of reliable partner that it needed in Afghanistan.

Abdullah remained content in a position of glory without power to promote national reconciliation, including with the Taliban, which ultimately produced no tangible results. Ghani had already commissioned a Pashtunist ally, Mohammad Masoum Stanikzai, as the head of the Afghan delegation to negotiate with the Taliban, and likeminded ethnic loyalist, Mohib, as a potential successor to him after the completion of his second term. Stanikzai had been a long-standing player in Afghanistan's murky politics, with many failures. Since the start of the Karzai-led administration, he had served in various ministerial and top security positions, although when in 2015 Ghani nominated him as minister of defence, his nomination was repeatedly rejected by the lower house of parliament (Wolesi Jirga).[57]

With Abdullah settling for a non-executive post and being sidelined, many of his close aides who had strongly stood by him in the 2014 election dispute became disillusioned with him. They concluded that he cared more about symbols and appearances, and lacked a clear notion of how to play a decisive role in leading Afghanistan out of its messy predicament. Mahmoud Saikal, disappointed after long years of serving his country, decided that he could no longer tolerate the direction that Afghanistan had taken under Karzai and Ghani. In his October 2018 letter to Ghani and Abdullah, while still serving as ambassador to the UN, he warned about the consequences of poor governance and sought the restoration of national trust, government reform and removal of ethnic prejudices, corruption, agents of external intelligence and criminals from the NUG. His letter received no response. With a heavy heart over the future of Afghanistan, he resigned for a second time from the Afghan government in April 2019. In his dismay, Saikal reflected not only the sentiment of many of his colleagues and fellow citizens but also that of the United States, whose Afghanistan campaign had moved from one disastrous phase to another amid mixed success in some other crucial areas.

6

State-building

Other Challenges, 2001-21

In both modern and premodern societies, therefore, but more systematically in the latter, problems that do get recognized often are not operationalized, or are operationalized weakly.

Chandler Morse[1]

The prevalence of poor leadership and governance, as well as endemic corruption, was accompanied by little or mixed success in some of the other crucial areas of state-building during Hamid Karzai's and Ashraf Ghani's leadership, under the aegis of the United States and its allies. They included, most significantly, the prevention of opium cultivation and production, the economy, women's status, human rights, social services (education and health in particular) and democratic freedoms, not to mention security as the big issue (discussed in chapter 7). Although a detailed discussion of these variables falls outside the ambit of this study, the purpose of this chapter is to provide a *snapshot* analysis of them for two important reasons. One is to glimpse what the Afghan governments and the US and allied partners did or did not achieve in these areas as they encompassed obvious policy goals of state-building. The other is to give an idea of where Afghanistan was in these respects by the time the US and its allies retreated and the Taliban returned to power.

The opium crisis

Despite all promises and efforts, the Afghan government and the US, along with its Western allies, could not prevent Afghanistan from burgeoning as a 'narco-state'. The country had previously experienced such a status during the first few years of the Taliban rule (1996–2001). But in July 2000, Taliban leader Mullah Mohammad Omar declared a religious verdict against the cultivation and production of opium, although in the face of popular backlash, the ban was largely dropped. The US was very mindful of Afghanistan as the main source of opium and heroin production and trade in the world. To assuage the situation, in 2004, Karzai said that 'the fight against drugs is actually the fight for Afghanistan', and he declared a 'jihad against narcotics'.[2]

However, the illegal sector continued to expand; Afghanistan rapidly became the world's largest producer of opium. In 2005, the country accounted for 63 per cent of the world's opium cultivation. In 2007, it produced 8,200 tons of opium, making it the biggest producer of the drug in the world, supplying 93 per cent of the global opiate market.[3] The United Nations Office on Drugs and Crime (UNODC) reported that opium cultivation increased in the following three years, constituting the nation's major economic activity. By 2010, the poppy trade formed 30–50 per cent of the Afghan economy and, in April 2013, it comprised around 15 per cent of the nation's gross domestic product (GDP),[4] accounting for more than 90 per cent of the global supply of heroin.[5] Further increases in opium production were predicted in the years ahead, particularly in the Pashtun-dominated southern provinces of Helmand, Kandahar, Uruzgan, Zabul and Farah, where the Taliban managed to gain most influence.[6] Consequently, the number of Afghan addicts also grew to an alarming roughly 3 million. According to one study, in 2015, 'it was estimated that drug use affected almost 31% of Afghan households'.[7] This trend entailed serious long-term political, social, economic and security consequences for the country. Opium and heroin production and drug trafficking became a lucrative source of income and power for a variety of groups. It not only funded the operations of the Taliban and other private militias, but also enriched 'ethnic warlords, and corrupt public officials',[8] including allegedly some members of the Karzai cartel (see chapter 4).

It was also evident as early as 2007–8 that the illicit Afghan drug industry was not only linked to international cartels but was also a significant impediment to the development of good governance and transparency, hampering sustainable economic development and fuelling instability.[9] The scale of this crisis prompted much focus by the US and its allies on assuaging the damage caused by the proliferation of opium, with the goal of eradicating it from Afghanistan altogether. The US adopted a Counternarcotics Strategy for Afghanistan, underlining the hardening of Washington's intention to implement large-scale eradication schemes, such as crop spraying and manual crop destruction.[10] However, many analysts argued that crop eradication, which targeted small cultivators, would decrease stability and drive cultivators into the arms of the Taliban.[11] This critique was based on two main arguments: first, poverty and increasing drought in much of Afghanistan meant that many poor farmers relied on the opium as their only source of income; and, second, the eradication of poppy crops would actually drive up the street price of opium, putting more money in the hands of the Taliban, traffickers and deceitful officials.[12]

Despite the problems inherent in crop eradication, many state actors involved in Afghanistan, including the US, the UK and Australia, continued to press for it as the only effective means to stem the tide of opium production and proliferation.[13] Others, such as the European Parliament and scholars from the think-tank Senlis

Council, pushed for an alternative solution, such as paying licensed farmers to cultivate poppies for legitimate medicines, such as codeine and morphine, of which there was a major shortage in the Third World.[14] Crop substitution that would encourage farmers to shift from opium to saffron cultivation was also advocated as another measure.[15] In spite of the debate about the appropriate methods of tackling poppy proliferation, it was clear that, from 2005, the opium crisis had progressed to such a level as to seriously undermine any opportunities to develop effective infrastructural foundations, including democratic institutions, in Afghanistan, as it encouraged corruption, illicit trade and a narco-dependent economy.

Urgent action needed to be taken. However, US support, along with that of its allies, for a range of measures from interdiction raids and alternative crop programmes to airstrikes on suspected heroin labs, failed to produce any tangible results. Between 2002 and 2017, 'the US government spent roughly $8.62 billion on counternarcotics efforts in Afghanistan. Despite this investment, the country remained the world's largest opium producer.'[16] Afghan opium and heroin continued to flow to the global market via neighbouring states and Russia. Defending his administration in 2007, Karzai blamed 'the international community' for the problem, by which he meant the US and its allies, for failing 'to come up with a coherent counter-narcotics strategy for his country' and for an 'explosion in the opium poppy cultivation'. He asserted that poppy cultivation had soared mostly in the provinces under the watch of foreign forces, especially Helmand Province, where British troops were fighting the Taliban, implying British ineptitude in allowing this to happen, an idea which was utterly rejected by London.[17]

Regardless, the opium industry continued its upward trajectory unabated under Ghani, although with a slight reduction in pace. By 2020, Afghanistan 'accounted for some 85 per cent of global opium production ... supplying some 80% of all opiate users in the world'. The total income from the source in Afghanistan was estimated at

$1.8–$2.7 billion, which did not include the sums accrued outside the country.[18] In other words, in nearly two decades, Afghan governments and their US and allied partners achieved very little by way of altering Afghanistan's reputation as a narco-state. Taliban 2.0 once again declared a poppy ban in March 2023. But analysts are sceptical about this, given the situation of poor farmers and the Taliban's dependence on income from poppy cultivation in the wake of the economic, financial, developmental and humanitarian crises facing Afghanistan under the Taliban.[19]

The economy

In this area too, progress was uneven, and in many ways negligible. Afghanistan certainly experienced an unprecedented phase of economic and trade growth during Karzai's and Ghani's time in office. The main factor catalysing this expansion was the injection of billions of dollars into the country in reconstruction, economic, security and humanitarian assistance, mostly from the US and partly from its allies and other donors, including India and Iran. Amounting to an average, over twenty years, of $50,000 for each Afghan citizen per annum[20] by the US alone, the expenditure included the costs of operations in fighting the Taliban and other anti-systemic groups, propping up the Afghan government, reconstruction projects and the resettlement of millions of refugees who returned from neighbouring countries, primarily Pakistan and Iran. This, together with the surge in foreign troops, civilian workers, private security firms, not to mention the narcotics industry, dramatically turbo-charged an artificial burst of economic activity in support of what was projected as the transformation of Afghanistan into a democratic, free market and anti-terror state. But this was largely a mirage. Overall, Afghanistan's economy remained very fragile, dependent mostly on foreign aid, foreign national spending, the narcotics industry and black-market operations.

The Afghan economy had hardly progressed much beyond being a rentier economy. The ruling cluster, involving political and entrepreneurial benefactors, many of whom returned from the diaspora to exploit new opportunities, as well as numerous domestic and foreign companies, especially in the field of communications and infrastructural development, found it a good time to set up a variety of profitable enterprises. As for the majority of the population, there was little improvement in their living conditions. Most continued to live in abject poverty. By 2020, Afghanistan's GDP was about $19 billion for an estimated population of 40 million, half of whom were under the age of seventeen, and the GDP per capita amounted to $517, up from $200 in 2003.[21] About 50 per cent of its inhabitants lived below the national poverty line in 2020, and for 'every 1,000 babies born in Afghanistan in 2021, 56 die[d] before their 5th birthday',[22] although average life expectancy rose from fifty-five to sixty-two. By all indicators, Afghanistan was still 'languishing at the bottom of international ranking by the human development index and the prospects for better life for Afghans look[ed] dim'.[23]

Concomitantly, the rise in economic activities caused a sizeable population shift from the country to the cities in pursuit of jobs and better lives, causing the main urban centres to expand enormously and become congested (Kabul in particular, whose population rose from some 2 million to 5 million within a decade, although the city had originally been designed to accommodate some half a million). The influx of unskilled rural migrants found it increasingly difficult to secure decent employment to cope with the rising costs of urban living. Most of the limited skilled manpower was absorbed by domestic and foreign entrepreneurs who offered them high salaries, creating what became known as the 'secondary civil service',[24] which functioned in considerable isolation from the concerns of society's mainstream.[25] The rural–urban dichotomy, social and economic disparity, and public disillusionment were stark.

There was an urgent need for a systematic and responsive mode of structural socio-economic change and development. Despite early attempts at taxation and monetary reforms, not much was achieved in the way of implementing a comprehensive and systematic economic plan with an emphasis on linking the centre to the peripheries and the latter to one another, stimulating job opportunities in the rural areas, and encouraging self-sufficiency, and national unity. Several compacts were concluded between the Afghan governments and the international community to improve the national economic outlook. A very important one was the 'Afghanistan Compact', a document outlining goals for the development of Afghanistan forged by the Afghan and foreign donor governments at a conference in London in 2006. Whereas the Bonn Agreement, as discussed in chapter 3, focused almost exclusively on a roadmap for the development of institutional structures for procedural democracy, the Afghanistan Compact evinced the international community's realization that, without increased security and a diminution of the drugs trade that contributes to instability in the region, no attempts at state-building would succeed. The compact pledged to reverse three main deficiencies in Afghanistan: security; governance, rule of law and human rights; and economic and social development.[26] However, neither this compact nor several other similar agreements bore much fruit as their implementation was undermined by the dysfunctionality and kleptocratic nature of governments in Kabul, growing insecurity and the half-hearted commitment of outside actors.

If Afghanistan was to have a fighting chance of becoming a self-sustaining independent state in the long run, it demanded both investment in the country's natural resources and expansion of skilled manpower.[27] As reported by the Pentagon in 2010, Afghanistan possessed mineral resources worth $1 trillion, although Afghan Minister of Mines Wahidullah Shahrani at the time estimated it to be more than $3 trillion.[28] It was nonetheless known since the late 1960s that Afghanistan was endowed with very sizeable iron, copper, gold, lithium and oil deposits, making mineral exploration in the country a worthwhile investment.

Following the US-led involvement, China showed an interest in tapping into Afghanistan's natural resources. It saw an opportunity to invest in the country's mineral deposits and to have a share in its growing economy, to which the US, as the dominant competitive power in Afghanistan, was not necessarily opposed. Initially, China invested around $130 million in the areas of irrigation, infrastructure, communications and power. And, more importantly, the China Metallurgical Group signed an agreement with the Karzai government in May 2008 for access to the Aynak copper mine in Logar Province, with an investment of $3 billion that was expected to yield $1 billion of annual revenue a year for Kabul.[29] In December 2011, the China National Petroleum Corporation secured approval for a billion-dollar deal to develop oil blocks in the Amur Darya Basin in the north, in association with the Afghan Watan group, which was owned by the Popal brothers, who were believed to be cousins of President Karzai.[30]

Similarly, in addition to the Indian government's reconstruction aid that rose to $2 billion during the two decades of US-led involvement, in November 2011, an Indian consortium spearheaded by the state-owned Steel Authority of India Ltd secured a contract for the Haji Gak iron-ore deposit – the largest in Asia – in the central province of Bamiyan. It was expected to invest $10 billion over the next thirty years. Further, in December 2014, the United States Agency for International Development (USAID) pledged to provide $125 million to design a roadmap for development of the Sheberghan Gas Development Project in the northern province of Jowzjan, across from Turkmenistan,[31] where, during the Soviet era, Russians had made hefty investments to exploit gas deposits, although on a barter basis.

However, many of these projects, and several others, barely came to fruition to benefit Afghanistan. As a potential driver of the Afghan economy, these resources were seriously undercut by poor govern-ance, political favouritism, corruption and local control, and conflicts over them as well as public dependence on the state[32] and, above all, increased insecurity. This played an important part in stymieing many other interested outside investors. Without a sizeable domestic source of income, the Afghan economy under Karzai and Ghani remained largely hostage to foreign handouts, and the narcotics industry.

There were also serious concerns about the lack of sufficient accountability and monitoring of America's growing military expend-iture and reconstruction aid amidst reports of substantial amounts being diverted into private pockets and bank accounts, or dummy projects, in an environment of rampant corruption and mismanage-ment. This prompted the US Congress to establish in 2008 a Special Inspector General for Afghanistan Reconstruction (SIGAR) to 'conduct robust, independent, and objective oversight of the US reconstruction investment in Afghanistan'.[33] By then, Congress had appropriated $38 billion in humanitarian and reconstruction assist-ance (which, over two decades of America's involvement, grew to $131 billion).[34] Ever since, SIGAR's audit and inspection reports have proved to be very critical of the way that the US reconstruction and budgetary aid implemented through USAID and the Department of Defense was considerably misappropriated by both American and Afghan sides.[35]

Having said this, it is not to deny that Afghanistan experienced a reconstruction boom at a level that it had not seen since its founda-tion. Both public and private sectors expanded enormously compared to any time in the past. Many infrastructural, industrial and social services projects – roads, bridges, hydro-electric dams, hospitals, clinics, educational institutions, telecommunications and manufac-turing firms, and hospitality enterprises – were initiated and built. More Afghans were employed and trained in different professions, with many of them benefiting from the reconstruction investment and activities. Backed by the US and its allies, Afghanistan was even admitted into the World Trade Organization in July 2016 as one of its least-developed countries – something that not even many middle-economy countries, like neighbouring Iran, could dream of.

However, given the amount of capital, foreign expertise, know-how and technology with which Afghanistan was endowed, there were more than sufficient resources to rebuild the country twice over for the benefit of the common good. Yet, this did not happen. The level of fraud, wastage, mismanagement, shoddy work practices, and administrative and supervisory failures was so high that the country saw only artificial, not structural, economic development. In some cases, projects were either substantially delayed or not completed. Of those that were completed, many suffered from serious defects and were littered with bomb damage, requiring them to be repaired at great cost.[36] Bribery in the form of kickbacks by Afghan officials and foreign and domestic companies, or their subcontractors, was pervasive. In other cases, the country lacked the capacity to absorb the influx of vast amounts of foreign money.[37] As a result, large sums frequently remained unspent and vulnerable to embezzlement by domestic and outside predators.

The rate of economic growth was very uneven. By 2014, Afghanistan's average annual growth of 9 per cent since 2002 was rapidly declining. The World Bank's World Development Indicators show that the annual GDP growth fell from 14.4 per cent in 2012 to 2 per cent in 2013. With foreign troop drawdown accelerating, it fell even further to 1.3 and 1.5 per cent in 2014 and 2015, respectively, to the serious concern of a meeting of Afghanistan's international donors, co-hosted by the European Union and the Afghan government in October 2016. Given American and international fatigue, this decline remained constant in the following years, although with a slight improvement in 2019, but then nosedived with the return of the Taliban to power.[38] In all, the economic expansion benefited mostly those in positions of power and influence, their dependents and supporters, and opportunist entrepreneurs; it did little to lift the majority of Afghans out of poverty.

After two decades of massive US-led investment, Afghanistan remained an impoverished country. According to Gallup surveys conducted in July and August 2022, even before Afghanistan was plunged into economic ruin under Taliban 2.0 (with 95–98 per cent of its population in need of outside help to survive), the country 'ranked as the least developed country in the world every year since 2017' (except 2020, during which no Gallup survey was conducted due to the Covid-19 global pandemic).[39] Most citizens lived on an average of $2.15 a day in 2017,[40] with little prospect of improvement. Thus, Afghanistan never graduated from being at the bottom of the list of the world's poorest countries from 2002 to 2021.[41]

Women's rights

Afghan women and their images were projected by the global media as icons of the new 'democratized' Afghanistan. This issue occupied a special place in the examination of civil society and human rights promotion in Afghanistan from 2002. Against the background of women's traditional deprivation in many walks of life under a mixture of Islamic and traditional rubrics, with the US intervention and advent of the Karzai leadership, the dawn of a new era for Afghan women was emphasized. The stints of women's emancipation initiated during the reign of King Amanullah in the 1920s, then under King Zahir Shah, especially from the late 1950s, and expanded during the rule of the People's Democratic Party of Afghanistan were very limited in scope, affecting only a small category of those women who were educated and mostly concentrated in the capital. However, even this much of a window of progress was entirely closed by the Taliban's first round of gender-apartheid rule. Karzai, along with some members of his cabinets, was Islamically and culturally restrained in his approach to women's rights and freedoms in the highly conservative Afghan micro-societies. He was nonetheless open minded about the issue, along with many of the expatriates in his administration, and inclined to subscribe to the George W. Bush administration's emphasis on improving Afghan women's lives after the fall of the Taliban. In a famous radio address to the nation on 17 November 2001, First Lady Laura Bush entered the political arena she had previously avoided in order to launch a fervent plea for 'a worldwide effort to focus on the brutality against women and children' in Afghanistan, arguing that 'the brutal oppression of women is the central goal of the terrorists'.[42] If the subduing of women was the central goal of the terrorists, she seemed to suggest, then saving women from this oppression was the central goal of democratizing Afghanistan and the 'war on terror'. 'Because of our recent military gains', Laura Bush argued:

> in much of Afghanistan, women are no longer imprisoned in their homes. They can listen to music and teach their daughters without fear of punishment. Yet, the terrorists who helped rule that country now plot and plan in many countries, and they must be stopped. The fight against terrorism is also a fight for the rights and dignity of women.[43]

As laudable as her address was on behalf of the women of Afghanistan, it also implied that the US had intervened not only to remove a direct security threat but also *specifically* to stand up for the rights of women to remove their *burqas*, to receive an education and to enjoy the emerging democratic freedoms under US auspices. Yet, her statement was premature. Seven years later, in 2008, Amnesty International would state:

> Afghan women and girls still face widespread discrimination from all segments of society, domestic violence, abduction and rape by armed individuals, trafficking, forced marriages, including ever

younger child marriages, and being traded in settlement of disputes and debts.[44]

Nonetheless, Laura Bush's address was followed by a deluge of media support for non-governmental organizations (NGOs) working with women in Afghanistan, and the image of the Afghan woman 'liberated' from her *burqa* became the paradigmatic proof of the 'success' of the US involvement and Karzai's administration in Afghanistan.[45]

In response to this domestic US focus on the plight of females, a large number of women's NGOs were founded or given increased funding in Afghanistan. Many of these organizations were seen as flagship civil society projects in the domestic US media and received a comparatively large amount of coverage, and at least rhetorical support in comparison to other civil society organizations in Afghanistan.

Many of the women's NGOs, some of which – like the Afghan Women's Education Center and the Afghan Women's Network – had been established in the 1990s, and others – like the US-based Women for Afghan Women – founded after the fall of the Taliban, were given a unique opportunity in support of women's causes.[46] They became active more as what Thomas Carothers calls 'advocacy NGOs', as opposed to 'development' or 'reconstruction' NGOs: that is, they focused much of their work on developing proto-democratic groups among women and lobbying Afghan governing bodies for greater attention to women's rights.[47] The human rights of women (and indeed of all Afghan citizens) were advocated as a fundamental aspect of the development of substantive democracy in Afghanistan, embedded within which were liberal principles of human rights, free expression and congregation, and respect for the rule of law.

There is no doubt that under the Karzai and Ghani administrations and US patronage some progress was made in relation to women's rights through initiatives such as the National Action Plan for Women and the landmark Afghan 2009 law criminalizing many acts of violence against women. Improvement in the areas of women's education, health, cultural and social freedoms enabled, for example, a visible number of women and girls to discard their veils in favour of modest headscarves, especially in the capital.

Confirming this point, but with serious reservations, a 2014 Amnesty International report stated:

> On women's rights, the limited progress of the past 12 years has been mainly due to the tireless work of Afghan women activists themselves. Women are now represented in public life and have better access to education. . . . But many of these advances are under threat . . . from conservative elements in the government and armed groups like the Taliban . . . or have already been rolled back. Few perpetrators of violence against women are brought to justice, while discrimination and domestic abuse are rife. Women human rights defenders face daily death threats and harassment with minimal official protection or remedy.[48]

In other words, the overall picture still remained exceedingly grim. Even the modest gains made were mostly concentrated in the small pool of educated women in the main urban centres, such as Kabul. Outside the capital, Islamic and cultural traditionalism still remained deeply entrenched.

Institutional discrimination persisted against women in the administration and the education sector persistently suffered from growing instability and violence raging across the country. Girls' schools in rural areas suffered repeated attacks, which were attributed to Taliban and other fundamentalist forces opposed to women's education.[49] Rape and sexual violence were used as a weapon of war. Little progress was made in improving some of the basic human rights of women; maternal mortality rates remained among the highest in the world,[50] as millions of women continued to live (like men and children in their families) in poverty.

The desperate situation of women seemed to disprove the self-praising rhetoric of the Bush administration that the 'rights and dignity' taken from them by the 'terrorists' had been restored. It also raised questions about the efficacy of those NGOs devoted to improving the human rights of women. The failures of the Afghan governments, and the US and national and international NGOs in this respect, while multifaceted, were heavily influenced by two factors. The first was the contradiction between the official rhetoric regarding the restoration of human rights to women and the scant attention paid to women's issues during the actual 'state-building' process from the end of 2001. The second was the prevalence of nepotism and elitism within a number of the NGOs themselves, and their perceived affiliation with the military forces 'occupying' the country, which contributed to distrust of many women's organizations, both foreign and local, and did little to foster greater attention to women's rights in the broader community. The resulting situation attested to the fact that while the Bonn process, involving holding elections and rewriting a constitution, were considered positive steps on the way to building a democracy, they did not in themselves ensure that citizens would experience the freedom to embrace and enjoy these new democratic structures.

Even so, compared to pre-2001, women's rights saw an upward trajectory legally, politically and socially over time. Many women availed themselves of the opportunities to enter the public arena and participate in the rebuilding of a supposedly new Afghanistan. Under the constitutional quota, women were elected to the 2005 and subsequent parliaments. In the 2018 parliamentary elections, sixty-nine women were voted to the 250-seat Wolesi Jirga from constituencies in the capital and the provinces.[51] Karzai successfully appointed one woman in his 2005 cabinet though his nomination for another in his 2009 cabinet was turned down by the Wolesi Jirga. There was a marked improvement under Ghani in this respect: four women were approved by the Wolesi Jirga in the 2015 National Unity Government

(NUG), with a similar number in Ghani's 2020 cabinet. Also, Ghani appointed several women to ambassadorial and senior policymaking posts. It is worth mentioning that Sima Samar, who was included in Karzai's first cabinet as Minister of Women's Affairs, was the first woman to hold that position at that level in Afghanistan's history, although the first female to hold a cabinet post was Kubra Noorzai, who served as Minister of Public Health from 1965 to 1969. Samar subsequently served as head of the Afghan Independent Human Rights Commission, with the task of improving not only human rights in general but also those of women. Along with these developments came women's participation in the private sector, where they opened their own businesses and made headway, among other things, in the creative and performance arts.

As freedom of expression increased with this more liberal atmosphere, and as media outlets – both digital and print – multiplied rapidly, a good number of young women emerged as newsreaders, programme producers and reporters. Despite some being funded by, and functioning as mouthpieces for not only the government but also various strongmen and outside players, dozens of television and radio stations, led by Tolo network, as well as daily, weekly and monthly publications, aided the process. Freedom of political expression and congregation, as well as the breakdown of some social taboos, together with the growing empowerment of women and such historically suppressed non-Pashtun minorities as the Panjshiris and Hazaras, turned out to be perhaps the most positive aspects of the US and allied involvement in Afghanistan and the Afghan governments they propped up. The trajectory was not always linear. It was punctuated by the political and power needs of Karzai and the authoritarian tendencies of Ghani. The patriarchal, cultural and Islamic restrictions still remained dominant, but the prospects for women and girls looked brighter than at any other time before Taliban 2.0's return of gender-apartheid policies, depriving them of all their basic rights.

Social services

Education

Another sector that saw substantial change was education.[52] Certainly, a great deal of stress was placed on, and hefty investment made in, this sector. The process commenced with help from the US and allied partners as well as the United Nations Educational, Scientific and Cultural Organization (UNESCO) and other relevant international agencies during Karzai's period in office and enhanced under Ghani. As a result, by 2020, more than 10 million students were enrolled in some 18,000 primary, middle and secondary schools around the country. Of this number, girls accounted for about 40 per cent of the elementary school students and 35 per cent of middle and high school students. Some 400,000 students were enrolled in public and private universities, as they mushroomed rapidly in a deregulated environment: some 39 of them public and another 126 private (including the American University of Afghanistan) operating at varying standards across the country. The oldest and traditionally the most reputable was Kabul University.[53]

As more young people were educated, a new generation – talented, and socio-politically aware and connected – arose on the horizon from the ranks of the segment of the population that formed the majority in Afghanistan. This was commendable, especially when considered in the context of war conditions, intimidation and destruction perpetrated by the Taliban and other conservative and extremist opposition groups, including Islamic State-Khorasan (IS-K).

However, this tells only part of the story. The quality of education and availability of qualified teachers, pedagogical and educational facilities varied considerably among the schools, colleges and universities.[54] While running three sessions a day, many schools suffered from a lack of basic educational and infrastructural facilities. For example, as observed by the author during several visits to the country before the Taliban boomeranged back into power, in some schools, even in Kabul, students were sitting on the bare ground, and studying with a minimum means of learning or writing. They were taught by dedicated teachers, but the educational credentials of some were highly questionable. Kabul University, which was once a credible centre of learning, research and research output prior to the outbreak of the conflicts from 1978, had lost much of its gloss by 2017. Its faculties had been funded unevenly, depending on their deans' connection and influence with powerful authorities inside and outside the university, that is the Ministry of Higher Education and 'strongmen', and were hostage to nepotistic politics of favour and disfavour so commonly practised in the country. As such, some of the faculties had managed to achieve a reasonable standard of teaching and research, in affiliation with American or European universities; but the same was not true in relation to some others, especially those focused on social sciences.

One of the bright spots was the establishment of the Afghan Center at Kabul University (ACKU), a valuable source of research and public awareness. ACKU was opened in 2012 after the completion of its $2 million building. It exemplified the best of what could be achieved, given its rich, digitized collection of material on Afghanistan.[55] Otherwise, many public and private universities lacked the necessary degree of quality control, as well as funding and infrastructural facilities beyond the basics. Some private universities also fell prey to political influence from their sources of funding and powerful individuals, as Afghanistan remained at the mercy of many self-serving manipulative power-holders.

Health

Public health had never been a very strong sector in Afghanistan, and it experienced severe deterioration under Taliban 1.0. But the sector attracted considerable attention and investment between 2002 and 2020. Although Afghanistan's infant mortality rate dropped from

86.951 per 1,000 in 2002 to 48.869 in 2020, it was still very high compared to the amount invested in the health sector,[56] which rose from $16 per capita in 2002 to $70 per capita in 2018.[57] The World Health Organization (WHO) reported that Afghanistan's 'health system has been steadily progressing over the last 17 years, with increasing coverage of health services throughout the country'.[58] During the period, more public and private hospitals and clinics were built, and more patients were treated, with substantial assistance from USAID and other foreign donor sources, including India and the WHO. Some 3,135 health facilities were functioning and accessible to a majority of the population. USAID, working through the Afghanistan Reconstruction Trust Fund – a multilateral donor platform – claims that it supported 'the delivery of basic health services to over 2,300 health facilities across the country'.[59]

However, as in the case of education, this tells only part of the story. A SIGAR report states that from July 2015 through to October 2018 the body visited 269 facilities in ten provinces and discovered serious shortcomings. It says:

> We found that although most facilities were operational and, except for one instance, included an operational pharmacy, two facilities were in potentially hazardous condition due to possible seismic activity and an explosion. Finally, at another facility, staff were not present because a staff member had been killed offsite earlier in the day. The facility was closed as a result. During our site visits we observed that many facilities had other deficiencies including a lack of access to utilities such as electricity or water; wall or ceiling defects; incinerators in poor condition, or a lack of resources.[60]

Thus, despite improvement over what had historically existed, the sector faced serious challenges from a 'critical shortage of key ingredients'. They ranged from qualified healthcare workers, especially in the area of women's health services, safe and well-equipped facilities, particularly in zones of conflict (primarily in the south), to supplies of medicines, equipment and vaccines. Furthermore, a World Bank report concluded that: 'Insecurity, gender imbalances, and lack of government revenue severely limit the availability of even most basic healthcare for most Afghans – and the situation has become particularly acute during the Covid-19 Pandemic.'[61] Covid-19 affected and killed thousands of Afghans. UNICEF reported that between April 2020 and 8 July 2021, a total of 131,586 people were infected with 5,561 deaths, although by June 2021 Afghanistan was officially registering an estimated 2,000 cases daily.[62] But by all accounts, these numbers were very much understated for a number of reasons. These included very limited testing, a massive shortage of vaccines and facilities, poor healthcare, and lack of reliable registration and access to clinics and hospitals in most rural areas.[63] Eyewitness accounts relate that thousands of Afghans who died of the disease were simply not reported, and families believed that many of the deaths, especially in remote areas of the country, were due to influenza or natural causes, as destined by God.

The accomplishments that were made in these areas – the opium crisis, the economy, the status of women and human rights, and social services – as part of state-building in Afghanistan were negligible compared to the amount of money that was spent on the country over two decades. During this period, America's lone contribution to Afghanistan's reconstruction came to about $131–$141 billion, and expenditure in fighting the war amounted to $2.313 trillion, with a 'trickle-down' financial and economic impact. These sums were by no means meagre. Most Afghan people and many critics of the US-led involvement inside and outside America were justified in asking: where did all this massive expenditure lead Afghanistan? The Karzai, Ghani and US governments have much to answer for. Afghanistan never gained the security that the Bush administration had promised it, either. The country simply moved from one phase of insecurity to another, as is now examined in chapter 7.

7

Strategy and Security

We've been engaged in a project that essentially is both counter-cultural and counter-historical to Afghan experience. We've created a central government there for the first time that's trying to extend its writ.

Eric S. Edelman[1]

The political system that was forged in alliance with the US and its allies in Afghanistan was intended to be the engine for state-building and for America's success in Afghanistan. It defied and confounded Washington's expectations, depriving America of instrumental agency for change on the ground. The Hamid Karzai and Ashraf Ghani leaderships proved to be inadequate, lacking the necessary vision and capability to forge effective governance or to build solid bridges between the central authority and micro-societies within the framework of a meaningful and fruitful partnership with the United States, as the main power in the country. But this was not all. The US played its part by not having a military strategy for what to do if the non-military dimensions of its approach to state-building failed to generate suitable transformative political, economic, social and, above all, security changes that would, in turn, generate appropriate conditions for statehood in Afghanistan. It had a military plan for the intervention which originally worked in overpowering the Taliban and Al Qaeda, but which lacked grounding in a well-thought-out strategy. It was guided by short-term rather than long-term considerations, without details in terms of the clarity of goals, methods and the means to achieve them, to deal appropriately with unforeseen contingencies, and it also lacked an endgame to bring the campaign to a responsible conclusion within a reasonable timeline. After the initial phase of the campaign, US military operations and, for that matter, those of the allies, took a slippery path from 2002, partly due to preparations for the invasion of Iraq and partly because of an unrealistic sense of euphoria in Washington that the Afghanistan situation was under control. This raises the question of whether the US military was ever in a position to win against the Taliban and their supporters, and help Afghanistan become its own security provider.

This chapter examines the approach of the US military, from which NATO allies took their cue for their operations, its inability to curb the capability of the Taliban and their fellow violent extremist groups, who until 2020 were designated as terrorists, and their Pakistani backers. The objective is not to cover the nuts and bolts of the battlefield confrontations, and the means and methods used by the two sides. It is rather to analyse why the US and its allies, including the Afghan security forces that they trained and equipped, could not stem the growing tide of the Taliban-led insurgency that finally, in a tribal mode of guerilla warfare or war by other means, prevailed. After all, the Taliban and their affiliates were not formidable and were not backed by a world power (as the Mujahideen had been by the US against the Soviet occupation in the 1980s), but rather by a fragile, although nuclear-armed, Pakistan.

No doubt, there was a general strategy or plan of action initially. The main goals were to capture or kill Osama bin Laden, dismantle Al Qaeda, get rid of the Taliban regime, and support the formation of a receptive and internationally recognized and publicly mandated government in Afghanistan, as developed within the Bonn process up to the 2004 presidential and 2005 parliamentary elections. This was expected to be achieved through a US 'light footprint' approach, enabling the US to avoid becoming entangled in a long-term military involvement. The US military, assisted by the International Security Assistance Force (ISAF), which was deployed by the US NATO allies for the security of Kabul in December 2001 and came under NATO's command in August 2003, played its part well in the process, although the failure to find and kill Bin Laden early enough was, as General James Mattis puts it, a big operational mistake.

However, this broad strategy, Karl Eikenberry argues, soon degenerated into 'small strategies' to deal with unforeseen developments that eventuated in the context of the failures of the political and reconstruction dimensions of state-building (as explained in the previous four chapters) against the backdrop of Afghanistan's national and regional complexities. General David Petraeus agrees with Eikenberry on the issue of degeneration of the initial strategy and adds:

> Our foundational mistake was our lack of commitment. In essence, we never adopted a sufficient, consistent, overarching approach that we stuck with from administration to administration, or even within individual administrations. ... By the time attention and resources were once again truly devoted to Afghanistan, some eight years after the initial invasion, we had missed an opportunity to take advantage of a protracted period of relatively little violence in Afghanistan, during which time the Taliban and other insurgent elements regrouped in Pakistan and then Afghanistan, and during which we could have made considerably greater strides in developing Afghan forces and institutions than we did.[2]

Petraeus differs from Eikenberry, who had three lengthy tours of duty in Afghanistan compared to Petraeus's short stint, on two counts. One is that he does not seem to take into consideration the historical and contemporary conditions militating against state-building in Afghanistan. The other is that the security situation in Afghanistan took a downward trajectory from 2003, in the wake of the US invasion of Iraq, with the US lacking sufficient forces to fight the Iraqi and Afghan wars simultaneously with the necessary effectiveness. Added to this were America's quandaries over acting decisively to curtail Pakistan's support of the Taliban and their partners. Let us now see how the US security-building and security operations took a downward slide.

As discussed in chapter 3, Operation Enduring Freedom (OEF) was launched in haste, without a firm grasp of Afghanistan's particularities in a complicated neighbourhood. Washington did not have the necessary time to draw up a comprehensive strategy based on an in-depth understanding of Afghanistan, and could not foresee the roadblocks that its national conditions and regional circumstances might generate. Former US Defense Secretary Robert Gates (2006–11) states:

> Our lack of understanding of Afghanistan, its culture, its tribal and ethnic politics, its power brokers, and their relationships, was profound. After ... twenty years [since helping defeat the Soviets there], I came to realize that in Afghanistan, as in Iraq, having decided to replace the regime, when it came to with 'what?', the American government had no idea what would follow. We had learned virtually nothing about the place in ... twenty years.[3]

The original military success against Al Qaeda and the Taliban, coupled with the unfolding Bonn process, caused an instant feeling of triumphalism. Reflecting this mode, President George W. Bush claimed, as early as April 2002, that the US was now engaged in 'helping to build an Afghanistan that is free from this evil [terrorism] and is a better place in which to live'. In contrast to the Bush administration's original opposition to 'nation-building' and a Marshall

Plan for Afghanistan, the president shortly thereafter changed tack by intimating that America was now acting in George Marshall's tradition of rebuilding Europe after victory in the Second World War, as there was a need for the 'military victory' to be followed by 'a moral victory that resulted in better lives for individual human beings'.[4] By 1 May 2003, Defense Secretary Donald Rumsfeld, who had favoured a 'light footprint' approach, confidently announced an end to 'major combat' in Afghanistan,[5] almost in parallel with Bush's declaration of 'mission accomplished' in Iraq. In step with Washington's civilian and military leaderships, Karzai also announced the dawn of an era for 'stabilization and reconstruction'.[6] Yet this was not in line with what was emerging on the ground.

By the first anniversary of the US-led campaign, there were troubling signs pointing to an increase in the activities of the Taliban and several related groups, as well as criminal gangs, including those who engaged in drug trafficking, money laundering and people smuggling. General Eikenberry, who was then US security coordinator for Afghanistan and chief of Military Cooperation-Afghanistan, could detect some disruptive developments on the horizon, and had concerns about this and the Bush leadership's intention to invade Iraq as a priority, potentially at the expense of the plans for Afghanistan. By the time of the March 2003 Iraq invasion, the security environment in Afghanistan was becoming challenging, especially in the Pashtun-dominated southern and eastern provinces bordering Pakistan, where a modestly sized US-led coalition force, together with ISAF, was grappling with increased insurgent activities.

The Taliban and their partners, including most importantly the Haqqani network and Gulbuddin Hekmatyar's Hezbi Islami group, were making a comeback with a vengeance. Pakistan's support for the insurgents was becoming increasingly evident in terms of the provision of safe havens, free cross-border movements and battlefield logistic and operational guidance and assistance. The Taliban-led guerrilla offensives were escalating beyond the capacity of the 8,000

American forces and 5,000 ISAF members, led by NATO from August 2003, as mandated by the UN, and the nascent security apparatus of the Karzai administration to contain them. In the fourth year of intervention, the US and allied forces were spread thinly across the land and were beginning to sustain increasing casualties. US commanders on the ground were calling for more troops and resources as well as some strident measures to prompt Islamabad to retrench its support for the insurgents and abide by its public stance against terrorism. In response, the US augmented troop deployment, which by the start of 2006 grew to some 21,000 for both combat operations and assistance to endow Afghanistan with a military and security capability as a prelude to winding down US and allied military involvement.

Meanwhile, US commanders were reporting a dramatic increase in the number of Taliban attacks in 2006, escalating by some 200–300 per cent from the year before, making the year the bloodiest since the toppling of the Taliban regime. They, along with some senior figures inside and outside the US Congress, were voicing the need for a comprehensive strategy to extend the fight to include Pakistan's tribal regions, that is the Federally Administered Tribal Areas (FATA) or what has been part of Pakistan's province of Khyber-Pakhtunkhwa since 2017. Most of the insurgents came from this area, constituting 'the greatest challenge to long-term security within Afghanistan.'[7] The complexity of the situation and fear of the US being caught in 'the Afghan trap' began to trouble Washington to the extent that prior to ending his second term, President Bush authorized deployment of an extra 10,000 troops over two years and doubled America's reconstruction aid to Afghanistan.

In the face of mounting challenges, the US-led coalition forces were in an uncoordinated state. A rift was brewing between the two sides of the Atlantic. It had started with Rumsfeld's famous 2003 statement about 'old' and 'new' Europe, berating those traditional allies – mainly France and Germany – for not supporting the US invasion of Iraq. Rumsfeld had begun complaining about the NATO allies not doing enough in Afghanistan. While having repeatedly resisted US military participation in nation-building type operations, by 2005 he could clearly see signs of the US getting involved in a protracted conflict in Afghanistan; he threatened to reduce the US troop deployment by 3,000 within the next few months as a way of pressuring the allies to do more. As mentioned in chapter 3, most of the allies had originally come to Afghanistan with no long-term commitment, but rather to assist the US on a short-term basis. Some newer NATO members (Eastern Europe and the Baltic states) were trying, through their proactive contributions, to enlist US support for tougher measures against Russia.

However, as changing circumstances called for long-term involvement, ISAF was cajoled into going beyond its initial mandate. From 2003, when NATO took over command of ISAF, the latter's role expanded in different stages, mostly in parallel with the US-led coalition forces, across Afghanistan. Made up of contributions from twenty-six countries, ISAF was moulded as a civil-military force. While US-led coalition forces were tasked mainly with counterterrorism missions, ISAF mostly operated in a counterinsurgency (COIN) framework.[8] Beyond acting in self-defence when attacked, ISAF's functions came to include the provision of assistance to build Afghanistan's security forces and securitize and administer fourteen of a total of twenty-three Provincial Reconstruction Teams (PRTs) that were established across Afghanistan between 2002 and 2014. The coalition forces managed the remaining nine PRTs. The PRTs were apportioned to different participating NATO and coalition member states and were funded from their nations' reconstruction and aid packages, some of which were funnelled through the United Nations Assistance Mission in Afghanistan (UNAMA).

Against this backdrop, Rumsfeld, who was one of the most controversial and powerful Secretaries of Defense since Robert McNamara during the Vietnam War, resigned in what appeared to be a forced exit, which was announced on 8 November 2006. Rumsfeld was a key figure in planning the intervention in Afghanistan and invasion of Iraq but had been facing growing criticism from within the military for his 'light footprint' approach. He was succeeded by Gates, a highly experienced intelligence veteran and analyst, who had served in various capacities under a number of American presidents.

During his first visit to Afghanistan in mid-January 2007, Gates was alarmed by the security situation and the Taliban's robustness, as he was briefed by General Eikenberry and other US commanders. Gates notes:

> I heard a consistent message from everyone: the Taliban insurgency was growing, their safe havens in Pakistan were a big problem, the spring of 2007 would be more violent than the previous year, and more troops were needed. I was told that NATO nations had not provided some 3,500 military trainers they had promised, and Eikenberry – who was due to rotate out less than a week after my visit – asked that the deployment of a battalion of the 10th Mountain Division (about 1,200 troops) be extended through the spring offensive [the start of the fighting season in Afghanistan].[9]

There was a request for even more troops. Gates says he was prepared to respond positively, but was cautioned by the accompanying chairman of the Joint Chiefs of Staff, General Peter Pace, who told him that any additional troop deployment in Afghanistan would 'increase the strain on the U.S. military'. Pace pointed out that with the concurrent surge in Iraq involving 160,000 troops, 'the Army and Marine Corps didn't have combat capability to spare'. As a result, Gates realized that he 'couldn't deliver in both places at once'.[10] This debunked further the mainstay of the US defence strategy that it could fight and win two major wars simultaneously.[11]

In meeting President Karzai, Gates relates that while he 'owed his position – and his life – to American support', 'he was very much a

Pashtun leader and an Afghan nationalist'.[12] He states that Karzai had deep concerns about some of the issues linked to US and allied military operations, which had already become a bone of contention between him and the international coalition. In addition to 'civilian casualties', those issues included the culturally and socially insensitive actions of private security contractors, night raids and the use of dogs on patrols. They also involved invasion of privacy and kicking down doors of houses while women and children were inside (something that struck at the heart of Pashtuns' norms of honour), moral lapses and human rights violations similar to those committed in Iraq.[13] Gates claims that dealing with Karzai was 'frustrating and maddening' for US commanders and diplomats, but the president was right about those issues and 'we were far too slow in picking up on these signals and taking action'. He intimates that 'Karzai knew he needed the coalition but he also was sensitive to actions that would anger the Afghan public, undermine their tolerance for the presence of foreign troops in their country, and reflect badly on him in the eyes of his countrymen.'[14]

In other words, as the insurgency was rapidly expanding and becoming deadly, and the security situation was declining to an alarming extent, the US and allied forces were falling short of understanding the complexity of operating in a country like Afghanistan. However, in contrast to Gates and Eikenberry, NATO's Secretary General Jaap de Hoop Scheffer was concurrently providing a mixed assessment of the situation, depending on who he was addressing. In a meeting with President Bush on 2 April 2008, he said 'we are prevailing in Afghanistan'[15] – something that the president wanted to hear as an affirmation of his own public utterances. Yet, in a speech at the Royal United Services Institute in London four months later, de Hoop Scheffer was underplaying his earlier optimistic assessment, stating:

We have . . . seen the Taliban and other extremist forces strengthen their positions in the tribal areas along the border with Afghanistan.

It is thus becoming ever clearer that success in Afghanistan can only be achieved if we engage Pakistan in a common effort against extremism which threatens the future of the entire region.

In the same speech, he raised serious concerns about the rate of casualties in fierce fighting in August and the first half of September 2008, when 'many NATO soldiers and many Afghans have lost their lives'.[16]

The hole in American operations was widening, with Washington's inability to meet repeated requests of NATO ISAF Commander General David D. McKiernan for more troops for combat operations, combat support operations and training of Afghan National Defense and Security Forces (ANDSF), which the US had primarily been building since 2002. In a September 2008 hearing of the House of Representatives Committee on Armed Services, Secretary Gates and Joint Chiefs of Staff Admiral Michael Glenn Mullen admitted to a shortage of helicopters, and said there was no capability to deploy more Marines in Afghanistan due to the burden of the Iraq war. Reflecting growing disquiet in Washington's political and defence circles, some committee members seriously questioned the efficacy of the entire US military and state-building approach. They noted that the democratic processes had not paid sufficient dividends, and that poor governance, corruption, the narcotics industry, economic stultification and the Afghan government's dependence on foreign aid for 90 per cent of its annual budget had continued in the country. Representative Michael Conaway of Texas questioned even the applicability of democracy in Afghanistan, stating:

Afghanistan is limited in natural resources, unless you consider rocks a natural resource. And I struggle with the idea that a democracy can be maintained in which the economy is, to a significant portion, drug-related and the corrosive effects that that has.[17]

189

Adding further to these woes was the lack of uniformity in assessing and reporting the realities on the ground to the decision-makers in Washington and allied capitals. Lack of coordination between allied forces and operations and training of the Afghan military was emerging as a major problem. By the time Bush's presidency ended, Democrat Barack Obama took office in January 2009, and Eikenberry returned to Afghanistan as ambassador in April, the insurgency was in full swing. It was no longer confined to the southern and eastern provinces. The Taliban had managed to expand their operations, striking targets in some of the northern and western parts of the country. According to some reports circulating at the time, they were being helped by some Pashtunist elements from within the Karzai government who had an interest in spreading the fighting into non-Pashtun areas.[18] The US and allied forces were truly on the back foot.

As explained in chapters 4 and 5, President Obama seemed personally troubled by the length of the war, with no victory in sight. Sharing the president's and Gates's concerns, Eikenberry also formed the view that the US campaign and Afghanistan were not moving in the right direction. Hence President Obama's initiation of the 2009 review of the Afghanistan policy. With prospects of a military victory fading, Obama now focused on finding a responsible way out of the war. Vice-President Joe Biden, National Security Advisor Tom Donilon, Special Assistant and Senior Coordinator for Afghanistan and Pakistan Douglas Lute, Ambassador Eikenberry and US Special Representative for Afghanistan and Pakistan Richard Holbrooke were on the same page as the president. However, commander of the joint US-led coalition and NATO ISAF forces General Stanley McChrystal (June 2009–June 2010), was of the view that:

While the situation is serious, success is still achievable. This starts with redefining both the fight itself and what we need for the fight. It is then sustained through a fundamentally new way of doing business. Finally, it will be realized when our new operational culture connects with the powerful will of the Afghan people.[19]

This was indeed in contrast to the assessment on the ground. In December 2010, Eikenberry invited this author (who was then visiting Kabul for fieldwork) to a dinner at his residence, where he had also gathered some of his senior military and USAID colleagues, to discuss the Afghanistan situation. There did not seem to be much optimism among them about the chances of success in Afghanistan. Eikenberry was personally very much abreast of the political, social and cultural roadblocks with which some of Washington's senior policy and military decision-makers had not entirely come to terms. In a subsequent conversation, he alluded to the fact that, despite Karzai being unpredictable and difficult to deal with, he was correct in reproaching some of the US-led coalition actions as counterproductive in terms of winning 'hearts and minds' in Afghanistan. In his opinion, the task of security-building had become more arduous and taxing than might otherwise have been the case.

McChrystal thought that 'the key to the insurgency was southern Afghanistan and if Kandahar and Helmand provinces could be flipped to government control that would then crush the Taliban, which he considered to be a national movement with its heart lying in the south'. So he argued that additional reinforcement of NATO forces was needed, to be deployed mainly in the south, 'to rip the heart out of the Taliban movement, along with strengthening the government, as decisive measures'.[20] He also believed that with the additional combat power and clever use of intelligence, based on his counterterrorism experience in Iraq where he was commander of the Joint Special Operations Command Task Force that found and killed Abu Musab Zarqawi,[21] he could dominate the south and effectively disrupt and destroy a lot of the Taliban command and control nation-wide as he had done in Iraq. Further, he thought that during the surge, the US military and NATO could accelerate the training of the Afghan National Army and press the reset button to build a more capable ANDSF to take over from the allied forces within two to three years. McChrystal essentially stood for a robust COIN strategy, with an intense focus on southern Afghanistan, despite Obama's reminding him that Al Qaeda was in the country's east. General Petraeus, who commanded US and allied forces in Afghanistan after McChrystal (June 2010–July 2011) and was the architect of the relatively successful surge in Iraq in 2007, also adhered to a similar strategy, despite differences between the two. However, 'if you asked him [McChrystal] when the surge began, where would the Afghan national security forces be in terms of capability two or three years later, Stan's view would have been, at a much higher state of capacity and readiness'.[22] Yet this is not how it turned out.

As mentioned in chapter 4, McChrystal requested an extra 40,000 troops to action his approach. After an intensive and at times acrimonious debate, Obama agreed to the dispatch of 30,000 troops, but on strict conditions. They included, most importantly, a drawdown of most of the US and allied troops, starting on 22 June 2011 and ending by the close of 2014 with transfer of combat responsibility to a more empowered ANDSF during this period, alongside a determined move towards a political settlement of the Afghanistan conflict. Only a small US contingent of 9,800 troops was to remain for a further year for training, support and anti-terrorism operations. The announcement of a specific withdrawal date in effect changed America's posture from conditions-based to time-based, with emphasis on COIN. It essentially proposed an *afghanization* of the war – an approach that had previously been tried but had not worked for the US in Vietnam or the USSR in Afghanistan. The Taliban, their affiliates and Pakistani supporters could only be very pleased with the development as it appeared to be a clear sign that Washington had had enough and wanted to exit from Afghanistan as soon as possible, something that they had anticipated would eventually come about.

In contrast, the US policy reset was hailed by some military and strategic analysts, who argued that the US now had the right strategy, number of troops and arsenal on the ground to herald a military victory. Included among them was General Jim Molan, former deputy of Petraeus in Iraq, and strategic specialist and advisor to the US military David Kilcullen.[23] Unfortunately, such optimism was misplaced, as events proved in the years ahead.

Regardless, Obama had reason to expect McChrystal and his successor, Petraeus, to smooth the way for a responsible drawdown. But neither of the generals lasted long enough in their posts to make a difference to the growing insurgency and mounting military and civilian casualties. McChrystal, who managed to develop a good rapport with various Afghan leaders from the top down, fell victim to his criticism of the president's top Afghanistan advisory team in a *Rolling Stone* magazine article and was relieved of his position by Obama.[24] Petraeus, who was still recovering from the exhaustion of his role in Iraq, lasted only one year in Afghanistan before he was appointed as CIA director.[25]

A string of five generals commanding allied forces followed Petraeus between February 2013 and July 2021: John Allen (July 2011–February 2013), Joseph Dunford Jr (February 2013–July 2014), John Campbell (July 2014–March 2016), John 'Mick' Nicholson Jr (March 2016–September 2018), and Scott Miller (September 2018–July 2021). The frequency of change in the military leadership had its own destabilizing effect on, and caused a degree of confusion among, US and allied forces, the Afghan governments and the ANDSF. It also indicated that Afghanistan was now a US foreign policy priority only in pursuit of exiting, rather than staying on course in the country. In the midst of all this, the US also finally achieved the main trigger and justification of its Afghanistan intervention: finding and eliminating the Al Qaeda leader after a decade of frantic searching.

Bin Laden's demise

The killing of Bin Laden on 2 May 2011, in a special operation by US Navy SEAL Team Six in the Pakistani city of Abbottabad (near Pakistan's Military Academy), in total secrecy so far as the Pakistani authorities were concerned, could not but mark a turning point in the US's Afghanistan campaign. Washington's pursuit of him for so long had played a pivotal part in widening and lengthening the American and allied involvement in Afghanistan. Having achieved its central objective, the Obama–Biden leadership, whose short-term electoral cycle and political needs varied from the military's long-term security considerations, now had even less in the way of compelling reasons to be as militarily committed to Afghanistan. Concurrently, US public opinion in support of the Afghan war had been precipitously declining below 50 per cent since 2009, along with general war fatigue settling across the NATO countries, as indicated by Gallup public opinion polls.[26]

The key question now was how to end the Afghanistan campaign. The US and its allies needed to make a respectable military exit, at the same time ensuring that Afghanistan did not remain vulnerable to the return to power of the Taliban. The latter possibility would have meant defeat – the waste of what had been achieved in Afghanistan at the expense of American and allied blood and money, not to mention the sacrifices of the Afghan people. This was not going to be an easy task to accomplish. Apart from the fact that Afghanistan remained a politically, economically and socially fragile country, many other factors undermined the US and allied security-building efforts. At the top of the list was Pakistan's determination to persist with its patronage of the Taliban and their allies, working towards a final victory. As far as Islamabad and its Afghan clients were concerned, time was on their side and triumph was now within reach.

Pakistan's role

The US failure decisively to impair Pakistan's support of the Taliban and their partners from the early days of the Afghanistan campaign constituted the most debilitating factor in the American and allied military efforts to stabilize and secure Afghanistan. Contrary to their public stance in support of the war on terrorism, the Pakistani military and intelligence brass never showed any resolve to do anything more than the minimum in this respect. The main game for them was to stay on course, no matter what, and succeed in Afghanistan in pursuit of Pakistan's long-standing regional ambitions. They paid only lip-service to US interests in order to maintain America's very generous military, economic and financial assistance, which was largely appropriated by them to bolster their powerful central position in the conduct of Pakistani domestic and foreign affairs,[27] rather than to improve living conditions for a majority of Pakistani citizens.

To keep Washington on side, Islamabad persistently highlighted Pakistan as a force for good and stability in the region and non-interference in Afghanistan. But at the same time, it never resiled from its long-standing policy of deepening and widening Pakistan's involvement in Afghanistan. As elaborated in chapter 2, the process started during the Soviet occupation of Afghanistan. Pakistan's military and intelligence apparatus backed the main Pashtun Mujahideen groups, and acted as a critical conduit for the US-led supply of arms, finance and training to those groups. Following the Soviet defeat, Islamabad shifted that support initially to Hekmatyar's group, and later to the Taliban and their partners. Islamabad publicly voiced support for the US's Afghanistan intervention and fight against terrorism. But double-crossing and outright denials of interference in Afghanistan formed an important aspect of its policy of plausible deniability.[28]

Pakistan's military dictator General Zia ul-Haq (1978–88) once confirmed this point. As related by US Secretary of State George Shultz (1982–95), in a telephone call in March 1980, President Ronald Reagan asked the Pakistani leader what he thought of the clause of non-interference in Afghanistan by its neighbours, referring mainly to Pakistan, in an agreement which was to be signed as the Geneva Peace Accords for the Soviet withdrawal from Afghanistan (see chapter 2). The general's response was that we will 'just lie' as before, claiming that 'Muslims have the right to lie in a good cause.'[29]

Islamabad pursued the same dictum in dealing with the US over its Afghanistan campaign and war on terrorism: publicly backing the US while supporting the Taliban and their affiliates that essentially sabotaged American war efforts. US Congressman Eliot L. Engel later stated:

> We entered into a questionable alliance with Pakistan which continued to arm and support the Taliban, providing the group safe haven and allowing it to strengthen its hand in Afghanistan.[30]

Whenever Washington pressed Islamabad diplomatically and materially, for example holding back and, on occasion, cutting financial and military assistance to Pakistan, especially during the Obama and Donald Trump administrations, to prompt it to do more to curtail its support of the Taliban's cross-border operations in Afghanistan, Islamabad resorted to two soothing diversionary tactics.

First, it repeatedly cited its anti-terrorism operations, which started in 2001 and continued intermittently until 2010, in Pakistan's semi-autonomous Federally Administrative Tribal Area (FATA), especially Waziristan, and the Northwest Frontier Province, bordering Afghanistan,[31] as proof of its opposition to terrorism. However, those actions were aimed mostly at suppressing anti-Pakistani government militancy and bringing the areas under Islamabad's jurisdiction, rather than acting against Afghan insurgents. The operations slowed down once the 'Pakistani government and tribal and militia leaders (including pro-Taliban elements)' reached an agreement known as the 'Shakai deal' in April 2004. Under the deal, the tribal leaders '"pledged loyalty" to the government in return for leniency', involving general amnesty to 'all except top-tier leaders of Al Qa'ida and the Taliban'. The 'tribal forces that were created to hunt down' the latter 'apparently failed to locate any foreign terrorists'.[32] Violence continued intermittently between tribal militias and government forces, and the deal brought no decline in the Taliban's cross-border movements and operations in Afghanistan. In 2006, the government reached another agreement with the tribal and militia leaders –the Waziristan Accord. 'Although violence directed against government troops on the Pakistani side of the border did decrease somewhat in the immediate aftermath of the signing, extra-judicial killings continued, and insurgent and terrorist actions within Afghanistan increased dramatically.'[33]

Second, while Pakistan's Inter-Services Intelligence (ISI) ostensibly cooperated with the CIA, Islamabad periodically announced in a timely fashion the capture of Al Qaeda operatives and released some of them to the US to assuage Washington's concerns. Releasees were not all necessarily high ranking; some were of less value than others. Meanwhile, the ISI retained in Pakistani custody or protection those that could be used for bargaining with Washington whenever appropriate. According to Seymour Hersh, they included Bin Laden, who Islamabad allegedly held 'hostage'[34] in Abbottabad as critical leverage to ensure the flow of Washington's aid and to camouflage its continued backing of the Taliban. However, Nelly Lahoud disputes the point about the Pakistani authorities' awareness of Bin Laden's presence in their midst. Lahoud, who has gone through Bin Laden's papers – taken by US Navy SEAL Team Six at the time of his killing – says that the Pakistani authorities may not have had full knowledge of Bin Laden's whereabouts, as his Abbottabad compound was guarded secretly by supportive Pakistani 'brothers'.[35] Yet it seems overwhelmingly unlikely that Bin Laden could have hidden in his compound, only a stone's throw from the Pakistan Military Academy, without the knowledge of Pakistani authorities, more specifically the ISI.

Some of the high-value figures that the ISI captured, either on its own or jointly with CIA agents, and who were handed over to the US included, for example, Ibn al-Shaikh al-Libi (January 2002), Abu Zubayda (March 2002), Ramzi bin al-Shibh (September 2002), and Mustafa al-Hawsawi (March 2003). However, the biggest catch of all was Khalid Sheikh Mohammed, the main operational architect of the 9/11 attacks (March 2003), whose capture pleased Washington enormously, and Walid Muhammad bin Attash (April 2003). President Bush hailed their arrest as a 'significant find'. Meanwhile, Adil al-Jazeeri (June 2003) and five other suspected Al Qaeda members who were also arrested and handed over to the US, along with Attash and Khalid Sheikh Mohammed, were not of such great importance. Islamabad continued this approach in the following years, exemplified by its imprisonment of the Taliban's deputy leader, Mullah Abdul Ghani Baradar, and subsequent release of him at America's request to negotiate the US–Taliban peace deal of February 2020.

Washington was appraised of Islamabad's duplicity from the early days, based on reports by CIA agents, who operated on both sides of the Afghanistan-Pakistan borderland, and by US commanders in Afghanistan, as well as by the Afghan National Directorate of Security (NDS), which worked in close conjunction with the CIA and other allied intelligence services. It was also largely aware of the whereabouts of the Taliban's leaders, their hiding places, and their top decision-making body, the Leadership Council (*shura*). The Council had visibly become functional in Quetta, the capital of Pakistan's Baluchistan Province, under the group's reclusive leader Mullah Mohammad Omar as far back as late 2002. Omar presided over the Council until his death in a Karachi hospital and burial in the Afghan province of Zabul in April 2013, although neither the Taliban nor Pakistani authorities confirmed this until July 2015.[36] Omar was succeeded by Mullah Akhtar Mansour who, while travelling from Iran to Pakistan on a Pakistani passport, was killed in a US drone strike on the Pakistan side of the border in May 2016. Replacing Mansour was Mullah Hibatullah Akhundzada. Previously based in Quetta, since the Taliban's resumption of power Akhundzada has operated from Kandahar and does not appear in public.

Washington knew about the pivotal role of the military and ISI in determining Pakistan's domestic and foreign policy priorities. But it seems that it underestimated their long-standing geopolitical ambitions in Afghanistan, and investment in the Taliban as a critical tool in this respect. Afghanistan–Pakistan relations had rarely been very cordial since the creation of Pakistan in 1947. As elaborated in chapter 2, the dispute over the Durand Line, with its complications for cross-border Pashtun ties, along with Kabul's push for an independent Pashtunistan as an Afghanistan proxy partially carved out of Pakistan, had frequently caused tension and occasional border skirmishes between the two sides. The beginning of the Afghanistan turmoil, with the 1978 pro-Soviet coup and subsequent Soviet invasion, had given Islamabad a unique opportunity to leverage its support for the Western-backed Mujahideen forces to press on with a policy of treating Afghanistan as 'strategic depth' in relation to India. This concept was not new. It was a compulsion that the Pakistan army had 'inherited from the British',[37] who had sought to instrumentalize it against Russian expansionism during the Great Game in the nineteenth century.

What held the US back from acting forcefully to compel Islamabad to cut ties with the Taliban and other related violent extremist groups? There would have been several considerations. First was America's dependence on Pakistan as the main artery for the transit of most of its war supplies to Afghanistan. Second was Pakistan's fragility as a nuclear-armed state. It was feared that any extensive cross-border operations to target the Taliban's safe havens, disrupt their supply lines or halt their cross-border movements could further destabilize an already fragile Pakistan, resulting in the country's possible disintegration and its relatively insecure nuclear arsenals (compared to those of other nuclear powers) falling into the wrong hands.[38] This was, indeed, the very argument that Islamabad also used to deter American actions. Third was the non-viability of closing the contentious Durand Line. As Eikenberry notes, Kabul would have been opposed to the closure so as not to deprive Afghanistan's Pashtuns of livelihoods and kindred linkages across the border.[39] Islamabad would have retaliated by hampering transit of American war supplies to Afghanistan. Fourth was the consideration that more than a minimum of US action could drive Pakistan further into the arms of China, with which Islamabad had already nurtured strategic ties in a common anti-India cause. Finally, there was the issue of resource availability in opening a new front, especially when the Iraq war was raging and Afghanistan's security was nosediving. Even after the end of the Iraq war in 2011, the US found it necessary to make a military comeback in Iraq to confront the rise of the so-called Islamic State over large chunks of Iraqi and Syrian territories from mid-2014.

These imperatives seemingly went to the heart of the Bush administration's reluctance and that of its successors to act decisively against Pakistan, despite an urgent need to deter the country as the most critical source of nourishment for the insurgency in Afghanistan. Whatever cross-border actions the US took, they were never on a scale that could prompt a change in Islamabad's Afghanistan policy or make a serious dent in the Taliban's resilience. The US drone attacks on targets inside Pakistan, which started under Bush in June 2004, were augmented by Obama and continued, although on a reduced scale, under Trump, hardly made a difference. Most of the hundreds of drone attacks were aimed at Al Qaeda operatives in the Afghan-Pakistan borderlands.[40] Their use proved to be very controversial, as the legality, the resultant high level of civilian casualties and the violation of Pakistan's sovereignty were widely questioned.[41] In the final analysis, America's reluctance or inability to do whatever was required to cut off Pakistan's patronage of the Taliban and their extremist partners, and seal the Afghan-Pakistan border, as treacherous as it was, proved to be central to the American and allied failure in Afghanistan.

Planning and operational shortcomings

As mentioned, Operation Enduring Freedom (OEF) was unleashed with little detailed clarity of goals, and 'means to achieve them, allocation of tasks/sub-tasks, logistics availability, resource allocation/

distribution and their employment, rate of availability of such resources, budgetary estimates, and evaluative mechanisms to measure operational success'.[42] It lacked an endgame and was conducted based mainly on short- rather than long-term considerations. Little or no concrete planning was done for how to deal with unexpected developments in a country whose difficult landscape had historically been inhospitable to outside interventions. Nor was sufficient thought given to the kind of transformative changes that could appropriately enable Afghanistan to become a self-sustaining, viable state in the medium to long run.

Afghanistan was a war-torn and destitute country. Its population had been widely traumatized, and their livelihoods destroyed. It lacked any institutional bases of stability. The US intervention within a 'light footprint' approach was destined to prove inadequate. If the Bush administration really intended to empower the Afghan people to live in peace and security within a democratic structure, Afghanistan's conditions required from the outset a much larger appropriate military and reconstruction involvement than what unfolded. In other words, a very 'heavy footprint' was needed to manage the country's transition at both macro and micro levels. As Richard Clarke asserts, '[t]he United States should have inserted forces into Afghanistan to cut off bin Laden's escape routes' and apprehend him and his deputies, as well as the Taliban leaders, in one way or another and establish 'a security presence throughout the country'.[43] But the US was too tight-fisted and too slow. During the first two years of OEF, the per capita funds that the US assigned for Afghanistan were $52 – a meagre amount compared to $1,390 and $814 per capita which were made available to Bosnia and Kosovo, respectively. The US was also very slow in training and equipping a capable Afghan security force. By 2004, '[t]he goal the Pentagon approved was only for a 4,800-man Afghan national army'. Washington's small footprint approach was more in accord with Rumsfeld's theories that 'small amounts of special forces and airpower could combine to do what large Army units had been called on to do in the past,[44] than in keeping with the reality of Afghanistan's existing conditions. The US did not want to appear as an 'invader' and end up in a quagmire, rather than providing what was needed to rapidly ensure security across Afghanistan at a time when the military was on the front foot in the country. It therefore acted expediently to achieve its basic objectives with minimum costs and duration. This was a gross miscalculation and a missed opportunity.

Another point of contention was that the US and its allies initially thought they were fighting only the Taliban and Al Qaeda. But they soon also found themselves in confrontation with the militant Haqqani network, named after its founder Jalaluddin Haqqani, and Hekmatyar's Hezbi Islami. Both groups wore the mantle of the Mujahideen's fight against the Soviets and their surrogates in the 1980s. Both were closely associated with Al Qaeda and the ISI, although Haqqani's network more so in this respect. Most of the Haqqani fighters came from Afghanistan's eastern provinces, in contrast with the Taliban's recruits who hailed largely from southern provinces, Kandahar and Helmand in particular. Hezbi Islami's combatants originated from a Pashtun mix. After many tactical flip-flops, both groups became affiliated with the Taliban following the US intervention. While Hezbi Islami continued to function according to the opportunistic aims of its leader, the Haqqanis consistently shared the common goal of the Taliban and ISI to 'liberate' Afghanistan and to reinstate the Taliban's Islamic Emirate rule. While branding it 'among the biggest threats to American and allied forces in Afghanistan,'[45] the Obama administration designated the Haqqani network a terrorist organization closely linked with the ISI in September 2012.[46] After the death of Jalaluddin in September 2018, the leadership of the group passed to his son, Sarajuddin Haqqani. Whereas Hekmatyar and his group joined Ghani's government in a *modus vivendi* in 2017, the Haqqani network persisted as a lethal force until mid-August 2021 when, in partnership with the Taliban, it assumed power in Afghanistan. As such, the US and its allied forces were locked into fighting on three fronts, as well as keeping a close eye on Al Qaeda and Islamic State-Khorasan (IS-K), which rose as another bloody anti-systemic actor, although in rivalry with the Taliban.

Further, there were problems in inter-force coordination and communications within the US-led forces. Since NATO's force contributions came from a range of countries, including those of East European members, they varied in their training and operational cultures.[47] They naturally could not be expected to coordinate and function uniformly even under a single NATO command in Afghanistan. The problem was aggravated by different lines of reporting that commanders of each force had to make to the overall commander in Afghanistan and his/her individual home authorities and NATO headquarters in Brussels. The same applied to the US commander, who had to report to various government agencies, most importantly the Defense Department and the White House, and to NATO's leadership. Quite often, the lines of communication were muddled by commanders under the overall commander in Afghanistan, as they filed their reports to their specific superiors in Washington and Europe.

When all this is considered in the context of reconstruction and diplomatic reporting in a similar fashion, confusion and crossed lines in communications generated their own difficulties. For example, just in the case of the US alone, at least three different sources from Afghanistan reported to Washington and to the White House: the military command, the embassy, and the CIA. They were not always on the same page due to inefficient inter-agency communication and alliance over common interests – a problem that also could not but bewilder their Afghan counterparts, who were able to exploit the resultant loopholes for their individual advantages. As Eikenberry points out, 'the lack of effective inter-force and inter-agency coordination could not but undermine the military's performance'.[48] Beyond this, as stated previously, the frequent change of commanders did not help cadre stability either, on whose vital support the ANDSF were very much dependent, especially following the start of the troop drawdown in 2011.

The inadequacy of strategic coordination was accompanied by constant troop shortages. Although Washington's troop deployment steadily grew to about 100,000 just prior to the drawdown in 2011, the same could not be said of European allied contributors. Repeated NATO meetings failed to secure more troops from some European members. In fact, several remained stubbornly unwilling to deploy their troops in danger zones in the south. Exemplifying this was the Dutch withdrawal from Uruzgan province in 2010. Faced with insufficient resources, Washington resorted to outsourcing a number of important security functions. It continued to arm and finance, as an exigency under the circumstances, a number of private security firms and local power-holders – 'strongmen' – and their militias. Both the security firms and armed groups operated independently of the Afghan central government, and the United States could not ensure control over them in the medium to long term. Over time, private contractors, who were often neither accountable nor effective, represented 69 per cent of the US Department of Defense's workforce in Afghanistan.[49]

Meanwhile, the role of local power-holders, with the power of extraction and dispensation, was pivotal in the running of the country during the entire period of US and allied involvement. Of the first group of thirty-two provincial governors appointed in 2002, at least twenty were leaders of armed groups, with most of the remainder having links to such leaders.[50] These figures thus benefited from both state-building and state weakness. Many such figures were elected into parliament, where they exercised disproportionate influence. This was the case throughout Karzai's era. Ghani tried to diminish the role of those who were still in positions of power and authority, but his efforts were undermined, partly through his ethnic bias, aimed at bolstering his own power and aggrandisement, and partly by the backlash that his actions generated. As mentioned in chapter 5, for example, one of the strongmen that Ghani took on was Atta Mohammad Nur, the powerful governor of Balkh Province in the north (2004–18). Ghani fired Nur in December 2017, but the latter's refusal to accept this precipitated a major governance crisis.[51] Nur finally made way for a loyalist Ghani appointee, but he still remained a powerful regional leader, whose help Ghani sought to save his government before its collapse in mid-August 2021. A similar tension existed between Ghani and his Uzbek vice-president Abdul Rashid Dostum, who was involved in notorious incidents. Ghani decided to distance himself from him, but in the end sought Dostum's assistance to save his government, which came to naught.[52] Under the circumstances, any attempt to curtail the power and influence of the strongmen proved to be half-hearted and largely unproductive.[53] The US and allied forces could not but be spectators, for the most part, in relation to the domestic political squabbles and power arrangements. From their perspective, with the insurgency raging and the US-led military strategy largely in disarray, any entrenched strongmen who were not supportive of the Taliban came to be seen as acceptable allies, which became a key element in America's exit strategy under Obama and remained so under Trump.

The ANDSF

Throughout its involvement, the United States exuded a degree of confidence about its efforts in building the Afghan National Defense and Security Forces (ANDSF), including the Border Guard and the Afghan Local Police, with a capacity to replace foreign combat forces. Yet by December 2012, when the US troop drawdown was under way, the situation looked so bleak that a Pentagon report said that only one of the Afghan National Army's twenty-three brigades was 'able to operate independently without air or other military support from the United States and [a] NATO partner'.[54] However, from that point, the US and NATO allies accelerated their investment in time, energy and capital to train, equip and expand the ANDSF. The NATO Training Mission-Afghanistan (NTM-A) emphasized qualitative improvement in increasing the training of non-commissioned officers, marksmanship and literacy training. By the end of 2014, when most of the allied forces had pulled out, the ANDSF's total strength was officially announced at 350,000. From 2013 onward, the ANDSF's combat capability markedly improved, enabling it to take the lead in some of the medium to large combat operations with a considerable amount of success. To enhance Afghanistan's self-reliant defensive capacity, the US also speeded up efforts to build the Afghan Air Force (AAF). As officially stated by NATO, by 2016, the AAF was expected to make 'significant progress towards becoming a professional, fully-independent, operationally capable and sustainable force'.[55] However, the ANDSF never achieved a level of capacity whereby it could keep the armed opposition at bay without guidance, logistics and combat back-up from the US and allied forces, with American air power serving instrumentally when needed.

The ANDSF was plagued with serious problems. For a start, it had been built in a piecemeal fashion by different foreign forces and subjected to varying logistic and operational orientations. It was not constructed, organized, trained and equipped within a coherent national framework. To reflect Afghanistan's demographic diversity, it was multi-ethnically composed, although not necessarily in the order of the sizes of different groups, raising occasional complaints from the Pashtuns about under-representation. The ANDSF perpetually suffered from a notable degree of desertion, internal ethnic, cultural and sectarian divisions, corruption, shortage of ammunition and, above all, lack of loyalty to corrupt, dysfunctional and ethnically imbalanced central governments that they were supposed to serve. It was also infiltrated by the opposition, resulting in fragging and 'green on blue' attacks. As it took on more fighting from 2014, foreign troops' casualties substantially decreased, but the ANDSF's rate of fatalities rose dramatically. In January 2019, Ashraf Ghani declared that more than 45,000 members of Afghanistan's security forces had been killed since he took over the presidency on 29 September 2014, compared to fewer than seventy-two international service members losing their lives.[56] This rate greatly increased following the signing of the February 2020 US–Taliban Doha Peace Agreement, as the Taliban and their partners took advantage of a ceasefire with the US and its allies and doubled their operations across the country. For the duration of the two decades of the war, an estimated 66,000 civilians and 47,245 Afghan security forces were killed. The insurgents' fatalities were put at 51,191, compared to 2,448 American troops, 1,144 allied soldiers, and 3,846 contractors who were killed. Seventy-two journalists and 444 aid workers also lost their lives during the same period.[57] These figures, however, do not include those combatants and civilians who died or committed suicide as a result of the secondary effects of the conflict. Additionally, there were thousands of combatants from all sides and Afghan civilians who were injured, many crippled for life, and who suffered from post-traumatic stress disorder.

Meanwhile, the ANDSF's size of about 300,000 proved to be misleading. It has now been revealed that the figure was inflated, as it included many 'ghost soldiers' and double counting based on corrupt practices by government officials and officers at different levels for pecuniary gain, which also inherently affected the ANDSF's strength and performance.[58] This was the case with all of the ANDSF's main components, although in varying degrees: the Afghan National Army (the largest element) and the Afghan National Police, including the Afghan Border Police and the Afghan National Civil Order Police. The latter two entities remained underdeveloped and poorly equipped for the task of ensuring the security of Afghanistan's borders, especially the frontier with Pakistan, and the civilian population. In addition, the Afghan Local Police that the United States and its allies, in conjunction with the Karzai government, established to operate locally in different parts of the country, were notoriously self-serving. A United Nations Development Programme (UNDP) report revealed in April 2015 'that Afghanistan government officials who headed oversight of the police suppressed complaints of corruption against the force and ... recommended their dismissal'. The report also expressed concern about why the UNDP's own division of the Law and Order Trust Fund of Afghanistan (LOTFA), which was funded by international donors between 2002 and 2015 with $3.6 billion to pay the salaries and other expenses of Afghan police, 'did not show' the report 'to senior U.N. officials after it was submitted in January' 2015. This also raised some serious questions about LOTFA's operations.[59]

The Afghan security apparatuses that performed with a noticeable measure of effectiveness were the Afghan NDS, along with the limited contingent of well-trained Special Forces. But even these forces were not free of internal abuses and were suspected of being penetrated, like other instruments of state power and the government, by the Taliban and their supporters. The NDS was mostly bankrolled by the CIA, with its main task being funding and arming militias to fight the Taliban. Many of these militias revolved around strongmen, some of whom not only engaged in turf war against one another but also pocketed much of the funding. The US military and the CIA were accused of 'turning a blind eye' to such anomalies.[60]

Complicating the situation further was the far less productive outcome of the internationally funded disarmament, demobilization and reintegration (DDR) programme. The DDR programme was established after 2003 as Afghanistan was awash with small and heavy weapons. It was managed and implemented by UNAMA, with assistance from ISAF. Its main targets were the government-linked, former armed groups that controlled different parts of the country, some of them remnants of the forces that had resisted the Taliban and the Soviet occupation, including, most importantly, the United Islamic National Front for the Salvation of Afghanistan (UINFSA). However, in an environment of growing national insecurity and unpredictability, a lack of strong government institutions post-Taliban, and fighting a rising insurgency, local commanders of these groups resisted the programme, and those running the programme could not entice people in many localities to volunteer for DDR. As a result, since the programme lacked the necessary power and means of imposition, it failed to be very productive.[61]

The Afghan security sector ultimately lacked what was necessary to operate with a reasonable degree of national unity, loyalty and purpose. A 2022 study reports that the ANDSF failure essentially reflected 'the structural shortcomings of Security Sector Reform (SSR) in Afghanistan and the overall international approach' in the country. 'SSR policies . . . sought to establish an adequate military and defense administration without sufficiently recognizing how structural shortcomings elsewhere would shape the effectiveness of the SSR programmes'. The study further concludes:

> The precarious strategic situation of the ANSF [also known as the ANDSF] was further compounded by the unilateral conduct of the United States under the Trump administration, with the 2020 Doha Agreement between the US and the Taliban demoralizing the remaining ANSF forces and motivating further desertions . . . [The ANSF's] ultimate failure and mass surrender to the Taliban was the inevitable outcome of an SSR programme that failed to be coordinated with other policy responses and was undermined by the diplomatic support for a government that had long lost its popular sway. The failure of SSR in Afghanistan ultimately embodies the failures of state-building in the country.[62]

For all the efforts of the US, along with its allies and Afghan partners, the broad 'light footprint' strategy that America initially adopted in its Afghanistan campaign, involving a reluctance to rapidly endow Afghanistan with its own security capability, proved glaringly inadequate. After the initial success, in the face of serious unforeseen impediments, the US lacked an appropriately resilient strategy. The strategic missteps were profound and excessive, and rectifying them was beyond the US's power capability. As the situation evolved, no amount of military investment or operations could possibly have led to a responsible and face-saving withdrawal, let alone a victory.

8

Conclusion

A Failed Project

A vital element in keeping the peace is our military establishment. Our arms must be might, ready for instant action, so that no potential aggressor may be tempted to risk his own destruction. . . . Yet we must not fail to comprehend its grave implications . . . we must guard against the acquisition of unwarranted influence . . . by the military-industrial complex. The potential for the disastrous rise of misplaced power exists and will persist.

Dwight D. Eisenhower[1]

The US intervention in Afghanistan, backed by NATO and non-NATO allies and the UN, was launched by hawkish Republican President George W. Bush primarily as a retaliatory action, to achieve two intertwined objectives. One was specifically to punish the perpetrators of 9/11 – Al Qaeda and, more prominently, its leader, Osama bin Laden, as the prime target – and their protectors, the ultra-extremist Taliban regime, and to ensure that Afghanistan was no longer a breeding ground and hub for terrorist groups. The other was to achieve this in conflation with the wider foreign policy goals of 'democracy promotion' and the 'war on terrorism'. The Bush administration viewed a combination of the two as not only mutually reinforcing but also imperative for cementing the post-Cold War position of the United States as the sole superpower, and central to creating a post-Cold War, America-centric world order. The original intention was to execute the Afghanistan campaign within a 'light footprint' approach in a relatively short period of time and in a cost-effective manner, yet it was also entangled with the two broader foreign policy aims.

After initial military success in deposing the Taliban regime and dispersing Al Qaeda, in partnership with the Afghan resistance forces, however, America's Afghan campaign faced serious, unforeseen impediments for which it lacked effective contingency plans. A failure to apprehend Bin Laden sooner rather than later and to help, in conjunction with receptive Afghan leaders, to put Afghanistan on a democratic and anti-terror war trajectory, as well as to stunt Pakistan's Afghanistan ambitions in a zone of frenemies and rivalries, enmeshed America in prolonged, complex processes of state-building and in fighting a robust, Pakistan-backed, Taliban-led insurgency. In this, the Bush administration's ideological and geopolitical preferences assumed greater importance than was necessary to assist in shaping Afghanistan's transition based on a sound understanding of the country's historical and prevailing realities and those of its region. From the time of the 2003 US invasion of Iraq as an extension of the 'war on terrorism', the Afghanistan campaign was relegated to secondary importance. It drifted in a direction that was not originally anticipated. The US and allied efforts faltered in contributing effectively to Afghanistan's transformation into a stable, secure, economically viable and self-sustaining state in a democratic and anti-terror alliance with the US.

Poor Afghan leadership, corrupt, dysfunctional governments, ethnic politics, the state–society dichotomy – functioning to benefit the leaders and their supporting elites rather than a majority of the impoverished and war-traumatized citizens – and other state-building anomalies in such areas as the opium industry, the economy, social services and the status of women, rapidly took hold in Afghanistan's transition. This was accompanied by serious US strategic missteps in crucial phases of the campaign, including troop and weapons shortages, slow and inadequate training and equipping of Afghan armed and security forces, and an indecisive policy in dealing with Pakistan. These variables generated increased opportunities for the Taliban-led insurgency to spread across the country and for Islamabad to maintain its patronage of the insurgents until final victory.

By the time Bush's Democrat successor Barack Obama took office in January 2009, the Afghanistan project was in serious trouble, with any chances of a victory fading. Afghanistan's political and security situation was deteriorating, and reconstruction processes, despite some earlier visible gains, were faltering. Obama had reason to conclude that the US was entangled in an endless and unwinnable war, and that it was now imperative to find a way out of the Afghan conundrum. He reset the US strategy to move from one of counter-terrorism and counterinsurgency, to *afghanize* the war, to maximize pressure on Pakistan, and to pave the way for a political settlement in pursuit of a respectable military exit. But it was too late to change the realities on the ground. The specific date that Obama set for withdrawal of most of the US and allied troops by the close of 2014 changed America's approach from one of a conditions-based to a time-bound involvement. This development clearly signalled to the Taliban and their supporters that the end of the US-led campaign was in sight.

The US assassination of Bin Laden just over 100 kilometres from Islamabad on 2 May 2011, strengthened Obama's resolve to draw down forces. While celebrated in Washington and in the allied capitals, the event constituted a setback for Pakistan in the sense that it lessened Islamabad's bargaining power vis-à-vis the US. But it did not diminish its commitment to the Taliban and their partners, while everything else in Afghanistan was moving in their favour. Against the backdrop of ongoing tensions and conflicts among the Afghan leaders and weaknesses of their governments – a chronic factor in the course of the historical evolution of mosaic Afghanistan – Obama's shift in strategy hardened the determination of the Taliban and their Pakistani patrons to stay on course. As the US and allied troop drawdown commenced in mid-2011, dropping their troop numbers from a peak of 147,000 to less than 20,000 to train and support Afghan forces by the turn of 2015, Washington in effect undercut its ability to pressure or persuade the Taliban to negotiate a viable political settlement with the governments in Kabul, which they had rejected as illegitimate puppets.

Peace agreement

However, the Taliban were now sufficiently emboldened to negotiate directly with a desperate US alone and largely on their terms. President Donald Trump's impulsive and impatient quest for an urgent, total pull-out provided them a unique opportunity. The handling of negotiations from the US side by the Afghan-American Republican, neoconservative old hand, Zalmay Khalilzad, proved disastrous. Hailing from a common Pashtun heritage with the Taliban, and under instructions to facilitate a complete troop exit before the end of Trump's first term in office with the aim of partly boosting the president's re-election chances, Khalilzad's eye was always on how to fulfil this imperative. He found the Taliban's deputy leader, Mullah Abdul Ghani Baradar, whom Islamabad had released from detention at Washington's request to head the Taliban negotiating team, a reasonably worldly figure and a reflection of what was promoted as the 'new Taliban', who were now supposedly more nuanced and averse to repeating their past mistakes and draconian rule. Hence, Khalilzad's conclusion of the infamous bilateral US–Taliban peace agreement of 29 February 2020, without the participation of the Afghan government.

Under this deal, which was signed in Doha, where the Taliban had been permitted to operate an office since 2013, and in the presence of US Secretary of State Mike Pompeo, the US gave the Taliban everything that they wanted. In return, the Taliban agreed to a ceasefire with the US and allied forces until their total withdrawal within fourteen months, and not to let Afghanistan be used for hostile actions against them, despite the Taliban's lack of control over many parts of Afghanistan at the time. The Taliban also made a non-binding pledge to enter an intra-Afghan dialogue for a negotiated settlement. This amounted to a hand-over of Afghanistan to the Taliban as America's peace partner at the expense of the US alliance with the Islamic Republic of Afghanistan and its government.

Although the Doha Agreement stated that the US did not recognize the 'Islamic Emirate of Afghanistan', this title was mentioned several times in the document. In effect, this amounted to America's de facto recognition of the Taliban as a legitimate, political and armed movement instead of a terrorist group, as it had been designated by Washington up to this point.

Khalilzad had been warned about the negative consequences of signing such an agreement seven months before its conclusion, but had brushed them aside. Mahmoud Saikal notes that at a dinner in Kabul on 28 July 2019, hosted by the former Afghan deputy foreign minister Jawed Ludin in honour of Ambassador Khalilzad, he asked the ambassador if the speculation was true that the US government was planning to sign a peace agreement with the Taliban, and if such an agreement included a mention of 'the Islamic Emirate of Afghanistan'. Khalilzad's response was affirmative, but he said that every time the title is mentioned, 'we clearly say we don't recognize it'. Saikal reminded him that the Taliban were 'fighting against the UN Security Council approved presence of the US/NATO forces in Afghanistan ... [and] that when a superpower signs an agreement with a rebel group it would raise the morale of the group and their regional supporters very high'. In the case of Afghanistan, it would embolden them to conquer the rest of the country, undermine the morale of the Afghan National Defense and Security Forces (ANDSF), and send out the wrong message to radical/extremist/terrorist groups in the region and around the world. He also told Khalilzad that 'withdrawal of the US/NATO forces should be based on the ... roadmap agreed at the 2010 NATO Summit in Lisbon'.[2] Khalilzad's response was 'how come your government leaders [President Ashraf Ghani and the Head of the High Council for National Reconciliation, Abdullah Abdullah] have said nothing about the agreement?' Regarding the Lisbon agreement, he said that President Trump was 'sensitive to agreements reached during the Obama administration'. Saikal made it clear to him that he (Saikal) was no longer with the government and cautioned him against signing such an agreement as it would be 'disastrous'.[3]

To alert some of the regional countries about the potential deal, Saikal records that on 6 August 2019, he conveyed his concerns to Vinay Kumar, the Indian ambassador in Afghanistan, in a WhatsApp message, who responded, 'We completely share your views and will convey them ... to Khalilzad ... as with other US interlocutors.'[4]

While Ghani may not have said anything to Khalilzad beforehand, he was furious when the agreement was signed and tried to abort it by resisting its implementation, largely for his own sake. But he was not in any position to deflect Washington's pressure. In analysing the contents of the signed agreement, many seasoned Afghan and non-Afghan scholars, observers and political figures subsequently repeated Saikal's early warnings, but to no avail.[5]

A calamitous ending

President Joe Biden, who had been advised by his Joint Chief of Staff General Mark Milley against withdrawal in view of the fragile state of the Afghan government and its military capability,[6] nonetheless decided to go ahead and implement the Trump-era peace agreement. Even in the wake of the Taliban's rapid territorial advances, Biden did not change his mind, except to extend the total troop withdrawal date by three months, primarily for logistical reasons and to make it coincide with the twentieth anniversary of 9/11. He seemed to be driven by a personal conviction that it was time that Afghans took care of their own security and governance, and that prolonging the US intervention would not make any difference.[7] In this, the president was also assured by Ghani's repeated assertions that his government would survive the foreign troop pull-out[8] and that he would personally never abandon his country as some of his predecessors had, referring mainly to King Amanullah's departure in the face of insurgency in 1928. Yet, Biden's evaluation was misplaced just as Ghani's assurances were delusional. Ghani's unpopularity and Machiavellian political manoeuvres to hold on to power, along with a lack of loyalty from the armed and security forces under pressure from the Taliban, had stripped him of credibility.

With the Taliban's success in briskly strangling and taking over major cities by conquering or winning over government commanders, and reaching the gates of Kabul, Ghani (accompanied by some of his loyalists, including National Security Advisor Hamdullah Mohib) fled the country to Abu Dhabi via Tashkent, Uzbekistan. The capital fell to the Taliban without a shot being fired on 15 August 2021. Ghani's departure completed the collapse of his administration and security forces. It also meant that any chance of making some kind of a deal with the Taliban evaporated, as was subsequently claimed by Khalilzad in defence of his actions.

Biden tried to justify the developments by declaring that America had achieved its fundamental intervention objective by preventing a repeat of 9/11. He took no responsibility for the chaotic and incompetent manner in which American and allied forces were withdrawn. Emergency operations were mounted to evacuate American and other allies' embassy staff and citizens, as well as many of their Afghan dependents who had worked with them over the years. The distressing images that emerged at Kabul airport were no less confronting and tragic than those at the end of America's Vietnam fiasco in 1975. The original goal of dismantling Al Qaeda and their equally terrorist Taliban protectors, and ensuring that Afghanistan would never again be a stomping ground for terrorist groups, was not acknowledged by Biden. He blamed the Trump administration for whatever happened, and Trump and his Republican Party condemned the Biden leadership for its catastrophic handling of the situation.[9] Biden's excuses were especially galling in the face of widespread branding of the Afghanistan campaign as a strategic blunder.[10] Thus, as humiliating as it was, a war conducted between a superpower and poor tribal forces, backed by a virtually bankrupt and deeply troubled Pakistan, ended for the US and its allies. It typified the loss of a small war by a big power.

Khalilzad badly misread – wittingly or unwittingly – the intentions of Taliban 2.0. He assumed, wrongly, that the Taliban had changed and their behaviour was likely to be moderated by the pro-Western changes that Afghanistan had experienced on America's watch. Given his long-standing involvement in, and study of, Afghanistan, he should have realized that the Taliban and their affiliates had never wavered in their commitment to reviving the Islamic Emirate of Afghanistan and enforcing their rule, as in the past, according to their unique, ultra-orthodox version of Islam and Sharia (Islamic Law). Indeed, the Taliban's core leaders had publicly made it clear that they did not believe in any form of representative government and were, instead, committed to traditional patriarchal rule, led by an Amir as the absolute ruler. Equally, he should have anticipated that the Taliban had not severed their intimate links with Al Qaeda, and that this time around they would be even more violent, exclusionary, misogynistic and ethno-tribally Pashtun supremacist than during their previous reign of terror in the 1990s. In their resolve to wipe out any vestiges of pro-Western changes, since their resumption of power the Taliban have done whatever it takes to bend Afghanistan's diverse population to their will under what amounts to a kind of totalitarian rule in the name of Islam.[11]

Khalilzad has been severely criticized for concluding the Doha Agreement with the Taliban. Loyalty to his American political masters did not allow him to foresee the deal's consequences for Afghanistan, for fighting terrorism and indeed for the reputation of the US and NATO. He now stands in an unfortunate position in history as a failed peacemaker who betrayed his birth country at the same time as letting down his adopted country, which now has to cope with the fallout of his actions. In his defence, he has blamed Ghani for fleeing the country and killing off any chances of a power-sharing arrangement with the Taliban,[12] just as Ghani has blamed Khalilzad for the whole debacle.[13]

However, Khalilzad and the Trump and Biden administrations are not the only actors that bear responsibility for what Afghanistan has become under the Taliban. Karzai and Ghani also stand out. As discussed in chapters 4 and 5, both presided over corrupt, dysfunctional governments and pursued policies that did little to promote national unity and viability. They had unprecedented opportunities to move Afghanistan towards a functioning state; instead they personalized, ethnicized and polarized politics to bolster their power. Karzai, nonetheless, unlike Ghani, stayed in Kabul following the Taliban takeover, along with the conciliatory Abdullah. Both he and Abdullah berated Ghani for his act of self-preservation and pusillanimity, and sought to present themselves as patriotic nationalists. But they have had no impact on the Taliban's mode of governance and behaviour. Under their strict watch, the Taliban tolerated them as symbols of political expediency to show that their regime is reasonable and therefore deserves international recognition.

Pakistan's interest

In contrast to the US and its NATO and Afghan allies, Pakistan finally attained its goal of 'strategic depth' through a proxy domination of Afghanistan. The perseverance of the country's military and

Inter-Services Intelligence (ISI) in standing by the Taliban and double-crossing the US paid off. They could now proactively seek Afghanistan's political, social, economic and security integration with Pakistan. In light of the Taliban's triumph, Islamabad rapidly moved to consolidate its gains. ISI Director General General Faiz Hameed visited Kabul in early September 2021,[14] for two main purposes. One was to sort out power distribution among the Taliban leaders, as there were reports of disputes between the Haqqani and core Kandahari Taliban leaders. The other was to oversee the Taliban operations in Panjshir Province, where the National Resistance Front (NRF), led by Ahmad Massoud, son of the legendary late Commander Ahmad Shah Massoud, had prevented the Taliban from taking over their stronghold. During Hameed's visit, the Taliban launched their indiscriminate, bloody offensive and occupied the centre of the province. Massoud and many of his inner circle and fighters made their way to Tajikistan in order to regroup and to continue their resistance to terrorism and Taliban's takeover.

To reap tangible dividends for having instrumentalized the Taliban, in August 2021, Islamabad established the Afghanistan Inter-Ministerial Coordination Cell (AICC – hereafter referred to as the Cell), which was formally announced in November. Its two main coordinators were Pakistan's National Security Advisor Moeed Yusuf and Special Representative for Afghanistan Mohammad Sadiq, a highly experienced and skilled diplomat, with years of accumulated insight into Afghanistan. Other Cell members came from ministries of the interior, foreign affairs, finance, commerce, customs, national logistics, civil aviation, state bank, frontier corps and the ISI and other security agencies. Directed by the prime minister's office, the Cell was ostensibly set up to operate as the 'policy planning and implementation hub for Pakistan's Afghan policy' to facilitate humanitarian help to Afghanistan.[15] But its main function was to implement Pakistan's key policy of ensuring that Afghanistan was organically linked to Pakistan, thereby also taking full advantage of Afghanistan's resources to assist Pakistan in its areas of energy deficiency, trade deficit, inflation and repayment of foreign loans. The Cell started to liaise with foreign governments, international organizations and non-governmental organizations (NGOs) on behalf of Afghanistan.

The Cell's members began to visit Kabul and other Afghan provinces regularly and summoned Taliban officials from time to time, either directly or through Pakistan's ambassador in Kabul, who played the role of viceroy, to discuss accountability. In mid-January 2022, Prime Minister Imran Khan directed different Pakistani agencies to export qualified and trained manpower to Afghanistan, especially in the fields of medicine, information technology, finance and accounting, as well as railways, minerals and pharmaceuticals.[16] Following his instruction, the Cell's conveners, along with some of its other members, visited Kabul in late January 2022, during which time they offered the Taliban capacity-building and training support in different sectors, including health, education, banking, customs, railways and aviation.

In conjunction with the Cell, on 27 June 2022, Imran Khan's replacement, Prime Minister Shehbaz Sharif, directed the authorities to import quality coal from Afghanistan to be paid for in Pakistani rupees, in order to fuel the country's power plants. The aim was not only to generate cheap electricity for Pakistan but also to prop up the country's dwindling foreign exchange to the order of over $2.2 billion annually in import bills by obtaining Afghanistan's high-quality coal at a bargain price of $90 per ton. When the inequitable nature of the deal was disclosed and criticized, the Taliban raised the export price of coal to $200 per ton. According to a Pakistani official, the rate of Afghanistan's daily coal exports to Pakistan by mid-2022 was 3,000 tons but was expected to rise to 20,000 tons when the mining of coal reached its full potential.[17] The financial profit for the Taliban was about $4 million a day, enough to boost their operational budget.

Further, weeks after the Taliban takeover and in conjunction with the Cell, Pakistan launched the regional process of the Ministerial Meeting of Afghanistan's Neighbours in Islamabad to gain wider support for its post-Taliban policies, and to advocate for regional and international engagement with the Taliban government. The second meeting of this process was held in Tehran in October 2021, during which the participants called for the formation of an inclusive government in Afghanistan. Its third meeting was hosted in Tunxi in March 2022 by Pakistan's main ally, China, which has been receptive to the Taliban as it has an interest in Afghanistan's natural resources.[18]

Parallel to the above endeavours, in December 2021 Pakistan hosted an Extraordinary Session of the Organisation of Islamic Cooperation (OIC) Council of Foreign Ministers on the humanitarian situation in Afghanistan.[19] But since only a few of the OIC's fifty-seven members had made modest contributions to the Afghanistan Humanitarian Trust Fund by late 2021, the meeting had more to do with Pakistan's diplomatic manoeuvrings to legitimize its role in Afghanistan as part of a wider policy of advocating international engagement with the Taliban.

Through the AICC and its tailor-made regional process, and in close coordination with the Taliban regime and regional players like China and Qatar, Islamabad has sought to wield widespread influence in managing Afghanistan. The AICC was certainly very active until early 2023, although following a bomb blast in January 2023 in a Peshawar mosque that killed more than a hundred people, and to which the Tehrik-e Taliban Pakistan (TTP) and the Afghan Taliban were rumoured to be linked, Sadiq resigned from the Cell.[20]

Islamabad's Afghanistan policy has by no means been risk-free, as occasional differences have surfaced between it and the Taliban over management of the disputed Durand border and the Taliban's camaraderie with the equally extremist TTP that has functioned as a radical Islamic challenge to Islamabad for years. Not surprisingly, since late 2022, Islamabad has voiced complaints to the Taliban about TTP's cross-border terrorism emanating from Afghanistan, with a call to stop it.[21] Yet Islamabad can take solace in the fact that just about all the Taliban leaders and commanders have lived and trained in Pakistan, with many of them intimately linked to the ISI, whose personnel and proxies are placed in the Taliban governance at all levels. In addition, since mid-July 2023, the Taliban have also begun a process of relocating TTP fighters to non-Pashtun provinces, especially in northern Afghanistan, in an attempt to *pashtunize* the whole of Afghanistan as the exclusive land of the Pashtuns and to boost security in those areas, to the dismay of their native inhabitants, and potential concern for the bordering Central Asian Republics. This has resulted in the shift of a troublesome problem from Pakistan to Afghanistan. However, the possible rise of a militant Pashtun nationalism on both sides of the Afghan-Pakistan border in pursuit of a wider Islamic Afghanistan touted by some Taliban leaders, could spell long-term danger for Pakistan.[22]

Resistance, and division

Having said this, the Taliban neither have the field free to themselves, nor are they a coherent group. Their totalitarian behaviour[23] has generated widespread domestic resentment and outside apprehension. Many Afghan women from urban centres, Kabul in particular, have expressed their public opposition from time to time, only to be confronted by the Taliban's repressive measures. In addition, several armed resistance groups have burgeoned. Although a discussion of these forces is beyond the ambit of this study, it is worth mentioning that the NRF, led by 34-year-old Ahmad Massoud, has been the most active. Educated at the British Royal Military Academy Sandhurst and with growing field experience, Massoud has firmly stated the NRF's policies as embodying the aspirations of a majority of the Afghan people, in particular the younger generation who form the bulk of the population. He claims that the NRF stands for a just and democratic transformation of Afghanistan as a responsible, constructive, multi-ethnic, and progressive sovereign Islamic state.[24]

The NRF's leadership is based in Tajikistan but its fighters, lately reported to number about 5,000, have been battling the Taliban in hit-and-run guerrilla operations in several north and north-eastern provinces, most importantly those of Panjshir, Badakhshan and Takhar. Its fighters originate mostly from those areas, and include some members of the Special Forces of the former administration. Neither the NRF nor any other resistance forces, such as the Afghanistan Freedom Front and the Afghanistan Islamic National and Liberation Movement, are at this stage materially backed by any outside sources. Their capability remains limited, although it is growing as the Taliban's repressive rule extends. The biggest challenge that the resistance forces currently face is the lack of sufficient coordination and unity. They are divided from within and between one another – critical impediments that need to be overcome – but something that has been a historical feature in Afghanistan.[25] The process of degrading the Taliban is expected to be long and arduous.

The Taliban, while lacking in both domestic and international legitimacy, are not a united entity either.[26] There are serious personality and ideological divisions among them, with the Haqqani group, led by Sarajuddin Haqqani, hailing mostly from eastern Afghanistan, and the core Taliban group emanating from Kandahar in the south, which includes Mullah Baradar and Defence Minister Mullah Mohammad Yaqoob, son of Mullah Mohammad Omar. The Haqqani leaders, who are very much in control of Kabul and the eastern provinces, have voiced occasional dissatisfaction with the Kandahar-based leadership of Mullah Haibatullah Akhunzada, who is supposedly the absolute Amir and commander-in-chief of the regime, and who has proven to be as hardline and reclusive as his predecessor, Mullah Omar.[27] This division has prompted the Taliban's chief spokesman, Zabihullah Mujahid, to refute that any discord exists, declaring unity behind Akhunzada.[28] All in all, the Taliban's rule and the interests of their Pakistani supporters are not based on firm and enduring foundations, as has also been the case with previous regimes in Afghanistan.

Regional reactions and implications

The success or failure of America's Afghanistan project did not concern only Afghanistan, the United States and Pakistan. America's adversaries – the Islamic Republic of Iran, Russia and China – closely watched the unfolding events in the country with great interest and concerns about America's motivation for wider regional and global objectives. They were wary of the processes of democratization and were not unhappy when the project eventually failed. They turned its shortcomings and loopholes to their advantage however they could. To secure strong influence, Tehran not only provided substantial reconstruction aid to Afghanistan, dispensed cash payments to President Karzai, and supported the main Shia groups in the country;[29] it also courted and supported certain receptive elements of the Taliban, especially from 2016. Iranian Foreign Minister Jawad Zarif confirmed this on the grounds that 'the Taliban will play an important role in the future of Afghanistan.'[30] Allegedly, Tehran also accommodated some members of Al Qaeda.[31] These actions were intended to make life difficult for the US in Afghanistan as part of Tehran's broader anti-American posture.

Similarly, there were reports that Russia paid some Taliban to kill American soldiers in Afghanistan.[32] Moscow also warmly supported Karzai's growing dissatisfaction with, and Ghani's increased coolness towards Washington in order to expand its relations with Kabul in an anti-US stance. Parallel to Khalilzad's peace mission, Moscow hosted several conferences on Afghanistan to promote its position as a peace-broker. Invited participants included not only Afghan personalities, a receptive Karzai among them, and Afghanistan's neighbours as well as India, but also the Taliban.[33] Beijing backed a peaceful resolution of the Afghan conflict, but with a firm eye on how and when the Afghan environment would become more profitable and receptive to it. It worked closely with its de facto ally, Pakistan, to ensure that the latter was not negatively impacted. Further, Beijing has shown interest in Pakistan linking Afghanistan to the China–Pakistan Economic Corridor of its Belt and Road Initiative as it also sees the country becoming part of the initiative. It is conceivable that the US and allied retreat incentivized Vladimir Putin to put into practice his plan of aggression against Ukraine, and Xi Jinping to become more assertive in challenging the US over its support of Taiwan and opposition to Chinese expansion in the South China Sea.

At the same time, the Afghanistan defeat shook America's Arab allies, especially in the Persian Gulf. Most members of the Gulf Cooperation Council, Saudi Arabia and the United Arab Emirates (UAE) in particular, were compelled to question the reliability of the US as their traditional security provider. They have increasingly seen the Chinese and Russian authoritarian models of governance and mode of operations as more attractive than America's faltering democratic system. Iran's full membership of the Shanghai Cooperation Organisation (SCO) in July 2023 was expected. But Saudi Arabia's announcement of its interest in linking to the SCO as a dialogue member, together with cooperating with Russia in the Organization of the Petroleum Exporting Countries Plus (OPEC+) to stabilize and raise oil prices, must have been unsettling for Washington. As, too, were the two visits in 2022 and 2023 of UAE President Mohammed bin Zayed Al Nahyan to Russia in order to expand relations, along with his remarks to the Russian leader that the UAE does not always follow the US.[34]

Lessons

Afghanistan was the first testing ground of America's involvement in democratic state-building and fighting terrorism in the immediate aftermath of 11 September 2001. The success or failure of the Afghan experiment thus had important implications for the future of not only Afghanistan but also America's broader foreign policy goals. The Afghanistan failure seriously dented US credibility. This raises the question of whether the Bush administration ever had any real intention in Afghanistan other than to start and use its intervention in that country to legitimize its wider and unmanageable foreign policy goals?

The most important lessons to be learned from the US's bitter Afghanistan experience are the following:

1. The need for a culturally sensitive form of democratic state-building, which is developed according to the specific social, cultural and political traditions of the country deeply rooted in its ethno-tribal and Islamic landscape. The centralized 'Western presidential' model of governance in Afghanistan completely failed to enfranchise the disparate ethnic and tribal communities in the country.

2. The need for greater attention to be paid to 'bottom-up' state-building, rather than purely 'top-down' democratic state institutions. In Afghanistan, the failure to build a widely based, well-educated indigenous civil society, and the dominance of Western paradigms of 'advocacy' NGOs could not generate the appropriate conditions whereby people could make the most of their civil liberties to engage with democratic practices. This was exacerbated by the lack of local governments which were fully integrated into a broader federalist rather than strong presidential system.

3. The need to recognize the fact that if the building of democratic institutions and processes was always to be compromised when it came into conflict with security objectives, democracy itself would be undermined. At various points in the state-building process in Afghanistan, the US used its power to influence outcomes in its quest for democratization, as exemplified by Khalilzad's activities. Furthermore, as Pakistan's relentless support of the Taliban became the centre of the nexus of instability and violence in Afghanistan, the contradiction between America's

democratic state-building rhetoric in Afghanistan and its concurrent wobbling towards a military-dominant Pakistan appeared not just hypocritical, but fundamentally damaging to any hope of helping Afghanistan to transform into a viable state.

4. The need to educate the public and establish the rule of law as a fundamental imperative for transition of a developing country into a viable state. Without such an imperative, any attempt at democratic state-building can only be futile, as the Afghanistan case shows.

5. Finally, state-building without transparent and well-regulated reconstruction and development aid in a post-conflict state is futile. One of the most significant problems to confront post-conflict reconstruction efforts in Afghanistan was not so much the lack of funding but rather of transparency around the destination of the funding that existed, leading to accusations of inefficiency and even open corruption in many sectors that the dominant figures, elites, companies and private security firms could harness to their benefit. This meant that Afghan citizens, particularly in rural areas, did not see a large improvement in their quality of life after the US intervention, and thus grew sceptical of the Karzai and Ghani governments, the US and NATO, and their combined ability to produce sorely needed improvements in their living conditions.

If Afghanistan's history and the US intervention tell us one thing, it is that no single group, with or without the support of an outside player, can succeed in creating the necessary conditions for modern statehood in the country. Only a multi-ethnic, popular-based coalition stands a chance of moving the country forward to stability, security, prosperity and national unity. The Taliban's rule by force and politics of exclusivity and ethno-tribal supremacy is doomed in the medium to long run, as has been the case historically with any other groups along different points of the political and social spectrum in the country. The future of Afghanistan rests on close cooperation between the internal forces of resistance and external pressure either to prompt the Taliban to change their ways for a negotiated political settlement or to endure internal and international alienation and eventually be driven out of the country, but at more unspeakable costs for the people of Afghanistan. As the situation stands, Afghanistan is at serious risk of becoming, as a June 2023 UN Security Council report warns, a terrorist nest under the Taliban,[35] to the deep regret of not only the Afghan people but also the international community. The US and its allies, who vowed to prevent Afghanistan from becoming such a nest, are very much on the back foot. The Taliban's Afghanistan is not the same as Islamic State (IS), which obliged the United States and Russia to lead two contrasting coalitions to at least disenfranchise it territorially if not ideologically and operationally. But the Taliban, who are as bad ideologically and practically as IS and its Khorasan branch (IS-K), are militarily better equipped and more battle-hardened than IS – courtesy of the US defeat in Afghanistan. Once again, the future of Afghanistan hangs in the balance.

Notes

1 Introduction: Big Power, Small War

1. 'Arrival of Afghan Prime Minister', Press Release 349, 24 June 1958, in *Department of State Bulletin*, Vol. 39, No. 995, 21 July 1958, p. 131, https://archive.org/details/sim_department-of-state-bulletin_1958-07-21_39_995/page/130/mode/2up
2. There is debate about whether it was an 'intervention' or 'invasion'. Because the US action had the support of the United Nations (UN) and that body has persistently referred to it as an 'intervention', this book has adopted the latter term.
3. Fifteen of whom were citizens of the Kingdom of Saudi Arabia, a de facto ally of the US since 1945.
4. Administration of President George W. Bush 2001–9, 'Highlights of Accomplishments and Results', December 2008, p. 3, https://georgewbush-whitehouse.archives.gov/infocus/bushrecord/documents/legacybooklet.pdf
5. No one is more vocal about this than the historian Francis Fukuyama, although the subsequent evolution of a multipolar world order with China and Russia challenging the US nullified many aspects of his thesis. See Francis Fukuyama, *The End of History and the Last Man*, New York: Free Press, 1992.
6. George W. Bush's National Security Advisor and subsequent Secretary of State, Condoleezza Rice, and Zalmay Khalilzad, advisor on Afghanistan, were also closely associated with this group.
7. Amin Saikal, 'A Mission for Moderates: How Three Threats Interlock', *International Herald Tribune*, 29 December 2003.
8. Guy Dinmore, 'Neocons Turn their Attention to Iran', *Financial Times*, 18 January 2005.
9. For a detailed discussion, see Amin Saikal, *Iran Rising: The Survival and Future of the Islamic Republic*, Princeton, NJ: Princeton University Press, 2021, chs 1–2.

10. For details, see Elisabeth Rosenthal and David E. Sanger, 'U.S. Plane in China after it Collides with Chinese Jet', *New York Times*, 2 April 2001.
11. 'Bush Statement on China, U.S. Spy Plane Incident', CNN.com./World, 2 April 2001, http://edition.cnn.com/2001/WORLD/asiapcf/east/04/02/bush.transcript/
12. David E. Sanger, 'U.S. Would Defend Taiwan', *New York Times*, 26 April 2001.
13. For a detailed account of an insider, see Richard A. Clarke, *Against All Enemies: Inside America's War on Terror*, New York: Free Press, 2004, especially ch. 6.
14. For a detailed discussion, see Michael Rubin, 'Taking Tea with the Taliban', American Enterprise Institute, 1 February 2010, https://www.aei.org/articles/taking-tea-with-the-taliban/
15. Gore Vidal, 'The Enemy Within', *Observer*, 27 October 2002, reprinted as 'UQ Wire: Gore Vidal's The Enemy Within', *Scoop*, 30 October 2002, https://www.scoop.co.nz/stories/HL0210/S00205/uq-wire-gore-vidals-the-enemy-within.htm?from-mobile=bottom-link-01
16. For details, see 'Joint Inquiry into Intelligence Community Activities Before and After the Terrorist Attacks of September 11, 2001', Hearings before the Select Committee on Intelligence, US Senate, and the Permanent Select Committee on Intelligence House of Representatives, S. Hrg. 107-1086, Vol. 1, 18, 19, 20, 24 and 26 September 2002, https://www.govinfo.gov/content/pkg/CHRG-107jhrg96166/html/CHRG-107jhrg96166.htm
17. Ahmed Rashid, 'Pakistan and the Taliban', in William Maley, ed., *Fundamentalism Reborn?* London: Hurst & Co., 1998, pp. 72–89, esp. pp. 84–9; Neamatollah Nojimi, 'The Rise and Fall of the Taliban', in Robert D. Crews and Amin Tarzi, eds, *The Taliban and the Crisis of Afghanistan*, Cambridge, MA: Harvard University Press, 2008, pp. 90–117.
18. For a detailed discussion, see Amin Saikal, 'Musharraf and Pakistan's Crisis', in Rajshree Jetly, ed., *Pakistan in Regional and Global Politics*, New Delhi: Routledge, 2009, pp. 1–19; 'Exploring Three Strategies for Afghanistan', Hearing before the Committee on Foreign Relations, US Senate, S. Hrg. 111-321, 16 September 2009, https://www.govinfo.gov/content/pkg/CHRG-111shrg55538/html/CHRG-111shrg55538.htm
19. Islamabad's objective in using this title was to indicate that the ethnic Pashtun Taliban, rather than the UINFSA, which was largely made up of non-Pashtun elements of Afghanistan's diverse population, were representative of the Afghan people. Interestingly, the UINFSA leadership team included some prominent Pashtuns, such as Haji Abdul Qadir, who previously was a commander of the Hezbi Islami Khalis faction which fought against the Soviet occupation in the 1980s.
20. 'Afghanistan: Building Stability, Avoiding Chaos', Hearing before the Committee on Foreign Relations, US Senate, S. Hrg. 107-708, 26 June 2002, https://www.govinfo.gov/content/pkg/CHRG-107shrg82115/html/CHRG-107shrg82115.htm
21. Anwar Iqbal, 'Afghan Army to Collapse in Six Months without US Help: Ghani', *Dawn*, 18 January 2018.
22. IS-K became active in Afghanistan from 2015 and have been responsible for some horrific suicide bombings and explosions, particularly in the Shia populated areas of Kabul and other parts of Afghanistan. IS-K's objective was to

ignite a sectarian conflict on top of wider fighting between the US and allied forces and those of the Taliban, and also indeed in opposition to the Taliban. For IS-K's background and activities, see Amira Jadoon with Andrew Mines, *The Islamic State in Afghanistan and Pakistan: Strategic Alliances and Rivalries*, Boulder, CO: Lynne Rienner, 2023; Antonio Giustozzi, 'The Islamic State in Khorasan', *Newsletter*, Italian Institute for International Political Studies, 27 June 2019, https://www.ispionline.it/en/publication/islamic-state-khorasan-23406

23. For a detailed discussion, see M. Nazif Shahrani, 'Introduction: The Impact of Four Decades of War and Violence on Afghan Society and Political Culture', in M. Nazif Shahrani, ed., *Modern Afghanistan: The Impact of 40 Years of War*, Bloomington, IN: Indiana University Press, 2018, pp. 1–17.

24. Amnesty International and International Commission of Jurists, *The Taliban's War on Women: The Crime against Humanity of Gender Persecution in Afghanistan*, London and Geneva: Amnesty International and International Commission of Jurists, 2023, https://www.amnesty.org.au/report-the-talibans-war-on-women-the-crime-against-humanity-of-gender-persecution-in-afghanistan/. This report accuses the Taliban of committing crimes against humanity in their treatment of women and girls.

25. Afghanistan International, 10 June 2023, https://twitter.com/mazdaki/status/1 610629589742813186?lang=en. Following this, General Mubin, who played a key role in the group's mid-August 2021 takeover of Kabul, was reportedly detained by the Taliban.

26. Jerry Dunleavy, 'U.S. Left Behind More than $7 Billion of Military Equipment in Taliban-Run Afghanistan', *Washington Examiner*, 8 March 2023, https://www.washingtonexaminer.com/restoring-america/courage-strength-optimism/us-left-behind-over-7-billion-military-equipment-taliban-afghanistan. Note, all dollar figures in the text are US dollars.

27. For a breakdown of the hardware, see Jack Detsch and Robbie Gramer, 'The U.S. Left Billions Worth of Weapons in Afghanistan', *Foreign Policy*, 28 April 2022, https://foreignpolicy.com/2022/04/28/the-u-s-left-billions-worth-of-weapons-in-afghanistan/

28. Gavin Butler, 'Taliban Officials Say their Army Will Include Suicide Bombers', *VICE*, 5 January 2022, https://www.vice.com/en/article/qjbjvp/taliban-army-will-include-suicide-bombers

29. 'Afghanistan: Nearly 20 Million Going Hungry', *UN News: Global Perspective Human Stories*, 9 May 2022, https://news.un.org/en/story/2022/05/1117812. See also SIGAR (Special Inspector General for Afghanistan Reconstruction), *Quarterly Report to the United States Congress*, Arlington, VA: SIGAR, 30 April 2023, esp. pp. 91–3, https://www.sigar.mil/pdf/quarterlyreports/2023-04-30qr. pdf

30. 'Afghanistan', *2022 Global Hunger Index*, https://www.globalhungerindex.org/afghanistan.html

31. United Nations Security Council, 'Fourteenth Report of the Analytical Support and Sanctions Monitoring Team Submitted Pursuant to Resolution 2665 (2022) Concerning the Taliban and Other Associated Individuals and Entities Constituting a Threat to the Peace Stability and Security of Afghanistan',

S/2023/370, 1 June 2023, p. 3, https://documents-dds-ny.un.org/doc/UNDOC/GEN/N23/125/36/PDF/N2312536.pdf?OpenElement

32. 'Remarks by President Biden on the Way Forward in Afghanistan', White House, 14 April 2021, https://www.whitehouse.gov/briefing-room/speeches-remarks/2021/04/14/remarks-by-president-biden-on-the-way-forward-in-afghanistan/

33. Robert Burns and Lolita C. Baldor, 'Joint Chiefs Chairman Calls Afghan War a "Strategic Failure"', *AP News*, 29 September 2021, https://apnews.com/article/joe-biden-bombings-kabul-taliban-terrorism-d1c939fc224a988dc6117ae4a70840e6

34. Karl Eikenberry, interview with the author, 7 October 2022.

35. Andrew Mack, 'Why Big Nations Lose Small Wars: The Politics of Asymmetric Conflict', *World Politics*, Vol. 27, No. 2, 1975, pp. 175–200, p. 177.

36. An Asia Foundation survey showed that in 2019, 85 per cent of Afghans had no sympathy for the Taliban. Mohammad Shoaib Haidary, 'Afghanistan is Losing Faith in the Taliban', *Fair Observer*, 27 October 2022, https://www.fairobserver.com/politics/afghanistan-is-losing-faith-in-the-taliban/

37. The term 'middle power' carries various connotations, depending on whether a state's status is measured hierarchically or horizontally in terms of power capability and influence. A classic definition pertinent to the discussion here is given by Martin Wight: 'A middle power is a power with such military strength, resources and strategic position that in peacetime the great powers bid for its support, and in wartime, while it has no hope of winning a war against a great power, it can hope to inflict costs on a great power out of proportion to what the great power can hope to gain by attacking it.' Martin Wight, *Power Politics*, edited by Hedley Bull and Carsten Holbraad, Leicester: Leicester University Press, 1978, p. 65. For further elaboration, see Amin Saikal, 'Iran: Aspirations and Constraints', in Adham Saouli, ed., *Unfulfilled Aspirations: Middle Power Politics in the Middle East*, London: Hurst & Co., 2020, pp. 113–34.

38. The most recent include Jonathan L. Lee, *Afghanistan: A History from 1260 to the Present*, London: Reaktion Books, 2022; Hassan Abbas, *The Return of the Taliban: Afghanistan after the Americans Left*, London: Yale University Press, 2023; Antonio Giustozzi, *The Taliban at War, 2001–2021*, London: Hurst & Co., 2022; Deepak Tripathi, *Afghanistan and the Vietnam Syndrome: Comparing US and Soviet Wars*, Cham: Springer, 2023; Carter Malkasian, *The American War in Afghanistan: A History*, New York: Oxford University Press, 2021; M. Nazif Shahrani, ed., *Modern Afghanistan: The Impact of 40 Years of War*, Bloomington, IN: Indiana University Press, 2018; Amin Saikal, *Modern Afghanistan: A History of Struggle and Survival*, 2nd edn, London: I.B. Tauris, 2012; Amin Saikal, *Zone of Crisis: Afghanistan, Pakistan, Iran and Iraq*, London: I.B. Tauris, 2014.

39. Including Saikal, *Modern Afghanistan*; Saikal, *Zone of Crisis*.

2 The Historical Context

1. Alexander Burnes, *Cabool: Being a Personal Narrative of a Journey to, and Residence in that City, in the Years 1836, 7, and 8*, Graz: Akademische Druck- u. Verlagsanstalt, 1842/1973, p. 144.

2. Philip Pettit, *The State*, Princeton, NJ: Princeton University Press, 2023, p. 2. Pettit's work provides a very comprehensive discussion of the state and its role from different theoretical and empirical angles.

3. For a detailed discussion, see Amin Saikal, 'Afghanistan's Geographic Possibilities', *Survival: Global Politics and Strategy*, Vol. 56, No. 3, 2014, pp. 141–56.

4. H.J. Mackinder, 'The Geographical Pivot of History', *Geographical Journal*, Vol. 23, No. 4, 1904, pp. 421–37.

5. See Arnold Fletcher, *Afghanistan: Highway of Conquest*, Ithaca, NY: Cornell University Press, 1965.

6. Henry Kissinger, *Years of Upheaval*, Boston, MA: Little, Brown and Co., 1982, p. 677.

7. For a detailed account, see Seth G. Jones, *In the Graveyard of Empires: America's War in Afghanistan*, New York: W.W. Norton, 2009.

8. Some Afghans have compared it with Switzerland largely due to its landlocked location, natural beauty and ethnic divisions, although any such comparison has been based on romanticization rather than reality. See Thomas Ruttig, 'All Together Now: Afghanistan is not Switzerland', *Foreign Policy*, 17 September 2010, https://foreignpolicy.com/2010/09/17/all-together-now-afghanistan-is-not-switzerland/

9. For an interesting discussion of this, see Raymond Frost, *The Backward Society*, London: Longmans, 1961, ch. 3; M. Nazif Shahrani, 'The State and Community Self-governance: Paths to Stability and Human Security in Post-2014 Afghanistan', in Srinjoy Bose, Nishank Motwani and William Maley, eds, *Afghanistan: Challenges and Prospects*, New York: Routledge, 2018, pp. 43–62; Louis Dupree, *Afghanistan*, Princeton, NJ: Princeton University Press, 1980, Part II.

10. 'Breakdown of Afghan Population as of 2020, by Ethnic Group', *Statista*, https://www.statista.com/statistics/1258799/afghanistan-share-of-population-by-ethnic-group/

11. The term 'Afghan' has become controversial since the appearance of the political ascendancy of the Taliban, as it refers to the Pashtuns and is not inclusive of the non-Pashtun segments of the Afghanistan population, some of whose figures have even questioned the validity of the name 'Afghanistan' for this reason.

12. Mountstuart Elphinstone, *An Account of the Kingdom of Caubul*, Vol. 1, Karachi: Oxford University Press, 1972, p. 205.

13. Mohammad Ali, *The Afghans*, Lahore: The Punjab Educational Press, 1965, p. 5.

14. Thomas J. Barfield has written a comprehensive study of Afghanistan in the context of *Asabiyyah* in his book *Afghanistan: A Cultural and Political History*, Princeton, NJ: Princeton University, 2010.

15. For a detailed social and cultural analysis of the Pathans or Pashtuns, see Anatol Lieven, *Pakistan: A Hard Country*, London: Allen Lane, 2011, pp. 371–401.

16. Lieven, *Pakistan*, p. 379.

17. 'Afghanistan Population 2023', *World Population Review*, https://worldpopulationreview.com/countries/afghanistan-population

18. For a detailed discussion of this, see Ravan Farhadi, 'Qadam-ha-ye Awshti bain-i Tajik ha' [Steps of Peace among the Tajiks], in Nasrine Abou-Bakre Gross, ed., *Qadam-ha-ye Awshti wa Massouliate-e Ma Afghan-ha* [Steps of Peace and our Responsibility as Afghans], Falls Church, VA: Kabultec, 2000, pp. 49–61.

19. This is comprehensively discussed from varying perspectives by several Afghan intellectuals and experienced policymakers in Abou-Bakre Gross, ed., *Qadam-ha-ye Awshti wa Massouliate-e Ma Afghan-ha* [Steps of Peace and our Responsibility as Afghans]. Also, see the discourse of another prominent Afghan historian, Ahmad A. Kohzad, *Men and Events: Through 18th and 19th Century, Afghanistan*, London: Forgotten Books, 2018.

20. Amin Saikal, *Modern Afghanistan: A History of Struggle and Survival*, 2nd edn, London: I.B. Tauris, 2012, pp. 19–22.

21. For a Pashtun historian's account of developments from 1747 to 1919 in Dari, see Abdul Hai Habibi, *Tarikhi Mukhtasari Afghanistan Az Zamnaha-i-e Qadeem Taa Istiqualal* [Short History of Afghanistan from Ancient Times to Independence], Peshawar: Khawar, 1989, pp. 204–315. For further details of Ahmad Shah's power assumption, empire-building and aftermath, see Mountstuart Elphinstone, *An Account of the Kingdom of Caubul*, Vol. 2, Karachi: Oxford University Press, 1972, pp. 279–352.

22. Martha Mundy, *Domestic Government: Kinship, Community and Polity in North Yemen*, London: I.B. Tauris, 1995, p. 107.

23. For a detailed discussion of Ahmad Shah's period and his sons' polygamic-based power rivalry and Anglo-Russian interventions, see Saikal, *Modern Afghanistan*, pp. 19–39; Jonathan L. Lee, *Afghanistan: A History from 1260 to the Present*, London: Reaktion Books, 2018, chs 3–5.

24. Summarizing the character of the 'Afghauns', at the time, Moutstuart Elphinstone wrote: 'their vices are revenge, envy, avarice, rapacity, and obstinacy; on the other hand, they are fond of liberty, faithful to their friends, kind to their dependents, hospitable, brave, hardy, frugal, laborious, and prudent; and they are less disposed than the nations in their neighbourhood to falsehood, intrigue and deceit'. Elphinstone, *An Account of the Kingdom of Caubul*, Vol. 1, pp. 330–1.

25. For an excellent discussion of the British rule of India, see Atul Kohli, *Imperialism and the Developing World: How Britain and the United States Shaped the Global Periphery*, New York: Oxford University Press, 2020, esp. ch. 3.

26. G.P. Tate, *The Kingdom of Afghanistan: A Historical Sketch*, Bombay: F.G. Pearson at the Times Press, 1911, p. 1.

27. For elaboration, see Hasan Kawun Kakar, *Government and Society in Afghanistan: The Reign of Amir 'Abd al-Rahman Khan*, Austin, TX: University of Texas Press, 1979.

28. For a discussion of this issue, see Habibi, *Junbushi Mashrotiat dar Afghanistan* [The Constitutionalist Movement in Afghanistan], Kabul: Government Press, 1364/1985.

29. For the plot and identity of the assassin, see Saikal, *Modern Afghanistan*, pp. 55–6.

30. For a detailed discussion of Amanullah's rule, see Saikal, *Modern Afghanistan*, ch. 3; Habibi, *Junbushi Mashrotiat dar Afghanistan*, ch. 3; Lee, *Afghanistan*, ch. 10. For a documentary account of Amanullah's success in gaining Afghanistan's full independence, see Azizuddin Wakil Populzai, *Negha-i ba Tarikh-i Atirdad-I Istiqlal* [A Glance at the History of Independence], Kabul: Government Press, 1368/1989.

31. Kalakani has become an object of veneration among some Tajiks since the return of the Taliban to power. For a first-hand narration by a note-taker from the time of events leading up to and enabling Kalakani to become king, see Robert D. McChesney, *Kabul Under Siege: Fayz Mohammad's Account of the 1929 Uprising*, Princeton, NJ: Markus Wiener Publishers, 1999. There is also a sympathetic description of Kalakani and events surrounding his rise to power and rule by a famous twentieth-century Afghan poet, also a noted historian and diplomat, Khalilullah Khalili, in Afzal Nasiri and Marie Khalili, eds and trans., *Memoirs of Khalilullah Khalili: An Afghan Philosopher Poet – A Conversation with his Daughter*, Virginia: Afzal Nasiri and Marie Khalili, 2013, esp. pp. 43–445.

32. For an excellent analysis of Amanullah's reforms and failure, see Leon B. Poullada, *Reform and Rebellion in Afghanistan, 1919–1929: King Amanullah's Failure to Modernize a Tribal Society*, Ithaca, NY: Cornell University Press, 1973.

33. Daoud's brother, Naim, was married to King Zahir's younger sister.

34. For a critical assessment of the political, social, cultural and economic situation between 1929 and 1953, see Mir Gholam Mohammad Ghobar, *Afghanistan in the Course of History*, Vol. 2, trans. Sherief A. Fayez, Alexandria, VA: Hashmat K. Ghobar, 2001.

35. Nikita Khrushchev, *Khrushchev Remembers: The Last Testament*, trans. Strobe Talbott, London: Andre Deutsch, 1974, pp. 298–300.

36. Ahamad Shah Massoud played a key role in the resistance to the Soviet invasion and to the Taliban and Al Qaeda before his assassination by Taliban-backed Al Qaeda agents on 9 September 2001. He was named a 'National Hero' after the fall of Taliban rule and has been described as the Afghan 'Napoleon'. For a detailed account of his life and ideals, see Sandy Gall, *Afghan Napoleon: The Life of Ahmad Shah Massoud*, London: Haus Publishing, 2021; and, in his own words, see Mohammad Eshaq, comp. and trans., *Nama-hai-e az Massoud Buzurg* [Some Letters from Great Massoud], Kabul: Matbai-e Maiwand, 1382/2003.

37. For an eyewitness account of Daoud's prime ministership and his departure, and the period of the democracy experiment, see Mir Mohammad Sidiq Farhang, *Khaterat-e Mir Mohammad Sidiq Farhang* [Memoirs of Mir Mohammad Sidiq Farhang], completed by Seyyed Mohammad Farooq Farhang and Seyyed Zia Farhang, Tehran: Tessa Press, 2015, pp. 368–431.

38. For a snapshot, see Alan Taylor, 'Afghanistan in the 1950s and '60s', *The Atlantic*, 2 July 2013, https://www.theatlantic.com/photo/2013/07/afghanistan-in-the-1950s-and-60s/100544/; John Kuroski, ed., '46 Fascinating Photos of 1960s Afghanistan Before the Taliban', *All that's Interesting*, 19 August 2021, https://allthatsinteresting.com/1960s-afghanistan

39. Prime Minister Maiwandwal subsequently emerged as a main critic of Zahir Shah for not relinquishing some of his powers in support of democratic development. When Daoud deposed the king and took power, Daoud's Parchami allies disliked the anti-communist Maiwandwal. Accused of plotting to overthrow the government, he was arrested and tortured to death by his Parchami interrogator. His death was presented as suicide, with a forced 'confession' and witness documents to substantiate his guilt. See Abdul Aziz Danishyar, ed., *The Afghanistan Republic Annual – 1974*, Kabul: Kabul Times Publishing Agency, 1974, pp. 82–8.

40. 'Afghanistan: Kingly Accomplishment', *Time*, 3 December 1965, https://content.time.com/time/subscriber/article/0,33009,842252,00.html

41. The signing of this treaty ended a long-running dispute that had complicated Afghanistan–Iran relations, although it has since flared up again during Taliban 2.0 rule. For the English text, see 'The Afghan-Iranian Helmand-River Water Treaty', 1973, https://www.internationalwaterlaw.org/documents/regional-docs/1973_Helmand_River_Water_Treaty-Afghanistan-Iran.pdf

42. For an insider's account of Zahir Shah's monarchy, see the memoirs of two brothers, Sayed Qassem Reshtia (1913–98) and Mir Mohammad Siddiq Farhang (1915–90). They were both historians who rose to political prominence when serving the government in different capacities under Zahir Shah's monarchy. Reshtia reached the position of deputy prime minister and Farhang ended his career as ambassador to Yugoslavia. They were both reformists of a kind, but from different standpoints. Whereas Reshtia functioned largely in compliance with the political wind of the time, Farhang's activism for change landed him in prison twice in 1933 and 1952–6 (during this latter period, Reshtia was in charge of the government press and information, located in Daoud's cabinet). See Sayed Qassem Reshtia, *Khatera-e Siyas-e, 1932–1992* [The Political Memoirs of Sayed Qassem Reshtia, Afghan Historian and Diplomat, Period of 1932–1992], completed by Mohammad Qawee Koshan, Alexandria, VA: American Sepedi Press, 1997; Farhang, *Khaterat-e Mir Mohammad Sidiq Farhang*.

43. Farhang, *Khaterat-e Mir Mohammad Sidiq Farhang*, pp. 431–79.

44. For a first-hand discussion of Daoud's growing distrust of the Soviet Union, his fear of Soviet backing of the PDPA to seize power through a coup, and confrontation with the Soviet leaders, see Abdul Samad Ghaus, *The Fall of Afghanistan: An Insider's Account*, Lincoln, NE: University of Nebraska Press, 1988, pp. 159–83. Ghaus was deputy foreign minister under Daoud.

45. See Amin Saikal, *The Rise and Fall of the Shah: Iran from Autocracy to Religious Rule*, Princeton, NJ: Princeton University Press, 2009, esp. pp. 143–5.

46. For details of Daoud's republican rule, see Saikal, *Modern Afghanistan*, ch. 7.

47. For an Afghan historian's details and personal experience of the PDPA coup and the growth of the jihadi resistance to it, see Nasry Haq Shinas, *Tahawulat-e Siasi Jihadi-e Afghanistan* [Political Developments of Jihad in Afghanistan], West Germany: The Islamic Society of Afghan Students and Refugees, 1365/1986.

48. For an account of KHAD and Najibullah as its head, see M. Hassan Kakar, *Afghanistan: The Soviet Invasion and the Afghan Response, 1979–1982*, Berkeley, CA: University of California Press, 1995, ch. 9.

49. Amin Saikal, *Iran at the Crossroads*, Cambridge: Polity Press, 2016, p. 75.

50. Christina Lamb, *Waiting for Allah: Pakistan's Struggle for Democracy – Benazir Bhutto and Pakistan*, London: Penguin Books, 1991, p. 224.

51. In a cable to Washington, Archer Blood conveyed the possibility of Hafizullah Amin switching to the US to reduce his overdependence on the USSR. See Peter Baker, 'Why Did Soviets Invade Afghanistan? Documents Offer History Lesson for Trump', *New York Times*, 29 January 2019.

52. For a discussion of how the invasion decision was made, see Pierre Bienaimé, 'The Politburo Approved the Soviet Invasion of Afghanistan 35 Years Ago Today', *Insider*, 13 December 2014, https://www.businessinsider.com/the-politburo-approved-the-soviet-invasion-of-afghanistan-35-years-ago-today-2014-12. For further details of the PDPA rule and the Soviet invasion and its aftermath, see Saikal, *Modern Afghanistan*, chs 8–9.

53. For George F. Kennan's view of the Soviet invasion, see 'George F. Kennan, on Washington's Reaction to the Afghan Crisis: "Was This Really Mature Statesmanship?"', *New York Times*, 1 February 1980, https://www.nytimes.com/1980/02/01/archives/george-f-kennan-on-washingtons-reaction-to-the-afghan-crisis-was.html

54. Jimmy Carter, 'Address to the Nation on the Soviet Invasion of Afghanistan', *The American Presidency Project*, 4 January 1980, https://www.presidency.ucsb.edu/documents/address-the-nation-the-soviet-invasion-afghanistan

55. The Soviet invasion occurred at a time when President Carter was also battling a serious challenge from Khomeini's Islamic government. The Iranian leader backed his militant supporters' overrunning of the US embassy in Tehran and taking 52 US personnel hostage, causing a 'hostage crisis' that lasted 440 days, humiliating the Carter administration.

56. For details, see Ronald Reagan, 'Evil Empire Speech', *Voices of Democracy: The U.S. Oratory Project*, 8 March 1983, https://voicesofdemocracy.umd.edu/reagan-evil-empire-speech-text/

57. See Julie Lowenstein, 'US Foreign Policy and the Soviet-Afghan War: A Revisionist History', Harvey M. Applebaum '59 Award, Yale University, 2016, p. 16, https://elischolar.library.yale.edu/cgi/viewcontent.cgi?article=1045&context=applebaum_award

58. Rachel Bronson, *Thicker than Oil: America's Uneasy Partnership with Saudi Arabia*, New York: Oxford University Press, 2006, p. 233.

59. For his detailed view, see Turki Al Faisal Al-Saud with Michael Field, *The Afghanistan File*, Cowes, UK: Arabian Publishing, 2021.

60. John K. Cooley, *Unholy Wars: Afghanistan, America and International Terrorism*, London: Pluto Press, 1999, p. 2.

61. Zeeshan Haider, 'Backlash Seen from Pakistani Mosques Assault', *Reuters*, 11 July 2007, https://www.reuters.com/article/us-pakistan-mosque-backlash-idUSISL13227720070711

62. Serge Schmemann, 'Gorbachev Says U.S. Arms Note is Not Adequate', *New York Times*, 26 February 1986.

63. Quoted in Steve Coll, *Ghost Wars: The Secret History of the CIA, Afghanistan, and Bin Laden, from the Soviet Invasion to September 10, 2001*, New York: Penguin Books, 2004, p. 235.

64. For a full eyewitness account of an Afghan major general at the time, see Stir Great General Mohammad Nabi 'Azemi, *Urdo wa Syassat dar sai daha-i akheer-I Afghanistan* [Army and Politics: In the Three Decades in Afghanistan], Vol. 2, Peshawar: Sabah Ketabkhanu, 1376/1997, pp. 405–34.

65. For a comprehensive study of the Soviet invasion of and defeat in Afghanistan, see Artemy M. Kalinovsky, *A Long Goodbye: The Soviet Withdrawal from Afghanistan*, Cambridge, MA: Harvard University Press, 2011.

66. For a detailed account, see Avinash Paliwal, 'Murder of a President: How India and the UN Mucked up Completely in Afghanistan', *Quartz India*, 30 October 2017, https://qz.com/india/1114676/najibullahs-failed-escape-how-india-and-the-un-mucked-up-completely-in-afghanistan/

67. Lieven, *Pakistan*, p. 162.

68. Sune Engel Rasmussen, 'Fear and Doubt as Notorious "Butcher of Kabul" Returns with Talk of Peace', *Guardian*, 5 May 2017. For details of human rights abuses during this period, see Human Rights Watch, *Blood-stained Hands: Past Atrocities in Kabul and Afghanistan's Legacy of Impunity*, 6 July 2005, esp. Section III, 'The Battle for Kabul: April 1992–March 1993', https://www.hrw.org/report/2005/07/06/blood-stained-hands/past-atrocities-kabul-and-afghanistans-legacy-impunity. For eyewitness accounts, see Afghanistan Justice Project, *Casting Shadows: War Crimes and Crimes against Humanity, 1978–2001*, 2005, esp. pp. 110–15, https://www.opensocietyfoundations.org/uploads/291156cd-c8e3-4620-a5e1-d3117ed7fb93/ajpreport_20050718.pdf

69. Taliban, the plural of Talib, means Islamic religious students.

70. 'Taliban Government in Afghanistan: Background and Issues for Congress', Congressional Research Service Report R46955, 2 November 2021, p. 1, https://crsreports.congress.gov/product/pdf/R/R46955

71. For a Taliban version of their rule and the events leading up to and after 9/11, see Abdul Salam Zaeef, *My Life with the Taliban*, edited by Alex Strick van Linschoten and Felix Kuehn, Melbourne: Scribe, 2010.

72. Saikal, *The Rise and Fall of the Shah*, p. 165.

73. Barton Gellman and Dana Priest, 'U.S. Strikes Terrorist-linked Sites in Afghanistan, Factory in Sudan', *Washington Post*, 21 August 1998.

74. For a detailed discussion, see Steve Coll, 'U.S.–Taliban Talks', *The New Yorker*, 17 February 2011, https://www.newyorker.com/magazine/2011/02/28/u-s-taliban-talks

75. 'Afghan Opposition Leader Holds Talks with French Leaders', 4 April 2001, AP Archive, YouTube, 22 July 2015, https://www.youtube.com/watch?v=D50hcLtoPE4. For details, see Gall, *Afghan Napoleon*, ch. 22.

76. Steven Erlanger, 'In Afghan Refugee Camp, Albright Hammers Taliban', *New York Times*, 19 November 1997.

77. Zalmay Khalilzad, 'Afghanistan: Time to Reengage', *Washington Post*, 7 October 1996.

78. Amin Saikal, 'Don't Cave In to the Taliban', *New York Times*, 18 October 2007.

79. Amin Saikal, 'The Role of Outside Actors in Afghanistan', *Middle East Policy*, Vol. 7, No. 4, 2000, pp. 50–7.

80. 'Afghanistan GDP – Gross Domestic Product', Countryeconomy.com, 2000, https://countryeconomy.com/gdp/afghanistan?year=2000#:~:text=The%20GDP%20figure%20in%202000,in%201999%2C%20it%20was%20%24135

81. 'Afghanistan', UNESCO Institute for Statistics, 2000, http://uis.unesco.org/en/country/af

3 Intervention, Post-Taliban Democratization and the 'War on Terror'

1. A.D. Lindsay, *The Essentials of Democracy*, London: Oxford University Press, 1930, p. 49.
2. For an informative discussion of Osama bin Laden, his Al Qaeda network, their plan for the 9/11 attacks and the aftermath up to America's killing of Bin Laden, see Nelly Lahoud, *The Bin Laden Papers: How Abbottabad Raid Revealed the Truth about Al-Qaeda, Its Leader and His Family*, New Haven, CT: Yale University Press, 2022, esp. part 1.
3. For an authoritative account of the CIA's involvement in the initial phase of the US Afghanistan campaign, see Robert L. Grenier, *88 Days to Kandahar: A CIA Diary*, New York: Simon & Schuster, 2015.
4. For a comprehensive account, see Bob Woodward, *Bush at War*, New York: Simon & Schuster, 2002, esp. sections 1–7. It also provides the cast of characters involved in the decision-making process, pp. xvii–xix.
5. For a discussion of this point, see Amin Saikal, 'Securing Afghanistan's Border', *Survival: Global Politics and Strategy*, Vol. 48, Issue 1, 2006, pp. 129–42.
6. 'Pakistani Leader Claims U.S. Threat After 9/11', *New York Times*, 22 September 2006.
7. For a detailed account of Armitage's message and the way Musharraf decided to support the US in fighting terrorism, see Pervez Musharraf, *In the Line of Fire: A Memoir*, London: Simon & Schuster, 2006, pp. 201–7.
8. Jim Mattis and Bing West, *Call Sign Chaos: Learning to Lead*, New York: Random House, 2021, p. 57.
9. Mattis and West, *Call Sign Chaos*, p. 72.
10. For detailed discussion of this and Camp Rhino operations, see Mattis and West, *Call Sign Chaos*, pp. 53–76.
11. Mattis and West, *Call Sign Chaos*, p. 71.
12. For a detailed account of this and Karzai's close relationship and joint operations with the US and its Special Forces, and his role in putting an Afghan face on the US intervention, which he claimed was not an 'occupation' during the southern phase of the American campaign, see Charles H. Briscoe, Richard L. Kiper, James A. Schroder and Kalev I. Sepp, *Weapon of Choice: U.S. Army Special Operations Forces in Afghanistan*, Fort Leavenworth, KS: Combat Studies Institute Press, 2003, p. 107, and ch. 3.
13. Mattis and West, *Call Sign Chaos*, pp. 74, 75.
14. Ali had previously served as a UINFSA commander but had been accused of 'criminal' activities and vacillating loyalty and was being monitored by Human Rights Watch. He was subsequently elected to Afghanistan's lower house of parliament in 2005 and played an important role in the Karzai and Ashraf Ghani administrations.
15. For a full account of the episode from Mattis's perspective, see Mattis and West, *Call Sign Chaos*, pp. 74-6.
16. For a brief description of Hazrat Ali, see 'Profiles of Afghan Power Brokers', CAP (Continuous Article Publishing), 26 October 2009, https://www.americanprogress.org/article/profiles-of-afghan-power-brokers/#10

17. Karl Eikenberry, interview with the author, 14 May 2022.
18. 'Tora Bora Revisited: How We Failed to get Bin Laden and Why It Matters Today', A Report to Members of the Committee on Foreign Relations, US Senate, 111th Congress, 30 November 2009, Washington: U.S. Government Printing Office, 2009, p. 1, https://www.govinfo.gov/content/pkg/CPRT-111SPRT53709/html/CPRT-111SPRT53709.htm
19. 'Stephen J. Hadley Looks Back on 9/11, Iraq, and Afghanistan', Council on Foreign Relations, 22 October 2014, https://www.cfr.org/event/stephen-j-hadley-looks-back-911-iraq-and-afghanistan
20. George W. Bush, 'President Delivers State of the Union Address', White House, 29 January 2002, https://georgewbush-whitehouse.archives.gov/news/releases/2002/01/20020129-11.html
21. George W. Bush, 'President Delivers "State of the Union"', White House, 28 January 2003, https://georgewbush-whitehouse.archives.gov/news/releases/2003/01/20030128-19.html
22. 'Failed States 2023', *World Population Review*, https://worldpopulationreview.com/country-rankings/failed-states. For a detailed discussion of what constitutes a failed state, see Robert I. Rotberg, ed., *When States Fail: Causes and Consequences*, Princeton, NJ: Princeton University Press, 2004.
23. For Bush's view and discussion of it, see William Schneider, 'Not Exactly a Bush Flip-Flop', *The Atlantic*, 1 October 2001, https://www.theatlantic.com/politics/archive/2001/10/not-exactly-a-bush-flip-flop/377745/; Paul D. Miller, 'Bush on Nation-building and Afghanistan', *Foreign Policy*, 17 November 2010, https://foreignpolicy.com/2010/11/17/bush-on-nation-building-and-afghanistan/
24. He was very clear about the linkage between the Afghanistan intervention and wider war on terrorism, saying: 'From the beginning of the war on terrorism, we have stressed the importance of understanding the nature of our enemy as a network. . . . [Al-Qaeda] is more analogous to a disease that has infected many parts of a healthy body. . . . You cannot simply cut out one infected area and declare victory, but success in one area can lead to success in others.' 'Afghanistan: Building Stability, Avoiding Chaos', Hearing before the Committee of Foreign Relations, US Senate, S. Hrg. 107-708, 26 June 2002, https://www.govinfo.gov/content/pkg/CHRG-107shrg82115/html/CHRG-107shrg82115.htm
25. 'Afghanistan Does Not Need Marshall Plan: Powell', *Zee News*, 8 December 2001, https://zeenews.india.com/entertainment/celebrity/jennifer-aniston-earned-more-than-angelina-jolie-in-2008_27801.html/amp
26. Jonathan Monten, 'The Roots of the Bush Doctrine: Power, Nationalism and Democracy Promotion in U.S. Strategy', *International Security*, Vol. 29, No. 4, 2005, pp. 112–56.
27. Cited in US Government, *The National Security Strategy of the United States of America*, September 2002, p. 1, https://georgewbush-whitehouse.archives.gov/nsc/nss/2002/nss1.html
28. George W. Bush, 'President Bush Discusses Progress in Afghanistan, Global War on Terror', White House, 15 February 2007, https://georgewbush-whitehouse.archives.gov/news/releases/2007/02/20070215-1.html

29. For the full text, see United Nations Security Council, 'Agreement on Provisional Arrangements in Afghanistan Pending the Re-Establishment of Permanent Government Institutions', S/2001/1154, 5 December 2001, https://peacemaker.un.org/sites/peacemaker.un.org/files/AF_011205_AgreementProvisionalArrangementsinAfghanistan%28en%29.pdf

30. Barnett R. Rubin, 'Crafting a Constitution for Afghanistan', *Journal of Democracy*, Vol. 15, No. 3, 2004, pp. 5–19, at p. 6.

31. Rubin, 'Crafting a Constitution', p. 6.

32. Amin Saikal, 'The United Nations and Democratization in Afghanistan', in Edward Newman and Roland Rich, eds, *The UN Role in Promoting Democracy: Between Ideals and Reality,* Tokyo: United Nations University Press, 2004, pp. 320–38, at pp. 326–7.

33. For a detailed account of this episode, see James Dobbins, 'Negotiating with Iran: Reflections from Personal Experience', *Washington Quarterly*, Vol. 33, No. 1, 2010, pp. 149–62.

34. Quoted in 'Filling the Vacuum: The Bonn Conference', *Frontline*, 2022, https://www.pbs.org/wgbh/pages/frontline/shows/campaign/withus/cbonn.html

35. ICG (International Crisis Group), *Afghanistan's Flawed Constitutional Process*, Report 56, Kabul/Brussels: ICG, 12 June 2003, pp. 11–12.

36. See, for example, Marin Strmecki, interview, 'Creating a Government', *Newshour with Jim Lehrer*, PBS, 21 December 2001; Ali A. Jalali, 'The Legacy of War and the Challenge of Peace Building', in Robert I. Rotberg, ed., *Building a New Afghanistan*, Washington, DC: Brookings Institution Press, 2007, pp. 22–55, at p. 30.

37. Charles H. Norchi, 'Toward the Rule of Law in Afghanistan: The Constitutive Process', in John D. Montgomery and Dennis A. Rondinelli, eds, *Beyond Reconstruction in Afghanistan: Lessons from Development Experience*, New York: Palgrave Macmillan, 2004, pp. 115–31, at p. 117.

38. Rubin, 'Crafting a Constitution', p. 7. For how many Loya Jirgas have been held and for what purpose as well as their functions and outcomes, acting more as legitimation than decision-making bodies in the course of Afghan history, see Mohammad Alam Faizzaad, *Jirga hai-e buzrurg milli-e Afghanistan (loya jirga haa)* [The Large National Gatherings of Afghanistan], Lahore: no publisher, 1368/1989.

39. Khalilzad was already praising the Loya Jirga as a panacea for Afghanistan's lack of democracy in 2000, before the intervention. Khalilzad argued that the US should bolster nascent democratic tendencies among moderate Afghans by lending support to 'the convening of a traditional Afghan grand assembly for resolving the Afghan conflict and for the selection of a broadly acceptable transitional government. Such an assembly, a *Loya Jirgha* [sic] would help bring together Afghans of different tribal, religious, and ethnic backgrounds and foster a common Afghan identity.' Zalmay Khalilzad and Daniel Byman, 'Afghanistan: The Consolidation of a Rogue State', *Washington Quarterly*, Vol. 23, No. 1, 2000, pp. 65–78, at pp. 76–7.

40. Human Rights Watch, 'Q & A on Afghanistan's Loya Jirga Process', 17 April 2002, https://www.hrw.org/legacy/press/2002/04/qna-loyagirga.pdf; M. Jamil Hanifi, 'Editing the Past: Colonial Production of Hegemony through the "Loya Jerga" in Afghanistan', *Iranian Studies*, Vol. 37, No. 2, 2004, pp. 295–322.

41. Norchi, 'Towards the Rule of Law', p. 118; Lauryn Oates and Isabelle Solon Helal, *At the Cross-roads of Conflict and Democracy: Women and Afghanistan's Constitutional Loya Jirga*, Montreal: Rights and Democracy, 2004, p. 16, https://publications.gc.ca/collections/Collection/E84-14-2004E.pdf. Oates and Helal claim that *shuras* are ad-hoc forms of decision-making which are generally comprised of village elders, landlords, khans and military commanders, and rarely include women.

42. For non-governmental commentary on the make-up of the transitional government see, for example, Human Rights Watch, 'Afghanistan: Analysis of New Cabinet', 20 June 2002, http://hrw.org/english/docs/2002/06/20/afghan4051.htm

43. Rubin, 'Crafting a Constitution', p. 10; Human Rights Watch News, 'Afghanistan: Loya Jirga off to a Shaky Start', 13 June 2002, http://hrw.org/english/docs/2002/06/13/afghan4039.htm; Oates and Helal, *At the Cross-roads*, p. 15.

44. Saikal, 'The UN and Democratization', p. 331. See also Carlotta Gall, 'Former Afghan King Rules Out All but Symbolic Role', *New York Times*, 11 June 2002; Camelia Entekhabi-Fard, 'As Afghan Council Proceeds, American Predicts a Strong President', *EurasiaNet*, 22 December 2003, https://eurasianet.org/as-afghan-council-proceeds-american-predicts-strong-president; S. Frederick Starr and Marin J. Strmecki, 'Afghan Democracy and Its First Missteps', *New York Times*, 14 June 2002.

45. Ahmed Rashid, 'Afghanistan's Former King Says He Will Not Seek Political Role', *Wall Street Journal*, 11 June 2002.

46. Camelia Entekhabi-Fard cited a student at Kabul University who declared at the time of the ELJ, 'I feel the United States and United Kingdom rigged our vote. I feel Karzai is dishonest and he is dealing with foreigners because he loves power. I loved him before but now I am confused.' Camelia Entekhabi-Fard, 'Accusations of American Meddling Mar Afghan Council', *EurasiaNet*, 6 December 2002, https://eurasianet.org/accusations-of-american-meddling-mar-afghan-council

47. Oates and Helal, *At the Cross-roads*, p. 12.

48. Cheryl Benard and Nina Hachigan, eds, *Democracy and Islam in the New Constitution of Afghanistan*, Conference Proceedings, Santa Monica, CA: RAND Corporation, 2003, p. 3. In addition to the editors, the authors were Khaled M. Abou El Fadl, Said Arjomand, Nathan Brown, Jerrold Green, Donald Horowitz, Michael Rich, Barnett Rubin and Birol Yesilada.

49. See for example Carlotta Gall, 'New Afghan Constitution Juggles Koran and Democracy', *New York Times*, 19 October 2003.

50. ICG (International Crisis Group), *Afghanistan: The Constitutional Loya Jirga*, Afghanistan Briefing, Kabul/Brussels: ICG, 12 December 2003, p. 10.

51. ICG, *Afghanistan: The Constitutional Loya Jirga*, p. 4.

52. Grant Kippen, 'The 2004 Presidential Election: On the Road to Democracy in Afghanistan', Centre for the Study of Democracy, Kingston: Queen's University, 2005, p. 6.

53. Amin Saikal and William Maley, 'The President Who Would be King', *New York Times*, 6 February 2008.

54. Rubin, 'Crafting a Constitution', p. 17.

55. Ali Wardak, 'Building a Post-war Justice System in Afghanistan', *Crime, Law and Social Change*, Vol. 41, 2004, pp. 319–41.

56. ICG, *Afghanistan's Flawed Constitutional Process*, p. 10.

57. Constitution of Afghanistan 2004, chapter 1, article 3, http://www.asianlii.org/af/legis/const/2004/1.html#A002n

58. Constitution of Afghanistan 2004, chapter 1, article 2(2).

59. Larry P. Goodson, 'Afghanistan in 2003: The Taliban Resurface and a New Constitution is Born', *Asian Survey*, Vol. 44, No. 1, 2004, pp. 14–22, at p. 20.

60. Oates and Helal, *At the Cross-roads*, p. 27.

61. Amnesty International, 'Afghanistan: Threats of Expulsion of Loya Jirga Delegate Unacceptable', Press Release, 17 December 2003, https://www.amnesty.org/en/documents/asa11/029/2003/en/; Human Rights Watch, 'Afghanistan: Constitutional Process Marred by Abuses', 8 January 2004, http://hrw.org/english/docs/2004/01/07/afghan6914.htm

62. Zalmay Khalilzad, 'Democracy Bubbles Up', *Wall Street Journal*, 25 March 2004.

63. See, for example, Saikal, 'The UN and Democratization', p. 335; William Maley, *Rescuing Afghanistan*, Sydney: University of NSW Press, 2006, p. 46.

64. It is important to note that, as Afghanistan did not have legislation defining 'crimes against humanity' and no court has ever found citizens guilty of 'crimes against humanity', this provision was unlikely to be applied with any force in Afghanistan.

65. 'Decree of the President of the Transitional State of Afghanistan on the Adoption of Electoral Law', 27 May 2004, chapter V, article 17, http://aceproject.org/ero-en/regions/asia/AF/Electoral%20Law%20Eng.pdf/view

66. Thomas Ruttig, 'The 2004 Afghan Presidential Elections and Challenges for the Forthcoming Parliamentary Elections', in Moonis Ahmar, ed., *The Challenge of Rebuilding Afghanistan*, Karachi: Bureau of Composition, Compilation and Translation, University of Karachi Press, 2005, p. 61.

67. Cheryl Benard, Seth G. Jones, Olga Oliker, Cathryn Quantic Thurston, Brooke K. Stearns and Kristen Cordell, *Women and Nation Building*, Santa Monica, CA: RAND Corporation, 2008, p. 162; Ruttig, 'The 2004 Afghan Presidential Elections', p. 62; Kenneth Katzman, *Afghanistan: Elections, Constitution, and Government*, Washington, DC: Congressional Research Service, 2006.

68. Ruttig, 'The 2004 Afghan Presidential Elections', p. 63.

69. Michael J. Metrinko, 'Elections in Afghanistan: Looking to the Future', Issue Paper No. XX, Carlisle, PA: US Army Peacekeeping and Stability Operations Institute, January 2008, p. 3, https://csl.armywarcollege.edu/usacsl/publications/ElectionsInAfghanistan.pdf

70. Hamish Nixon and Richard Ponzio, 'Building Democracy in Afghanistan: The Statebuilding Agenda and International Engagement', *International Peacekeeping*, Vol. 14, No. 1, 2007, pp. 26–40, at p. 30.

71. Astri Suhrke, 'Democratizing a Dependent State: The Case of Afghanistan', *Democratization*, Vol. 15, No. 3, 2008, pp. 630–48, at p. 641.

72. Nixon and Ponzio, 'Building Democracy', p. 32.

73. Andrew Reynolds, 'Electoral Systems Today: The Curious Case of Afghanistan', *Journal of Democracy*, Vol. 17, No. 2, 2006, pp. 104–17, at p. 114.

74. 'Election Watch: Election Results (September–December 2005)', *Journal of Democracy*, Vol. 17, No. 1, 2006, pp. 177–8, at p. 177.
75. Larry P. Goodson, 'Building Democracy after Conflict: Bullets, Ballots, and Poppies in Afghanistan', *Journal of Democracy*, Vol. 16, No. 1, 2005, pp. 24–38, at p. 31.
76. Katzman, *Afghanistan: Elections, Constitution, and Government*, p. 4; Reynolds, 'Electoral Systems Today', p. 112.
77. See Sam Zarifi and Charmain Mohamed, *Afghan Election Diary*, Human Rights Watch, 19 September 2005, http://www.hrw.org/campaigns/afghanistan/blog.htm
78. Khalilzad, 'Democracy Bubbles Up'.
79. Zalmay Khalilzad, 'How to Nation-build: Ten Lessons from Afghanistan', *The National Interest*, No. 80, Summer 2005, pp. 19–27, at p. 19.
80. 'The Afghan Success', Editorial, *Wall Street Journal*, 19 September 2005, p. A16.
81. See for example, Suhrke, 'Democratizing a Dependent State'; Kathy Gannon, 'Afghanistan Unbound', *Foreign Affairs*, Vol. 83, No. 3, 2004, pp. 35–46; ICG, *Afghanistan's Flawed Constitutional Process*; ICG, *Afghanistan: The Constitutional Loya Jirga*; Human Rights Watch, 'Q & A on Afghanistan's Loya Jirga Process'; Human Rights Watch, 'Afghanistan: Analysis of New Cabinet'; Human Rights Watch, 'Afghanistan: Constitutional Process'; S. Frederick Starr and Marin J. Strmecki, 'Afghan Democracy and Its First Missteps', *New York Times*, 14 June 2002; Entekhabi-Fard, 'Accusations of American Meddling'; Oates and Helal, *At the Cross-roads*; Amnesty International, 'Threats of Expulsion'; Nixon and Ponzio, 'Building Democracy'.
82. Saikal, 'The United Nations and Democratization', p. 337.
83. Thomas Carothers, *Aiding Democracy Abroad: The Learning Curve*, Washington, DC: Carnegie Endowment for International Peace, 1999, p. 85.
84. Antonella Deledda, 'Afghanistan – The End of the Bonn Process', *Transition Studies Review*, Vol. 13, No. 1, 2006, pp. 155–71.
85. Nixon and Ponzio, 'Building Democracy', p. 31.
86. Nixon and Ponzio, 'Building Democracy', p. 32.
87. United Nations University, 'Lessons from the National Solidarity Programme in Afghanistan', Research Brief, June 2014, https://www.wider.unu.edu/publication/lessons-national-solidarity-programme-afghanistan
88. Nixon and Ponzio, 'Building Democracy', p. 35.
89. Carothers, *Aiding Democracy Abroad*, pp. 210–11.
90. Jude Howell, 'The Global War on Terror, Development and Civil Society', *Journal of International Development*, Vol. 18, No. 1, 2005, pp. 121–35, at p. 126. As Howell argues, the 'war on terror' has resulted in a complete othering of Muslim organizations, even those focusing on providing basic humanitarian aid to citizens in war-torn countries such as Afghanistan, a fact which undermines the neutrality and independence of transnational NGOs.
91. Howell, 'The Global War on Terror', p. 129.
92. 'Storm over Berlusconi "Inferior Muslims" Remarks', *Independent*, 27 September 2001.
93. Naftali Bendavid, 'Officials' Religious Remarks Raise Fears of Intolerance', *Chicago Tribune*, 24 February 2002. For a broader discussion, see Amin Saikal,

Islam and the West: Conflict or Cooperation? London: Palgrave Macmillan, 2003.

94. Woodward, *Bush at War*, p. 49.
95. Joyce Battle, 'Iraq: Declassified Documents of U.S. Support for Hussein', *Washington Post*, 27 February 2003.
96. David Von Drehle and R. Jeffrey Smith, 'U.S. Strikes Iraq for Plot to Kill Bush', *Washington Post*, 27 June 1993.
97. As George W. Bush famously said; 'After all this is the guy [Saddam Hussein] who tried to kill my dad.' See 'Saddam Tried To Kill My Dad', *Sydney Morning Herald*, 27 September 2002.
98. Quoted in JoAnne Allen, 'Greenspan Clarifies Iraq War and Oil Link', *Reuters*, 17 September 2007, https://www.reuters.com/article/uk-greenspan-idUKN1728646120070917. For details, see Alan Greenspan, *The Age of Turbulence: Adventures in a New World*, London: Penguin Books, 2007.
99. Woodward, *Bush at War*, p. 49.
100. For example, American military personnel engaged in unspeakable moral and physical atrocities at Abu Ghraib. See Seymour M. Hersh, 'Torture at Abu Ghraib: American Soldiers Brutalized Iraqis: How Far Up Does the Responsibility Go?', *The New Yorker*, 30 April 2004, https://www.newyorker.com/magazine/2004/05/10/torture-at-abu-ghraib
101. Loren Thompson, 'Iraq: The Biggest Mistake in American Military History', *Forbes*, 15 December 2011, https://www.forbes.com/sites/lorenthompson/2011/12/15/the-biggest-mistake-in-american-military-history/?sh=167d9bf32d3b; James P. Pfiffner, 'US Blunders in Iraq: De-Baathification and Disbanding the Army', *Intelligence and National Security*, Vol. 25, No. 1, 2010, pp. 76–85.
102. 'U.S. Lessons Learned in Afghanistan', Hearing Before the Committee on Foreign Affairs, House of Representatives, 15 January 2020, https://www.govinfo.gov/content/pkg/CHRG-116hhrg38915/html/CHRG-116hhrg38915.htm
103. Eikenberry, interview with the author, 14 May 2022.
104. Richard A. Clarke, *Against All Enemies: Inside America's War on Terror*, New York: Free Press, 2004, p. 276.
105. Quoted in Idrees Ali, Jonathan Landay and Steve Holland, 'America's Longest War: 20 Years of Missteps in Afghanistan', *Reuters*, 17 August 2021, https://www.reuters.com/world/asia-pacific/americas-longest-war-20-years-missteps-afghanistan-2021-08-16/
106. Eikenberry, interview with the author, 14 May 2022.
107. Eikenberry, interview with the author, 14 May 2022.

4 Dysfunctional Governance: The Hamid Karzai Era, 2001-14

1. A.L.O.E. (Charlotte Maria Tucker), *War and Peace: A Tale of the Retreat from Caubul*, London: Thomas Nelson and Sons, 1878, p. 10.
2. Karl Eikenberry, interview with the author, 22 February 2022.
3. To be precise, NATO did not take over responsibility for ISAF until 11 August 2003; before that, ISAF existed outside NATO.

4. James Kirchick, 'The Man Who Would Be King', *New Republic*, 27 February 2008, https://newrepublic.com/article/60876/the-man-who-would-be-king

5. Zalmay Khalilzad, *The Envoy: From Kabul to the White House, My Journey Through A Turbulent World*, New York: St. Martin's Press, 2016, pp. 132, 133.

6. Khalilzad, *The Envoy*, p. 132.

7. Karl Eikenberry, interview with the author, 14 May 2022.

8. Khalilzad, *The Envoy*, p. 132.

9. Ivan Watson, 'Ambassador Khalilzad, the "Viceroy of Afghanistan"', *NPR*, 22 October 2004, https://www.npr.org/templates/story/story.php?storyId=4122620

10. Jon Boone, 'WikiLeaks Cables Portray Hamid Karzai as Corrupt and Erratic', *Guardian*, 3 December 2010; Malou Innocent and Danny Markus, 'Afghanistan Corruption Breeds Failure', CATO Institute, 22 May 2012, https://www.cato.org/commentary/afghanistans-corruption-breeds-failure; Amrullah Saleh, 'The Crisis of Politics of Ethnicity in Afghanistan', *Al Jazeera*, 26 June 2012, https://www.aljazeera.com/opinions/2012/6/26/the-crisis-and-politics-of-ethnicity-in-afghanistan. Meanwhile, Mahmoud Saikal was among the early senior government officials who resigned in 2006 from his post as deputy foreign minister in protest over incompetence and corruption.

11. For a comprehensive discussion, see Cornelius Friesendorf and Jorg Krempel (translator: Lynn Benstead), *Militarized versus Civilian Policing: Problems of Reforming the Afghan National Police*, Frankfurt: Peace Research Institute of Frankfurt, 2011.

12. For allegations of corruption on the part of some members of Karzai's family, see James Risen, 'Reports Link Karzai's Brother to Heroin Trade', *New York Times*, 4 October 2008.

13. During my fieldwork at the end of 2010, I conducted discussions about the Afghan situation with a number of well-placed figures who confirmed these points. See Amin Saikal, *Zone of Crisis: Afghanistan, Pakistan, Iran and Iraq*, London: I.B. Tauris, 2014, p. 39. Amrullah Saleh, former Afghan vice-president under Ashraf Ghani, and head of the Afghan Intelligence for many years under Karzai, claimed that 'For the last five years, the president has been hand-picking people who flatter him and consider him to be a larger-than-life figure. Karzai has suppressed the voice of discontent and criticism within his own administration. He has surrounded himself with a large number of operators who lack a political base and who do not stick to one vision.' For this, and other opinions about Karzai, see Frud Bezhan, 'Remembering Karzai', 23 RadioFreeEurope RadioLiberty, September 2014, https://www.rferl.org/a/afghanistan-hamid-karzai-legacy/26602469.html

14. Ali Arouzi, 'Karzai: A "Prisoner in His Palace"', *NBC News*, 1 August 2012, https://www.nbcnews.com/news/world/karzai-prisoner-his-palace-flna923777

15. Rajan Menon, 'Afghanistan's Minor Miracle', *Los Angeles Times*, 14 December 2004.

16. See Ahmad Reshad Jalali, 'Corruption and Nepotism the Biggest Threats to Afghanistan', Pajhwok Afghan News, 9 November 2015, https://pajhwok.

com/opinion/corruption-and-nepotism-the-biggest-threats-to-afghanistan/. For more details, see Joshua Partlow, *A Kingdom of Their Own: The Family Karzai and the Afghan Disaster*, New York: Knopf, 2017.

17. For details, see Saikal, *Zone of Crisis*, pp. 38–44.

18. See, for example, Thomas Ruttig, Martine van Bijlert and Gran Hewad, 'A Hasty Process: New Independent Election Commission Announced', Afghanistan Analysts Network, 30 July 2013, https://www.afghanistan-analysts.org/en/reports/political-landscape/a-process-fast-and-patchy-new-independent-elections-commission-announced/

19. Saikal, *Zone of Crisis*, p. 40. The term 'Karzai cartel' is commonly used to describe the Karzai family. For example, see Simon Tisdall, 'Ahmed Wali Karzai, the Corrupt and Lawless Face of Modern Afghanistan', *Guardian*, 13 July 2011; and 'Dying for the Karzai Cartel', *National Review Online*, Hudson Institute, 20 May 2010, https://www.hudson.org/national-security-defense/dying-for-the-karzai-cartel

20. See Michael Hughes, 'Afghan in Exile: Taking a Stand against the Karzai Cartel', *Huffington Post*, 12 May 2011; 'Karzai's Brother Said to be on CIA Payroll', *Reuters*, 28 October 2009, https://www.reuters.com/article/us-afghanistan-usa-cia-idUKTRE59R07T20091028

21. Quoted in 'Afghanistan's Narco War: Breaking the Link between Drug Traffickers and Insurgents', Report to the Committee on Foreign Relations, US Senate, S. Prt. 111-29, 10 August 2009, https://www.govinfo.gov/content/pkg/CPRT-111SPRT51521/html/CPRT-111SPRT51521.htm

22. James Risen, 'Intrigue in Karzai Family as an Afghan Era Closes', *New York Times*, 3 June 2012.

23. For details, see Risen, 'Intrigue in Karzai Family'; and Saikal, *Zone of Crisis*, pp. 38–40.

24. Andrew Higgins, 'Officials Puzzle over Millions of Dollars Leaving Afghanistan by Plane for Dubai', *RAWA News*, 25 February 2010, http://www.rawa.org/temp/runews/2010/02/25/officials-puzzle-over-millions-of-dollars-leaving-afghanistan-by-plane-for-dubai.html

25. 'Afghanistan GDP – Gross Domestic Product', Countryeconomy.com, 2011, https://countryeconomy.com/gdp/afghanistan?year=2011

26. Kevin Sieff, 'Karzai Acknowledges CIA Payments', *Washington Post*, 4 May 2013.

27. Julian Borger, 'Ghost Money from MI6 and CIA May Fuel Afghan Corruption, Say Diplomats', *Guardian*, 30 April 2013.

28. Jon Boone, 'Hamid Karzai Admits Office Gets "Bags of Money" from Iran', *Guardian*, 26 October 2010.

29. Hamid Shalizi, 'Karzai Says His Office Gets "Bags of Money" from Iran', *Reuters*, 25 October 2010, https://www.reuters.com/article/us-afghanistan-karzai-idUSTRE69O27Z20101025

30. For the status of Shah Shuja Durrani, see Amin Saikal, *Modern Afghanistan: A History of Struggle and Survival*, 2nd edn, London: I.B. Tauris, 2012, pp. 32–4. See also Emile Simpson, 'Checked Out: Why Hamid Karzai's Fickle Recklessness Imperils the Future of Afghanistan', *Foreign Policy*, 29 November 2013, https://foreignpolicy.com/2013/11/29/checked-out/

31. UNODC (United Nations Office on Drugs and Crime), *Corruption in Afghanistan: Recent Patterns and Trends*, Vienna: UNODC, 2012, p. 10, https://www.unodc.org/documents/lpo-brazil//Topics_corruption/Publicacoes/Corruption_in_Afghanistan_FINAL.pdf
32. UNODC, *Corruption in Afghanistan*, pp. 4–5.
33. The author personally observed one instance of this during a visit to the outskirts of Kabul in December 2010.
34. For a comprehensive discussion, see Fatima Ayub, Sari Kouvo and Rachel Wareham, *Security Sector Reform in Afghanistan*, Brussels: International Center for Transitional Justice and Initiative for Peacebuilding, April 2009, https://www.ictj.org/sites/default/files/ICTJ-Afghanistan-Security-Reform-2009-English.pdf
35. World Bank, *Afghanistan – Public Expenditure Review 2010: Second Generation of Public Expenditure Reforms*, Report No. 53892-AF, in consultation with the UK Department for International Development, April 2010, p. 4, https://documents1.worldbank.org/curated/en/588341468180890921/pdf/538920ESW0P1021IC0disclosed06191101.pdf
36. Many bribes demanded exceeded $1,000, which was double the average Afghan salary per annum. See UNODC, *Corruption in Afghanistan*, p. 5.
37. Rod Nordland and Dexter Filkins, 'Antigraft Units, Backed by U.S., Draw Karzai's Ire', *New York Times*, 6 August 2010.
38. Rod Nordland, 'Afghan Government Drops Corruption Charges Against Aide', *New York Times*, 8 November 2010.
39. Dexter Filkins and Mark Mazzetti, 'Karzai Aide in Corruption Inquiry is Tied to CIA', *New York Times*, 25 August 2010.
40. See Jon Boone, 'The Financial Scandal that Broke Afghanistan's Kabul Bank', *Guardian*, 17 June 2011.
41. Sayed Ziafatullah Saeedi, 'How Afghanistan Judiciary Lost Its Independence', *The Diplomat*, 5 June 2019, https://thediplomat.com/2019/06/how-afghanistans-judiciary-lost-its-independence/; Kenneth Katzman, *Afghanistan: Politics, Elections, and Government Performance*, Washington, DC: CRS Congressional Research Service, 5 May 2011.
42. 'Afghan MPs Reject Most of Karzai Cabinet Nominees', *BBC News*, 2 January 2010, http://news.bbc.co.uk/2/hi/south_asia/8437677.stm
43. See Paraag Shukla, 'Afghan Parliament Stymied by Protests, Infighting', *Institute for the Study of War*, 1 September 2011, https://www.understandingwar.org/otherwork/isw-brief-afghan-parliament-stymied-protests-infighting
44. M. Hussain, 'Afghanistan Parliamentary Elections, Immunity and Prosecution of Parliamentarians', Heinrich Böll Stiftung, 27 March 2011, www.boell-afghanistan.org/web/52-323/html
45. For a discussion of the 2010 parliamentary elections, see ICG, *Afghanistan's Elections Stalemate*, Asia Briefing No. 117, Kabul/Brussels: ICG, 23 February 2011, https://icg-prod.s3.amazonaws.com/b117-afghanistan-s-elections-stalemate.pdf
45. 'September Election Has Distanced People from Govt: Study', *TOLOnews*, 23 March 2011.
47. Alissa J. Rubin and Abdul Waheed Wafa, 'Karzai Annuls Afghan Court Reviewing 2010 Polls', *New York Times*, 10 August 2011.

48. See Alissa J. Rubin, 'Afghan Leader Forces Out Top 2 Security Officials', *New York Times*, 6 June 2010.

49. 'Wikileaks Cables say Afghan President Karzai "Paranoid"', *BBC News*, 3 December 2010, https://www.bbc.com/news/world-south-asia-11906216

50. Gregg Carlstrom, 'Afghanistan's Governance Problem: New US Research Concludes Corruption and Inefficiency Still Hallmarks of Afghan State', *Al Jazeera*, 13 May 2010.

51. See, for details, Christopher Helman and Hank Tucker, 'The War in Afghanistan Cost America $300 Million Per Day for 20 Years, with Big Bills Yet to Come', *Forbes*, 16 August 2021, https://www.forbes.com/sites/hanktucker/2021/08/16/the-war-in-afghanistan-cost-america-300-million-per-day-for-20-years-with-big-bills-yet-to-come/?sh=50330327f8dd

52. See Quentin Sommerville, 'Afghan Corruption has Doubled since 2007, Survey Says', *BBC News*, 8 July 2010, https://www.bbc.com/news/10549258

53. For evidence of fraud, see Ghaith Abdul-Ahad, 'New Evidence of Widespread Fraud in Afghanistan Election Uncovered', *Guardian*, 29 September 2009.

54. Following this ECC decision, Karzai moved towards substantially curtailing its independence. See Grant Kippen, 'Afghanistan: President Karzai Modifying Election Law in His Favor', *EurasiaNet*, 4 March 2010, www.unhcr.org/refworld/docid/4b966e768.html

55. Peter Beaumont and Jon Boone, 'US Diplomat "Forced Out" over Stance on Afghan Election Fraud', *Guardian*, 1 October 2009.

56. Kenneth Katzman and Clayton Thomas, 'Afghanistan: Post-Taliban Governance, Security, and U.S. Policy', Congressional Research Service, CRS 7-5700, 13 December 2017, pp. 24–5.

57. Barack Obama, 'Remarks by the President in Address to the Nation on the Way Forward in Afghanistan and Pakistan', White House, Office of the Press Secretary, 1 December 2009, https://obamawhitehouse.archives.gov/the-press-office/remarks-president-address-nation-way-forward-afghanistan-and-pakistan

58. Obama, 'Remarks by the President'.

59. 'Factbox: How Obama's Afghan Strategy is Shaping Up', *Reuters*, 1 December 2009, https://www.reuters.com/article/us-afghanistan-usa-factbox/factbox-how-obamas-afghan-strategy-is-shaping-up-idUSTRE5AT3R220091130

60. Karl Eikenberry, interview with the author, 7 October 2022.

61. Ben Farmer, 'Hamid Karzai Reaches Out to "Taliban Brothers" in Afghanistan', *The Telegraph* (London), 3 November 2009.

62. For key points of the BSA, see Charles Recknagel, 'Explainer: Key Points in U.S.–Afghan Bilateral Security Agreement', RadioFreeEurope RadioLiberty, 30 September 2014, https://www.rferl.org/a/explainer-bsa-afghan-us-security-agreement-bsa/26613884.html

63. Emma Graham-Harrison, 'Taliban Urge Afghan President Hamid Karzai to Reject US Security Deal', *Guardian*, 3 December 2013.

64. Karl Eikenberry, interview with the author, 14 May 2022.

65. Emma Graham-Harrison, 'Afghan Finance Minister Breaks Down in Tears as he Denies Corruption', *Guardian*, 10 August 2012.

66. Emma Graham-Harrison, 'Afghan President Flies to Washington for Tough Talks on Military Future', *Guardian*, 8 January 2013.

67. Sudarsan Raghavan, 'Hamid Karzai is Trying to Find His Place in the New Afghanistan', *Washington Post*, 27 December 2022.

68. Shashank Bengali, 'Afghan President Hamid Karzai Relieved His Term is Winding Down', *Los Angeles Times*, 18 May 2014.

5 Dysfunctional Governance: The Ashraf Ghani Era, 2014–21

1. John Stuart Mill, *Three Essays on Liberty, Representative Government, the Subjugation of Women*, London: Oxford University Press, 1975, p. ix.

2. For details, see George Packer, 'Afghanistan's Theorist-in-Chief', *The New Yorker*, 27 June 2016, https://www.newyorker.com/magazine/2016/07/04/ashraf-ghani-afghanistans-theorist-in-chief

3. Quoted in Ismail Khan, 'Analysis: Ghani Playing it Safe', *Dawn*, 14 December 2015, https://www.dawn.com/news/1226271

4. 'Ghani Again Mistaken Rudaki Poem in Tajikistan', *Afghanistan Times*, 30 March 2021, https://www.afghanistantimes.af/ghani-again-mistaken-rudaki-poem-in-tajikistan/

5. Ashraf Ghani and Clare Lockhart, *Fixing Failed States: A Framework for Rebuilding a Fractured World*, New York: Oxford University Press, 2008.

6. 'World Thinkers 2013: The Results of Prospect's World Thinkers Poll', *Prospect Magazine*, 24 April 2013, https://www.prospectmagazine.co.uk/magazine/world-thinkers-2013

7. Pompeo also claims that 'When I met with him the first time during my CIA days, I told him straight up: "You're squandering your time on K Street and Capitol Hill when you should be hustling for allies in Herat and Mazar-e-Sharif." He had come to see the ability to procure American money and friends as the main factor for staying in power and continuing his grift.' Mike Pompeo, *Never Give an Inch: Fighting for the America I Love*, New York: Broadside Books, 2023, p. 365.

8. Mahmoud Saikal, 'Afghanistan in Transition: An Insider's Account', unpublished diary, 2 May 2017, p. 197.

9. For details of the conference's concluding statement, see 'Tokyo Conference on Afghanistan: The Tokyo Declaration – Partnership for Self-Reliance in Afghanistan From Transition to Transformation', Tokyo: Ministry of Foreign Affairs of Japan, 8 July 2012, https://www.mofa.go.jp/region/middle_e/afghanistan/tokyo_conference_2012/tokyo_declaration_en1.html

10. A long-standing Pashtun activist, Khan subsequently formed a splinter group by the same name and represented Ghazni Province (his birthplace) as an elected member of the Wolesi Jirga. He joined Abdullah's team following internal differences that led to the break-up of another coalition that he had entered in the run-up to the 2014 election.

11. Subsequently, the Afghan national security advisor Rangain Dadfar Spanta, and Rahmatullah Nabil, director of national directorate of security under Ghani, revealed that Abdullah had won the election during the first round, but a plot was hatched to lower the percentage of his votes and drag him to the second round. Fawad Nassiha, 'Yadasht-i Spanta, rawayat-i 'dast-i awal' az syyast-i Afghanistan-i ma'asser' [Notes of Spanta, Firsthand Witness Concerning the Politics of Modern Afghanistan], *BBC News* (Persian),

7 December 2017, https://www.bbc.com/persian/afghanistan-42263617; Faridullah Hussainkhail, 'Former NDS Chief "Spills Beans" on 2014 Presidential Elections', *TOLONews*, 21 November 2017, https://tolonews.com/afghanistan/former-nds-chief-'spills-beans'-2014-presidential-elections

12. See Ahmad Mukhtar, 'Election Scandal Brings Down Afghan Official', *CBS News*, 23 June 2014, https://www.cbsnews.com/news/afghanistan-election-ziaul-haq-amarkhel-resigns-amid-fraud-scandal/

13. British ambassador Sir Richard Stagg, for example, wanted a quick resolution rather than electoral justice. Mahmoud Saikal, 'Afghanistan in Transition', p. 96.

14. Mahmoud Saikal, 'Afghanistan in Transition', p. 170.

15. Mahmoud Saikal, 'Afghanistan in Transition', p. 188.

16. Mahmoud Saikal, 'Afghanistan in Transition', p. 194.

17. Mahmoud Saikal, 'Afghanistan in Transition', p. 194.

18. Mahmoud Saikal, 'Afghanistan in Transition', p. 211.

19. Mahmoud Saikal, 'Afghanistan in Transition', p. 189.

20. Mahmoud Saikal, 'Afghanistan in Transition', p. 205.

21. Mahmoud Saikal, 'Afghanistan in Transition', p. 215.

22. Mahmoud Saikal, 'Afghanistan in Transition', p. 232.

23. Mahmoud Saikal, 'Afghanistan in Transition', p. 233.

24. Mahmoud Saikal, 'Afghanistan in Transition', p. 252.

25. John R. Evans, 'Bilateral Security Agreement: A New Era of Afghan–U.S. Cooperation', *Brookings*, 30 September 2014, https://www.brookings.edu/articles/bilateral-security-agreement-a-new-era-of-afghan-u-s-cooperation/

26. For the full text, see 'U.S.–Afghanistan Joint Statement', White House, Office of the Press Secretary, 24 March 2015, https://obamawhitehouse.archives.gov/the-press-office/2015/03/24/us-afghanistan-joint-statement

27. For details, see Jennifer Brick Murtazashvili, 'The Collapse of Afghanistan', *Journal of Democracy*, Vol. 33, No. 1, 2022, pp. 40–54.

28. Ghani's bias in favour of Pashtuns was evidenced in a 2017 leaked memo from inside the presidential palace. See 'Leaked Memo Fuels Accusations of Ethnic Bias in Afghan Government', *Reuters*, 21 September 2017, www.reuters.com/article/us-afghanistan-politics/leaked-memo-fuels-accusations-of-ethnic-bias-in-afghan-government-idUSKCN1BW15U

29. Mujib Mashal and Najim Rahim, 'Afghan President Fires a Powerful Governor from Post he Held 13 Years', *New York Times*, 18 December 2017; 'Afghanistan's Acting Foreign Minister Resigns', RadioFreeEurope RadioLiberty, 23 October 2019, https://www.rferl.org/a/afghanistan-s-acting-foreign-minister-resigns/30232957.html

30. Scott Smith, 'Ashraf Ghani's Pakistan Outreach: Fighting Against the Odds', United States Institute of Peace, 29 June 2015, https://www.usip.org/publications/2015/06/ashraf-ghanis-pakistan-outreach

31. Thomas Gibbons-Neff, 'Ex-official Levels New Corruption Accusations at Afghan Government', *New York Times*, 26 May 2019.

32. Tamim Hamid, 'Ghani Fails to Tackle Corruption, Investigation Shows', *TOLONews*, 8 September 2018, https://tolonews.com/afghanistan/ghani-fails-tackle-corruption-investigation-shows

33. United Nations Security Council, 'Statement by the President of the Security Council', S/PRST/2018/15, 23 July 2018, https://documents-dds-ny.un.org/doc/UNDOC/GEN/N18/235/24/PDF/N1823524.pdf?OpenElement

34. Simon Tisdall, 'Afghanistan is the Dirty Little Secret of the US Presidential Campaign', *Guardian*, 26 October 2016.

35. David Nakamura and Abby Phillip, 'Trump Announces New Strategy for Afghanistan that Calls for a Troop Increase', *Washington Post*, 21 August 2017.

36. Nakamura and Phillip, 'Trump Announces New Strategy'.

37. Donald Trump, 'Remarks by President Trump on the Strategy in Afghanistan and South Asia', Fort Myer, Arlington, VA, 21 August 2017, https://trump-whitehouse.archives.gov/briefings-statements/remarks-president-trump-strategy-afghanistan-south-asia/

38. Pompeo, *Never Give an Inch*, p. 366.

39. Pompeo, *Never Give an Inch*, p. 372.

40. Pompeo, *Never Give an Inch*, p. 372.

41. John Bolton, *The Room Where It Happened: A White House Memoir*, New York: Simon & Schuster, 2020, p. 214. For a more elaborate account of Bolton's relations with Khalilzad and views on negotiations with the Taliban, also see esp. pp. 213–14, 428–30, 434–9.

42. Pompeo, *Never Give an Inch*, p. 374.

43. For details, see Henry Kissinger, *Diplomacy*, New York: Simon & Schuster, 1994, ch. 27.

44. Khalilzad's shuttle diplomacy was similar to that of former US Secretary of State Kissinger, who brought about Israeli-Egyptian and Israeli-Syrian military disengagements in the wake of the 1973 Arab-Israeli War. For a full discussion, see Henry Kissinger, *Years of Upheaval*, Boston, MA: Little, Brown and Co., 1982, ch. 18; Edward R.F. Sheehan, 'How Kissinger Did It: Step by Step in the Middle East', *Foreign Policy*, No. 22, Spring 1976, pp. 3–70.

45. 'Agreement for Bringing Peace to Afghanistan between the Islamic Emirate of Afghanistan Which is Not Recognized by the United States as a State and is Known as the Taliban and the United States of America', US State Department, 29 February 2020, https://www.state.gov/wp-content/uploads/2020/02/Agreement-For-Bringing-Peace-to-Afghanistan-02.29.20.pdf

46. For a good analytical discussion of this, see Deepak Tripathi, *Afghanistan and the Vietnam Syndrome: Comparing US and Soviet Wars*, Cham: Springer, 2023, esp. chs 2 and 4.

47. US Department of State, 'Joint Declaration between the Islamic Republic of Afghanistan and the United States of America for Bringing Peace to Afghanistan', 29 February 2020, https://www.state.gov/wp-content/uploads/2020/02/02.29.20-US-Afghanistan-Joint-Declaration.pdf

48. Mahmoud Saikal, 'Naziraan mi goyand; cherra moufiqyat-i rawund-i sulh-i Afghanistan ba payman-i jaded ar syyasit-i dakhil-i wabasta ast' [Observers Say, Why is the Peace Deal Linked to the New Declaration in Domestic Politics?], *BBC News* (Persian), 1 March 2021, https://www.bbc.com/persian/blog-viewpoints-56203114

49. Khalilzad subsequently rejected 'claims that the government or key Afghan figures were kept in the dark about key negotiations. He says President Ashraf Ghani, former President Hamid Karzai, Peace Council chief Abdullah

Abdullah, and other leading political figures were all kept informed about the developments in the peace talks and various aspects of the agreement, including its two secret annexes'. See Zarif Nazar, 'Former U.S. Envoy Defends Controversial Peace Deal with Taliban', RadioFreeEurope RadioLiberty, 14 August 2022, https://www.rferl.org/a/afghanistan-khalilzad-defends-taliban-deal/31988305.html

50. Pompeo, *Never Give an Inch*, pp. 364–5.
51. Pompeo, *Never Give an Inch*, pp. 376, 378.
52. 'Pompeo Says Ashraf Ghani "Stole" the Election', *Afghan Online Press*, 14 January 2023, http://www.aopnews.com/us-afghanistan-relations/pompeo-says-ashraf-ghani-stole-the-election/
53. Quoted in Brian W. Everstine, 'U.S. Cuts Aid to Afghanistan Amid Political Stalemate', *Air & Space Forces Magazine*, 24 March 2020, https://www.airand-spaceforces.com/u-s-cuts-aid-to-afghanistan-amid-political-stalemate/
54. Pompeo, *Never Give an Inch*, p. 378.
55. For detailed analysis, see Ali Yawar Adili, 'End of the Post-election Impasse? Ghani and Abdullah's New Power-sharing Formula', *Afghanistan Analysts Network*, 20 May 2020, https://www.afghanistan-analysts.org/en/reports/polit-ical-landscape/end-of-the-post-election-impasse-ghani-and-abdullahs-new-power-sharing-formula/
56. Pompeo, *Never Give an Inch*, p. 378.
57. Zabihullah Moosakhail, 'Parliament Rejects Stanikzai as Afghanistan's Defense Minister', *Khaama Press News Agency*, 4 July 2015, https://www.khaama.com/breaking-news-parliament-rejects-stanikzai-as-afghanistans-defense-minister-3596/

6 State-building: Other Challenges, 2001–21

1. Chandler Morse, 'Becoming versus Being Modern: An Essay on Institutional Change and Economic Development', in Chandler Morse, Douglas E. Ashford, Frederick T. Bent, William H. Friedland, John W. Lewis and David B. Macklin, *Modernization by Design: Social Change in the Twentieth Century*, Ithaca, NY: Cornell University Press, 1969, pp. 238–382, at p. 316.
2. UNODC (United Nations Office on Drugs and Crime), *Afghanistan: Opium Survey 2007*, October 2007, p. iv, https://www.unodc.org/documents/crop-monitoring/Afghanistan-Opium-Survey-2007.pdf; Luke Harding, 'Karzai Asks West for Cash Support', *Guardian*, 31 March 2004; 'Afghan Police Raid Heroin Labs, Seize Tons of Opium Poppy', *ABC News*, 7 April 2004, https://www.abc.net.au/news/2004-04-07/afghan-police-raid-heroin-labs-seize-tons-of-opium/166016; 'Afghanistan: Are the British Counternarcotics Efforts Going Wobbly?', Hearing before the Subcommittee on Criminal Justice, Drug Policy and Human Resources, House of Representatives, 1 April 2004, https://www.govinfo.gov/content/pkg/CHRG-108hhrg96745/html/CHRG-108hhrg96745.htm
3. UNODC, *Afghanistan: Opium Survey 2007*, p. iii.
4. Ben Farmer, 'Opium Crop in Afghanistan Heading for Record Levels', *The Telegraph*, 15 April 2013.
5. Farmer, 'Opium Crop'.

6. UNODC, *Afghanistan: Opium Risk Assessment 2013*, Vienna and Kabul: UNODC and Islamic Republic of Afghanistan Ministry of Counter Narcotics, April 2013, pp. 1–2.

7. Cited as part of a comprehensive analysis in Nasar Ahmad Shayan, Aziz ur-Rahman Niazi, Hooman Moheb, Hamid Mohammadi, Khaja Wazir Ahmad Saddiqi, Osman Dag et al., 'Epidemiology of Drug Use in Herat – Afghanistan', *Addiction and Health*, Vol. 14, No. 2, 2022, pp. 68–77, https://www.ncbi.nlm.nih.gov/pmc/articles/PMC9743815/. See also UNODC, *Drug Use in Afghanistan: 2009 Survey: Executive Summary*, June 2010, pp. 5–6, https://www.unodc.org/documents/data-and-analysis/Studies/Afghan-Drug-Survey-2009-Executive-Summary-web.pdf

8. Jonathan Landay, 'Profits and Poppy: Afghanistan's Illegal Drug Trade a Boon for Taliban', *Reuters*, 16 August 2021, https://www.reuters.com/world/asia-pacific/profits-poppy-afghanistans-illegal-drug-trade-boon-taliban-2021-08-16/

9. Barnett R. Rubin and Jake Sherman, *Counter-narcotics to Stabilize Afghanistan: The False Promise of Crop Eradication*, New York: Center on International Cooperation, 2008, pp. 21–3, http://milnewstbay.pbworks.com/f/counternar-coticsfinal.pdf

10. US Department of State, *US Counternarcotics Strategy for Afghanistan*, August 2007, https://2001-2009.state.gov/documents/organization/90671.pdf

11. Martin Jelsma, 'Learning Lessons from the Taliban Opium Ban', *International Journal of Drug Policy*, Vol. 16, No. 2, 2005, pp. 98–103.

12. On the issue of corrupt Afghan officials involved in profiting from the drug industry, see 'Afghanistan's Narco War: Breaking the Link between Drug Traffickers and Insurgents', Report to the Committee on Foreign Relations, US Senate, S. Prt. 111-29, 10 August 2009, https://www.govinfo.gov/content/pkg/CPRT-111SPRT51521/html/CPRT-111SPRT51521.htm

13. Dennis Shanahan, 'Kevin Rudd in Bucharest for NATO Summit on Afghanistan', *The Australian*, 3 April 2008; Rubin and Sherman, *Counter-narcotics to Stabilize Afghanistan*, p. 25; Declan Walsh and Ian Black, 'Eradication or Legalisation? How to Solve Afghanistan's Opium Crisis', *Guardian*, 29 August 2007; 'Minister Voices Afghan Opium Fear', *BBC News*, 2 May 2008, http://news.bbc.co.uk/2/hi/health/7377817.stm

14. Peter van Ham and Jorrit Kamminga, 'Poppies for Peace: Reforming Afghanistan's Opium Industry', *Washington Quarterly*, Vol. 30, No. 1, 2006/7, pp. 69–82.

15. Pashton Zargon, 'Can Saffron Replace Poppy?', *The New Humanitarian*, 6 August 2008, https://www.thenewhumanitarian.org/report/79647/afghani-stan-can-saffron-replace-poppy

16. For an elaborate report, see SIGAR (Special Inspector General for Afghanistan Reconstruction), *Counternarcotics: Lessons from the U.S. Experience in Afghanistan*, June 2018, https://www.sigar.mil/interactive-reports/counternar-cotics/index.html

17. Aunohita Mojumdar, Alex Barker and James Blitz, 'Karzai Blasts West over Opium Policy', *Financial Times*, 30 August 2007.

18. For a comprehensive coverage, see UNODC, *Drug Situation in Afghanistan in 2021: Latest Findings and Emerging Threats*, Vienna: UNODC, 2021, pp. 4, 9,

https://www.unodc.org/documents/data-and-analysis/Afghanistan/Afghanistan_brief_Nov_2021.pdf

19. Mujtaba Haris, 'Broken Promises: Afghanistan's Drugs Trade Thrives Despite the Taliban's Anti-drugs Pledge', Afghan Institute for Strategic Studies, 29 May 2023, https://aissonline.org/en/opinions/broken-pro.../1152

20. Christopher Helman and Hank Tucker, 'The War in Afghanistan Cost America $300 Million Per Day for 20 Years, with Big Bills Yet to Come', Forbes, 16 August 2021, https://www.forbes.com/sites/hanktucker/2021/08/16/the-war-in-afghanistan-cost-america-300-million-per-day-for-20-years-with-big-bills-yet-to-come/?sh=3b086e747f8d

21. 'Afghanistan GDP Per Capita 1960–2023', macrotrends, 2023, https://www.macrotrends.net/countries/AFG/afghanistan/gdp-per-capita. For details of the breakdown of the economy, see 'Afghanistan Economy', CountryReports, 2023, https://www.countryreports.org/country/Afghanistan/economy.htm#:~:text=Is%20Afghanistan%20a%20wealthy%20country,highly%20dependent%20on%20foreign%20aid

22. Asian Development Bank, Poverty Data: Afghanistan, 2022, https://www.adb.org/countries/afghanistan/poverty; World Bank, 'GDP (Current US$) – Afghanistan', World Bank Data, 2021, https://data.worldbank.org/indicator/NY.GDP.MKTP.CD?locations=AF

23. UNDP (United Nations Development Programme), Pitfalls and Promise: Minerals Extraction in Afghanistan: Afghanistan Human Development Report 2020, Kabul: UNDP Afghanistan, 9 September 2020, p. 8, https://afghanistan.un.org/sites/default/files/2020-09/NHDR_2020_%20English_0.pdf

24. Sayed Hashmatullah Hashimi and Gerhard Lauth, Civil Service Reform in Afghanistan: Roles and Functions of the Civil Service Sector, Kabul: Afghanistan Research and Evaluation Unit and Deutsche Gesellschaft fur Internationale Zusammenarbeit (GIZ) GmbH, August 2016, p. 2.

25. For a discussion of the difficulties of public service reform, see Francis Fukuyama's interview with Nader Nadery, Ghani's senior advisor on public relations and strategic affairs. 'Frankly Fukuyama: Could a US-backed Afghanistan Have Survived?', YouTube, 22 June 2023, https://www.youtube.com/watch?v=1Tv-5u1PgJc

26. 'The Afghanistan Compact', Building on Success: The London Conference on Afghanistan, 31 January–1 February 2006, p. 2, https://www.diplomatie.gouv.fr/IMG/pdf/afghanistan_compact.pdf

27. For details, see Omar Joya, 'Natural Resources: What Strategy for Afghanistan?', Policy Paper, Kabul: Samuel Hall, January 2013, https://s3.amazonaws.com/rgi-documents/a7f164345eed951712a5a1f433087b1de4704f7e.pdf

28. 'Karzai: Japan Gets Priority in Afghan Mining', NBC News, 20 June 2010, https://www.nbcnews.com/id/wbna37803781

29. Ben Arnoldy: 'Can Afghanistan Economy Thrive without Poppy?', Christian Science Monitor, 5 March 2010, https://www.csmonitor.com/World/Asia-South-Central/2010/0305/Can-Afghanistan-economy-thrive-without-poppy

30. James Risen, 'Karzai's Relatives Use Ties to Gain Power in Afghanistan', NBC News, 6 October 2010, https://www.nbcnews.com/id/wbna39528462

31. Power Engineering International, 'US Development Agency Funds Gas-fired Project in Afghanistan', Power Engineering International, 16 December 2014,

https://www.powerengineeringint.com/gas-oil-fired/us-development-agency-funds-gas-fired-project-in-afghanistan/

32. For a discussion of 'rentierism' and the resource curse, see Michael Herb, 'No Representation without Taxation? Rents, Development, and Democracy', *Comparative Politics*, Vol. 37, No. 3, 2005, pp. 297–316.

33. SIGAR, 'About SIGAR', High-risk List Afghanistan, 2016, https://www.sigar.mil/interactive-reports/high-risk-list/sigar.html

34. For details, see Craig Whitlock, 'Built to Fail: The Afghanistan Papers – A Secret History of the War', *Washington Post*, 9 December 2019.

35. For a detailed account, see SIGAR, *Quarterly Report to the United States Congress*, 30 January 2014, https://www.sigar.mil/pdf/quarterlyreports/2014jan30qr.pdf; SIGAR, *Quarterly Report to the United States Congress*, 30 January 2017, https://www.sigar.mil/pdf/quarterlyreports/2017-01-30qr.pdf

36. For example, during the first fifteen years of its involvement, the US had constructed, paved, repaired or funded some 16,000 km of roads at the cost of nearly $3 billion, which was once hailed 'as key to bringing economic growth and security'. But, due to 'poor conditions, including government corruption, lack of funding and insecurity', and poor maintenance, by 2016 the highways were in very bad condition and of little benefit. Erin Cunningham, 'The U.S. Spent Billions Building Roads in Afghanistan. Now Many of Them are Beyond Repair', *Washington Post*, 30 October 2016.

37. For an objective discussion, see Astri Suhrke, *When More is Less: The International Project in Afghanistan*, New York: Columbia University Press, 2011.

38. World Bank, 'GDP (Constant 2015 US$) – Afghanistan', World Bank Data, 2015, https://data.worldbank.org/indicator/NY.GDP.MKTP.KD?locations=AF

39. 'Afghans Sink Deeper into Despair under Taliban's Control', Gallup Blog, 1 December 2022, https://news.gallup.com/opinion/gallup/406121/afghans-sink-deeper-despair-taliban-control.aspx. For detailed data, see UNCTAD (United Nations Conference on Trade and Development), 'General Profile: Afghanistan', 2022, https://unctadstat.unctad.org/countryprofile/generalprofile/en-gb/004/index.html; UNCTAD, 'UN List of Least Developed Countries', 2022, https://unctad.org/topic/least-developed-countries/list

40. World Bank, 'Afghanistan', World Bank Data, 2023, https://data.worldbank.org/country/AF

41. For a definition and criteria regarding what constitutes a least developed country and explanatory and statistical details in relation specifically to Afghanistan, see UNCTAD, *The Least Developed Countries Report 2020*, Geneva: United Nations, 2020, https://unctad.org/system/files/official-document/ldcr2020_en.pdf

42. Laura Bush, 'Text: Laura Bush on Taliban Oppression of Women', Radio Address, 17 November 2001, https://www.washingtonpost.com/wp-srv/nation/specials/attacked/transcripts/laurabushtext_111701.html

43. Bush, 'Text: Laura Bush'.

44. Amnesty International, 'Afghanistan: Women's Human Rights Defenders Continue to Struggle for Women's Rights', 7 March 2008, https://www.amnesty.org/fr/wp-content/uploads/2021/07/asa110032008eng.pdf

45. *Business Week, Newsweek, Time* and the *New York Times* magazine featured *burqa*-clad women on their covers in the weeks immediately following the October 2001 intervention in Afghanistan. In the period between 11 September 2001 and 1 January 2002, ninety-three news articles on the plight of Afghan women appeared in major American newspapers, compared with just fifteen in the eighteen-month period between 1 January 2000 and 11 September 2001. See Carol A. Stabile and Deepa Kumar, 'Unveiling Imperialism: Media, Gender and the War on Afghanistan', *Media, Culture & Society*, Vol. 27, No. 5, 2005, pp. 765–82. For a nuanced critique of the US government and media obsession with the 'unveiling' of Afghan women in the aftermath of the US intervention, see Lila Abu-Lughod, 'Do Muslim Women Really Need Saving? Anthropological Reflections on Cultural Relativism and Its Others', *American Anthropologist*, Vol. 104, No. 3, 2002, pp. 783–90.
46. Others included the Afghan Women's Mission, the Afghan Gender Café, the Afghan Women's Council, Humanitarian Assistance for Women and Children of Afghanistan, Parwaz, and Women's Alliance for Peace and Human Rights in Afghanistan. In addition, the long-standing Revolutionary Association of the Women of Afghanistan (RAWA), although slightly different to the above organizations in its overtly political message, had also expanded its activities since 2001.
47. Thomas Carothers, *Aiding Democracy Abroad: The Learning Curve*, Washington, DC: Carnegie Endowment for International Peace, 1999, pp. 211–15.
48. Amnesty International, 'Too Many Missed Opportunities: Human Rights in Afghanistan under Karzai', 3 April 2014, https://www.amnesty.org/en/latest/press-release/2014/04/too-many-missed-opportunities-human-rights-afghanistan-under-karzai/
49. Human Rights Watch, 'Lessons in Terror: Attacks on Education in Afghanistan', July 2006, https://www.hrw.org/reports/2006/afghanistan0706/afghanistan-0706brochure.pdf
50. See World Bank, 'Maternal Mortality Ratio (Modeled Estimate, Per 100,000 Live Births) – Afghanistan', World Bank Data, 2023, https://data.worldbank.org/indicator/SH.STA.MMRT?locations=AF
51. Freedom House, 'Freedom in the World 2020: Afghanistan', Freedom House, 2020, https://freedomhouse.org/country/afghanistan/freedom-world/2020
52. For a historical discussion of the sector, see Mir Hekmatullah Sadat, 'History of Education in Afghanistan', reliefweb, 1 March 2004, https://reliefweb.int/report/afghanistan/history-education-afghanistan
53. Counselor Corporation, 'List of Universities in Afghanistan', no date, https://counselorcorporation.com/list-of-universities-in-afghanistan/
54. For details, see Farhat Easar, Hadia Azizi, Khudaynazar Rahmani, Mujtaba Moradi, Rajab Taieb, and Wasal Naser Faqiryar, 'Education in Afghanistan since 2001: Evolution and Rollbacks', Kabul: Rumi Organisation for Research, 2023.
55. ACKU materialized due to the tireless efforts of Nancy Dupree (1927–2017), an American historian of Afghanistan, and her husband, Louis Dupree (1925–89), a distinguished scholar of anthropology, Afghan culture and history. Both had been long involved in publishing, promoting education and providing relief assistance in Afghanistan.

56. 'Afghanistan Infant Mortality Rate 1950-2023', macrotrends, 2023, https://www.macrotrends.net/countries/AFG/afghanistan/infant-mortality-rate#:~:text=The%20current%20infant%20mortality%20rate,a%202.99%25%20decline%20from%202021

57. 'Afghanistan Healthcare Spending 2002–2023', macrotrends, 2023, https://www.macrotrends.net/countries/AFG/afghanistan/healthcare-spending#:~:text=Afghanistan%20healthcare%20spending%20for%202019,a%202.18%25%20increase%20from%202015

58. WHO (World Health Organization), 'Afghanistan: Health System', WHO, 2023, https://www.emro.who.int/afg/programmes/health-system-strengthening.html

59. USAID (United States Agency for International Development), 'Health', USAID, 2023, https://www.usaid.gov/afghanistan/our-work/health

60. SIGAR, *Health Facilities in Afghanistan: Observations from Site Visits at 269 Clinics and Hospitals*, SIGAR: Arlington, VA, March 2020, p. i, https://www.sigar.mil/pdf/special%20projects/SIGAR-20-28-SP.pdf

61. World Bank, 'Delivering Strong and Sustained Health Gains in Afghanistan: The Sehatmandi Project', World Bank, 23 October 2020, https://www.worldbank.org/en/results/2020/10/23/delivering-strong-and-sustained-health-gains-in-afghanistan-the-sehatmandi-project

62. UNICEF, '1.4 Million Doses of COVID-19 Vaccine Arrive in Afghanistan through COVAX Global Dose-sharing Mechanism', UNICEF, 9 July 2021, https://www.unicef.org/press-releases/14-million-doses-covid-19-vaccine-arrive-afghanistan-through-covax-global-dose

63. See Edouard Mathieu, Hannah Ritchie, Lucas Rodes-Guirao, Cameron Appel, Daniel Gavrilov, Charlie Giattino et al., 'Afghanistan: What is the Daily Number of Confirmed Cases?', Our World in Data, https://ourworldindata.org/coronavirus/country/afghanistan

7 Strategy and Security

1. 'Secretary Gates and Admiral Mullen Testify', Hearing on Security and Stability in Afghanistan and Iraq, September 2008, https://www.understandingwar.org/publications/commentaries/secretary-gates-and-admiral-mullen-testify

2. David Petraeus, 'Afghanistan Did Not Have to Turn Out This Way', *The Atlantic*, 8 August 2022, https://www.theatlantic.com/international/archive/2022/08/us-withdrawal-afghanistan-strategy-shortcomings/670980/

3. Robert Gates, *Duty: Memoirs of a Secretary at War*, New York: Alfred A. Knopf, 2014, p. 336.

4. George W. Bush, 'President Outlines War Effort', US Department of State, Archive, 17 April 2002, https://2001-2009.state.gov/s/ct/rls/rm/9505.htm

5. 'Rumsfeld: Major Combat over in Afghanistan', *CNN*, 1 May 2003, https://edition.cnn.com/2003/WORLD/asiapcf/central/05/01/afghan.combat/

6. Quoted in Council on Foreign Relations, *The U.S. War in Afghanistan: 1999–2021,* no date, https://www.cfr.org/timeline/us-war-afghanistan

7. K. Alan Kronstadt, *Pakistan–U.S. Relations*, Congressional Research Service, 6 February 2009, p. 11, https://sgp.fas.org/crs/row/RL33498.pdf; Julian E. Barnes, 'Defense Chiefs Call for Wider War on Militants', *Los Angeles Times*, 11 September 2008.

8. For an explanation of COIN and its role, see Karl W. Eikenberry, 'Reassessing the All-volunteer Force', *Washington Quarterly*, Vol. 36, No. 1, Winter 2013, pp. 7–24, at pp. 17–18.

9. Gates, *Duty*, p. 200.

10. Gates, *Duty*, p. 200.

11. For a discussion, see John Hudson, 'U.S. Can't Fight Two Wars at the Same Time Anymore', *The Atlantic*, 3 January 2012.

12. Gates, *Duty*, p. 201.

13. Gates, *Duty*, p. 201. In the case of Iraq, the torture and humiliation of Iraqi prisoners at Abu Ghraib by their American interrogators exemplified the worst of American human rights violations. For details, see Seymour M. Hersh, 'Torture at Abu Ghraib: American Soldiers Brutalized Iraqis: How Far Up Does the Responsibility Go?', *The New Yorker*, 30 April 2004, https://www.newyorker.com/magazine/2004/05/10/torture-at-abu-ghraib. There has been no investigation of American soldiers' behaviour in Afghanistan, although one has been instigated in Australia in relation to alleged war crimes by its soldiers, with one soldier charged in this respect. See Inspector-General of the Australian Defence Force, *Afghanistan Inquiry Report*, Canberra: Commonwealth of Australia, 2020, https://www.defence.gov.au/sites/default/files/2021-10/IGADF-Afghanistan-Inquiry-Public-Release-Version.pdf. In September 2012, two US marines were charged over urinating on the bodies of dead Taliban fighters. Adam Gabbatt, 'US Marines Charged over Urinating on Bodies of Dead Taliban in Afghanistan', *Guardian*, 24 September 2012.

14. Gates, *Duty*, pp. 201–2.

15. White House, 'President Bush Meets with NATO Secretary General Jaap de Hoop Scheffer', Office of the Press Secretary, White House, 2 April 2008, https://georgewbush-whitehouse.archives.gov/news/releases/2008/04/20080402-4.html

16. Jaap de Hoop Scheffer, 'Speech by NATO Secretary General Jaap de Hoop Scheffer at the Royal United Services Institute (RUSI)', Opinions, North Atlantic Treaty Organization, 18 September 2008, https://www.nato.int/docu/speech/2008/s080918a.html

17. 'Security and Stability in Afghanistan and Iraq: Developments in U.S. Strategy and Operations and the Way Ahead', Hearing before the Committee on Armed Services, House of Representatives, 110th Congress, Second Session, 10 September 2008, p. 28, https://www.govinfo.gov/content/pkg/CHRG-110hhrg45827/pdf/CHRG-110hhrg45827.pdf

18. Amin Saikal, 'Bloody Conflict Looms in Afghan North', *Guardian*, 19 October 2009.

19. General Stanley A. McChrystal, 'Commander's Initial Assessment', National Security Archive, 30 August 2009, pp. 1–4, https://nsarchive.gwu.edu/sites/default/files/documents/qy3fic-cl4be/15.pdf

20. Karl Eikenberry, interview with the author, 7 October 2022.

21. Abu Musab Zarqawi, a Jordanian, was affiliated with Al Qaeda and had formed the so-called Islamic State of Iraq (*al-dawla Islmiyya fil Iraq*), a precursor to Islamic State of Iraq and Syria (ISIS), as a brutal militant organization fighting the US forces in the context of fuelling a Sunni-Shia conflict in Iraq.
22. Eikenberry, interview with the author, 7 October 2022.
23. See 'David Kilcullen on Afghanistan', interview, ABC (Australia), 28 August 2010, https://www.abc.net.au/radionational/programs/saturdayextra/david-kilcullen-on-afghanistan/3023810. In regard to his earlier assertion about the winnability of the Afghan war, see George Packer, 'Kilcullen on Afghanistan: "It's Still Winnable, but Only Just"', *The New Yorker*, 14 November 2008, https://www.newyorker.com/news/george-packer/kilcullen-on-afghanistan-its-still-winnable-but-only-just
24. Michael Hastings, 'The Runaway General: The Profile that Brought Down McChrystal', *Rolling Stone*, 22 June 2010, https://www.rollingstone.com/politics/politics-news/the-runaway-general-the-profile-that-brought-down-mcchrystal-192609/
25. Petraeus resigned from the CIA post in November 2012 after admitting having an extramarital affair with his biographer, Paula Broadwell, who had accompanied him in Afghanistan. See Terri Pouse, 'Who's Who in the David Petraeus "Love Pentagon" Scandal', *Time*, 13 November 2012.
26. Frank Newport, 'American Public Opinion and the Afghanistan Situation', *Gallup News*, 27 August 2021, https://news.gallup.com/opinion/polling-matters/354182/american-public-opinion-afghanistan-situation.aspx
27. Between 2001 and 2009, Pakistan became one of the largest recipients of US aid, with $5.3 billion in overt assistance, which included some $3.1 billion in development and humanitarian aid, and $6.7 billion in military reimbursements for its 'support of counterterrorism efforts.' For details, see Kronstadt, *Pakistan–U.S. Relations*, pp. 94–5.
28. For a detailed discussion, see Thomas F. Lynch III, 'The Decades-long "Double-double Game": Pakistan, the United States, and the Taliban', *Military Review*, July–August 2018, pp. 64–78, https://www.armyupress.army.mil/Portals/7/military-review/Archives/English/JA-18/Lynch-Pakistan-US-Taliban.pdf
29. George P. Shultz, *Turmoil and Triumph: Diplomacy, Power, and the Victory of the American Ideal*, New York: Charles Scribner's Sons, 1993, p. 1091.
30. 'U.S. Lessons Learned in Afghanistan', Hearing before the Committee on Foreign Affairs, House of Representatives, 15 January 2020, https://www.govinfo.gov/content/pkg/CHRG-116hhrg38915/html/CHRG-116hhrg38915.htm
31. For a detailed discussion of FATA's geographical, historical and political status, see Amina Khan, 'FATA: Voice of the Unheard – Path-dependency and Why History Matters', *Strategic Studies*, Vol. 31, No. 1/2, 2011, pp. 40–74; Shuja Nawaz, 'Learning by Doing: The Pakistan Army's Experience with Counterinsurgency', Washington, DC: Atlantic Council, February 2011, https://www.files.ethz.ch/isn/126743/020111_ACUS_Nawaz_PakistanCounterinsurgency.pdf
32. Evagoras C. Leventis, 'The Waziristan Accord', *Middle East Review of International Affairs*, Vol. 11, No. 4, 2007, pp. 19–37, at p. 25.
33. Leventis, 'The Waziristan Accord', p. 26.

34. Seymour M. Hersh, 'The Killing of Osama bin Laden', *London Review of Books*, Vol. 37, No. 10, 21 May 2015.

35. Nelly Lahoud, *The Bin Laden Papers: How the Abbottabad Raid Revealed the Truth about Al-Qaeda, Its Leader and His Family*, New Haven, CT: Yale University Press, 2022, pp. 270–71.

36. Mullah Omar's death was first disclosed by the Afghan NDS. 'Taliban Admit Covering Up Death of Mullah Omar', *BBC News*, 31 August 2015, https://www.bbc.com/news/world-asia-34105565

37. For a detailed and very insightful discussion of Pakistan's role in support of the Taliban and other armed opposition groups, especially the Haqqani network, see C. Christine Fair, *Fighting to the End: The Pakistan Army's Way of War*, Oxford: Oxford University Press, 2014, esp. chapter 5.

38. For a detailed discussion, see Marvin Kalb, 'The Agonizing Problem of Pakistan's Nukes', *Brookings Institute*, 28 September 2021, https://www.brookings.edu/articles/the-agonizing-problem-of-pakistans-nukes/

39. Eikenberry, interview with the author, 14 May 2022.

40. For the complexity of this area, see Amin Tarzi, 'Political Struggles over the Afghanistan–Pakistan Borderlands', in Shahzad Bashir and Robert D. Crews, eds, *Under the Drones: Modern Lives in the Afghanistan–Pakistan Borderlands*, Cambridge, MA: Harvard University Press, 2012, pp. 17–29.

41. For details, see New America, 'The Drone War in Pakistan', *New America*, 21 May 2016, https://www.newamerica.org/international-security/reports/americas-counterterrorism-wars/the-drone-war-in-pakistan/; Wali Aslam, 'The US Drone Strikes and On-the-ground Consequences in Pakistan', *Peace in Progress*, No. 19, February 2014, https://www.icip.cat/perlapau/en/article/the-us-drone-strikes-and-on-the-ground-consequences-in-pakistan/?pdf; Rafat Mahmood and Michael Jetter, 'Gone With the Wind: The Consequences of US Drone Strikes in Pakistan', *The Economic Journal*, Vol. 133, No. 650, 2023, pp. 787–811.

42. Anant Mishra, 'How Washington Misunderstood "Strategy" in Afghanistan', Canberra: Australian Army Research Centre, 24 May 2022, https://researchcentre.army.gov.au/library/land-power-forum/how-washington-misunderstood-strategy-afghanistan

43. Richard A. Clarke, *Against All Enemies: Inside America's War on Terror*, New York: Free Press, 2004, pp. 277–8.

44. Clarke, *Against All Enemies*, p. 278.

45. 'Haqqani Network Designated Terrorist Organization by U.S.', *Associated Press*, 7 September 2012, https://www.politico.com/story/2012/09/haqqani-network-designated-terrorist-organization-by-us-080911

46. Bill Roggio, 'US Adds Haqqani Network to List of Terror Groups', *Long War Journal*, 7 September 2012, https://www.longwarjournal.org/archives/2012/09/us_adds_haqqani_netw_1.php

47. For a discussion, see Gopal Ratnam, 'Poor Planning, Coordination Cited in Afghan Intervention: U.S., German Officials Note Lessons from 15-year War', United States Institute of Peace, 16 December 2015, https://www.usip.org/publications/2015/12/poor-planning-coordination-cited-afghan-intervention; Eikenberry, interview with the author, 7 October 2022.

48. Eikenberry, interview with the author, 7 October 2022.

49. Moshe Schwartz, *Department of Defense Contractors in Iraq and Afghanistan: Background and Analysis*, Congressional Research Service, 2 July 2010, p. 10, https://apps.dtic.mil/sti/pdfs/ADA512802.pdf; Amin Saikal, 'The Role of Sub-national Actors in Afghanistan', in Klejda Mulaj, ed., *Violent Non-state Actors in World Politics*, London: Hurst & Co., 2010, pp. 239–56.

50. Antonio Giustozzi, *Empires of Mud: War and Warlords in Afghanistan*, London: Hurst & Co., 2009, p. 91.

51. For details, see Mujib Mashal and Najim Rahim, 'Afghan President Fires a Powerful Governor from Post He Held 13 Years', *New York Times*, 18 December 2017.

52. 'Afghan Tensions Rise as Protest in North Turns Violent', *Reuters*, 4 July 2018, https://www.reuters.com/article/uk-afghanistan-protests-idUKKBN1JU15Z. See also 'Warlord Accused of Rights Abuses Awarded Afghanistan's Highest Military Rank', RadioFreeEurope RadioLiberty, 15 July 2020, https://www.rferl. org/a/warlord-accused-of-rights-abuses-awarded-afghanistan-s-highest-military-rank/30727645.html

53. For a discussion on the prevalence of warlordism in Afghanistan, see Roger Mac Ginty, 'Warlords and the Liberal Peace: State-building in Afghanistan', *Conflict, Security & Development*, Vol. 10, No. 4, 2010, pp. 577–98. For a history of warlordism in Afghanistan, see Giustozzi, *Empires of Mud*.

54. Elisabeth Bumiller, 'Pentagon Says Afghan Forces Still Need Assistance', *New York Times*, 10 December 2012.

55. 'Afghan National Security Forces (ANSF)', NATO and ISAF, Media Backgrounder, 26 October 2010, https://www.nato.int/nato_static_fl2014/ assets/pdf/pdf_2010_11/20110310_101122-media-backgrounder-ANSF.pdf

56. 'Afghanistan's Ghani Says 45,000 Security Personnel Killed Since 2014', *BBC News*, 15 January 2019, https://www.bbc.com/news/world-asia-47005558. For a detailed account and analysis, see Anthony H. Cordesman, 'The State of the Fighting in the Afghan War in Mid-2019', Centre for Strategic and International Studies, 13 August 2019, https://www.csis.org/analysis/state-fighting-afghan-war-mid-2019

57. Ellen Knickmeyer, 'Costs of the Afghanistan War, in Lives and Dollars', *AP Press News*, August 17, 2021, https://apnews.com/article/middle-east-business-afghanistan-43d8f53b35e80ec18c130cd683e1a38f

58. SIGAR (Special Inspector General for Afghanistan Reconstruction), *Collapse of the Afghan National Defense and Security Forces: An Assessment of the Factors That Led to Its Demise*, Arlington, VA: SIGAR, May 2022, esp. p. 35, https:// www.sigar.mil/pdf/evaluations/SIGAR-22-22-IP.pdf

59. Jessica Donati and Hamid Shalizi, 'UN Investigation Finds Corruption in Afghan Police Oversight Division', *Reuters*, 19 April 2015, https://www.reuters. com/article/us-afghanistan-corruption-idUSKBN0NA06C20150419

60. Sune Engel Rasmussen, 'Afghanistan Funds Abused Militias as US Military "Ignores" Situation, Officials Say', *Guardian*, 26 December 2016.

61. For a detailed study, see Deedee Derksen, *The Politics of Disarmament and Rearmament in Afghanistan*, Washington, DC: United States Institute of Peace, 2015, https://www.usip.org/sites/default/files/PW110-The-Politics-of-Disarmament-and-Rearmament-in-Afghanistan.pdf

62. European Foundation for South Asian Studies, 'Building the State? Security Sector Reform in Afghanistan between 2001 and 2021', Amsterdam: European Foundation for South Asian Studies, April 2022, https://www. efsas.org/publications/articles-by-efsas/state-security-sector-reform-afghani-stan-2001-2021/. For a comprehensive analysis of the weaknesses and disintegration of the Afghan security forces, see SIGAR, *Why the Afghan Security Forces Collapsed*, Arlington, VA: SIGAR, 28 February 2023, https:// www.sigar.mil/pdf/evaluations/SIGAR-23-16-IP.pdf

8 Conclusion: A Failed Project

1. Dwight D. Eisenhower, 'President Dwight D. Eisenhower's Farewell Address (1961)', Milestone Documents, National Archives, https://www.archives.gov/ milestone-documents/president-dwight-d-eisenhowers-farewell-address
2. For details, see 'Lisbon Summit Declaration', NATO, Press Release, 20 November 2010, https://www.nato.int/cps/en/natohq/official_texts_68828. htm
3. Mahmoud Saikal, WhatsApp correspondence with the author, 9 July 2023.
4. Mahmoud Saikal, WhatsApp correspondence with the author, 9 July 2023.
5. For confirmation of this point and a thorough analysis of the peace agreement, see Michael Semple, Robin L. Raphel and Shams Rasikh, 'An Independent Assessment of the Afghanistan Peace Process June 2018–May 2021', Political Settlements and Research Programme (PSRP), June 2021, https://www. politicalsettlements.org/wp-content/uploads/2021/07/An-independent-assessment-of-the-Afghanistan-peace-process.pdf
6. Helene Cooper and Eric Schmitt, 'Military Officials Say They Urged Biden Against Afghanistan Withdrawal', *New York Times*, 28 September 2021.
7. For details see Joe Biden, 'Remarks by President Biden on the Drawdown of U.S. Forces in Afghanistan', White House, 8 July 2021, https://www.whitehouse. gov/briefing-room/speeches-remarks/2021/07/08/remarks-by-president-biden-on-the-drawdown-of-u-s-forces-in-afghanistan/
8. Mike Glenn, 'At Pentagon, Afghan President Ghani Expresses Confidence His Country Will Survive U.S. Pullout', *Washington Times*, 25 June 2021.
9. Lindsay Wise, 'Congressional Republicans Blame Biden for Bungling Afghanistan Pullout', *Wall Street Journal*, 13 August 2021.
10. For a full discussion, see 'Statement of Robert P. Storch, Inspector General, Department of Defense', Hearing on 'The Biden Administration's Disastrous Withdrawal from Afghanistan, Part 1: Review by the Inspectors General', House Committee on Oversight and Accountability, US Congress, 19 April 2023, https://oversight.house.gov/wp-content/uploads/2023/04/Storch-HCOA-041923.pdf
11. For an on-the-ground assessment after two years of the Taliban's rule and its massive human rights violations and brutal draconian impositions, see UNAMA (United Nations Assistance Mission in Afghanistan), 'Human Rights Situation in Afghanistan: May–June 2023 Update', 17 July 2023, https:// reliefweb.int/report/afghanistan/unama-human-rights-situation-afghanistan-may-june-2023-update-endarips

12. Ayesha Tanzeem, 'Khalilzad: Ghani's "Intransigence," Afghan Elite's "Selfishness" Led to Collapse', *Voice of America*, 27 October 2021, https://www.voanews.com/a/khalilzad-ghani-intransigence-afghan-elite-selfishness-led-to-collapse/6288276.html

13. 'Ex-President Ghani Blames Khalilzad for his Ouster', *Afghanistan Times*, 11 August 2022, https://www.afghanistantimes.af/ex-president-ghani-blames-khalilzad-for-his-ouster/

14. 'Everything Will Be Okay: Pakistan's Intelligence Chief Faiz Hameed During Visit to Kabul', *India Today*, 5 September 2021, https://www.indiatoday.in/world/story/pakistan-intelligence-chief-faiz-hameed-visit-kabul-1849323-2021-09-05

15. Nasim Zehra, 'Afghanistan Inter-ministerial Coordination Cell: A Reason for Hope', *Arab News Pakistan*, 1 December 2021, https://www.arabnews.pk/node/1979121

16. Humayun Salimi, 'Pakistan's PM Directs Authorities to Send Manpower to Afghanistan', *Arezo News*, 15 January 2022, https://arezo.news/en/afghanistan/pakistans-pm-directs-authorities-to-send-manpower-to-afghanistan/

17. Ahmad Khan Dawlatyar, 'Coal on Afghanistan–Pakistan Line', Ankara Center for Crisis and Policy Studies, 23 July 2022, https://www.ankasam.org/coal-crisis-on-afghanistan-pakistan-line/?lang=en

18. Burc Eruygur, '4th Ministerial Meeting of Afghanistan's Neighbors Voices Need for Joint Mechanism to Provide Humanitarian Aid', *AA*, 14 April 2023, https://www.aa.com.tr/en/asia-pacific/4th-ministerial-meeting-of-afghani-stan-s-neighbors-voices-need-for-joint-mechanism-to-provide-humani-tarian-aid/2871719

19. See 'Pakistan Warns of Consequences from Afghan "Economic Meltdown"', *Al Jazeera*, 19 December 2021, https://www.aljazeera.com/news/2021/12/19/islamic-countries-hold-meeting-to-discuss-aid-to-afghanistan

20. Sophia Saifi, Rhea Mogul and Saleem Mehsud, 'Death Toll from Blast in Pakistan Mosque Rises to at Least 100 as Country Faces "National Security Crisis"', *CNN*, 31 January 2023, https://edition.cnn.com/2023/01/31/asia/paki-stan-peshawar-mosque-blast-tuesday-intl-hnk/index.html

21. For a discussion, see Samina Ahmed, 'The Pakistani Taliban Test Ties between Islamabad and Kabul', *Commentary*, International Crisis Group, 29 March 2023, https://www.crisisgroup.org/asia/south-asia/pakistan/pakistani-taliban-test-ties-between-islamabad-and-kabul

22. For details, see Amin Saikal, 'Afghanistan and Pakistan: The Question of Pashtun Nationalism?', *Journal of Muslim Minority Affairs*, Vol. 30, Issue 1, 2010, pp. 5–17.

23. UNAMA, 'Human Rights Situation in Afghanistan'.

24. See Ahmad Massoud, 'What is Missing from Afghan Peace Talks', *New York Times*, 14 April 2020; 'Fireside Chat with Ahmad Massoud', Aspen Institute Security Forum, July 2023, https://www.youtube.com/watch?v=ftGPxaKNZFg. See also Lynne O'Donnell, 'Afghan Resistance Leaders see "No Option" but War', *Foreign Policy*, 29 September 2022, https://foreignpolicy.com/2022/09/29/afghanistan-taliban-resistance-terrorism-jihad/

25. In late 2022, the NRF undertook a comprehensive reform of its organizational structure. By mid-2023, it established a fifty-member multi-ethnic political

council, a military council, a women's council, a think-tank and an active executive council consisting of political, military, intelligence, victims of conflict, and administrative/finance committees.

26. Nishhank Motwani, 'Taliban Leaders Still Lack Legitimacy', *East Asia Forum*, 20 October 2022.
27. For details, see Steve Coll, 'Who Are the Taliban Now?', *New York Review of Books*, 22 June 2023; Vanda Felbab-Brown, 'Afghanistan in 2023: Taliban Internal Power Struggles and Militancy', *Brookings*, 3 February 2023, https://www.brookings.edu/articles/afghanistan-in-2023-taliban-internal-power-struggles-and-militancy/
28. Rahim Faiez, 'Ruling Taliban Displays Rare Division in Public over Bans', *Associated Press*, 16 February 2023, https://apnews.com/article/kabul-united-states-government-taliban-6f34fa4d93635d3500d91918624d4191; Pamela Constable, 'Taliban Moving Senior Officials to Kandahar: Will it Mean a Harder Line?', *Washington Post*, 4 June 2023.
29. For details, see Alireza Nader, Ali G. Scotten, Ahmad Idrees Rahmani, Robert Stewart and Leila Mahnad, *Iran's Influence in Afghanistan: Implications for the US Drawdown*, Santa Monica, CA: RAND Corporation, 2014, ch. 2.
30. Iranian Foreign Minister Jawad Zarif, interview with the author, Tehran, January 2017.
31. For a discussion, see Assaf Moghadam, 'Marriage of Convenience: The Evolution of Iran and al-Qa'ida's Tactical Cooperation', *CTC Sentinel*, Vol. 10, Issue 4, 2017, pp. 12–18, https://ctc.westpoint.edu/marriage-of-convenience-the-evolution-of-iran-and-al-qaidas-tactical-cooperation/
32. Charles Savage, Eric Schmitt and Michael Schwirtz, 'Russia Secretly Offered Afghan Militants Bounties to Kill U.S. Troops, Intelligence Says', *New York Times*, 20 June 2020.
33. See Amin Saikal and Kirill Nourzhanov, *The Afghanistan Spectre: The Security of Central Asia*, London: I.B. Tauris/Bloomsbury, 2021, pp. 125–6.
34. 'UAE President Tells Russia's Putin: We Wish to Strengthen Ties', *Reuters*, 16 June 2023, https://www.reuters.com/world/uae-president-tells-russias-putin-we-wish-strengthen-ties-2023-06-16/
35. United Nations Security Council, 'Fourteenth Report of the Analytical Support and Sanctions Monitoring Team Submitted Pursuant to Resolution 2665 (2022) Concerning the Taliban and Other Associated Individuals and Entities Constituting a Threat to the Peace Stability and Security of Afghanistan', S/2023/370, 1 June 2023, https://documents-dds-ny.un.org/doc/UNDOC/GEN/N23/125/36/PDF/N2312536.pdf?OpenElement

Bibliography

A.L.O.E. (Charlotte Maria Tucker). *War and Peace: A Tale of the Retreat from Caubul*, London: Thomas Nelson and Sons, 1878.

Abbas, Hassan. *The Return of the Taliban: Afghanistan after the Americans Left*, London: Yale University Press, 2023.

Abdul-Ahad, Ghaith. 'New Evidence of Widespread Fraud in Afghanistan Election Uncovered', *Guardian*, 29 September 2009.

Abu-Lughod, Lila. 'Do Muslim Women Really Need Saving? Anthropological Reflections on Cultural Relativism and Its Others', *American Anthropologist*, Vol. 104, No. 3, 2002, pp. 783–90.

Adili, Ali Yawar. 'End of the Post-election Impasse? Ghani and Abdullah's New Power-sharing Formula', *Afghanistan Analysts Network*, 20 May 2020, https://www.afghanistan-analysts.org/en/reports/political-landscape/end-of-the-post-election-impasse-ghani-and-abdullahs-new-power-sharing-formula/

Administration of President George W. Bush 2001–2009. 'Highlights of Accomplishments and Results', December 2008, https://georgewbush-white-house.archives.gov/infocus/bushrecord/documents/legacybooklet.pdf

'Afghan MPs Reject Most of Karzai Cabinet Nominees'. *BBC News*, 2 January 2010, http://news.bbc.co.uk/2/hi/south_asia/8437677.stm

'Afghan National Security Forces (ANSF)'. NATO and ISAF, Media Backgrounder, 26 October 2010, https://www.nato.int/nato_static_fl2014/assets/pdf/pdf_2010_11/20110310_101122-media-backgrounder-ANSF.pdf

'Afghan Opposition Leader Holds Talks with French Leaders', 4 April 2001. AP Archive, YouTube, 22 July 2015, https://www.youtube.com/watch?v=D50hcLtoPE4

'Afghan Police Raid Heroin Labs, Seize Tons of Opium Poppy'. *ABC News*, 7 April 2004, https://www.abc.net.au/news/2004-04-07/afghan-police-raid-heroin-labs-seize-tons-of-opium/166016

'Afghan Tensions Rise as Protest in North Turns Violent'. *Reuters*, 4 July 2018, https://www.reuters.com/article/uk-afghanistan-protests-idUKKBN1JU15Z

'Afghanistan'. *2022 Global Hunger Index*, https://www.globalhungerindex.org/afghanistan.html

'Afghanistan'. UNESCO Institute for Statistics, 2000, http://uis.unesco.org/en/country/af

'Afghanistan: Are the British Counternarcotics Efforts Going Wobbly?'. Hearing before the Subcommittee on Criminal Justice, Drug Policy and Human Resources, House of Representatives, 1 April 2004, https://www.govinfo.gov/content/pkg/CHRG-108hhrg96745/html/CHRG-108hhrg96745.htm

'Afghanistan: Building Stability, Avoiding Chaos'. Hearing before the Committee on Foreign Relations, US Senate, S. Hrg. 107-708, 26 June 2002, https://www.govinfo.gov/content/pkg/CHRG-107shrg82115/html/CHRG-107shrg82115.htm

'Afghanistan Does Not Need Marshall Plan: Powell'. *Zee News*, 8 December 2001, https://zeenews.india.com/entertainment/celebrity/jennifer-aniston-earned-more-than-angelina-jolie-in-2008_27801.html/amp

'Afghanistan Economy'. CountryReports, 2023, https://www.countryreports.org/country/Afghanistan/economy.htm#:~:text=Is%20Afghanistan%20a%20wealthy%20country,highly%20dependent%20on%20foreign%20aid

'Afghanistan GDP – Gross Domestic Product'. Countryeconomy.com, 2000, https://countryeconomy.com/gdp/afghanistan?year=2000#:~:text=The%20GDP%20figure%20in%202000,in%201999%2C%20it%20was%20%24135

'Afghanistan GDP – Gross Domestic Product'. Countryeconomy.com, 2011, https://countryeconomy.com/gdp/afghanistan?year=2011

'Afghanistan GDP Per Capita 1960-2023'. macrotrends, 2023, https://www.macrotrends.net/countries/AFG/afghanistan/gdp-per-capita

'Afghanistan Healthcare Spending 2002–2023'. macrotrends, 2023, https://www.macrotrends.net/countries/AFG/afghanistan/healthcare-spending#:~:text=Afghanistan%20healthcare%20spending%20for%202019,a%202.18%25%20increase%20from%202015

'Afghanistan Infant Mortality Rate 1950–2023'. macrotrends, 2023, https://www.macrotrends.net/countries/AFG/afghanistan/infant-mortality-rate#:~:text=The%20current%20infant%20mortality%20rate,a%202.99%25%20decline%20from%202021

'Afghanistan: Kingly Accomplishment'. *Time*, 3 December 1965, https://content.time.com/time/subscriber/article/0,33009,842252,00.html

'Afghanistan: Nearly 20 Million Going Hungry'. *UN News: Global Perspective Human Stories*, 9 May 2022, https://news.un.org/en/story/2022/05/1117812

'Afghanistan Population 2023'. *World Population Review*, https://worldpopulation-review.com/countries/afghanistan-population

'Afghanistan's Acting Foreign Minister Resigns'. RadioFreeEurope RadioLiberty, 23 October 2019, https://www.rferl.org/a/afghanistan-s-acting-foreign-minister-resigns/30232957.html

'Afghanistan's Ghani Says 45,000 Security Personnel Killed Since 2014'. *BBC News*, 15 January 2019, https://www.bbc.com/news/world-asia-47005558

'Afghanistan's Narco War: Breaking the Link between Drug Traffickers and Insurgents'. Report to the Committee on Foreign Relations, US Senate, S. Prt. 111-29, 10 August 2009, https://www.govinfo.gov/content/pkg/CPRT-111SPRT51521/html/CPRT-111SPRT51521.htm

Afghanistan International. 10 June 2023, https://twitter.com/mazdaki/status/1610 629589742813186?lang=en

Afghanistan Justice Project. 'Casting Shadows: War Crimes and Crimes against Humanity: 1978–2001', 2005, https://www.opensocietyfoundations.org/uploads/291156cd-c8e3-4620-a5e1-d3117ed7fb93/ajpreport_20050718.pdf

'Afghans Sink Deeper into Despair Under Taliban's Control'. Gallup Blog, 1 December 2022, https://news.gallup.com/opinion/gallup/406121/afghans-sink-deeper-despair-taliban-control.aspx

'Agreement for Bringing Peace to Afghanistan between the Islamic Emirate of Afghanistan Which is Not Recognized by the United States as a State and is Known as the Taliban and the United States of America'. US State Department, 29 February 2020, https://www.state.gov/wp-content/uploads/2020/02/Agreement-For-Bringing-Peace-to-Afghanistan-02.29.20.pdf

Ahmed, Samina. 'The Pakistani Taliban Test Ties between Islamabad and Kabul', *Commentary*, International Crisis Group, 29 March 2023, https://www.crisis-group.org/asia/south-asia/pakistan/pakistani-taliban-test-ties-between-islam-abad-and-kabul

Al-Saud, Turki Al Faisal, with Michael Field. *The Afghanistan File*, Cowes, UK: Arabian Publishing Ltd, 2021.

Ali, Idrees, Jonathan Landay and Steve Holland. 'America's Longest War: 20 Years of Missteps in Afghanistan', *Reuters*, 17 August 2021, https://www.reuters.com/world/asia-pacific/americas-longest-war-20-years-missteps-afghanistan-2021-08-16/

Ali, Mohammad. *The Afghans*, Lahore: Punjab Educational Press, 1965.

Allen, JoAnne. 'Greenspan Clarifies Iraq War and Oil Link', *Reuters*, 17 September 2007, https://www.reuters.com/article/uk-greenspan-idUKN1728646120070917.

Amnesty International. 'Afghanistan: Threats of Expulsion of Loya Jirga Delegate Unacceptable', Press Release, 17 December 2003, https://www.amnesty.org/en/documents/asa11/029/2003/en/

Amnesty International. 'Afghanistan: Women's Human Rights Defenders Continue to Struggle for Women's Rights', 7 March 2008, https://www.amnesty.org/fr/wp-content/uploads/2021/07/asa110032008eng.pdf

Amnesty International. 'Too Many Missed Opportunities: Human Rights in Afghanistan under Karzai', 3 April 2014, https://www.amnesty.org/en/latest/press-release/2014/04/too-many-missed-opportunities-human-rights-afghani-stan-under-karzai/

Amnesty International and International Commission of Jurists. 'The Taliban's War on Women: The Crime against Humanity of Gender Persecution in Afghanistan', London and Geneva: Amnesty International and International Commission of Jurists, 26 May 2023, https://www.amnesty.org.au/report-the-talibans-war-on-women-the-crime-against-humanity-of-gender-persecution-in-afghanistan/

Arnoldy, Ben. 'Can Afghanistan Economy Thrive without Poppy?', *Christian Science Monitor*, 5 March 2010, https://www.csmonitor.com/World/Asia-South-Central/2010/0305/Can-Afghanistan-economy-thrive-without-poppy

Arouzi, Ali. 'Karzai: A "Prisoner In His Palace"', *NBC News*, 1 August 2012, https://www.nbcnews.com/news/world/karzai-prisoner-his-palace-flna923777

'Arrival of Afghan Prime Minister'. Press Release 349, 24 June 1958, in *Department of State Bulletin*, Vol. 39, No. 995, 21 July 1958, p. 131, https://archive.org/details/sim_department-of-state-bulletin_1958-07-21_39_995/page/130/mode/2up

Asian Development Bank. *Poverty Data: Afghanistan*, 2022, https://www.adb.org/countries/afghanistan/poverty

Aslam, Wali. 'The US Drone Strikes and On-the-ground Consequences in Pakistan', *Peace in Progress*, No. 19, February 2014, https://www.icip.cat/perlapau/en/article/the-us-drone-strikes-and-on-the-ground-consequences-in-pakistan/?pdf

Ayub, Fatima, Sari Kouvo and Rachel Wareham. *Security Sector Reform in Afghanistan*, Brussels: International Center for Transitional Justice and Initiative for Peacebuilding, April 2009, https://www.ictj.org/sites/default/files/ICTJ-Afghanistan-Security-Reform-2009-English.pdf

'Azemi, Stir Great General Mohammad Nabi. *Urdo wa Syassat dar sai daha-i akheer-I Afghanistan* [Army and Politics: In the Three Decades in Afghanistan], Vol. 2, Peshawar: Sabah Ketabkhanu, 1376/1997.

Baker, Peter. 'Why Did Soviets Invade Afghanistan? Documents Offer History Lesson for Trump', *New York Times*, 29 January 2019.

Barfield, Thomas J. *Afghanistan: A Cultural and Political History*, Princeton, NJ: Princeton University Press, 2010.

Barnes, Julian E. 'Defense Chiefs Call for Wider War on Militants', *Los Angeles Times*, 11 September 2008.

Battle, Joyce. 'Iraq: Declassified Documents of U.S. Support for Hussein', *Washington Post*, 27 February 2003.

Beaumont, Peter, and Jon Boone. 'US Diplomat "Forced Out" over Stance on Afghan Election Fraud', *Guardian*, October 1, 2009.

Benard, Cheryl, and Nina Hachigan, eds. *Democracy and Islam in the New Constitution of Afghanistan*, Conference Proceedings, Santa Monica, CA: RAND Corporation, 2003.

Benard, Cheryl, Seth G. Jones, Olga Oliker, Cathryn Quantic Thurston, Brooke K. Stearns and Kristen Cordell. *Women and Nation Building*, Santa Monica, CA: RAND Corporation, 2008.

Bendavid, Naftali. 'Officials' Religious Remarks Raise Fears of Intolerance', *Chicago Tribune*, February 2002.

Bengali, Shashank. 'Afghan President Hamid Karzai Relieved His Term is Winding Down', *Los Angeles Times*, 18 May 2014.

Bezhan, Frud. 'Remembering Karzai', 23 RadioFreeEurope RadioLiberty, September 2014, https://www.rferl.org/a/afghanistan-hamid-karzai-legacy/26602469.html

Biden, Joe. 'Remarks by President Biden on the Drawdown of U.S. Forces in Afghanistan', White House, 8 July 2021, https://www.whitehouse.gov/briefing-room/speeches-remarks/2021/07/08/remarks-by-president-biden-on-the-drawdown-of-u-s-forces-in-afghanistan/

Bienaimé, Pierre. 'The Politburo Approved the Soviet Invasion of Afghanistan 35 Years Ago Today', *Insider*, 13 December 2014, https://www.businessinsider.com/the-politburo-approved-the-soviet-invasion-of-afghanistan-35-years-ago-today-2014-12

Bolton, John. *The Room Where It Happened: A White House Memoir*, New York: Simon & Schuster, 2020.

Boone, Jon. 'Hamid Karzai Admits Office Gets "Bags of Money" from Iran', *Guardian*, 26 October 2010.

Boone, Jon. 'The Financial Scandal that Broke Afghanistan's Kabul Bank', *Guardian*, 17 June 2011.

Boone, Jon. 'WikiLeaks Cables Portray Hamid Karzai as Corrupt and Erratic', *Guardian*, 3 December 2010.

Borger, Julian. 'Ghost Money from MI6 and CIA May Fuel Afghan Corruption, Say Diplomats', *Guardian*, 30 April 2013.

'Breakdown of Afghan Population as of 2020, by Ethnic Group'. *Statista*, https://www.statista.com/statistics/1258799/afghanistan-share-of-population-by-ethnic-group/.

Briscoe, Charles H., Richard L. Kiper, James A. Schroder and Kalev I. Sepp. *Weapon of Choice: U.S. Army Special Operations Forces in Afghanista*n, Fort Leavenworth, KS: Combat Studies Institute Press, 2003.

Bronson, Rachel. *Thicker than Oil: America's Uneasy Partnership with Saudi Arabia*, New York: Oxford University Press, 2006.

Bumiller, Elisabeth. 'Pentagon Says Afghan Forces Still Need Assistance', *New York Times*, 10 December 2012.

Burnes, Alexander. *Cabool: Being a Personal Narrative of a Journey to, and Residence in that City, in the Years 1836, 7, and 8*, Graz: Akademische Druck- u. Verlagsanstalt, 1842/1973.

Burns, Robert, and Lolita C. Baldor. 'Joint Chiefs Chairman Calls Afghan War a "Strategic Failure"', *AP News*, 29 September 2021, https://apnews.com/article/joe-biden-bombings-kabul-taliban-terrorism-d1c939fc224a988dc6117ae4a70840e6

Bush, George W. 'President Bush Discusses Progress in Afghanistan, Global War on Terror', White House, 15 February 2007, https://georgewbush-whitehouse.archives.gov/news/releases/2007/02/20070215-1.html

Bush, George W. 'President Delivers "State of the Union"', White House, 28 January 2003, https://georgewbush-whitehouse.archives.gov/news/releases/2003/01/20030128-19.html

Bush, George W. 'President Delivers State of the Union Address', White House, 29 January 2002, https://georgewbush-whitehouse.archives.gov/news/releases/2002/01/20020129-11.html

Bush, George W. 'President Outlines War Effort', US Department of State, Archive, 17 April 2002, https://2001-2009.state.gov/s/ct/rls/rm/9505.htm

Bush, Laura. 'Text: Laura Bush on Taliban Oppression of Women', Radio Address, 17 November 2001, https://www.washingtonpost.com/wp-srv/nation/specials/attacked/transcripts/laurabushtext_111701.html

'Bush Statement on China, U.S. Spy Plane Incident'. CNN.com./World, 2 April 2001, http://edition.cnn.com/2001/WORLD/asiapcf/east/04/02/bush.transcript/

Butler, Gavin. 'Taliban Officials Say their Army Will Include Suicide Bombers', *VICE*, 5 January 2022, https://www.vice.com/en/article/qjbjvp/taliban-army-will-include-suicide-bombers

Carlstrom, Gregg. 'Afghanistan's Governance Problem: New US Research Concludes Corruption and Inefficiency Still Hallmarks of Afghan State', *Al Jazeera*, 13 May 2010.

Carothers, Thomas. *Aiding Democracy Abroad: The Learning Curve*, Washington, DC: Carnegie Endowment for International Peace, 1999.

Carter, Jimmy. 'Address to the Nation on the Soviet Invasion of Afghanistan', *The American Presidency Project*, 4 January 1980, https://www.presidency.ucsb.edu/documents/address-the-nation-the-soviet-invasion-afghanistan

Clarke, Richard A. *Against All Enemies: Inside America's War on Terror*, New York: Free Press, 2004.

Coll, Steve. *Ghost Wars: The Secret History of the CIA, Afghanistan, and Bin Laden, from the Soviet Invasion to September 10, 2001*, New York: Penguin Books, 2004.

Coll, Steve. 'U.S.–Taliban Talks', *The New Yorker*, 17 February 2011, https://www.newyorker.com/magazine/2011/02/28/u-s-taliban-talks

Coll, Steve. 'Who Are the Taliban Now?', *New York Review of Books*, 22 June 2023.

Constable, Pamela. 'Taliban Moving Senior Officials to Kandahar: Will it Mean a Harder Line?' *Washington Post*, 4 June 2023.

Constitution of Afghanistan 2004. http://www.asianlii.org/af/legis/const/2004/1.html#A002n

Cooley, John K. *Unholy Wars: Afghanistan, America and International Terrorism*, London: Pluto Press, 1999.

Cooper, Helene, and Eric Schmitt. 'Military Officials Say They Urged Biden Against Afghanistan Withdrawal', *New York Times*, 28 September 2021.

Cordesman, Anthony H. 'The State of the Fighting in the Afghan War in Mid-2019', Centre for Strategic and International Studies, 13 August 2019, https://www.csis.org/analysis/state-fighting-afghan-war-mid-2019

Council on Foreign Relations. *The U.S. War in Afghanistan: 1999–2021*, no date, https://www.cfr.org/timeline/us-war-afghanistan

Counselor Corporation. 'List of Universities in Afghanistan', no date, https://counselorcorporation.com/list-of-universities-in-afghanistan/

Cunningham, Erin. 'The U.S. Spent Billions Building Roads in Afghanistan. Now Many of Them are Beyond Repair', *Washington Post*, 30 October 2016.

Danishyar, Abdul Aziz, ed. *The Afghanistan Republic Annual – 1974*, Kabul: Kabul Times Publishing Agency, 1974.

'David Kilcullen on Afghanistan'. Interview, ABC (Australia), 28 August 2010, https://www.abc.net.au/radionational/programs/saturdayextra/david-kilcullen-on-afghanistan/3023810

Dawlatyar, Ahmad Khan. 'Coal on Afghanistan-Pakistan Line', Ankara Center for Crisis and Policy Studies, 23 July 2022, https://www.ankasam.org/coal-crisis-on-afghanistan-pakistan-line/?lang=en

De Hoop Scheffer, Jaap. 'Speech by NATO Secretary General Jaap de Hoop Scheffer at the Royal United Services Institute (RUSI)', Opinions, North Atlantic Treaty Organization, 18 September 2008, https://www.nato.int/docu/speech/2008/s080918a.html

'Decree of the President of the Transitional State of Afghanistan on the Adoption of Electoral Law'. 27 May 2004, http://aceproject.org/ero-en/regions/asia/AF/Electoral%20Law%20Eng.pdf/view

Deledda, Antonella. 'Afghanistan – The End of the Bonn Process', *Transition Studies Review*, Vol. 13, No. 1, 2006, pp. 155–71.

Derksen, Deedee. *The Politics of Disarmament and Rearmament in Afghanistan*, Washington, DC: United States Institute of Peace, 2015, https://www.usip.org/sites/default/files/PW110-The-Politics-of-Disarmament-and-Rearmament-in-Afghanistan.pdf

Detsch, Jack, and Robbie Gramer. 'The U.S. Left Billions Worth of Weapons in Afghanistan', *Foreign Policy*, 28 April 2022, https://foreignpolicy.com/2022/04/28/the-u-s-left-billions-worth-of-weapons-in-afghanistan/

Dinmore, Guy. 'Neocons Turn their Attention to Iran', *Financial Times*, 18 January 2005.

Dobbins, James. 'Negotiating with Iran: Reflections from Personal Experience', *Washington Quarterly*, Vol. 33, No. 1, 2010, pp. 149–62.

Donati, Jessica, and Hamid Shalizi. 'UN Investigation Finds Corruption in Afghan Police Oversight Division', *Reuters*, 19 April 2015, https://www.reuters.com/article/us-afghanistan-corruption-idUSKBN0NA06C20150419

Dunleavy, Jerry. 'U.S Left Behind More than $7 Billion of Military Equipment in Taliban-Run Afghanistan', *Washington Examiner*, 8 March 2023, https://www.washingtonexaminer.com/restoring-america/courage-strength-optimism/us-left-behind-over-7-billion-military-equipment-taliban-afghanistan

Dupree, Louis. *Afghanistan*, Princeton, NJ: Princeton University Press, 1980.

'Dying for the Karzai Cartel'. *National Review Online*, Hudson Institute, 20 May 2010, https://www.hudson.org/national-security-defense/dying-for-the-karzai-cartel

Easar, Farhat, Hadia Azizi, Khudaynazar Rahmani, Mujtaba Moradi, Rajab Taieb, and Wasal Naser Faqiryar. 'Education in Afghanistan since 2001: Evolution and Rollbacks', Kabul: Rumi Organisation for Research, 2023.

Eikenberry, Karl W. 'Reassessing the All-volunteer Force', *Washington Quarterly*, Vol. 36, No. 1, Winter 2013, pp. 7–24.

Eisenhower, Dwight D. 'President Dwight D. Eisenhower's Farewell Address (1961)', Milestone Documents, National Archives, https://www.archives.gov/milestone-documents/president-dwight-d-eisenhowers-farewell-address

'Election Watch: Election Results (September–December 2005)'. *Journal of Democracy*, Vol. 17, No. 1, 2006, pp. 177–8.

Elphinstone, Mountstuart. *An Account of the Kingdom of Caubul*, Vol. 1, Karachi: Oxford University Press, 1972.

Elphinstone, Mountstuart. *An Account of the Kingdom of Caubul*, Vol. 2, Karachi: Oxford University Press, 1972.

Entekhabi-Fard, Camelia. 'Accusations of American Meddling Mar Afghan Council', *EurasiaNet*, 6 December 2002, https://eurasianet.org/accusations-of-american-meddling-mar-afghan-council

Entekhabi-Fard, Camelia. 'As Afghan Council Proceeds, American Predicts a Strong President', *EurasiaNet*, 22 December 2003, https://eurasianet.org/as-afghan-council-proceeds-american-predicts-strong-president

Erlanger, Steven. 'In Afghan Refugee Camp, Albright Hammers Taliban', *New York Times*, 19 November 1997.

Eruygur, Burc. '4th Ministerial Meeting of Afghanistan's Neighbors Voices Need for Joint Mechanism to Provide Humanitarian Aid', *AA*, 14 April 2023, https://

www.aa.com.tr/en/asia-pacific/4th-ministerial-meeting-of-afghanistan-s-neighbors-voices-need-for-joint-mechanism-to-provide-humanitarian-aid/2871719

Eshaq, Mohammad, comp. and trans. *Nama-hai-e az Massoud Buzurg* [Letters from Great Massoud], Kabul: Matbai-e Maiwand, 1382/2003.

European Foundation for South Asian Studies. 'Building the State? Security Sector Reform in Afghanistan between 2001 and 2021'. Amsterdam: European Foundation for South Asian Studies, April 2022, https://www.efsas.org/publications/articles-by-efsas/state-security-sector-reform-afghanistan-2001-2021/

Evans, John R. 'Bilateral Security Agreement: A New Era of Afghan–U.S. Cooperation', *Brookings*, 30 September 2014, https://www.brookings.edu/articles/bilateral-security-agreement-a-new-era-of-afghan-u-s-cooperation/

Everstine, Brian W. 'U.S. Cuts Aid to Afghanistan Amid Political Stalemate', *Air & Space Forces Magazine*, 24 March 2020, https://www.airandspaceforces.com/u-s-cuts-aid-to-afghanistan-amid-political-stalemate/

'Everything Will Be Okay: Pakistan's Intelligence Chief Faiz Hameed During Visit to Kabul', *India Today*, 5 September 2021, https://www.indiatoday.in/world/story/pakistan-intelligence-chief-faiz-hameed-visit-kabul-1849323-2021-09-05

'Ex-President Ghani Blames Khalilzad for his Ouster'. *Afghanistan Times*, 11 August 2022, https://www.afghanistantimes.af/ex-president-ghani-blames-khalilzad-for-his-ouster/

'Exploring Three Strategies for Afghanistan'. Hearing before the Committee on Foreign Relations, US Senate, S. Hrg. 111-321, 16 September 2009, https://www.govinfo.gov/content/pkg/CHRG-111shrg55538/html/CHRG-111shrg55538.htm

Faiez, Rahim. 'Ruling Taliban Displays Rare Division in Public over Bans', *Associated Press*, 16 February 2023, https://apnews.com/article/kabul-united-states-government-taliban-6f34fa4d93635d3500d91918624d4191

'Factbox: How Obama's Afghan Strategy is Shaping Up'. *Reuters*, 1 December 2009, https://www.reuters.com/article/us-afghanistan-usa-factbox/factbox-how-obamas-afghan-strategy-is-shaping-up-idUSTRE5AT3R220091130

'Failed States 2023'. *World Population Review*, https://worldpopulationreview.com/country-rankings/failed-states

Fair, C. Christine. *Fighting to the End: The Pakistan Army's Way of War*, Oxford: Oxford University Press, 2014.

Faizzaad, Mohammad Alam. *Jirga hai-e buzrurg milli-e Afghanistan (loya jirga haa)* [The Large National Gatherings of Afghanistan], Lahore: no publisher, 1368/1990.

Farhadi, Ravan. 'Qadam-ha-ye Awshti bain-i Tajik ha' [Steps of Peace among the Tajiks], in Nasrine Abou-Bakre Gross, ed., *Qadam-ha-ye Awshti wa Massouliate-e Ma Afghan-ha* [Steps of Peace and our Responsibility as Afghans], Falls Church, VA: Kabultec, 2000, pp. 49–61.

Farhang, Mir Mohammad Sidiq. *Khaterat-e Mir Mohammad Sidiq Farhang* [Memoirs of Mir Mohammad Sidiq Farhang], completed by Seyyed Mohammad Farooq Farhang and Seyyed Zia Farhang, Tehran: Tessa Press, 2015.

Farmer, Ben. 'Hamid Karzai Reaches Out to "Taliban Brothers" in Afghanistan', *The Telegraph*, 3 November 2009.

Farmer, Ben. 'Opium Crop in Afghanistan Heading for Record Levels', *The Telegraph*, 15 April 2013.

Felbab-Brown, Vanda. 'Afghanistan in 2023: Taliban Internal Power Struggles and Militancy', *Brookings*, 3 February 2023, https://www.brookings.edu/articles/afghanistan-in-2023-taliban-internal-power-struggles-and-militancy/

Filkins, Dexter, and Mark Mazzetti. 'Karzai Aide in Corruption Inquiry is Tied to CIA', *New York Times*, 25 August 2010.

'Filling the Vacuum: The Bonn Conference'. *Frontline*, 2022, https://www.pbs.org/wgbh/pages/frontline/shows/campaign/withus/cbonn.html

Fletcher, Arnold. *Afghanistan: Highway of Conquest*, Ithaca, NY: Cornell University Press, 1965.

Freedom House. 'Freedom in the World 2020: Afghanistan'. 2020, https://freedomhouse.org/country/afghanistan/freedom-world/2020

Frost, Raymond. *The Backward Society*, London: Longmans, 1961.

Fukuyama, Francis. *The End of History and the Last Man*, New York: Free Press, 1992.

Fukuyama, Francis. 'Could a US-backed Afghanistan Have Survived?' Frankly Fukuyama, YouTube, 22 June 2023, https://www.youtube.com/watch?v=1Tv-5u1PgJc

Gabbatt, Adam. 'US Marines Charged over Urinating on Bodies of Dead Taliban in Afghanistan', *Guardian*, 24 September 2012.

Gall, Carlotta. 'Former Afghan King Rules Out All But Symbolic Role', *New York Times*, 11 June 2002.

Gall, Carlotta. 'New Afghan Constitution Juggles Koran and Democracy', *New York Times*, 19 October 2003.

Gall, Sandy. *Afghan Napoleon: The Life of Ahmad Shah Massoud*, London: Haus Publishing Ltd, 2021.

Gannon, Kathy. 'Afghanistan Unbound', *Foreign Affairs*, Vol. 83, No. 3, 2004, pp. 35–46.

Gates, Robert. *Duty: Memoirs of A Secretary at War*, New York: Alfred A. Knopf, 2014.

Gellman, Barton, and Dana Priest. 'U.S. Strikes Terrorist-linked Sites in Afghanistan, Factory in Sudan', *Washington Post*, 21 August 1998.

'Ghani Again Mistaken Rudaki Poem in Tajikistan', *Afghanistan Times*, 30 March 2021, https://www.afghanistantimes.af/ghani-again-mistaken-rudaki-poem-in-tajikistan/

'George F. Kennan, on Washington's Reaction to the Afghan Crisis: "Was This Really Mature Statesmanship?"'. *New York Times*, 1 February 1980, https://www.nytimes.com/1980/02/01/archives/george-f-kennan-on-washingtons-reaction-to-the-afghan-crisis-was.html

Ghani, Ashraf, and Clare Lockhart. *Fixing Failed States: A Framework for Rebuilding a Fractured World*, New York: Oxford University Press, 2008.

Ghaus, Abdul Samad. *The Fall of Afghanistan: An Insider's Account*, Lincoln, NE: University of Nebraska Press, 1988.

Ghobar, Mir Gholam Mohammad. *Afghanistan in the Course of History*, Vol. 2, trans. Sherief A. Fayez, Alexandria, VA: Hashmat K. Ghobar, 2001.

Gibbons-Neff, Thomas. 'Ex-official Levels New Corruption Accusations at Afghan Government', *New York Times*, 26 May 2019.

Giustozzi, Antonio. *Empires of Mud: War and Warlords in Afghanistan*, London: Hurst & Co., 2009.

Giustozzi, Antonio. 'The Islamic State in Khorasan', *Newsletter*, Italian Institute for International Political Studies, 27 June 2019, https://www.ispionline.it/en/publication/islamic-state-khorasan-23406

Giustozzi, Antonio. *The Taliban at War, 2001–2021*, London: Hurst & Co., 2022.

Glenn, Mike. 'At Pentagon, Afghan President Ghani Expresses Confidence His Country Will Survive U.S. Pullout', *Washington Times*, 25 June 2021.

Goodson, Larry P. 'Afghanistan in 2003: The Taliban Resurface and a New Constitution is Born', *Asian Survey*, Vol. 44, No. 1, 2004, pp. 14–22.

Goodson, Larry P. 'Building Democracy after Conflict: Bullets, Ballots, and Poppies in Afghanistan', *Journal of Democracy*, Vol. 16, No. 1, 2005, pp. 24–38.

Graham-Harrison, Emma. 'Afghan Finance Minister Breaks Down in Tears as He Denies Corruption', *Guardian*, 10 August 2012.

Graham-Harrison, Emma. 'Afghan President Flies to Washington for Tough Talks on Military Future', *Guardian*, 8 January 2013.

Graham-Harrison, Emma. 'Taliban Urge Afghan President Hamid Karzai to Reject US Security Deal', *Guardian*, 3 December 2013.

Grenier, Robert L. *88 Days to Kandahar: A CIA Diary*, New York: Simon & Schuster, 2015.

Greenspan, Alan. *The Age of Turbulence: Adventures in a New World*, London: Penguin Books, 2007.

Gross, Abou-Bakre, ed. *Qadam-ha-ye Awshti wa Massouliate-e Ma Afghan-ha* [Steps of Peace and our Responsibility as Afghans], Falls Church, VA: Kabultec, 2000.

Habibi, Abdul Hai. *Junbushi Mashrotiat dar Afghanistan* [The Constitutionalist Movement in Afghanistan], Kabul: Government Press, 1364/1985.

Habibi, Abdul Hai. *Tarikhi Mukhtasari Afghanistan Az Zamnaha-i-e Qadeem Taa Istiqualal* [Short History of Afghanistan from Ancient Times to Independence], Peshawar: Khawar, 1989.

Haidary, Mohammad Shoaib. 'Afghanistan is Losing Faith in the Taliban', *Fair Observer*, 27 October 2022, https://www.fairobserver.com/politics/afghanistan-is-losing-faith-in-the-taliban/

Haider, Zeeshan 'Backlash Seen from Pakistani Mosques Assault', *Reuters*, 11 July 2007.

Hamid, Tamim. 'Ghani Fails to Tackle Corruption, Investigation Shows', *TOLONews*, 8 September 2018, https://tolonews.com/afghanistan/ghani-fails-tackle-corruption-investigation-shows

Hanifi, M. Jamil. 'Editing the Past: Colonial Production of Hegemony through the "Loya Jerga" in Afghanistan', *Iranian Studies*, Vol. 37, No. 2, 2004, pp. 295–322.

'Haqqani Network Designated Terrorist Organization by U.S'. *Associated Press*, 7 September 2012, https://www.politico.com/story/2012/09/haqqani-network-designated-terrorist-organization-by-us-080911

Harding, Luke. 'Karzai Asks West for Cash Support', *Guardian*, 31 March 2004.

Haris, Mujtaba. 'Broken Promises: Afghanistan's Drugs Trade Thrives Despite the Taliban's Anti-drugs Pledge', Afghan Institute for Strategic Studies, 29 May 2023, https://aissonline.org/en/opinions/broken-pro.../1152

Hashimi, Sayed Hashmatullah, and Gerhard Lauth. *Civil Service Reform in Afghanistan: Roles and Functions of the Civil Service Sector*, Kabul: Afghanistan Research and Evaluation Unit and Deutsche fur Internationale Zusammenarbeit (GIZ) GmbH, August 2016.

Hastings, Michael. 'The Runaway General: The Profile that Brought Down McChrystal', *Rolling Stone*, 22 June 2010, https://www.rollingstone.com/politics/politics-news/the-runaway-general-the-profile-that-brought-down-mcchrystal-192609/

Helman, Christopher, and Hank Tucker. 'The War in Afghanistan Cost America $300 Million Per Day for 20 Years, with Big Bills Yet to Come', *Forbes*, 16 August 2021, https://www.forbes.com/sites/hanktucker/2021/08/16/the-war-in-afghanistan-cost-america-300-million-per-day-for-20-years-with-big-bills-yet-to-come/?sh=50330327f8dd

Herb, Michael. 'No Representation without Taxation? Rents, Development, and Democracy', *Comparative Politics*, Vol. 37, No. 3, 2005, pp. 297–316.

Hersh, Seymour M. 'The Killing of Osama bin Laden', *London Review of Books*, Vol. 37, No. 10, 21 May 2015.

Hersh, Seymour M. 'Torture at Abu Ghraib: American Soldiers Brutalized Iraqis: How Far Up Does the Responsibility Go?', *The New Yorker*, 30 April 2004, https://www.newyorker.com/magazine/2004/05/10/torture-at-abu-ghraib

Higgins, Andrew. 'Officials Puzzle over Millions of Dollars Leaving Afghanistan by Plane for Dubai', *RAWA News*, 25 February 2010, http://www.rawa.org/temp/runews/2010/02/25/officials-puzzle-over-millions-of-dollars-leaving-afghanistan-by-plane-for-dubai.html

Howell, Jude. 'The Global War on Terror, Development and Civil Society', *Journal of International Development*, Vol. 18, No. 1, 2005, pp. 121–35.

Hudson, John. 'U.S. Can't Fight Two Wars at the Same Time Anymore', *The Atlantic*, 3 January 2012.

Hughes, Michael. 'Afghan in Exile: Taking a Stand against the Karzai Cartel', *Huffington Post*, 12 May 2011.

Human Rights Watch. 'Afghanistan: Analysis of New Cabinet', 20 June 2002, http://hrw.org/english/docs/2002/06/20/afghan4051.htm

Human Rights Watch. 'Afghanistan: Constitutional Process Marred by Abuses', 8 January 2004, http://hrw.org/english/docs/2004/01/07/afghan6914.htm

Human Rights Watch. 'Blood-stained Hands: Past Atrocities in Kabul and Afghanistan's Legacy of Impunity', 6 July 2005, https://www.hrw.org/report/2005/07/06/blood-stained-hands-past-atrocities-kabul-and-afghanistans-legacy-impunity

Human Rights Watch. 'Lessons in Terror: Attacks on Education in Afghanistan', July, 2006, https://www.hrw.org/reports/2006/afghanistan0706/afghanistan0706brochure.pdf

Human Rights Watch. 'Q & A on Afghanistan's Loya Jirga Process', 17 April 2002, https://www.hrw.org/legacy/press/2002/04/qna-loyagirga.pdf

Human Rights Watch News. 'Afghanistan: Loya Jirga off to a Shaky Start', 13 June 2002, http://hrw.org/english/docs/2002/06/13/afghan4039.htm

Hussain, M. 'Afghanistan Parliamentary Elections, Immunity and Prosecution of Parliamentarians', Heinrich Böll Stiftung, 27 March 2011, www.boell-afghanistan.org/web/52-323/html

Hussainkhail, Faridullah. 'Former NDS Chief "Spills Beans" on 2014 Presidential Elections', *TOLONews*, 21 November 2017, https://tolonews.com/afghanistan/former-nds-chief-'spills-beans'-2014-presidential-elections

ICG (International Crisis Group). *Afghanistan: The Constitutional Loya Jirga*, Afghanistan Briefing, Kabul/Brussels: ICG, 12 December 2003.

ICG (International Crisis Group). *Afghanistan's Elections Stalemate*, Asia Briefing No. 117, Kabul/Brussels: ICG, 23 February 2011, https://icg-prod.s3.amazonaws.com/b117-afghanistan-s-elections-stalemate.pdf

ICG (International Crisis Group). *Afghanistan's Flawed Constitutional Process*, Report 56, Kabul/Brussels: ICG, 12 June 2003.

Innocent, Malou, and Danny Markus. 'Afghanistan Corruption Breeds Failure', CATO Institute, 22 May 2012, https://www.cato.org/commentary/afghanistans-corruption-breeds-failure

Inspector-General of the Australian Defence Force. *Afghanistan Inquiry Report*, Canberra: Commonwealth of Australia, 2020, https://www.defence.gov.au/sites/default/files/2021-10/IGADF-Afghanistan-Inquiry-Public-Release-Version.pdf

Iqbal, Anwar. 'Afghan Army to Collapse in Six Months without US Help: Ghani', *Dawn*, 18 January 2018.

Jadoon, Amira, with Andrew Mines. *The Islamic State in Afghanistan and Pakistan: Strategic Alliances and Rivalries*, Boulder, CO: Lynne Rienner, 2023.

Jalali, Ahmad Reshad. 'Corruption and Nepotism the Biggest Threats to Afghanistan', Pajhwok Afghan News, 9 November 2015, https://pajhwok.com/opinion/corruption-and-nepotism-the-biggest-threats-to-afghanistan/

Jalali, Ali A. 'The Legacy of War and the Challenge of Peace Building', in Robert I. Rotberg, ed., *Building a New Afghanistan*, Washington, DC: Brookings Institution Press, 2007, pp. 22–55.

Jelsma, Martin. 'Learning Lessons from the Taliban Opium Ban', *International Journal of Drug Policy*, Vol. 16, No. 2, 2005, pp. 98–103.

'Joint Inquiry into Intelligence Community Activities Before and After the Terrorist Attacks of September 11, 2001'. Hearings before the Select Committee on Intelligence, US Senate, and the Permanent Select Committee on Intelligence House of Representatives, S. Hrg. 107-1086, Vol. 1, 18, 19, 20, 24, and 26 September 2002, https://www.govinfo.gov/content/pkg/CHRG-107jhrg96166/html/CHRG-107jhrg96166.htm

Jones, Seth G. *In the Graveyard of Empires: America's War in Afghanistan*, New York: W.W. Norton, 2009.

Joya, Omar. 'Natural Resources: What Strategy for Afghanistan', Policy Paper, Kabul: Samuel Hall, January 2013, https://s3.amazonaws.com/rgi-documents/a7f164345eed951712a5a1f433087b1de4704f7e.pdf

Kakar, Hasan Kawun. *Government and Society in Afghanistan: The Reign of Amir 'Abd al-Rahman Khan*, Austin, TX: University of Texas Press, 1979.

Kakar, M. Hassan. *Afghanistan: The Soviet Invasion and the Afghan Response, 1979–1982*, Berkeley, CA: University of California Press.

Kalb, Marvin. 'The Agonizing Problem of Pakistan's Nukes', *Brookings Institute*, 28 September 2021, https://www.brookings.edu/articles/the-agonizing-problem-of-pakistans-nukes/

Kalinovsky, Artemy M. *A Long Goodbye: The Soviet Withdrawal from Afghanistan*, Cambridge, MA: Harvard University Press, 2011.

'Karzai: Japan Gets Priority in Afghan Mining'. *NBC News*, 20 June 2010, https://www.nbcnews.com/id/wbna37803781

'Karzai's Brother Said to be on CIA Payroll'. *Reuters*, 28 October 2009, https://www.reuters.com/article/us-afghanistan-usa-cia-idUKTRE59R07T20091028

Katzman, Kenneth. *Afghanistan: Elections, Constitution, and Government*, Washington, DC: Congressional Research Service, 2006.

Katzman, Kenneth. *Afghanistan: Politics, Elections, and Government Performance*, Washington, DC: CRS Congressional Research Service, 5 May 2011.

Katzman, Kenneth, and Clayton Thomas. 'Afghanistan: Post-Taliban Governance, Security, and U.S. Policy', *Congressional Research Service*, CRS 7-5700, 13 December 2017.

Khalilzad, Zalmay. 'Afghanistan: Time to Reengage', *Washington Post*, 7 October 1996.

Khalilzad, Zalmay. 'Democracy Bubbles Up', *Wall Street Journal*, 25 March 2004.

Khalilzad, Zalmay. 'How to Nation-build: Ten Lessons from Afghanistan', *The National Interest*, No. 80, Summer 2005, pp. 19–27.

Khalilzad, Zalmay. *The Envoy: From Kabul to the White House, My Journey Through a Turbulent World*, New York: St. Martin's Press, 2016.

Khalilzad, Zalmay, and Daniel Byman. 'Afghanistan: The Consolidation of a Rogue State', *Washington Quarterly*, Vol. 23, No. 1, 2000, pp. 65–78.

Khan, Amina. 'FATA: Voice of the Unheard – Path-dependency and Why History Matters', *Strategic Studies*, Vol. 31, No. 1/2, 2011, pp. 40–74.

Khan, Ismail. 'Analysis: Ghani Playing it Safe', *Dawn*, 14 December 2015, https://www.dawn.com/news/1226271

Khrushchev, Nikita. *Khrushchev Remembers: The Last Testament*, trans. Strobe Talbott, London: Andre Deutsch, 1974.

Kippen, Grant. 'Afghanistan: President Karzai Modifying Election Law in His Favor', *EurasiaNet*, 4 March 2010, www.unhcr.org/refworld/docid/4b966e768.html

Kippen, Grant. 'The 2004 Presidential Election: On the Road to Democracy in Afghanistan', Centre for the Study of Democracy, Kingston: Queen's University, 2005.

Kirchick, James. 'The Man Who Would Be King', *New Republic*, 27 February 2008, https://newrepublic.com/article/60876/the-man-who-would-be-king

Kissinger, Henry. *Diplomacy*, New York: Simon & Schuster, 1994.

Kissinger, Henry. *Years of Upheaval*, Boston, MA: Little, Brown and Company, 1982.

Knickmeyer, Ellen. 'Costs of the Afghanistan War, in Lives and Dollars', *AP Press News*, 17 August 2021, https://apnews.com/article/middle-east-business-afghanistan-43d8f53b35e80ec18c130cd683e1a38f

Kohli, Atul. *Imperialism and the Developing World: How Britain and the United States Shaped the Global Periphery*, New York: Oxford University Press, 2020.

Kohzad, Ahmad A. *Men and Events: Through 18th and 19th Century, Afghanistan*, London: Forgotten Books, 2018.

Kronstadt, K. Alan. *Pakistan–U.S. Relations*, Congressional Research Service, 6 February 2009, https://sgp.fas.org/crs/row/RL33498.pdf

Kuroski, John, ed. '46 Fascinating Photos of 1960s Afghanistan Before the Taliban', *All that's Interesting*, 19 August 2021, https://allthatsinteresting.com/1960s-afghanistan

Lahoud, Nelly. *The Bin Laden Papers: How the Abbottabad Raid Revealed the Truth about Al-Qaeda, Its Leader and His Family*, New Haven, CT: Yale University Press, 2022.

Lamb, Christina. *Waiting for Allah: Pakistan's Struggle for Democracy: Benazir Bhutto and Pakistan*, London: Penguin Books, 1991.

Landay, Jonathan. 'Profits and Poppy: Afghanistan's Illegal Drug Trade a Boon for Taliban', *Reuters*, 16 August 2021, https://www.reuters.com/world/asia-pacific/profits-poppy-afghanistans-illegal-drug-trade-boon-taliban-2021-08-16/

'Leaked Memo Fuels Accusations of Ethnic Bias in Afghan Government'. *Reuters*, 21 September 2017, www.reuters.com/article/us-afghanistan-politics/leaked-memo-fuels-accusations-of-ethnic-bias-in-afghan-government-idUSKCN-1BW15U

Lee, Jonathan L. *Afghanistan: A History from 1260 to the Present*, London: Reaktion Books, 2022.

Leventis, Evagoras C. 'The Waziristan Accord', *Middle East Review of International Affairs*, Vol. 11, No. 4, 2007, pp. 19–37.

Lieven, Anatol. *Pakistan: A Hard Country*, London: Allen Lane, 2011.

Lindsay, A.D. *The Essentials of Democracy*, London: Oxford University Press, 1930.

'Lisbon Summit Declaration'. NATO, Press Release, 20 November 2010, https://www.nato.int/cps/en/natohq/official_texts_68828.htm

Lowenstein, Julie. 'US Foreign Policy and the Soviet–Afghan War: A Revisionist History', Harvey M. Applebaum '59 Award, Yale University, 2016, https://elischolar.library.yale.edu/cgi/viewcontent.cgi?article=1045&context=applebaum_award

Lynch III, Thomas F. 'The Decades-long "Double-double Game": Pakistan, the United States, and the Taliban', *Military Review*, July–August 2018, pp. 64–78, https://www.armyupress.army.mil/Portals/7/military-review/Archives/English/JA-18/Lynch-Pakistan-US-Taliban.pdf

Mac Ginty, Roger. 'Warlords and the Liberal Peace: State-building in Afghanistan', *Conflict, Security & Development*, Vol. 10, No. 4, 2010, pp. 577–98.

McChesney, Robert D. *Kabul Under Siege: Fayz Mohammad's Account of the 1929 Uprising*, Princeton, NJ: Markus Wiener Publishers, 1999.

McChrystal, General Stanley A. 'Commander's Initial Assessment', National Security Archive, 30 August 2009, https://nsarchive.gwu.edu/sites/default/files/documents/qy3fic-cl4be/15.pdf

Mack, Andrew. 'Why Big Nations Lose Small Wars: The Politics of Asymmetric Conflict', *World Politics*, Vol. 27, No. 2, 1975, pp. 175–200.

Mackinder, H.J. 'The Geographical Pivot of History', *Geographical Journal*, Vol. 23, No. 4, 1904, pp. 421–37.

Mahmood, Rafat, and Michael Jetter. 'Gone with the Wind: The Consequences of US Drone Strikes in Pakistan', *Economic Journal*, Vol. 133, No. 650, 2023, pp. 787–811.

Maley, William. *Rescuing Afghanistan*, Sydney: University of NSW Press, 2006.

Malkasian, Carter. *The American War in Afghanistan: A History*, New York: Oxford University Press, 2021.

Mashal, Mujib, and Najim Rahim. 'Afghan President Fires a Powerful Governor From Post He Held 13 Years', *New York Times*, 18 December 2017.

BIBLIOGRAPHY

Massoud, Ahmad. 'What is Missing from Afghan Peace Talks', *New York Times*, 14 April 2020; 'Fireside Chat with Ahmad Massoud', The Aspen Institute Security Forum, July 2023, https://www.youtube.com/watch?v=ftGPxaKNZFg

Mathieu, Edouard, Hannah Ritchie, Lucas Rodes-Guirao, Cameron Appel, Daniel Gavrilov et al. 'Afghanistan: What is the Daily Number of Confirmed Cases?', Our World in Data, https://ourworldindata.org/coronavirus/country/afghanistan

Mattis, Jim, and Bing West. *Call Sign Chaos: Learning to Lead*, New York: Random House, 2021.

Menon, Rajan. 'Afghanistan's Minor Miracle', *Los Angeles Times*, 14 December 2004.

Metrinko, Michael J. 'Elections in Afghanistan: Looking to the Future', Issue Paper No. XX, Carlisle, PA: US Army Peacekeeping and Stability Operations Institute, January 2008, https://csl.armywarcollege.edu/usacsl/publications/ElectionsIn Afghanistan.pdf

Mill, John Stuart. *Three Essays on Liberty, Representative Government, the Subjugation of Women*, London: Oxford University Press, 1975.

Miller, Paul D. 'Bush on Nation-building and Afghanistan', *Foreign Policy*, 17 November 2010, https://foreignpolicy.com/2010/11/17/bush-on-nation-building-and-afghanistan/

'Minister Voices Afghan Opium Fear'. *BBC News*, 2 May 2008, http://news.bbc.co.uk/2/hi/health/7377817.stm

Mishra, Anant. 'How Washington Misunderstood "Strategy" in Afghanistan', Canberra: Australian Army Research Centre, 24 May 2022, https://research-centre.army.gov.au/library/land-power-forum/how-washington-misunder-stood-strategy-afghanistan

Moghadam, Assaf. 'Marriage of Convenience: The Evolution of Iran and al-Qa'ida's Tactical Cooperation', *CTC Sentinel*, Vol. 10, Issue 4, 2017, pp. 12–18, https://ctc.westpoint.edu/marriage-of-convenience-the-evolution-of-iran-and-al-qaidas-tactical-cooperation/

Mojumdar, Aunohita, Alex Barker and James Blitz. 'Karzai Blasts West over Opium Policy', *Financial Times*, 30 August 2007.

Monten, Jonathan. 'The Roots of the Bush Doctrine: Power, Nationalism and Democracy Promotion in U.S. Strategy', *International Security*, Vol. 29, No. 4, 2005, pp. 112–56.

Moosakhail, Zabihullah. 'Parliament Rejects Stanikzai as Afghanistan's Defense Minister', *Khaama Press News Agency*, 4 July 2015, https://www.khaama.com/breaking-news-parliament-rejects-stanikzai-as-afghanistans-defense-minister-3596/

Morse, Chandler. 'Becoming Versus Being Modern: An Essay on Institutional Change and Economic Development', in Chandler Morse, Douglas E. Ashford, Frederick T. Bent, William H. Friedland, John W. Lewis and David B. Macklin, *Modernization by Design: Social Change in the Twentieth Century*, Ithaca, NY: Cornell University Press, 1969, pp. 238–382.

Motwani, Nishhank. 'Taliban Leaders Still Lack Legitimacy', *East Asia Forum*, 20 October 2022.

Mukhtar, Ahmad. 'Election Scandal Brings Down Afghan Official', *CBS News*, 23 June 2014, https://www.cbsnews.com/news/afghanistan-election-ziaul-haq-amarkhel-resigns-amid-fraud-scandal/

Mundy, Martha. *Domestic Government: Kinship, Community and Polity in North Yemen*, London: I.B. Tauris, 1995.

Murtazashvili, Jennifer Brick. 'The Collapse of Afghanistan', *Journal of Democracy*, Vol. 33, No. 1, 2022, pp. 40–54.

Musharraf, Pervez. *In the Line of Fire: A Memoir*, London: Simon & Schuster, 2006.

Nader, Alireza, Ali G. Scotten, Ahmad Idrees Rahmani, Robert Stewart and Leila Mahnad. *Iran's Influence in Afghanistan: Implications for the US Drawdown*, Santa Monica, CA: RAND Corporation, 2014.

Nakamura, David, and Abby Phillip. 'Trump Announces New Strategy for Afghanistan that Calls for a Troop Increase', *Washington Post*, 21 August 2017.

Nasiri, Afzal, and Marie Khalili, eds and trans. *Memoirs of Khalilullah Khalili: An Afghan Philosopher Poet – A Conversation with his Daughter*, Virginia: Afzal Nasiri and Marie Khalili, 2013.

Nassiha, Fawad. 'Yadasht-i Spanta, rawayat-i 'dast-i awal' az syyast-i Afghanistan-i ma'asser' [Notes of Spanta, Firsthand Witness Concerning the Politics of Modern Afghanistan], *BBC News* (Persian), 7 December 2017, https://www.bbc.com/persian/afghanistan-42263617

Nawaz, Shuja. 'Learning by Doing: The Pakistan Army's Experience with Counterinsurgency', Washington, DC: Atlantic Council, February 2011, https://www.files.ethz.ch/isn/126743/020111_ACUS_Nawaz_PakistanCounterinsurgency.pdf

Nazar, Zarif. 'Former U.S. Envoy Defends Controversial Peace Deal with Taliban', RadioFreeEurope RadioLiberty, 14 August 2022, https://www.rferl.org/a/afghanistan-khalilzad-defends-taliban-deal/31988305.html

New America. 'The Drone War in Pakistan', *New America*, 21 May 2016, https://www.newamerica.org/international-security/reports/americas-counterterrorism-wars/the-drone-war-in-pakistan/

Newport, Frank. 'American Public Opinion and the Afghanistan Situation', *Gallup News*, 27 August 2021, https://news.gallup.com/opinion/polling-matters/354182/american-public-opinion-afghanistan-situation.aspx

Nixon, Hamish, and Richard Ponzio. 'Building Democracy in Afghanistan: The Statebuilding Agenda and International Engagement', *International Peacekeeping*, Vol. 14, No. 1, 2007, pp. 26–40.

Nojumi, Neamatollah. 'The Rise and Fall of the Taliban', in Robert D. Crews and Amin Tarzi, eds, *The Taliban and the Crisis of Afghanistan*, Cambridge, MA: Harvard University Press, 2008, pp. 90–117.

Norchi, Charles H. 'Toward the Rule of Law in Afghanistan: The Constitutive Process', in John D. Montgomery and Dennis A. Rondinelli, eds, *Beyond Reconstruction in Afghanistan: Lessons from Development Experience*, New York: Palgrave Macmillan, 2004, pp. 115–31.

Nordland, Rod. 'Afghan Government Drops Corruption Charges Against Aide', *New York Times*, 8 November 2010.

Nordland, Rod, and Dexter Filkins. 'Antigraft Units, Backed by U.S., Draw Karzai's Ire', *New York Times*, 6 August 2010.

Nourzhanov, Kirill, and Amin Saikal. *The Afghanistan Spectre: The Security of Central Asia*, London: I.B. Tauris/Bloomsbury, 2021, pp. 125–6.

O'Donnell, Lynne. 'Afghan Resistance Leaders see "No Option" but War', *Foreign Policy*, 29 September 2022, https://foreignpolicy.com/2022/09/29/afghanistan-taliban-resistance-terrorism-jihad/

Oates, Lauryn, and Isabelle Solon Helal. *At the Cross-roads of Conflict and Democracy: Women and Afghanistan's Constitutional Loya Jirga*, Montreal: Rights and Democracy, 2004, https://publications.gc.ca/collections/Collection/E84-14-2004E.pdf

Obama, Barack. 'Remarks by the President in Address to the Nation on the Way Forward in Afghanistan and Pakistan', White House, Office of the Press Secretary, 1 December 2009, https://obamawhitehouse.archives.gov/the-press-office/remarks-president-address-nation-way-forward-afghanistan-and-pakistan

Packer, George. 'Afghanistan's Theorist-in-chief', *The New Yorker*, 27 June 2016, https://www.newyorker.com/magazine/2016/07/04/ashraf-ghani-afghanistans-theorist-in-chief

Packer, George. 'Kilcullen on Afghanistan: "It's Still Winnable, But Only Just"', *The New Yorker*, 14 November 2008, https://www.newyorker.com/news/george-packer/kilcullen-on-afghanistan-its-still-winnable-but-only-just

'Pakistan Warns of Consequences from Afghan "Economic Meltdown"'. *Al Jazeera*, 19 December 2021, https://www.aljazeera.com/news/2021/12/19/islamic-countries-hold-meeting-to-discuss-aid-to-afghanistan

'Pakistani Leader Claims U.S. Threat After 9/11'. *New York Times*, 22 September 2006.

Paliwal, Avinash. 'Murder of a President: How India and the UN Mucked Up Completely in Afghanistan', *Quartz India*, 30 October 2017, https://qz.com/india/1114676/najibullahs-failed-escape-how-india-and-the-un-mucked-up-completely-in-afghanistan/

Partlow, Joshua. *A Kingdom of Their Own: The Family Karzai and the Afghan Disaster*, New York: Knopf, 2017.

Petraeus, David. 'Afghanistan Did Not Have to Turn Out this Way', *The Atlantic*, 8 August 2022, https://www.theatlantic.com/international/archive/2022/08/us-withdrawal-afghanistan-strategy-shortcomings/670980/

Pettit, Philip. *The State*, Princeton, NJ: Princeton University Press, 2023.

Pfiffner, James P. 'US Blunders in Iraq: De-Baathification and Disbanding the Army', *Intelligence and National Security*, Vol. 25, No. 1, 2010, pp. 76–85.

Pompeo, Mike. *Never Give an Inch: Fighting for the America I Love*, New York: Broadside Books, 2023.

'Pompeo Says Ashraf Ghani "Stole" the Election'. *Afghan Online Press*, 14 January 2023, http://www.aopnews.com/us-afghanistan-relations/pompeo-says-ashraf-ghani-stole-the-election/

Populzai, Azizuddin Wakil. *Negha-I ba Tarikh-I Atirdad-I Istiqlal* [A Glance at the History of Independence], Kabul: Government Press, 1368/1989.

Poullada, Leon B. *Reform and Rebellion in Afghanistan, 1919–1929: King Amanullah's Failure to Modernize a Tribal Society*, Ithaca, NY: Cornell University Press, 1973.

Pouse, Terri. 'Who's Who in the David Petraeus "Love Pentagon" Scandal', *Time*, 13 November 2012.

Power Engineering International. 'US Development Agency Funds Gas-fired Project in Afghanistan', *Power Engineering International*, 16 December 2014, https://www.powerengineeringint.com/gas-oil-fired/us-development-agency-funds-gas-fired-project-in-afghanistan/

'Profiles of Afghan Power Brokers'. CAP (Continuous Article Publishing), October 26, 2009, https://www.americanprogress.org/article/profiles-of-afghan-power-brokers/#10

Raghavan, Sudarsan. 'Hamid Karzai is Trying to Find His Place in the New Afghanistan', *Washington Post*, 27 December 2022.

Rashid, Ahmed. 'Afghanistan's Former King Says He Will Not Seek Political Role', *Wall Street Journal*, 11 June 2002.

Rashid, Ahmed. 'Pakistan and the Taliban', in William Maley, ed., *Fundamentalism Reborn?* London: Hurst & Co., 1998, pp. 72–89.

Rasmussen, Sune Engel. 'Afghanistan Funds Abused Militias as US Military "Ignores" Situation, Officials Say', *Guardian*, 26 December 2016.

Rasmussen, Sune Engel. 'Fear and Doubt as Notorious "Butcher of Kabul" Returns with Talk of Peace', *Guardian*, 5 May 2017.

Ratnam, Gopal. 'Poor Planning, Coordination Cited in Afghan Intervention: U.S., German Officials Note Lessons from 15-year War', United States Institute of Peace, 16 December 2015, https://www.usip.org/publications/2015/12/poor-planning-coordination-cited-afghan-intervention

Reagan, Ronald. 'Evil Empire Speech', *Voices of Democracy: The U.S. Oratory Project*, 8 March 1983, https://voicesofdemocracy.umd.edu/reagan-evil-empire-speech-text/

Recknagel, Charles. 'Explainer: Key Points In U.S.–Afghan Bilateral Security Agreement', RadioFree Europe RadioLiberty, 30 September 2014, https://www.rferl.org/a/explainer-bsa-afghan-us-security-agreement-bsa/26613884.html

'Remarks by President Biden on the Way Forward in Afghanistan', White House, 14 April 2021, https://www.whitehouse.gov/briefing-room/speeches-remarks/2021/04/14/remarks-by-president-biden-on-the-way-forward-in-afghanistan/

Reynolds, Andrew. 'Electoral Systems Today: The Curious Case of Afghanistan', *Journal of Democracy*, Vol. 17, No. 2, 2006, p. 104–17.

Risen, James. 'Intrigue in Karzai Family as an Afghan Era Closes', *New York Times*, 3 June 2012.

Risen, James. 'Karzai's Relatives Use Ties to Gain Power in Afghanistan', *NBC News*, 6 October 2010, https://www.nbcnews.com/id/wbna39528462

Risen, James. 'Reports Link Karzai's Brother to Heroin Trade', *New York Times*, 4 October 2008.

Reshtia, Sayed Qassem. *Khatera-e Siyas-e, 1932–1992* [The Political Memoirs of Sayed Qassem Reshtia, Afghan Historian and Diplomat, Period of 1932–1992], completed by Mohammad Qawee Koshan, Alexandria, VA: American Sepedi Press, 1997.

Roggio, Bill. 'US Adds Haqqani Network to List of Terror Groups', *Long War Journal*, 7 September 2012, https://www.longwarjournal.org/archives/2012/09/us_adds_haqqani_netw_1.php

Rosenthal, Elisabeth, and David E. Sanger. 'U.S. Plane in China after it Collides with Chinese Jet', *New York Times*, 2 April 2001.

Rotberg, Robert I., ed. *When States Fail: Causes and Consequences*, Princeton, NJ: Princeton University Press, 2004.

Rubin, Alissa J. 'Afghan Leader Forces Out Top 2 Security Officials', *New York Times*, 6 June 2010.

Rubin, Alissa J., and Abdul Waheed Wafa. 'Karzai Annuls Afghan Court Reviewing 2010 Polls', *New York Times*, 10 August 2011.

Rubin, Barnett R. 'Crafting a Constitution for Afghanistan', *Journal of Democracy*, Vol. 15, No. 3, 2004, pp. 5–19.

Rubin, Barnett R., and Jake Sherman. *Counter-narcotics to Stabilize Afghanistan: The False Promise of Crop Eradication*, New York: Center on International Cooperation, 2008, http://milnewstbay.pbworks.com/f/counternarcoticsfinal.pdf

Rubin, Michael. 'Taking Tea with the Taliban', American Enterprise Institute, 1 February 2010, https://www.aei.org/articles/taking-tea-with-the-taliban/

'Rumsfeld: Major Combat over in Afghanistan'. *CNN*, 1 May 2003, https://edition.cnn.com/2003/WORLD/asiapcf/central/05/01/afghan.combat/

Ruttig, Thomas. 'All Together Now: Afghanistan is not Switzerland', *Foreign Policy*, 17 September 2010, https://foreignpolicy.com/2010/09/17/all-together-now-afghanistan-is-not-switzerland/

Ruttig, Thomas. 'The 2004 Afghan Presidential Elections and Challenges for the Forthcoming Parliamentary Elections', in Moonis Ahmar, ed., *The Challenge of Rebuilding Afghanistan*, Karachi: Bureau of Composition, Compilation and Translation, University of Karachi Press, 2005.

Ruttig, Thomas, Martine van Bijlert and Gran Hewad. 'A Hasty Process: New Independent Election Commission Announced', Afghanistan Analysts Network, 30 July 2013, https://www.afghanistan-analysts.org/en/reports/political-landscape/a-process-fast-and-patchy-new-independent-elections-commission-announced/

Sadat, Mir Hekmatullah. 'History of Education in Afghanistan', reliefweb, 1 March 2004, https://reliefweb.int/report/afghanistan/history-education-afghanistan

'Saddam Tried to Kill My Dad'. *Sydney Morning Herald*, 27 September 2022.

Saeedi, Sayed Ziafatullah. 'How Afghanistan Judiciary Lost Its Independence', *The Diplomat*, 5 June 2019, https://thediplomat.com/2019/06/how-afghanistans-judiciary-lost-its-independence/

Saifi, Sophia, Rhea Mogul and Saleem Mehsud. 'Death Toll from Blast in Pakistan Mosque Rises to at Least 100 as Country Faces "National Security Crisis"', *CNN*, 31 January 2023, https://edition.cnn.com/2023/01/31/asia/pakistan-peshawar-mosque-blast-tuesday-intl-hnk/index.html

Saikal, Amin. 'A Mission for Moderates: How Three Threats Interlock', *International Herald Tribune*, 29 December 2003.

Saikal, Amin. 'Afghanistan and Pakistan: The Question of Pashtun Nationalism?', *Journal of Muslim Minority Affairs*, Vol. 30, Issue 1, 2010, pp. 5–17.

Saikal, Amin. 'Afghanistan's Geographic Possibilities', *Survival: Global Politics and Strategy*, Vol. 56, No. 3, 2014, pp. 141–56.

Saikal, Amin. 'Bloody Conflict Looms in Afghan North', *Guardian*, 19 October 2009.

Saikal, Amin. 'Don't Cave in to the Taliban', *New York Times*, 18 October 2007.

Saikal, Amin. 'Iran: Aspirations and Constraints', in Adham Saouli, ed., *Unfulfilled Aspirations: Middle Power Politics in the Middle East*, London: Hurst & Co., 2020, pp. 113–34.

Saikal, Amin. *Iran at the Crossroads*, Cambridge: Polity Press, 2016.

Saikal, Amin. *Iran Rising: The Survival and Future of the Islamic Republic*, Princeton, NJ: Princeton University Press, 2021.

Saikal, Amin. *Islam and the West: Conflict or Cooperation?* London: Palgrave Macmillan, 2003.

Saikal, Amin. *Modern Afghanistan: A History of Struggle and Survival*, 2nd edn, London: I.B. Tauris, 2012.

Saikal, Amin. 'Musharraf and Pakistan's Crisis', in Rajshree Jetly, ed., *Pakistan in Regional and Global Politics*, New Delhi: Routledge, 2009, pp. 1–19.

Saikal, Amin. 'Securing Afghanistan's Border', *Survival: Global Politics and Strategy*, Vol. 48, Issue 1, 2006, pp. 129–42.

Saikal, Amin. *The Rise and Fall of the Shah: Iran from Autocracy to Religious Rule*, Princeton, NJ: Princeton University Press, 2009.

Saikal, Amin. 'The Role of Outside Actors in Afghanistan', *Middle East Policy*, Vol. 7, No. 4, 2000, pp. 50–7.

Saikal, Amin. 'The Role of Sub-national Actors in Afghanistan', in Klejda Mulaj, ed., *Violent Non-state Actors in World Politics*, London: Hurst & Co., 2010, pp. 239–56.

Saikal, Amin. 'The United Nations and Democratization in Afghanistan', in Edward Newman and Roland Rich, eds, *The UN Role in Promoting Democracy: Between Ideals and Reality*, Tokyo: United Nations University Press, 2004, pp. 320–38.

Saikal, Amin. *Zone of Crisis: Afghanistan, Pakistan, Iran and Iraq*, London: I.B. Tauris, 2014.

Saikal, Amin, and William Maley. 'The President Who Would be King', *New York Times*, 6 February 2008.

Saikal, Mahmoud. 'Afghanistan in Transition: An Insider's Account', unpublished diary, 2 May 2017.

Saikal, Mahmoud. 'Naziraan mi goyand; cherra moufiqyat-i rawund-i sulh-i Afghanistan ba payman-i jaded ar syyasit-i dakhil-i wabasta ast' [Observers Say, Why is the Peace Deal Linked to the New Declaration in Domestic Politics?], *BBC News* (Persian), 1 March 2021, https://www.bbc.com/persian/blog-view-points-56203114

Saleh, Amrullah. 'The Crisis of Politics of Ethnicity in Afghanistan', *Al Jazeera*, 26 June 2012, https://www.aljazeera.com/opinions/2012/6/26/the-crisis-and-poli-tics-of-ethnicity-in-afghanistan

Salimi, Humayun. 'Pakistan's PM Directs Authorities to Send Manpower to Afghanistan', *Arezo News*, 15 January 2022, https://arezo.news/en/afghanistan/pakistans-pm-directs-authorities-to-send-manpower-to-afghanistan/

Sanger, David E. 'U.S. Would Defend Taiwan', *New York Times*, 26 April 2001.

Savage, Charles, Eric Schmitt and Michael Schwirtz. 'Russia Secretly Offered Afghan Militants Bounties to Kill U.S. Troops, Intelligence Says', *New York Times*, 20 June 2020.

Schmemann, Serge. 'Gorbachev Says U.S. Arms Note is Not Adequate', *New York Times*, 26 February 1986.

Schneider, William. 'Not Exactly a Bush Flip-flop', *The Atlantic*, 1 October 2001, https://www.theatlantic.com/politics/archive/2001/10/not-exactly-a-bush-flip-flop/377745/

Schwartz, Moshe. *Department of Defense Contractors in Iraq and Afghanistan: Background and Analysis*, Congressional Research Service, 2 July 2010, https://apps.dtic.mil/sti/pdfs/ADA512802.pdf

'Secretary Gates and Admiral Mullen Testify'. Hearing on Security and Stability in Afghanistan and Iraq, September 2008, https://www.understandingwar.org/publications/commentaries/secretary-gates-and-admiral-mullen-testify

'Security and Stability in Afghanistan and Iraq: Developments in U.S. Strategy and Operations and the Way Ahead'. Hearing before the Committee on Armed Services, House of Representatives, 110th Congress, Second Session, 10 September 2008, https://www.govinfo.gov/content/pkg/CHRG-110hhrg45827/pdf/CHRG-110hhrg45827.pdf

Semple, Michael, Robin L. Raphel and Shams Rasikh. 'An Independent Assessment of the Afghanistan Peace Process June 2018–May 2021', Political Settlements and Research Programme (PSRP), June 2021, https://www.politicalsettlements.org/wp-content/uploads/2021/07/An-independent-assessment-of-the-Afghanistan-peace-process.pdf

'September Election Has Distanced People from Govt: Study'. *TOLOnews*, 23 March 2011.

Shahrani, M. Nazif. 'Introduction: The Impact of Four Decades of War and Violence on Afghan Society and Political Culture', in M. Nazif Shahrani, ed., *Modern Afghanistan: The Impact of 40 Years of War*, Bloomington, IN: Indiana University Press, 2018, pp. 1–17.

Shahrani, M. Nazif, ed. *Modern Afghanistan: The Impact of 40 Years of War*, Bloomington, IN: Indiana University Press, 2018.

Shahrani, M. Nazif. 'The State and Community Self-Governance: Paths to Stability and Human Security in Post-2014 Afghanistan', in Srinjoy Bose, Nishank Motwani and William Maley, eds, *Afghanistan: Challenges and Prospects*, New York: Routledge, 2018, pp. 43–62.

Shalizi, Hamid. 'Karzai Says His Office Gets "Bags of Money" from Iran', *Reuters*, 25 October 2010, https://www.reuters.com/article/us-afghanistan-karzai-idUS-TRE69O27Z20101025

Shanahan, Dennis. 'Kevin Rudd in Bucharest for NATO Summit on Afghanistan', *The Australian*, 3 April 2008.

Shayan, Nasar Ahmad, Aziz ur-Rahman Niazi, Hooman Moheb, Hamid Mohammadi, Khaja Wazir Ahmad Saddiqi, Osman Dag et al. 'Epidemiology of Drug Use in Herat – Afghanistan', *Addiction and Health*, Vol. 14, No. 2, 2022, pp. 68–77, https://www.ncbi.nlm.nih.gov/pmc/articles/PMC9743815/

Sheehan, Edward R.F. 'How Kissinger Did It: Step by Step in the Middle East', *Foreign Policy*, No. 22, Spring 1976, pp. 3–70.

Shinas, Nasry Haq. *Tahawulat-e Siasi Jihadi-e Afghanistan* [Political Developments of Jihad in Afghanistan], West Germany: The Islamic Society of Afghan Students and Refugees, 1365/1986.

Shukla, Paraag. 'Afghan Parliament Stymied by Protests, Infighting', *Institute for the Study of War*, 1 September 2011, https://www.understandingwar.org/otherwork/isw-brief-afghan-parliament-stymied-protests-infighting

Shultz, George P. *Turmoil and Triumph: Diplomacy, Power, and the Victory of the American Ideal*, New York: Charles Scribner's Sons, 1993.

Sieff, Kevin. 'Karzai Acknowledges CIA Payments', *Washington Post*, 4 May 2013.

SIGAR (Special Inspector General for Afghanistan Reconstruction). 'About SIGAR', *High-risk List Afghanistan*, 2016, https://www.sigar.mil/interactive-reports/high-risk-list/sigar.html

SIGAR (Special Inspector General for Afghanistan Reconstruction). *Collapse of the Afghan National Defense and Security Forces: An Assessment of the Factors That Led to Its Demise*, SIGAR 22-22-IP Evaluation Report, Arlington, VA: SIGAR, May 2022, https://www.sigar.mil/pdf/evaluations/SIGAR-22-22-IP.pdf

SIGAR (Special Inspector General for Afghanistan Reconstruction). *Counternarcotics: Lessons from the U.S. Experience in Afghanistan*, June 2018, https://www.sigar.mil/interactive-reports/counternarcotics/index.html

SIGAR (Special Inspector General for Afghanistan Reconstruction). *Health Facilities in Afghanistan: Observations from Site Visits at 269 Clinics and Hospitals*, SIGAR: Arlington, VA, March 2020, https://www.sigar.mil/pdf/special%20projects/SIGAR-20-28-SP.pdf

SIGAR (Special Inspector General for Afghanistan Reconstruction). *Quarterly Report to the United States Congress*, 30 January 2014, https://www.sigar.mil/pdf/quarterlyreports/2014jan30qr.pdf

SIGAR (Special Inspector General for Afghanistan Reconstruction). *Quarterly Report to the United States Congress*, 30 January 2017, https://www.sigar.mil/pdf/quarterlyreports/2017-01-30qr.pdf

SIGAR (Special Inspector General for Afghanistan Reconstruction). *Quarterly Report to the United States Congress*, Arlington, VA: SIGAR, 30 April 2023, https://www.sigar.mil/pdf/quarterlyreports/2023-04-30qr.pdf

SIGAR (Special Inspector General for Afghanistan Reconstruction). *Why the Afghan Security Forces Collapsed*, Arlington, VA: SIGAR, 28 February 2023, https://www.sigar.mil/pdf/evaluations/SIGAR-23-16-IP.pdf

Simpson, Emile. 'Checked Out: Why Hamid Karzai's Fickle Recklessness Imperils the Future of Afghanistan', *Foreign Policy*, 29 November 2013, https://foreignpolicy.com/2013/11/29/checked-out/

Smith, Scott. 'Ashraf Ghani's Pakistan Outreach: Fighting Against the Odds', United States Institute of Peace, 29 June 2015, https://www.usip.org/publications/2015/06/ashraf-ghanis-pakistan-outreach

Sommerville, Quentin. 'Afghan Corruption has Doubled since 2007, Survey Says', *BBC News*, 8 July 2010, https://www.bbc.com/news/10549258

Stabile, Carol A., and Deepa Kumar. 'Unveiling Imperialism: Media, Gender and the War on Afghanistan', *Media, Culture & Society*, Vol. 27, No. 5, 2005, pp. 765–82.

Starr, S. Frederick, and Marin J. Strmecki. 'Afghan Democracy and Its First Missteps', *New York Times*, 14 June 2002.

'Statement of Robert P. Storch, Inspector General, Department of Defence'. Hearing on 'The Biden Administration's Disastrous Withdrawal from Afghanistan, Part 1: Review by the Inspectors General', House Committee on Oversight and Accountability, US Congress, 19 April 2023, https://oversight.house.gov/wp-content/uploads/2023/04/Storch-HCOA-041923.pdf

'Stephen J. Hadley Looks Back on 9/11, Iraq, and Afghanistan'. Council on Foreign Relations, 22 October 2014, https://www.cfr.org/event/stephen-j-hadley-looks-back-911-iraq-and-afghanistan

'Storm over Berlusconi "Inferior Muslims" Remarks'. *Independent*, 27 September 2001.

Strmecki, Marin. Interview, 'Creating a Government', *Newshour with Jim Lehrer*, PBS, 21 December 2001.

Suhrke, Astri. 'Democratizing a Dependent State: The Case of Afghanistan', *Democratization*, Vol. 15, No. 3, 2008, pp. 630–48.

Suhrke, Astri. *When More is Less: The International Project in Afghanistan*, New York: Columbia University Press, 2011.

'Taliban Admit Covering Up Death of Mullah Omar'. *BBC News*, 31 August 2015, https://www.bbc.com/news/world-asia-34105565

'Taliban Government in Afghanistan: Background and Issues for Congress'. Congressional Research Service Report R46955, 2 November 2021, https://crsreports.congress.gov/product/pdf/R/R46955

Tanzeem, Ayesha. 'Khalilzad: Ghani's "Intransigence," Afghan Elite's "Selfishness" Led to Collapse', *Voice of America*, 27 October 2021, https://www.voanews.com/a/khalilzad-ghani-intransigence-afghan-elite-selfishness-led-to-collapse/6288276.html

Tarzi, Amin. 'Political Struggles over the Afghanistan-Pakistan Borderlands', in Shahzad Bashir and Robert D. Crews, eds, *Under the Drones: Modern Lives in the Afghanistan-Pakistan Borderlands*, Cambridge, MA: Harvard University Press, 2012, pp. 17–29.

Tate, G.P. *The Kingdom of Afghanistan: A Historical Sketch*, Bombay: F.G. Pearson at the Times Press, 1911.

Taylor, Alan. 'Afghanistan in the 1950s and '60s', *The Atlantic*, 2 July 2013, https://www.theatlantic.com/photo/2013/07/afghanistan-in-the-1950s-and-60s/100544/

'The Afghan Success'. Editorial, *Wall Street Journal*, 19 September 2005, p. A16.

'The Afghan-Iranian Helmand-River Water Treaty'. 1973, https://www.internationalwaterlaw.org/documents/regionaldocs/1973_Helmand_River_Water_Treaty-Afghanistan-Iran.pdf

'The Afghanistan Compact'. Building on Success: The London Conference on Afghanistan, 31 January–1 February 2006, https://www.diplomatie.gouv.fr/IMG/pdf/afghanistan_compact.pdf

Thompson, Loren. 'Iraq: The Biggest Mistake in American Military History', *Forbes*, 15 December 2011, https://www.forbes.com/sites/lorenthompson/2011/12/15/the-biggest-mistake-in-american-military-history/?sh=167d9bf32d3b

Tisdall, Simon. 'Afghanistan is the Dirty Little Secret of the US Presidential Campaign', *Guardian*, 26 October 2016.

Tisdall, Simon 'Ahmed Wali Karzai, the Corrupt and Lawless Face of Modern Afghanistan', *Guardian*, 13 July 2011.

'Tokyo Conference on Afghanistan: The Tokyo Declaration – Partnership for Self-reliance in Afghanistan from Transition to Transformation'. Tokyo: Ministry of Foreign Affairs of Japan, 8 July 2012, https://www.mofa.go.jp/region/middle_e/afghanistan/tokyo_conference_2012/tokyo_declaration_en1.html

'Tora Bora Revisited: How We Failed to get Bin Laden and Why It Matters Today'. Report to Members of the Committee on Foreign Relations, US Senate, 111th Congress, 30 November 2009, Washington: U.S. Government Printing Office,

2009, https://www.govinfo.gov/content/pkg/CPRT-111SPRT53709/html/CPRT-111SPRT53709.htm

Tripathi, Deepak. *Afghanistan and the Vietnam Syndrome: Comparing US and Soviet Wars*, Cham: Springer, 2023.

Trump, Donald. 'Remarks by President Trump on the Strategy in Afghanistan and South Asia', Fort Myer, Arlington, VA, August 21, 2017, https://trumpwhitehouse.archives.gov/briefings-statements/remarks-president-trump-strategy-afghanistan-south-asia/

'UAE President Tells Russia's Putin: We Wish to Strengthen Ties'. *Reuters*, 16 June 2023, https://www.reuters.com/world/uae-president-tells-russias-putin-we-wish-strengthen-ties-2023-06-16/

UNAMA (United Nations Assistance Mission in Afghanistan). 'Human Rights Situation in Afghanistan: May–June 2023 Update', 17 July 2023, https://reliefweb.int/report/afghanistan/unama-human-rights-situation-afghanistan-may-june-2023-update-endarips

UNCTAD (United Nations Conference on Trade and Development). 'General Profile: Afghanistan', 2022, https://unctadstat.unctad.org/countryprofile/generalprofile/en-gb/004/index.html

UNCTAD (United Nations Conference on Trade and Development). *The Least Developed Countries Report 2020*, Geneva: United Nations, 2020, https://unctad.org/system/files/official-document/ldcr2020_en.pdf

UNCTAD (United Nations Conference on Trade and Development). 'UN List of Least Developed Countries', 2022, https://unctad.org/topic/least-developed-countries/list

UNDP (United Nations Development Programme). *Pitfalls and Promise: Minerals Extraction in Afghanistan: Afghanistan Human Development Report 2020*, Kabul: UNDP Afghanistan, 9 September 2020, https://afghanistan.un.org/sites/default/files/2020-09/NHDR_2020_%20English_0.pdf

UNICEF. '1.4 Million Doses of COVID-19 Vaccine Arrive in Afghanistan through COVAX Global Dose-sharing Mechanism', UNICEF, 9 July 2021, https://www.unicef.org/press-releases/14-million-doses-covid-19-vaccine-arrive-afghanistan-through-covax-global-dose#:~:text=KABUL%2C%209%20July%202021%20-%20More,to%20the%20Government%20of%20Afghanistan

United Nations Security Council. 'Agreement on Provisional Arrangements in Afghanistan Pending the Re-establishment of Permanent Government Institutions', S/2001/1154, 5 December 2001, https://peacemaker.un.org/sites/peacemaker.un.org/files/AF_011205_AgreementProvisionalArrangementsinAfghanistan%28en%29.pdf

United Nations Security Council. 'Fourteenth Report of the Analytical Support and Sanctions Monitoring Team Submitted Pursuant to Resolution 2665 (2022) Concerning the Taliban and Other Associated Individuals and Entities Constituting a Threat to the Peace Stability and Security of Afghanistan', S/2023/370, 1 June 2023, https://documents-dds-ny.un.org/doc/UNDOC/GEN/N23/125/36/PDF/N2312536.pdf?OpenElement

United Nations Security Council. 'Statement by the President of the Security Council', S/PRST/2018/15, 23 July 2018, https://documents-dds-ny.un.org/doc/UNDOC/GEN/N18/235/24/PDF/N1823524.pdf?OpenElement

BIBLIOGRAPHY

United Nations University. 'Lessons from the National Solidarity Programme in Afghanistan', Research Brief, June 2014, https://www.wider.unu.edu/publication/lessons-national-solidarity-programme-afghanistan

UNODC (United Nations Office on Drugs and Crime). *Afghanistan: Opium Risk Assessment 2013*, Vienna and Kabul: UNODC and Islamic Republic of Afghanistan Ministry of Counter Narcotics, April 2013.

UNODC (United Nations Office on Drugs and Crime). *Afghanistan: Opium Survey 2007*, October 2007, https://www.unodc.org/documents/crop-monitoring/Afghanistan-Opium-Survey-2007.pdf

UNODC (United Nations Office on Drugs and Crime). *Corruption in Afghanistan: Recent Patterns and Trends*, Vienna: UNODC, 2012, https://www.unodc.org/documents/lpo-brazil//Topics_corruption/Publicacoes/Corruption_in_Afghanistan_FINAL.pdf

UNODC (United Nations Office on Drugs and Crime). *Drug Situation in Afghanistan in 2021: Latest Findings and Emerging Threats*, UNODC, 2021, https://www.unodc.org/documents/data-and-analysis/Afghanistan/Afghanistan_brief_Nov_2021.pdf

UNODC (United Nations Office on Drugs and Crime). *Drug Use in Afghanistan: 2009 Survey: Executive Summary*, June 2010, https://www.unodc.org/documents/data-and-analysis/Studies/Afghan-Drug-Survey-2009-Executive-Summary-web.pdf

US Department of State. 'Joint Declaration between the Islamic Republic of Afghanistan and the United States of America for Bringing Peace to Afghanistan', 29 February 2020, https://www.state.gov/wp-content/uploads/2020/02/02.29.20-US-Afghanistan-Joint-Declaration.pdf

US Department of State. *US Counternarcotics Strategy for Afghanistan*, August 2007, https://2001-2009.state.gov/documents/organization/90671.pdf

US Government. *The National Security Strategy of the United States of America*, September 2002 https://georgewbush-whitehouse.archives.gov/nsc/nss/2002/nss1.html

'U.S. Lessons Learned in Afghanistan'. Hearing before the Committee on Foreign Affairs, House of Representatives, 15 January 2020, https://www.govinfo.gov/content/pkg/CHRG-116hhrg38915/html/CHRG-116hhrg38915.htm

'U.S.–Afghanistan Joint Statement'. White House, Office of the Press Secretary, 24 March 2015, https://obamawhitehouse.archives.gov/the-press-office/2015/03/24/us-afghanistan-joint-statement

USAID (United States Agency for International Development). 'Health', USAID, 2023, https://www.usaid.gov/afghanistan/our-work/health

van Ham, Peter, and Jorrit Kamminga. 'Poppies for Peace: Reforming Afghanistan's Opium Industry', *Washington Quarterly*, Vol. 30, No. 1, 2006/2007, pp. 69–82.

Vidal, Gore. 'The Enemy Within', *Observer*, 27 October 2002, reprinted as 'UQ Wire: Gore Vidal's The Enemy Within', *Scoop*, 30 October 2002, https://www.scoop.co.nz/stories/HL0210/S00205/uq-wire-gore-vidals-the-enemy-within.htm?from-mobile=bottom-link-01

Von Drehle, David, and R. Jeffrey Smith. 'U.S. Strikes Iraq for Plot to Kill Bush', *Washington Post*, 27 June 1993.

Walsh, Declan, and Ian Black. 'Eradication or Legalisation? How to Solve Afghanistan's Opium Crisis', *Guardian*, 29 August 2007.

Wardak, Ali. 'Building a Post-war Justice System in Afghanistan', *Crime, Law and Social Change*, Vol. 41, 2004, pp. 319–41.

'Warlord Accused of Rights Abuses Awarded Afghanistan's Highest Military Rank'. RadioFreeEurope RadioLiberty, 15 July 2020, https://www.rferl.org/a/warlord-accused-of-rights-abuses-awarded-afghanistan-s-highest-military-rank/30727645.html

Watson, Ivan. 'Ambassador Khalilzad, the "Viceroy of Afghanistan"', *NPR*, 22 October 2004, https://www.npr.org/templates/story/story.php?storyId=4122620

White House. 'President Bush Meets with NATO Secretary General Jaap de Hoop Scheffer'. Office of the Press Secretary, White House, 2 April 2008, https://georgewbush-whitehouse.archives.gov/news/releases/2008/04/20080402-4.html

Whitlock, Craig. 'Built to Fail: The Afghanistan Papers: A Secret History of the War', *Washington Post*, 9 December 2019.

WHO (World Health Organization). 'Afghanistan: Health System', WHO, 2023, https://www.emro.who.int/afg/programmes/health-system-strengthening.html

Wight, Martin. *Power Politics*, Hedley Bull and Carsten Holbraad, eds, Leicester: Leicester University Press, 1978.

'Wikileaks Cables say Afghan President Karzai "Paranoid"'. *BBC News*, 3 December 2010, https://www.bbc.com/news/world-south-asia-11906216

Wise, Lindsay. 'Congressional Republicans Blame Biden for Bungling Afghanistan Pullout', *Wall Street Journal*, 13 August 2021.

Woodward, Bob. *Bush at War*, New York: Simon & Schuster, 2002.

World Bank. 'Afghanistan', *World Bank Data*, 2023, https://data.worldbank.org/country/AF

World Bank. *Afghanistan – Public Expenditure Review 2010: Second Generation of Public Expenditure Reforms*, Report No. 53892-AF, in consultation with the UK Department for International Development, April 2010, https://documents1.worldbank.org/curated/en/588341468180890921/pdf/538920ESW0P1021IC0disclosed06191101.pdf

World Bank. 'Delivering Strong and Sustained Health Gains in Afghanistan: The Sehatmandi Project', World Bank, 23 October 2020, https://www.worldbank.org/en/results/2020/10/23/delivering-strong-and-sustained-health-gains-in-afghanistan-the-sehatmandi-project

World Bank. 'GDP (Constant 2015 US$) – Afghanistan', *World Bank Data*, 2015, https://data.worldbank.org/indicator/NY.GDP.MKTP.KD?locations=AF

World Bank. 'GDP (Current US$) – Afghanistan', *World Bank Data*, 2021, https://data.worldbank.org/indicator/NY.GDP.MKTP.CD?locations=AF

World Bank. 'Maternal Mortality Ratio (Modeled Estimate, Per 100,000 Live Births) – Afghanistan'. *World Bank Data*, 2023, https://data.worldbank.org/indicator/SH.STA.MMRT?locations=AF.

'World Thinkers 2013: The Results of Prospect's World Thinkers Poll'. *Prospect Magazine*, 24 April 2013, https://www.prospectmagazine.co.uk/magazine/world-thinkers-2013

Zaeef, Abdul Salam. *My Life with the Taliban*, eds Alex Strick van Linschoten and Felix Kuehn, Melbourne: Scribe, 2010.

BIBLIOGRAPHY

Zargon, Pashton. 'Can Saffron Replace Poppy?', *The New Humanitarian*, 6 August 2008, https://www.thenewhumanitarian.org/report/79647/afghanistan-can-saffron-replace-poppy

Zarifi, Sam, and Charmain Mohamed. *Afghan Election Diary*, Human Rights Watch, 19 September 2005, http://www.hrw.org/campaigns/afghanistan/blog.htm

Zehra, Nasim. 'Afghanistan Inter-ministerial Coordination Cell: A Reason for Hope', *Arab News Pakistan*, 1 December 2021, https://www.arabnews.pk/node/1979121

Index